Outlaw Heroes
as Liminal Figures
of Film and Television

Outlaw Heroes as Liminal Figures of Film and Television

Rebecca A. Umland

McFarland & Company, Inc., Publishers
Jefferson, North Carolina

LIBRARY OF CONGRESS CATALOGUING-IN-PUBLICATION DATA

Names: Umland, Rebecca A., author.
Title: Outlaw heroes as liminal figures of film and television / Rebecca A. Umland.
Description: Jefferson, North Carolina : McFarland & Company, Inc., Publishers, 2016 | Includes bibliographical references and index.
Identifiers: LCCN 2016009359 | ISBN 9780786479887 (softcover : acid free paper) ∞
Subjects: LCSH: Heroes in motion pictures. | Heroes in literature. | Heroes on television. | Liminality in motion pictures. | Liminality on television. | Motion pictures—United States—History. | Television programs—United States—History.
Classification: LCC PN1995.9.H44 U45 2016 | DDC 791.43/652—dc23
LC record available at https://lccn.loc.gov/2016009359

BRITISH LIBRARY CATALOGUING DATA ARE AVAILABLE

ISBN (print) 978-0-7864-7988-7
ISBN (ebook) 978-1-4766-2351-1

© 2016 Rebecca A. Umland. All rights reserved

No part of this book may be reproduced or transmitted in any form or by any means, electronic or mechanical, including photocopying or recording, or by any information storage and retrieval system, without permission in writing from the publisher.

Front cover: Poster art for the 2008 film *The Dark Knight* (Warner Bros./Photofest)

Printed in the United States of America

McFarland & Company, Inc., Publishers
Box 611, Jefferson, North Carolina 28640
www.mcfarlandpub.com

For Sam and John, true knights

Acknowledgments

I owe a debt of gratitude to the students who asked excellent questions in the "Quester Hero in Literature and Film" seminar I taught in the spring of 2013. Their curiosity and insights helped me formulate some fundamental questions that pertain to this book, especially those related to the type of hero examined in these pages and what makes him a compelling figure. Joel Cardenas, my graduate research assistant during the fall of 2013, worked diligently to help me locate reviews of the films discussed in this study. Thanks to Jessi Miller for her excellent help, and to Alta Kramer at the Calvin T. Ryan Library for locating and delivering promptly my many requests for materials, some of which, I am sure, required considerable effort to find.

I am grateful also to the University of Nebraska at Kearney Department of English, the College of Fine Arts and Humanities, and the Graduate College for support of this project. The developmental leave I was granted in the spring of 2015 provided the time to complete this book in a timely fashion. Finally, I must express my deep appreciation for the support of my husband, Samuel Umland, whose encouragement, encyclopedic memory, and seemingly inexhaustible knowledge of film and literature helped me enormously—more than he knows.

Table of Contents

Acknowledgments vi
Introduction 1

Part I: The Legacy of the True Knight and the Liminal Outlaw Hero 9

CHAPTER 1
- The Typology of the True Knight: Sir Thomas Malory's Lancelot 11

CHAPTER 2
- Chivalry, the Medieval Revival and the Popular Imagination 22

CHAPTER 3
- True Knighthood and the Liminal Outlaw Hero in Classic Hollywood Film 33

CHAPTER 4
- Remediation: The Rise of Television and the Liminal Outlaw Hero 54

Part II: The Liminal Outlaw Hero and the Rise of the Urban Western 89

CHAPTER 5
- Poetic Justice and the *Dirty Harry* Franchise (1971–1988) 93

CHAPTER 6
- "Now cracks a noble heart": Revenge Fantasy in the *Death Wish* Series (1974–1994) 136

Part III: The Liminal Outlaw Hero in the Modern Action Film 183

CHAPTER 7
- Reconciling Opposites in the *Rambo* Franchise (1982–2008) 187

CHAPTER 8
- Dark Days and the Dark Knight in Gotham City (2005–2012) 222

Chapter Notes 261
Works Cited 275
Index 281

Introduction

The romanticized outlaw hero has enjoyed an enduring appeal in the popular imagination, although the concept of this figure varies widely, perhaps being most frequently represented by the towering archetype of Robin Hood or his epigone, the celebrated Jesse James. In fact, in *The Western Hero in History and Legend*, Kent Ladd Steckmesser goes so far as to assert, "The most familiar characterization of our American outlaws is that they are Robin Hoods" (248). Both of these figures, even though they were transformed into folk heroes, are criminals who operate outside the law. Regardless of their legendary generosity to the common folk and their popularity with the masses, they are in fact guilty of thieving and/or murder. This book explores a more narrow concept of the outlaw hero: one that does not place him entirely outside the law, but rather in a liminal space, an anthropological concept of a threshold between past and future, or between conflicting social values and/or individual experiences and desires. Sandor Klapcsik discusses liminality as "a *constant oscillation*, crossing back and forth, between social, textual, and cultural positions" and as a "space of continuous transference, an *infinite process* formed by *transgressions* across evanescent, porous, evasive borderlines" (*Liminality in Fantastic Fiction* 3). In his *Romance of the Road: The Literature of the American Highway* Ronald Primeau employs this concept of the "liminal" to examine the road journey as an intermediate space, or border, in the process of self-discovery, one that liberates travellers from "a social structure that impinges upon dreams and aspirations," suspending them "not only in space and time but between what they think they know about the past and what they have reason to suspect will be inevitable when they get home" (69). This study maintains that a particular type of outlaw hero—the "liminal" outlaw hero—occupies a temporal and spatial area that allows him to achieve justice, while managing to remain detached from a corrupt or inept system. His audience appeal resides in his ability to negotiate between conflicting ideologies as he serves the shared values of community, paradoxically by stepping outside of it, while still managing to preserve his own individual freedom.

In *A Certain Tendency of the Hollywood Cinema, 1930–1980*, Robert Ray discusses "American culture's traditional dichotomy of individual and community that had generated the most significant pair of competing myths: the outlaw hero and the official hero" (58–59). The outlaw hero is the "gunfighter" or "loner" who represents the American impulse toward independence and "freedom from entanglements," while the contrasting official hero—often a "farmer or family man"—espouses a belief in "collective action" and the "legal process" rather than privileging an individual code of right and wrong (59). According to Ray, these two antithetical paradigms are perhaps best represented in "disguised westerns" such as *Casablanca* (1942), with Rick Blaine (Humphrey Bogart) and Victor Laszlo (Paul Henreid) as outlaw and official heroes, respectively, and the real western represented by the classic *Shane* (1953), which presents its incarnations through the film's titular figure (Alan Ladd) and his opposite, Joe Starrett (Van Heflen). To understand where this particular type of outlaw hero originated, and why he has enjoyed such lasting appeal for film audiences, we must turn to what is perhaps the most enduring image of justice, war, and heroism in the western world: the medieval knight.

Like the outlaw hero, the earlier figure of the knight errant occupies a permanent place in the western imagination, at times appearing in surprising guises. While the traditional knight is at home in the world of medieval romance or the historical battlefield, he has other incarnations, one of which is the liminal outlaw hero in Hollywood film. As Leo Braudy maintains in *From Chivalry to Terrorism: War and the Changing Nature of Masculinity* the modern outlaw hero—from Shane to Rambo—owes a debt to the medieval figure of the solitary knight on an adventure, who undertakes "the quest for truth that is both outside himself and within" (92). Although the historical concept of knighthood itself is both complex and varied, the particular figure of the *errant* knight, whose ardent, solitary quest is the pursuit of what Emerson identifies as moral perfectionism, remains a romanticized and persistent character. Not all versions of knighthood feature a quester in pursuit of an ideal or truth in the external world that tests or verifies his own internal moral imperative, but the figure of the errant knight, or the typology that Beverly Kennedy, in her 1985 study *Knighthood in the Morte D'Arthur*, identifies as the "true knight," best represented by the character of Lancelot, does just this.

The inadequacy of the law to achieve true justice in a time of crisis is what the end of Sir Thomas Malory's *Le Morte D'Arthur*, in particular, dramatizes so effectively. When the legal system fails, or conflicts with a higher justice, the "worshipful knight" (in some important ways analogous, as we shall see, to Ray's "official hero") must attain help from the "true knight" (the forerunner of the "outlaw hero") who adheres to a private code outside the legal and social entanglements of a culture; the latter is almost always represented by his efforts to avoid a commitment to a woman and the domestic ties that would ensue from such a relationship. Malory's text, probably completed in 1469 but published by William Caxton in 1485, reflects the tumultuous and conflicting period in English history during the time of the War of the Roses, and Malory himself was an outlaw knight, writing his now famous romance while in prison. Likewise, *Casablanca* and *Shane* reflect the crisis of American culture enmeshed in wars that it attempted, initially, to evade (World War II and the Korean War).

A certain type of hero is called upon to resolve conflicting impulses the audience might feel in times of crisis, as Ray observes in his discussion, but long before Rick Blaine or Shane impressed themselves in the American consciousness, Malory's "true knight," Lancelot, was cast as this type of hero. At the end of *Le Morte D'Arthur*, Lancelot establishes the pattern of the individual who, although operating on a principle that conflicts with the community of Camelot's legal decree, acts in accord with true justice, thus showing that the imperatives of the society that requires his service must be avoided for him to maintain his own innate, individual sense of right. This is *not* to say that the liminal outlaw heroes discussed in the ensuing chapters are knights, but that they borrow certain traits from the figure of the true knight. The urban western and frequently the modern action film are heavily reliant on the western and the mythology of the American past it promoted. But the western itself has roots in the distant past, as the early chapters of this book attempt to show, and often the figure of the medieval knight is consciously invoked.

Therefore, Lancelot's avoidance of what he alludes to as the marital "couch," Rick's stroll into the sunset with Renault in one of Hollywood's memorable moments, and Shane's lonely exit on horseback, are examples of the tension between two paradigmatic codes of behavior. Yet their solitude authenticates them as liminal outlaw heroes—the elect who serve a higher calling. Lancelot's romance ends in the ascetic life of sainthood, *Casablanca* concludes as a buddy movie, serving an ostensibly altruistic end, and Shane, having brought peace to the community through a violent climax, vanishes into the mythic past. In Hollywood cinema, this attempt to reconcile contradictory impulses is one that itself captures an essential conflict in American thought. Ray's point, that the ideology of the official hero, "We are a nation of laws, not of men," and that of the outlaw hero, "I don't know what the law says, but I do know what's right and wrong" (62), owes a debt, as we shall see in our examination of the true knight, Lancelot, to the conflict dramatized in Malory's text.

A study of the figure of a certain type of the Hollywood outlaw hero, then—narrowly defined in this context as the individual who brings justice and order to a community from which he remains distanced—shows that, while he evolves to meet the changing demands of audiences, his essential character and purpose remain constant. He negotiates between freedom and responsibility, the desire to remain individual, while still serving the greater social good. It will first be established that this particular type of liminal outlaw hero owes a debt to the typology of the true knight, which is especially apparent in sequential films, primarily urban westerns (films that employ the conventions of westerns, transposed onto contemporary urban life), but also in action films (which subject the liminal outlaw hero to a series of physical challenges and violent exploits). Certain traits embodied in Kennedy's true knight are manifest in the Hollywood liminal outlaw hero, often through violence, as Richard Slotkin demonstrates in the third book of his trilogy about the shaping of American ideology, *Gunfighter Nation: The Myth of the Frontier in Twentieth-Century America*. Because this particular typology of outlaw hero exists in a liminal space between the group collective and the wilderness of the fully realized, renegade outlaw, and because he manages to vindicate the law while preserving his own integrity, the films that feature this type of hero frequently take the form of integrative propaganda, that is, propaganda that attempts to justify, retrospectively, actions already taken or to serve as a corrective for those actions. This function is especially clear in *Casablanca* and *Shane*, and remains prevalent in the later films that feature this typology.

"Part I: The Legacy of the True Knight and the Liminal Outlaw Hero" provides an overview of the social significance and continued interest in the figure of the knight. Chapter 1, "The Typology of the True Knight: Sir Thomas Malory's Lancelot," discusses briefly the historical inception and rise of the knight in the Middle Ages, and then focuses on Beverley Kennedy's important identification of typologies of knighthood as they are presented in Sir Thomas Malory's *Le Morte D'Arthur*. Lancelot in that text is a model of what Kennedy identifies as true or spiritual knight, certain defining features of which can be seen to persist in the liminal outlaw hero, especially as he tries to negotiate between conflicting codes imposed upon him. Chapter 2, "Chivalry, the Medieval Revival and the Popular Imagination," shows the enduring appeal and transmission of this typology through the survival of the errant knight in the popular imagination, promoted by the medieval revival that flourished in the 19th century and continues today. The third chapter, "True Knighthood and the Liminal Outlaw Hero in Classic Hollywood Film," focuses on two highly influential films which feature heroes who embody certain traits of the true knight—Rick Blaine of *Casablanca* (1942) and the heroic gunfighter of

Shane (1953) in what Robert Ray calls a "disguised western" and a "real western," respectively. Chapter 4, "Remediation: The Rise of Television and the Liminal Outlaw Hero," shows an even broader transmission of the liminal outlaw hero through the vehicle of serialized television, using as apt examples *The Lone Ranger* (1949–1957) and *Have Gun–Will Travel* (1957–1963). As we shall see, both successful television series feature heroes who operate outside of the law proper, but who manage to achieve a finer sense of justice than the legal system often affords. The Lone Ranger's very name underscores his individuality; an ex–Texas Ranger who vows to accomplish what the law often cannot achieve, he adheres to a personal code that exceeds the law. Paladin, the protagonist of *Have Gun–Will Travel*, is a gun for hire, yet his erudition and courtesy, along with his strict personal code of ethics, places him in the liminal space between the law and the outlaw. Again, the overt link between this television hero and medieval knighthood, suggested by his name, makes explicit the continuation of this typology.

The outlaw hero featured prominently, of course, in classic Hollywood films and television westerns, but this popular genre had declined in box office sales during the 1960s and 1970s. Reasons for the decline of the western are still a matter of speculation and debate. J. Fred MacDonald's *Who Shot the Sheriff? The Rise and Fall of the Television Western* examines the demise of the genre after its long period of dominance on prime time television. Studies such as those edited by Andrew Patrick Nelson, including *Contemporary Westerns: Film and Television Since 1990*, demonstrate that westerns have enjoyed some resurgence of popularity in the past few decades; however, several conventions of the western genre appear in more recent popular genre which evolved, in some ways, out of the western: the urban western, exemplified by the popularity and iconic status of the *Dirty Harry* and *Death Wish* films (1971–1988 and 1974–1994, respectively); the *Rambo* franchise (1982–2008); and the *Batman: Dark Knight* trilogy (2005–2012). In each case, the hero negotiates between conflicting values, reconciling competing ideological stances. Rambo, for instance, is a veteran of an unpopular war; he returns to a culture that has become alien to him and which he finds corrupt, yet he is later recruited to serve the country in which he no longer feels at home. As a liminal outlaw hero, he both glorifies and exposes the weaknesses of post–Vietnam American culture and strives to preserve his own integrity, while reluctantly helping the group (military) security initiatives, resorting to violent means to do so. In context, *Rambo* functions as integrative propaganda because it both descries and upholds the American involvement in the Vietnam War. Certain essential character traits of each liminal outlaw hero in these film series are established in the first of the sequence and remain unchanged in the sequels—a testimony to their appeal—making them especially effective in ascertaining the lasting attraction of this type of outlaw hero, whose role is conciliatory, to resolve apparent contradictions in the culture.

"Part II: The Liminal Outlaw Hero and the Rise of the Urban Western" focuses, then, on two representative film franchises from the urban western genre that feature the liminal outlaw hero, demonstrating the endurance of this type of character, and how certain traits remain essentially unchanged. Chapters 5 and 6 discuss two highly successful urban westerns that debuted in the 1970s but continued into the 1980s and 1990s: Clint Eastwood as Harry Callahan, an unconventional San Francisco police inspector, and Charles Bronson as Paul Kersey, a liberal New York architect turned vigilante.

In "Part III: The Liminal Outlaw Hero in the Modern Action Film," chapters 7 and 8 explore two action heroes who occupy a liminal space as outlaw heroes, and who have enjoyed phenomenal success: John Rambo, the veteran rebel, whose screen life ran from 1982 to 2008 (with a new film announced in the planning stages) and Batman in the *Dark Knight* trilogy (2005–2012). I will show that the two striking features this type of liminal outlaw hero owes to the true knight are the rescue, almost always through violence, of the official hero and/or the legal system, and the insistence that he must remain an *errant*, solitary figure, free of entanglements that would impede his ability to function in this capacity, which is why, despite romantic interests, he remains unattached to any woman.

Such a narrow definition asks us to distinguish this type of liminal outlaw hero, who adjudicates between a legal and judicial system that is inadequate and/or corrupt, and a more refined sense of what is right, and another type of heroic figure who serves the law but is not antagonistic toward it. For instance, Dirty Harry Callahan is a police officer, but his beliefs and actions are frequently in direct opposition to authority and the judicial system, often causing conflict with the representatives of official justice. By contrast, the hero of the successful action series *Die Hard* (1988–2013), New York police officer John McLane (Bruce Willis), is not shown to be primarily in direct conflict with the law; moreover, the *Die Hard* films do not retain the hero's single status, but work toward reconciling McLane with his estranged wife and family. The difference between a figure like John McLane and Harry Callahan, then, is the way in which the *Dirty Harry* films emphasize the conflict between the individual and the law, which nonetheless depends upon this type of liminal outlaw hero to serve a higher justice. John Carpenter's *Escape from New York* (1981) and *Escape from L.A.* (1996) are set in a near dystopian future and feature Snake Plissken (Kurt Russell), an ex-U.S. special forces soldier who is released from a maximum security prison in order to rescue the president of the United States or, in the second film, the president's daughter. The outsider, Snake, is pressed into the rescue of the highest government official, or his daughter, but these very successful action-hero films differ from those that present the liminal outlaw hero who metes out justice where the law fails, because Snake himself is a convicted criminal (and does not deny his guilt); therefore, he does not adhere to the model of this study, despite any extenuating circumstances that might exonerate him. Moreover, he has no wish to rescue the "official hero," whom he deems, rightly, corrupt; instead, he is forced to do so. Snake operates in the face of almost total corruption and dissolution; in the world of these films, there is really no ideal left to uphold. In the scenario of the liminal outlaw hero, there may be plenty of corrupt officials, but there is also some cause worthy of this hero's help.

An exploration of these examples of feature film franchises that have enjoyed enormous box office success demonstrates best that while the topical issues in each work change to appeal to audience interest and taste, these two qualities of the liminal outlaw hero remain consistent. An examination of the films in these series shows us that the villains are subject to change, the setting shifts, and timely issues comprise the storyline; however, the nature of the hero in relation to the law, and his own keen sense of what he must do to preserve his individuality, remains fixed, and this is the true formula for box office success. Audiences return again and again to enjoy, vicariously, the liminal outlaw hero's ability to reconcile the frequent oppositional desire for individual freedom and responsibility to a larger cause. Thus, despite Hollywood's propensity to adapt to cultural trends, it recognizes the enduring traits of this type of liminal outlaw hero, whose essential role is to reconcile contradictory impulses inherent in American thought: the collective health of community and the individual desire for freedom, a conflict that the typology of the true knight, with his errant lifestyle and inherent sense of his own election, has embodied for centuries.

The stories a culture chooses to tell itself about its past, present, and future shape and affirm its identity. Movies function as a *speculum*—a mirror of images that help its viewers understand what it values, and why. It shows ideals, impediments to those ideals, and how the tension between individuality and community is a fundamental truth that asks for resolution to a conflict that is more of an ideological than a political one. The larger question posed by the pervasive and continued popularity of the liminal outlaw hero is this relationship between individual freedom and service to a larger community ideal, as Ray's work so ably shows in his discussion of the "official" and "outlaw" hero typologies. This is a fundamental issue in the inception and development of America as an idea, but its roots necessarily reach back to a more distant past. Hollywood cinema continues to be one way that opposing ideological impulses to cherish individual freedom on the one hand, while recognizing the importance of cooperation in the service of a larger collective community on the other hand, can be expressed, and films that feature the liminal outlaw hero offer one attempt to reconcile these ideals. This is why Right and Left cycle films that were made after the decline of the western, as Ray discusses them, have more in common than would first meet the eye.

In his excellent study *The Invisible Hand in Popular Culture: Liberty vs. Authority in American Film and TV*, Paul Cantor explores the related issue of governance and the expression of what he identifies as a libertarian impulse that espouses less as more, as it is presented in Hollywood television and film. Challenging the idea that Hollywood picture production is more or less unimaginative, Cantor demonstrates that the popular film and television media sometimes probe fundamental ideological issues about freedom and self-governance, manifesting, at times, a refreshingly original, even subversive view of the world. According to Cantor, "cultural elitists," many of them film critics, wrongly denigrate popular cinematic art: "Elitists who profess to believe in democracy nevertheless have no faith in common people to make sound decisions on their own, even in a matter as simple as choosing the films and television shows they watch. How can people be trusted to choose their government if they cannot be trusted to choose their entertainment?" (xiv). Film and television engage viewers in fundamental issues of freedom and governance, and the figure of the liminal outlaw hero enjoys a central position because of his function as adjudicator between official systems and individual choice.

Lancelot, the true knight, shares with gunfighters (Shane, Paladin), vigilante heroes (the Lone Ranger, Paul Kersey, Batman), ex-patriots (Rick Blaine, Rambo), and a righteous police inspector (Harry Callahan) concerns about freedom and order, the law and justice, morality and vengeance, that continue to appeal to audiences, despite the apparent boundaries of history, genre, and culture. This book, focusing on these examples of the liminal outlaw hero, examines reasons why this might be so.

Part I

The Legacy of the True Knight and the Liminal Outlaw Hero

"The past is never dead. It's not even past."
—William Faulkner, *Requiem for a Nun* (1951)

CHAPTER 1

The Typology of the True Knight: Sir Thomas Malory's Lancelot

Knighthood is a concept that has endured in the western imagination, and found expression in a variety of ways. The actual history of knighthood itself is complex, and its rich literary heritage is equally diverse and complicated. The social structure of the European Middle Ages consisted of the priesthood (whose function was the contemplative life of prayer), the peasants and laborers (who tilled the soil), and the warrior class (who fought battles).

Most scholars agree that knighthood dates back to a period from the 10th or 11th century, with a warrior of a lower social class who was enlisted to fight for a landowner or nobleman in exchange for material reward. Following the extensive study presented in Maurice Keen's chapter "The Secular Origins of Chivalry" (*Chivalry* 18–43), for instance, historian Frances Gies states, "The economic prototype of the knight, then, was a free man, holding land, and owing feudal military service.... The soldiers of the earlier period may or may not properly be called knights, but the full development of knighthood came only with the acquisition of class identity" (*The Knight in History* 4). The Germanic ideal of *comitatus*, exemplified by the old heroic poem *Beowulf*, consisted of the bond between a lord and his men; the men fought for their lord, and the lord rewarded them with booty and even with land. It was the acquisition of the latter that afforded the vassal-knight the wealth and means to gain social status and procure both superior weapons and horses for warfare. Leo Braudy, in his comprehensive study, *From Chivalry to Terrorism: War and the Changing Nature of Masculinity*, likewise points out that at first such warriors came from a "low social position," one that likened them to the classical Roman concept of the *miles*, a paid military servant or slave; in Old English, the term for knight, "cniht," originally meant a young male servant, which also demonstrates the lower status of this figure (66), a point that Gies also emphasizes (14).

However, by the 12th century, an important shift in status had begun: "From a fighting class who served the nobility, knights had risen to a position that even nobles envied and coveted" (Braudy 67). The knight gained status and power, attracting the attention not only of nobles, but also of the Church and the monarchy, both entities seeing the advantage of enlisting the aid of knights, or the potential danger of an unchecked powerful warrior class. Although knighthood began as a secular concept, it became transformed when the medieval Church sanctioned its violence by enlisting this class of knights for the Crusades.

It is this rise of the "Christian knight," perhaps, that marks the origin of "chivalry," as distinct from earlier knighthood, even though the concept of the chivalric is difficult to define with precision because of its cultural over-exposure (much like that of the Freudian Oedipal complex), a point that Richard W. Kaeuper emphasizes in his insightful "Historical Introduction" to *A Knight's Own Book of Chivalry*, a treatise on chivalry written by a 14th-century French knight, Geoffroi de Charny (2–3). Keen defines chivalry as "an ethos in which martial, aristocratic, and Christian forces were fused together" (*Chivalry* 16). Again, we turn to Braudy for an apt summary of this shift: he avers that while the chivalric code of knighthood may have been secular and "ethical" in its inception, rather than religious: "when it was united with the crusading impulse, it gave the actions of the warrior a transcendent defense, combining military aggression with both divine favor and moral validation" (75). The function and character of the knight evolved from the very early Middle Ages to reflect changing social and political forces, and to conform to images of the ideal man in relation to the world—both this one and the next—as the medieval Christian Church began to exert a greater influence in the secular sphere. The evolution of knighthood in Europe, then, is frequently discussed in three stages: its earliest form of the "armored, mounted solider in the turmoil-filled ninth and tenth centuries," followed by its maturation in the "eleventh through thirteenth centuries, the age of the architects of the King Arthur legend," the time in which the knight became "the cornerstone" of feudalism and also acquired both secular and spiritual prestige, and finally by its decline due to social changes that marked the end of the Middle Ages (Gies 3).

Beyond its historical existence, knighthood continued to exert a pronounced influence in popular culture and in imaginative literature, ultimately serving as an emblem of ideal courtesy and courage: the valiant warrior who is also mannered and charismatic has never lost its appeal. Braudy points to the pervasive influence of the imaginative figure of the Christian knight, one who placed a premium on piety as well as prowess:

The literary and artistic myth of his autonomy, the solitary knight on a quest to do what he believes is right, owes its genesis to the effort of Christianity and chivalry to reshape the warrior heritage into a new system of values.... It's the model that persists in the present, when the hero in westerns and action films is so often depicted as a bystander, a loner who doesn't want to become involved in the fray, but finally must, because of personal relation and moral obligation. The artistic preoccupation in both Western and Japanese culture with the solitary adventurer, as well as the lure of aloneness in increasingly complex urban societies, owes a crucial debt to the chivalric model of the warrior ... whose primary function is not in fighting but in the quest for a truth that is both outside himself and within. So the western gunfighter Shane ... is drawn to defend his weaker friends, and even Rambo (in *Rambo III*) is in a Buddhist monastery when he receives the call to action back in Vietnam [*From Chivalry to Terrorism* 92–93].

Thus, the model of knighthood that has enjoyed the most enduring appeal, as Braudy's assertion shows us, is the figure of the *errant* knight, whose solitary quest is not only for adventure, but also to realize fully his own potential, the pursuit of what Emerson calls moral perfectionism. The figure of the errant, spiritual knight derives from a typology that Beverly Kennedy, in *Knighthood in the Morte D'Arthur*, identifies as the "true knight." In understanding the distinction Kennedy makes among three main types of medieval knight that evolved in the Middle Ages and populate the pages of Malory's late medieval romance, it is clear that it is the true knight, exemplified by the celebrated figure of Lancelot, that has enjoyed the most enduring presence in literature and culture. Although it is imaginative literature of epic proportions, and not a nonfiction account, Malory's text is recognized as a central document for an understanding of knighthood, and an accurate reflection of many of its tenets. Richard W. Kaeuper asserts that Geoffroi of Charny's text on chivalry forms part of a "trinity of works very close to knighthood," along with the biography of another famous medieval knight, the *History of William Marshal*, and Sir Thomas Malory's *Morte D'Arthur* (*A Knight's Own Book of Chivalry* 42). The figure of Lancelot in Malory's 15th-century text continues to haunt the popular imagination, and the liminal outlaw hero in Hollywood film is, as we shall see, his worthy descendant.

In *Knighthood in the Morte D'Arthur* Kennedy traces the evolution of three typologies of knighthood found in Malory's text: the heroic, the worshipful and the true knight, all of which reflect important changes in the social and political structure of medieval Europe already summarized above. In Malory's text, Kennedy observes that Gawain exemplifies the oldest form of knighthood, the heroic, which espouses the values of feudalism, in this case using the social organization of the clan, derivative of the most famous models of such a type, Beowulf and Roland (83). The heroic knight's code is that of loyalty; he insists upon his right to revenge, and he is at home on the battlefield (97). In his article "Chivalry and the *Morte Darthur*," Richard Barber likewise notes that this type of knight in Malory's work derives from an earlier Germanic ideal of the "culture of the war-band" conceptualizing knighthood as battle (*A Companion to Malory* 20).

Another type, the worshipful or social knight, exemplified by Sir Tristram, but also by King Arthur himself, combines the feudal and courtly codes; this knight takes a pragmatic, rationalist approach to his profession, observing the manners of courtesy in the company of ladies and the rules of the political and judicial system in, for instance, jousts and tournaments (97). The rise of the worshipful knight, a late development of the institution of knighthood, corresponds with the interests the monarchy showed toward this powerful class of individuals, and the efforts to co-opt them—following the earlier lead of the Church's military orders of crusader knights—by founding various "Orders" that inducted worthy members to serve the monarchy.[1] The site of the worshipful knight in Malory's *Morte* is, of course, the court (or Camelot), and the Pentecostal Oath Arthur asks of his knights embodies the principles of this typology:

> thenne the kyng stablysshed all his knyghtes and gaf them that were of londes not ryche, he gaf them londes, and charged hem neuer to doo outraagyousyte nor mordre, and alweyes to flee treason. Also by no meane to be cruel, but to gyue mercy vnto hym that asketh mercy, vpon payn of forfeture of their worship and lordship of Kyng Arthur foreuermore, and alweyes to doo ladyes, damoysels, and gentylwymmen socour vpon payne of dethe. Also that no man take noo batails in a wrongful quarel for noo lawe, ne for noo worldes goodes. Vnto this were all the knyghtes sworne of the Table Round, both old and young, and euery yere were they sworne at the hyghe feest of Pentecost [III.15.27–38; III.15.33–46].[2]

This oath emphasizes an adherence to upholding the rights of the collective community, and recognition of Arthur as the figurehead of the law: "worship" is attained through acts that serve the communal good, and the monarchy itself, and adherence to a standard that applies to all of the knights. Furthermore, it is Arthur who invests the authority in the knights to hold lands and govern them in his name.

Kennedy's third type of knight, best represented by Lancelot, is the true or spiritual knight, the figure who has perhaps enjoyed the most lasting influence in the western imagination, and who is certainly the most complexly problematic for the reader. Much of this must be credited to Malory's own inventiveness in drawing such a richly developed character, which departs extensively from his French sources.[3] He is the most courteous and honorable of knights, yet he betrays his king, and his own knighthood, for the sake of his tragic love. He espouses the virtue of chastity but cannot avoid his illicit love for the queen.[4] According to Kennedy, the true knight, influenced by the Church's dictates, understands both the feudal and courtly codes of the heroic and worshipful knights, but pays homage to God, viewing knighthood as a spiritual calling. He is neither "primitive nor fatalistic" in his thinking, like the heroic knight, nor pragmatic and rationalistic, like the worshipful knight, but is rather mystical and providential, maintaining that God takes an active stand in the affairs of men. Corbenic, the Grail castle, is "a visible sign of God's grace" (97). Lancelot, we will remember, was destined to achieve the Holy Grail, but because of his sin with the queen, his illegitimate son, Galahad, fulfills this role instead.[5] Moreover, early in Malory's text, Lancelot, in a rare moment of extended speech, states very clearly his view of knighthood. When a damsel asks him why he has never taken a wife, and repeats a rumor that Guinevere "hath ordeyned by enchauntment that ye shal neuer loue none other but her" (VI.12.11; VI.10.41–42) Lancelot replies:

> I maye not warne peple to speke of me what it pleaseth hem. But for to be a wedded man, I thynke hit not, for thenne I must couche with her, and leue armes and turnementys, batayls, and aduentures. And as for to say for to take my plesaunce with peramours, that wylle I refuse, in pryncypal for drede of God. For knyghtes that ben auouturous or lecherous shal not be happy ne fortunate vnto the werrys, for outher they shalle be ouercome with a symplyer knyghte than they be hemself, outher els they shal by vnhap and her cursydnes slee better men than they ben hemself, and soo who that vseth peramours shalle be vnhappy, and all thing is vnhappy that is about hem [VI.12.14–22; VI.10.1–11].

In the above treatise, the insistence that God judges a knight's actions as worthy of reward or "cursydnes" is in accord with the belief of a historical knight, Geoffroi of Charny, as Kaeuper explains it: "Charny reminds his contemporaries such perfection [to which knights should aspire] can never be attributed to human effort alone, but rather to God's wonderful grace," an expression of Charny's insistence on "absolute divine election" (*A Knight's Own Book of Chivalry* 30). Lancelot also believes that a true knight must be both chaste and fearful of God to fulfill his calling, but that he must avoid marriage, a commitment that would interfere with his pursuit of his vocation. This conviction is compromised, of course, by his tragic love of the queen, but Lancelot remains, until the end of his life, a conflicted character because of these two loves. And despite the fact that the love is adulterous, Malory, speaking of Lancelot and Guinevere, praises their "old loue" that was in "Kynge Arthurs days," for its "trouthe and feythfulnes," rather than the fickle nature of love in his own time. Guinevere, Malory maintains, "was a true louer, and therefor she had a good ende" (XVIII.25.30–38; XVIII.25.28–35).[6]

The final sections of Malory's *Morte* introduce the civil strife and the ensuing demise of the Round Table. Much of the *Morte* has been shown to be a reflection of the tumultuous times in which Malory lived. The internal struggle that fells Arthur's realm mirrors the War of the Roses that raged in England, for the duration of Malory's life, between two powerful factions—the Houses of Lancaster and York. Malory himself was a knight, and a knight who spent several years in prison—where he composed at least most of his text—because of shifting political fortunes in this war. Therefore, the *Morte* embodies timeless ideals, but also the topical issues of 15th-century England, and of Malory's own fascinating part in that time.[7] The concluding books of the work, as Kennedy discusses in detail, depict how three separate trials accusing Guinevere of treason, and the clash of knightly codes of conduct, result in tragedy. In the first two instances—that of the poisoned apple, in which the queen is falsely accused of poisoning Sir Patryse, and the episode in which a jealous knight, Sir Mellyagraunce, mistakenly accuses Guinevere of adultery with Sir Kay—Arthur, the worshipful knight, cannot defend her because his role is that of adjudicator. Moreover, in both cases Arthur's honor, his "worship," is at stake, but Lancelot—the true knight—can and does come to the queen's defense. As Kennedy points out, in the first trial, the moral and legal issues are the same; in the second case, they are separable, but the legal issue, and ensuing trial by combat, is straightforward: Mellyagraunce accuses the queen of adultery with the wrong knight, so technically, his legal claim is false, and Lancelot is once again the victor (347).

The final trial, however, dramatizes the conflict between true justice and what the law itself will allow, as well as precipitating the tragic end of the *Morte*; it places these three typologies of knighthood, and the code of behavior represented by each, into conflict when the treacherous knights, Agrauayn (Aggravaine) and Mordred, force the adultery issue—which Arthur suspected but wished not to acknowledge—into the public light, as Malory makes clear: "For as the Frensshe book sayth, the kynge was ful lothe therto that ony noyse shold be vpon Syr Launcelot and his queen, for the kynge had a demynge, but he wold not here of hit. For Syr Launcelot had done soo moche for hym and the quene soo many tymes that, wete ye wel, the kynge loued hym passingly wel" (XX.2.36–39; XX.2.36–41). The two treacherous knights, motivated by their own desire to advance themselves, wish to cause a division between Arthur and Lancelot, yet they insist that their concern is for Arthur's name, maintaining that, as his kin, they can no longer stand by and watch him dishonored. Hence, they persuade Arthur to allow them to set a trap for the lovers. Although Lancelot is found in the queen's chamber, Malory makes clear that on this particular occasion, it is doubtful the two were engaged in amorous activity: "And thenne, as the Frensshe book sayth, the quene and Launcelot were togyders. And whether they were abedde or at other maner of disportes my lyst not herof make no mencyon, for loue that tyme was not as is nowadays" (XX.3.33–36; XX.3.4–8).

Unlike the previous two episodes in which the knight is called upon to serve as her champion, this time Lancelot is accused along with the queen; Arthur, having acquiesced to the heroic code of clan loyalty, also fulfills his role as worshipful knight, making a series of decisions that causes the calamitous consequences. He insists upon adhering to the law, ordering the queen to be burned at the stake for treason against the crown. Later, he capitulates to the vengeful Gawain by making war after Lancelot, in the act of rescuing the queen from the stake, inadvertently slays Gawain's brothers, Gareth and Gaheris. Arthur nonetheless laments the demise of the Round Table that will be a consequence of the strife between the two factions: "And moche more I am soryer for my good knyghtes losse than for the losse of my fayre quene, for quenes I myghte haue ynowe, but suche a felaushyp of good knyghtes shalle neuer be togyders in no company" (XX.9.25–27; XX.II.29–32). The female is expendable, but the social order of knighthood is what Arthur most regrets losing, a pattern that is continued, as we shall see, through time and into modern Hollywood cinema.

Lancelot becomes the model of the liminal outlaw hero when he answers a higher moral imperative to save Guinevere from the impure motives of the Orkney clan and the inadequate judgment of Arthur himself, and then taking refuge at his French castle, Joyous Garde; being forced into exile after returning the queen to Arthur by the Pope's edict; and finally, slaying, reluctantly, the vengeful Gawain. The strife between Arthur and Lancelot, instigated by the hatred and envy of Mordred and Aggravayne, then continued by Gawain's thirst for revenge and in accordance with the clan mentality of the heroic knight, creates the split in the kingdom that allows for Mordred, the usurper, to incite Civil War that brings about the demise of the Round Table. Readers witness the tragic events unfold, hoping to the end that a solution can be found that will avert the calamity. Lancelot, who has repeatedly defended Camelot and its ideals and tried to serve true justice, can finally only revert to his own inner sanctity, and that of the Christian ideals he has espoused throughout the text. It is surely no coincidence that the result of this clash of codes makes the end of Camelot seem inevitable, and leads to the lovers' lives of renunciation, Guinevere living out her days as a nun, and Lancelot's life ending as a saintly hermit, full of sorrow and remorse. Although his love for the queen has impeded his ability to earn a complete vision of the grail, he does at last achieve the blessedness to which he has aspired throughout Malory's text. His death and the reception of his soul into heaven at the conclusion of Malory's work imitate those of medieval saints' lives and martyrs. The night Lancelot dies, the Bishop of Canterbury has a dream of Lancelot being escorted to Heaven by a host of angels, with the gates opening to receive his soul. When he tells this to Sir Bors and the other followers of Lancelot who discover Lancelot's corpse, they find that he "laye as he had smyled, and the swettest sauour aboute hym that euer they felt" (XXI.12.18–23; XXI.12.26–34) the sweet odor a sign of his sainthood. Moreover, the corpse of Lancelot is on display for fifteen days, with apparently no decay, another sign of his election. In the end, Lancelot fulfills his higher spiritual calling, after a life of conflict and earthly renown. Finally, separation from social and legal entanglements is the only way Lancelot can resolve the conflict between his own innate sense of honor, the legal obligations imposed by Arthur's worshipful code, and Gawain's blind adherence to the heroic code of loyalty to his kinsmen and revenge for the death of his brothers.

Thus, Lancelot, the true knight, proves himself to be the champion of Arthur's ideals, the only one who can, in the end, serve the higher principles to which the Round Table aspires. As Andrew Lynch observes in "Malory's *Morte Darthur* and History,"

> To the modern outsider, and to an outraged enemy such as Gawain becomes, it would seem that Lancelot is a traitor to Arthur, since he has "held" the queen and fought against the king to keep her from his judgment and control. But Malory clearly does not see things that way. To him, Lancelot has saved Guenevere from an unjust death wished on her by liars and false counselors, and saved Arthur from the shame of allowing it to happen. "Lancelot is in real fact the only character who continues to be loyal to King Arthur throughout the war" (Radulescu 2003: 133). He is allowed an autonomy of action that exceeds the interpretation of loyalty as strict obedience to a lord [*A Companion to Arthurian Literature* 301].

In agreement with this statement, Kennedy goes so far as to assert that throughout the final section of Malory's text, Lancelot fulfills "the kingly ideal which Arthur could not fulfill—that of the *rex pius et Justus*" (*Knighthood* 332)— citing also earlier examples of the king's willingness to shed needless blood and his failure to bring the law to bear on his own kinsmen, the Orkney clan, as well as his choices in the concluding books that point to this. In the end, it is Lancelot who displays the kingly virtues of striving for true justice and piety, reverence for God.

The liminal outlaw hero, exemplified by Lancelot, serves an important role in American culture and ideology. Robert Ray's *A Certain Tendency of the Hollywood Cinema, 1930–1980* points out "American culture's traditional dichotomy of individual and community that had generated the most significant pair of competing myths: the outlaw hero and the official hero" (58–59). The outlaw hero is the "gunfighter" or "loner" who represents the American impulse toward independence and "freedom from entanglements," while the contrasting official hero—often a "farmer or family man"—espouses a belief in "collective action" and the "legal process" rather than an individual code of right and wrong (59). These two antithetical paradigms prevail in "disguised westerns" (*Casablanca*, 1942), with Rick Blaine (Humphrey Bogart) and Victor Laszlo (Paul Henreid) as outlaw and official heroes, respectively; it is also in classic westerns, such as *Shane* (1953), which Ray identifies as a composite "screen memory" (70) of classic Hollywood. *Shane* presents these two competing types through the film's titular figure (Alan Ladd) and his opposite, Joe Starrett (Van Heflen).

There are compelling reasons that suggest this particular type of outlaw hero in Hollywood film draws inspiration from the typology of the errant or "true knight." Ray rightly shows that the outlaw hero in Hollywood film owes a debt to Huck Finn (105), who escapes the entanglements and prejudices of culture; Huck avoids getting "civilized" when, at the end of Twain's novel, he evades domesticity by lighting out for the western territories. The outlaw hero, like Huck, avoids the confining ties of the feminine, but while Huck Finn can evade the ties of culture and community by fleeing their influence, he is powerless to affect change and bring about justice, as the medieval true knight and the later liminal outlaw hero can. Reaching farther back into the collective memory, Ray also points to the figure of Robin Hood as a model for the outlaw hero, as he, too, avoids the entrapment of a deadening culture (125). Robin Hood, himself a mythic figure with a rich and varied literary history, is sometimes portrayed as the champion of a virtuous absent monarch (Richard the Lionheart), and in opposition to a corrupt usurper king and/or his henchmen, but his arena of operation is most often outside the community, not within it. Moreover, Robin Hood is almost always associated with a community of fellow outlaws, rather than living the solitary way of the errant knight. Lancelot, conversely, spends more time away from the Round Table than he does at its official seat, Camelot, adhering to his own imperative that he should seek adventure, which also provides the means to avoid romantic entanglements, as well as social obligations and observances. Finally, Robin Hood does not experience a deep conflict between a romantic passion for a woman and adherence to a higher ideal, nor does he occupy the liminal space of the errant knight or gunfighter. Thus, while the significance of Robin Hood in the cultural imagination in the west can scarcely be over-estimated and does inform our understanding of the outlaw hero, certain features that Kennedy associates particularly with the "true knight," epitomized by the problematic Lancelot, exert a more pronounced influence over the portrayal of a more narrowly defined but enduring portrayal of the liminal-space outlaw hero figure of Hollywood film.

First, in order to fulfill a calling or vocation, both the true knight and this type of outlaw hero remain free of domestic obligations—cast instead as errant figures—and thus lead a life of solitude; second, both recognize a moral imperative that supersedes social convention and the law, but maintain what is, at times, a strained or uneasy alliance with the legal system, and come to its rescue to achieve true justice, while still preserving their individualism. When the law does not deliver justice, this type of hero is thus able to rectify the wrong, often, as Richard Slotkin explores in depth in *Gunfighter Nation: The Myth of the Frontier in Twentieth-Century America*, through force. Specifically, the liminal outlaw hero derives from the true knight, rather than the Robin Hood archetype because, while he holds himself to a higher standard than that which the social culture and the law demand, he is often the figure who must vindicate the representative of that culture or law, upholding social customs and/or coming to the aid of the figurehead of the law. In this way, both the true knight and the liminal outlaw hero are called upon to reconcile contradictions or tensions that exist between the individual and the community. To do this, both must exist in the liminal space that allows them to preserve their individuality, yet they must also be able to join the common effort of the collective group when called upon to do so, something that a figure who has transgressed the law cannot do.

The inadequacy of the law to dispense true justice in a time of crisis is what the end of the *Morte* dramatizes so effectively. When the law fails, or conflicts with a higher moral imperative, the "worshipful knight" (analogous to Ray's "official hero") must attain help from the "true knight" (the forerunner of the "outlaw hero") who adheres to a private code outside the legal and social entanglements of a culture. In the end, Lancelot rescues Arthur's queen from a punishment more severe than the text itself can support, but he cannot save the kingdom of Camelot from its internal strife. His own quest to serve a higher ideal than the one demanded of the political and social system of which he partakes, augments the tragic division in his character. Readers see that Lancelot, in his love for the queen, compromises his own ideals of knighthood, yet his service to others and to God exceeds that of the heroic and worshipful knights. His dilemma, and the attempt to reconcile contradictory impulses, is one that is mirrored in an essential conflict in American thought. Ray's point that the ideology of the official hero, "We are a nation of laws, not of men," and that of the outlaw hero, "I don't know what the law says, but I do know what is right and wrong"(62), shares similarities with the conflict dramatized in Malory's text.

But how can we explain the continuation of these traits of the true knight from Malory's text to classic Hollywood and the modern cinema? Malory's *Morte D'Arthur*, written and published at the end of the 15th century, signals the end of an era—the Middle Ages proper—and with it, one might suppose, the death of chivalry. As we shall see, however, in the next chapter, the ideals of knighthood retained a firm hold over the popular imagination, becoming even more pervasive with the medieval revival that flourished in the 19th century and beyond. Malory's text was so strong as to obliterate many of its predecessors; his influence on writers from the 19th century to the present is considerable, and his most complex and compelling figuration of chivalry resides in the character of Lancelot du Lake.

CHAPTER 2

Chivalry, the Medieval Revival and the Popular Imagination

A scrutiny of Sir Thomas Malory's life proves it to be as fascinating as the fiction he composed, his character as perplexing and contradictory as that of his greatest knight, Lancelot. Two full-length studies of Malory's life and times mentioned in the previous chapter (those of Felicity Riddy and P.J.C. Field) offer the fullest accounts, but much remains unknown because of a paucity of reliable records. In addition, there were several figures during this time with the same name. However, only one character seems to be viable as the author of the *Morte D'Arthur*, Sir Thomas Malory of Newbold Revel in Warwickshire. A succinct version of what is certain or near certain about Malory's biographical facts can be found in P.J.C. Field's "The Malory Life-Records" (*A Companion to Malory* 115–130) and in the self-references Malory included in the *Morte*.

According to Field, Malory was born into an established gentrified family (who held lands in three counties) "within a year either way of 1416" (115), and he died in prison in 1471, probably on March 12, although other records indicate March 14 (117). Malory was twice elected to Parliament, and was clearly esteemed by his peers: surviving documents list him as a witness for various legal transactions. Surviving records also indicate that Malory was knighted in 1441; this is when he is first shown to bear the title "Sir," whereas just the year before he is not recognized as such (119). However, a contradictory side of Malory's character emerged, beginning in 1450. "Then, with the new decade, Malory's life, for no known reason, underwent a startling change," when he was accused of a number of crimes: an attempted ambush of the Duke of Buckingham, cattle theft, rape, and breaking into Combe Abbey, "insulting the monks, and stealing a great deal of money" ("The Life Records" 119) but, curiously, it seems that Malory was either never tried or condemned for many of these crimes, which seem to be generated by the politics of the War of the Roses. Malory's entire life unfolded against the backdrop of this violent era in England's history, and he is known to have changed allegiance between the Lancastrians and Yorkists. At any rate, for crimes real and/or imagined, Malory spent the last two decades of his life in—and sometimes out of—prison, either by escape (twice), bail, or general pardon, although he was excluded from a royal pardon twice (1468 and 1470), the reason why he died in prison, having composed much or all of the *Morte* while incarcerated (117).

The contradictions in Malory's life, then, are intriguing: he was a writer of considerable talent, a landowner and a knight who was elected to public office—indicating the esteem he commanded from his peers—and yet he spent a large part of his adult life as a prisoner under heavy guard, accused of unsavory crimes. What is most significant about Malory and the transmission of his *Morte D'Arthur* is that he possessed a charismatic personality, exhibited a sincere reverence for knighthood, and wrote a text of striking originality that conveys something of his own complexity of character and of the principles of chivalry for which he already expresses a nostalgia, writing his work at the close of the Middle Ages. Therefore, the yearning for an ideal rooted in the past—what will come to be known as "medievalism"—had arguably already found expression in Malory's own late 15th-century work.[1]

Malory's text was completed by 1470, as we know from its concluding colophon (supplied by the editor and publisher, William Caxton) that indicates it was finished in the ninth year of the reign of King Edward IV. Caxton, responsible for the first book that was printed in England, published *Le Morte D'Arthur* in 1485, ostensibly due to public demand for it.[2] Malory, in providing unity to disparate sources through his own original vision of the chivalric deeds of Arthur and his Round Table knights, gave to posterity what we can call the "received legend." He is the writer who is responsible for providing what later ages came to know as the traditional Arthurian story.[3] That Malory's text enjoyed continued popularity can be deduced by the fact that it was reproduced five times after its initial publication. In his article "The Reception of Malory's *Morte Darthur*," A.S.G. Edwards, tracing its publication history, states that it was reprinted in 1498, 1529, 1559, 1582, and finally in 1634, with the Stansby edition that marked the beginning of a long hiatus (*A Companion to Malory* 241–242). Since printed books were costly and in these early years available only to the privileged, we can assume that Malory's was valued, to be in such demand as to warrant five new editions.

Despite this success of Malory's book, the Arthurian legend in imaginative literature experienced a decline over a period of several centuries, largely because it was exploited for political and monetary gain. The Tudors, who won victory in the War of the Roses and began manufacturing propaganda to recast recent history in their own favor (propagating what became known as the "Tudor Myth") made untenable claims to have descended from Arthur himself; monks at Glastonbury Abbey averred that they had discovered the tomb of Arthur and Guinevere there. Such exaggerations opened up the legend to literary parody, although it remained always a vital presence in the *popular* imagination, nor was its influence on the literature of the Renaissance and Restoration completely extinguished. The legend, albeit in a somewhat disguised form, is present in Spenser's famed epic Renaissance poem *The Faerie Queene* (1596), for instance, as discussed in detail by Charles Bowie Millican in his book titled *Spenser and the Table Round: A Study in the Contemporaneous Background for Spenser's Use of the Arthurian Legend* (Harvard Studies in Comparative Literature VIII, 1932; rpt, New York: Octagon Books, 1967). In the 17th century, John Milton, the great English epic poet who authored *Paradise Lost* (1667, 1674), contemplated the Arthurian legend for his subject (Book IX, ll. 28–47), but chose instead the more ambitious task of rewriting *Genesis*. Edwards discusses the continued interest in the Arthurian corpus as it can be witnessed by the fact that an elaborate twelve-day entertainment designed for Queen Elizabeth I "was clearly structured around Arthurian legend; but at one point it reveals a specifically Malorian influence" (*A Companion to Malory* 244), and that Elizabethan popular ballads contain references to the legend (245). Although Malory was dependent upon the French Vulgate Cycle, five prose romances composed in the early 13th century, it was clearly the Englishness of his Arthur, as derived from indigenous English sources—Geoffrey of Monmouth's *History of the Kings of Britain*, *The Alliterative Morte Arthure*, *The Stanzaic Morte Arthur*—that helped to keep the *Matter of Britain* from fading out of the collective cultural memory during the two centuries after Stansby's 1634 edition.

The renewed interest in the King Arthur legend in general, but in Malory's text in particular, was due in part to the larger Gothic Revival that occurred in the latter half of the 18th century. This movement found expression in its preoccupation with history and antiquarianism, in its preference for the medieval over the classical in architectural design, and in its interest in uncovering, preserving, and editing ancient texts, evinced by organizations such as the Early English Text Society.[4] In the early decades of the 19th century, Caxton's Malory was reprinted three times in two years: twice in 1816 by the J. Walker & Company, and in 1817 an edition was published by Longman and Company, with an introduction and notes by the then poet laureate of England, Robert Southey. Southey's edition was very popular with the Romantic poets—Keats and Wordsworth, for instance—and with the mid-century writers, such as

William Morris and Lord Tennyson. Other editions continued to appear throughout the 19th century, including those of Thomas Wright (1858) and Sir Edward Strachey (1868) further evidence of the resurgence of interest in Malory's Arthurian work.

In the early decades of the 19th century, it was the romances of Sir Walter Scott that re-envisioned and popularized the chivalric ideal. As Mark Girouard remarks, "One of Scott's greatest achievements was to bring chivalry up to date, and popularize a type of character which could reasonably be called chivalrous, but was acceptable as a model both by himself and his contemporaries" (*The Return to Camelot: Chivalry and the English Gentleman* 34). Scott was an antiquarian, as well as an occasional editor of medieval texts, but it is his imaginative literature in the form of poems and romances set in the medieval past—such as *Marmion* (1808) and *Ivanhoe* (1820)—that served as the most powerful forms of transmission for the chivalric ideal of knighthood.

One example of the way in which Scott's fiction impacted his contemporaries can be seen in the work of Kenhelm Digby, who composed a very popular treatise, *The Broad-Stone of Honour, or Rules for the Gentlemen of England* (1822), later printed in revised and expanded form as *The Broad Stone of Honour: Or, the True Sense and Practice of Chivalry* (1828–29 and 1844–48). In his chapter of the same name, Mark Girouard asserts that while Scott saw chivalry as essentially belonging to a distant past, with only some of its elements persisting in the present day in the conduct of gentlemen, "to Digby it was a permanently valid code, which expressed itself in different ways in different centuries, but remained essentially the same" (*Chivalry* 60). As Girouard points out, Digby was convinced that it was possible for the modern gentleman to adhere to the same standard of conduct imposed on knights in the age of chivalry, namely "belief and trust in God, generosity, high honour, independence, truthfulness, loyalty to friends and leaders, hardihood and contempt of luxury, courtesy, modesty, humanity, and respect for women" (*Chivalry* 61–62). Digby's text was admired by leading artists and critics of the day: romantic poet laureate William Wordsworth, art critic John Ruskin, and the Pre-Raphaelite poets and painters William Morris and Edward Burne-Jones (*Chivalry* 63).

New editions of Malory, along with Scott's reinterpretation of chivalry for his readers, is thus shown to have precipitated the apex of the Arthurian Revival that occurred in the middle of the 19th century, largely by the composition of the epic poem *Idylls of the King* by poet laureate Alfred, Lord Tennyson. This work was first published serially over a period of several decades (from 1859 to 1885) and then as a complete work, with "rehearsal" poems included in earlier collections of his verse. In its final form, *Idylls of the King* consists of twelve narrative poems (idylls) along with a "Dedication" and a coda, "To the

Queen." The *Idylls* offer a complete re-visioning of the Arthurian legend, catered to appeal to Victorian sensibilities. However, Tennyson was by no means the only poet to compose Arthurian poems.

William Morris' first collection of verse, *The Defence of Guenevere and Other Poems* (1858), features four finely crafted poems which specifically use Malory as their source: the titular poem ("The Defence of Guenevere"), "King Arthur's Tomb," "Sir Galahad, A Christmas Mystery," and "The Chapel in Lyoness," with others in the volume that reference the legend as well. Although it was generally savaged by critics of the day, Morris' *The Defence of Guenevere and Other Poems* contains what are now considered some of his finest verse. Morris finds moments of undeveloped dramatic potential in Malory's work, then expands and develops them, providing psychological depth and a poignant sympathy for his characters. The first two poems probe the problem of the adulterous love between Lancelot and Guinevere, and Morris portrays the lovers with sympathy, even having his Guenevere declare to her accusing audience in the poem, that Arthur bought her "with his great name and little love" (l. 83). The latter two poems were met with less hostility by Morris' Victorian readers, perhaps because they focused on the chaste knight, Galahad, and the value of a brotherhood of knights. What a comparison of the reception of Morris' poems with Tennyson's shows us is the importance of reworking the medieval material to suit audience tastes. The negative reaction to Morris' *Defence* volume was clearly focused on the sexuality and violence contained in it, while Tennyson's characters, especially the women, are recognizably Victorian, or judged according to Victorian standards of conduct. Even earlier than Morris and Tennyson, Matthew Arnold had published his *Tristan and Iseult* (1852), and Morris' friend, Algernon Charles Swinburne, composed a considerable *corpus* of Arthurian verse, notably *Tristram of Lyonesse* (1882) and *The Tale of Balen* (1896), which offer a consciously opposing view of these respective knights as they are portrayed in Tennyson's work. Swinburne's *Tristram* poem is a book-length narrative verse poem, divided into a "Prelude" and nine sections; it recreates the entire story of the fated lovers, and his treatment is unapologetically romantic and positive, in opposition to Tennyson's depiction of Tristram and his lover, Iseult of Ireland, as adulterous materialists. Likewise, Swinburne's Balen is heroic and stoic in his acceptance of his fate, while Tennyson shows him as ultimately weak-willed and unable to adhere to Arthur's ideals.

Hence, the many accomplished poets who found the medieval past, and Arthurian legend in particular, a lucrative source for their verse, testifies to the enduring appeal of the ideals and conflicts this material offered. Still, it was Tennyson's *Idylls* that interpreted the Arthurian legend for his contemporary audience, winning the admiration of the public, and the royal family as well. Using Malory as his primary (though not exclusive) source, Tennyson infused his twelve Arthurian idylls with Victorian values and concerns, exploring the idea of inspired leadership and espousing the importance of social order, emphasizing the role of women as the upholders of the moral fabric of society and insisting on a sexual code of conduct appropriate for both genders. He purges the medieval Catholicism found in Malory's grail section in order to cater to a middle-class, largely Protestant audience, and presents an Arthur who is second to none. Tennyson removes the taint of illegitimacy surrounding Arthur's conception and birth, and insists upon the king's chastity as well as his high moral standards. For instance, Mordred is not, as in Malory's work, Arthur's illegitimate son through an incestuous *liaison* but, as in earlier English accounts, he is the nephew of the king. As Tennyson insists in his coda to the *Idylls*, his Arthur, like Victoria's royal consort, Prince Albert, and Tennyson's best friend, Arthur Henry Hallam, represents human perfection, "ideal manhood closed in real man" ("To the Queen").

Just as Malory's work reflects the struggles and values of 15th-century England, so Tennyson's *Idylls* provide us with those of Victorian England. A comparison of the chivalric code in Malory's text (the Pentecostal Oath) with the tenets Tennyson's Arthur imposes upon his knights, illustrates that the writer of each age conceives of central chivalric values that are bound up with those of his own time and audience, as Girouard points out in his discussion of Scott's updated version of chivalry in the early part of the century. In Tennyson's "Guinevere," which features their final meeting in the *Idylls* in the gathering gloom of the apocalyptic end, Arthur reminds his queen of the oath he had imposed upon his knights:

> I made them lay their hands in mine and swear
> To reverence the King, as if he were
> Their conscience, and their conscience as their King,
> To break the heathen and uphold the Christ,
> To ride abroad redressing human wrongs.
> To speak no slander, no, nor listen to it,
> To honor his own word as if his God's,
> To lead sweet lives in purest chastity,
> To love one maiden only, cleave to her,
> And worship her by years of noble deeds,
> Until they won her; for indeed I knew
> Of no more subtle master under heaven,
> Than is the maiden passion for a maid,

> Not only to keep down the base in man,
> But teach high thought, and amiable words
> And courtliness, and the desire of fame,
> And love of truth, and all that makes a man [ll. 464–480].

From this excerpt, we can detect significant differences between the rather simple, straightforward, worshipful code of Malory's oath, with its emphasis on basic tenets such as the avoidance of murder or treason, showing mercy to any knights who ask it, and protecting women who are in need. Tennyson's Arthur emphasizes obedience to a strong leader as a *moral* imperative, not in adherence to the feudal or contractual one in Malory but one that rests upon the importance of chastity, "the maiden passion for a maid," as a motive for courage and valor. The emphasis on women as the moral center that inspires manliness and virtue on the part of the knights reflects the Victorian reverence for family as a microcosm of the larger social order, the fear of female sexual passion, and the importance placed upon public duty—by being bound by the tenets of inspired leadership—over private desire.[5]

As mentioned above, Tennyson's Arthur is the "blameless king," who contrasts sharply with the very human, fallible figure found in Malory's text, in which Arthur has illegitimate sons and makes other errors in judgment that contribute to the demise of his order. In contrast to Malory, Tennyson blames the adultery between Lancelot and Guinevere for the fall of the Round Table, as Arthur admonishes his adulterous queen: "Then came thy shameful sin with Lancelot; / Then came the sin of Tristram and Isolt, / Then others, following these, my mightiest knights, / And drawing foul ensample from fair names, / Sinn'd also, till the loathsome opposite / Of all my heart had destined did obtain, / And all thro' thee!" ("Guinevere" 484–490). The corrupting influence of unchecked feminine passion is made explicit when Arthur likens a faithless wife to a venereal disease (a reference to the Victorian concern about the precipitous rise in the number of prostitutes in its culture) should the husband refuse to cast her off, as he himself must now forsake the fallen Guinevere: "She like a new disease, unknown to men, / Creeps, no precaution used, among the crowd, / Makes wicked lightnings of her eyes, and saps / The fealty of our friends; and stirs the pulse / With devil's leaps, and poisons half the young" ("Guinevere" ll. 515–519).

Malory shows that the demise of the Round Table occurs through the treachery of Mordred and Aggravaine who are the sowers of discord; Gawain, Arthur, and Lancelot adhere to the typologies they represent, and the clash of these brings about the final fall of Arthur's order. Moreover, the lovers enter into the spiritual life after Arthur's demise; Lancelot even enjoys the death of a saint. Tennyson's Lancelot, by contrast, vanishes from the *Idylls* after "The Last Tournament" (the tenth of twelve idylls), and the final meeting and parting of Malory's lovers at the convent in Almesbury (after Arthur's death) is replaced in Tennyson's text by the last encounter there between Guinevere and Arthur.[6] Significantly, the *Idylls* conclude, not with the death of Guinevere and then Lancelot, but—sublimely—with Arthur being borne in a barge to a mysterious destiny, as witnessed by his last surviving knight, Sir Bedivere:

> Thereat once more he moved about, and clomb
> Even to the highest he could climb, and saw,
> Straining his eyes beneath an arch of hand,
> Or thought he saw, the speck that bare the King,
> Down that long water opening on the deep
> Somewhere far off, pass on and on, and go
> From less to less and vanish into light.
> And the new sun rose bringing the new year
> ["The Passing of Arthur" ll. 462–469].

As we can see, while Tennyson employs Malory as his source, he reinterprets the characters and events to suit Victorian sensibilities and to reflect the values of his readership, making the Arthurian legend a popular text for his contemporaries, not unlike Malory's own reworking of his source materials. This demonstrates that the *Matter of Britain* is mythopoeic—that is, it lends itself always to revitalization, while containing an inherently interesting story that transcends the boundaries of history and culture. Malory gave to posterity his "hoole book," a compelling and coherent story of a utopian world of chivalric ideals brought to a tragic end by its own internal strife; Tennyson demonstrated for later writers that the story of Arthur and the Round Table could speak to audiences anew. While certain topical issues influence the manner in which each writer presents the material, the question of what constitutes honor, and the ideal of knighthood, remains an inherent feature in all retellings of the medieval *corpus* of Arthur and his *entourage*. Thus, the figure of the knight, the inception of which we have seen in the previous chapter that focused on medieval chivalry in Malory, retained its hold on the collective imagination of writers and readers despite very pronounced changes in culture and taste.

Medieval mania prevailed in Victorian England, evinced not only by the number of Arthurian literary texts it produced, but also by the many representations of medieval and Arthurian subjects in pictorial art and in recreations of medieval chivalric pageantry. The most famous example of the latter, that of the ill-fated Eglinton Tournament held in Scotland in 1839, was an elaborately planned and orchestrated jousting match in which bad weather and ill-tempers resulted in a ridiculous fiasco that was lampooned by an amused press, as Mark Girouard discusses in Chapter 7, "The Eglinton Tournament." This type of re-enactment may be cited as an early forerunner of activities conducted by the Society for Creative Anachronism, founded in 1966. In pictorial art, the Pre-Raphaelite poets and painters, among them Dante Gabriel Rossetti, William Morris, and Edward Burne-Jones, created and popularized medieval subjects, but especially drew upon Malory's Arthurian work.[7] Several illustrated editions of Tennyson's *Idylls* had appeared, the most notable being those of Gustave Dore (1875), and the early photographer Julia Margaret Cameron (Tennyson's friend) who had earlier created her own visual photographic illustrations of the poems.

When an idea becomes fanatical, it opens itself to parody, as was the case with the Arthurian legend after the Middle Ages, with absurd Tudor claims that the monarchy could trace its roots to Arthur himself, for instance. Chivalric hysteria, which thrived from the early decades of the 19th century, had reached such a pitch by its end as to become the target of parody by Mark Twain, in his *A Connecticut Yankee in King Arthur's Court* (1889), the first time-travel novel, in which the main character (Hank Morgan), having received a blow on the head, traverses back in time to Camelot. Twain's novel enjoys a complex relationship with the medieval past. Its sole target is not the superstitions of the Middle Ages, with its oppression of the peasants, and the tyranny of Church and monarchy; rather, the novel also serves as an invective against more contemporary issues, primarily slavery. Twain attacks the over sentimentality of the 19th-century view of the medieval past as idyllic, but shows his own age to be far from a utopian world.[8] He has little patience for the enormous popularity of Tennyson's *Idylls* in England and America, yet in his novel Twain clearly shows us, from Hank Morgan's unscrupulous use of technology, that the fruits of "progress" are not always used ethically. What Twain's novel does show us is how deeply ingrained the image of chivalry had become through the revitalized efforts of writers and artists in the 19th century.

The Arthurian revival, and the chivalric ideal that is central to it, continued into modern times, dispersed through the culture in a myriad number of ways: in codified form via groups such as the Boy Scouts, founded by Robert Baden-Powell, and in actual chivalric behavior, such as that reportedly displayed by doomed males on the sinking *Titanic* in 1912. Chivalry for modern audiences emphasizes self-sacrifice and duty over desire, standing by one's post in the service of a higher social imperative. In the first half of the 20th century, it was T.H. White's *The Once and Future King* (1958) that offered a new interpretation of the Arthurian legend for modern audiences. Like Tennyson's *Idylls*, White's novel was first published in installments, and later released as a whole: *The Sword in the Stone* (1938), *The Queen of Air and Darkness* (1939), *The Ill-Made Knight* (1940), and *The Candle in the Wind* (1958), with a final section, *The Book of Merlyn*, being published separately in 1977, although it was composed much earlier. Also like Tennyson, White relied primarily on Malory's text, which he greatly admired, for his understanding of the Arthurian legend, although he, too, infuses the story with his own innovations, making it appeal to a 20th-century audience. White's is perhaps the strongest pacifist version of the legend, which makes sense considering the fact that he began the work between the two world wars. Writing also to a post–Freudian audience, White provided his characters with formative childhoods, and emphasizes the psychology of character. It is White's work that is the basis for popularizing the legend as it was dispersed through the Disney cartoon *The Sword in the Stone* (1963) and the musical *Camelot* (1960), which in 1967 was released as a film version of the same name. The degree to which White's novel revitalized the Arthurian legend for modern audiences can scarcely be over-estimated.

The alluring quality of Arthurian chivalry in particular can be witnessed by the renewal of the legend in literary and cinematic adaptations, which will be discussed in greater detail in ensuing chapters, and in re-enactments by antiquarian societies (the Society for Creative Anachronism, mentioned above, is one example) and live entertainment. In their insightful article "Twice Knightly: Democratizing the Middle Ages for Middle-Class America," Susan Aronstein and Nancy Coiner claim to be "in search of the late twentieth-century American version of what Umberto Eco calls the recurrent dream of the Middle Ages," based on Eco's assertion in his essay "Dreaming the Middle Ages," that post-medieval eras have always re-imagined the distant past to meet their own needs—hence "medievalism" (*Studies in Medievalism: Medievalism in North America* VI, 212). Aronstein and Coiner examine two instances of the reinterpretation of the Middle Ages in contemporary American culture: "Fantasyland," part of Disneyland in southern California, and the Excalibur Hotel and Casino in Las Vegas, both places of "ritualized play" (220) designed for children and adults, respectively. Fantasyland includes a ritual re-enactment of the young Arthur pulling the sword from the stone that proves his election, that he is the right ruler of the kingdom; the Excalibur offers a nightly tournament in King Arthur's Arena, along with a medieval feast for spectators. During the Disneyland ritual, a young boy is chosen from the assembled crowd to succeed Arthur, who has been called away, and is named king in his stead for a day ("Twice-Knightly" 219). In the Excalibur event, a young man from the present time enters the arena and expresses his desire to have lived during the time of chivalry, in King Arthur's court. Merlin appears and grants him his wish via a dream-vision, and a jousting tournament ensues, after which the victorious young man's fantasy concludes with his marriage to Arthur and Guinevere's daughter ("Twice Knightly" 223–224).

Returning to Eco's point that the Middle Ages are always re-imagined by later audiences, and their own aim to find how the myth of chivalry informs late 20th-century American sensibilities, Aronstein and Coiner conclude that the examples of Fantasyland and the Excalibur tournament show how the Middle Ages are adapted to contain central American values, and incorporate into the Arthurian material that which is an inherent part of American history:

> The success of these sites stems from the fact that medieval narrative forms, particularly the romance narrative, provide the basis for our own cultural myth. It is no accident that the only other era in history that Americans revisit frequently, the Western frontier, is based on a narrative that is essentially medieval romance in Western clothing. The Middle Ages speak to us as Americans because its dominant myth provided the plot and values for our own story [229].

The errant knight of medieval romance sought adventure; he roamed the world in search of ways to increase his honor and renown. The westerner in the myth of the American frontier also enjoyed the vast expansiveness of land and the opportunities it afforded to authenticate himself. Both the errant knight and the liminal outlaw hero in the west had to strive to preserve their individuality while serving a social cause. Finally, both were dependent upon their horses and weapons as an integral part of their identity.

The chivalric ideal embodied in the Arthurian legend and exemplified by the fantasy of the Middle Ages and the American West alike, functions as a means to mediate between the real and ideal. As we have seen, Lancelot, the true knight, strives to maintain his ideal version of the chivalric code, even in the face of the harsh social and political pressures that come to a violent climax at the end of Malory's *Morte*. His position is liminal, in that he attempts to bring about a just end for the queen in the face of a harsh judicial pronouncement against her. To defend an ideal is at the heart of true knighthood; it is also the way in the myth of the American west. The ideal of chivalry lived on after the Middle Ages that gave birth to it waned. In the ensuing chapters, we will see how vital and potent the figure of the true knight is, and the incarnations he has assumed in Hollywood cinema and television.

CHAPTER 3

True Knighthood and the Liminal Outlaw Hero in Classic Hollywood Film

The liminal outlaw hero in Hollywood film evolves to meet the changing demands of audiences, but certain features of this figure persist, and these account for his lasting appeal. Two films from the classic Hollywood era provide examples of main characters who serve as strong precursors to the type of liminal hero that will be discussed in detail in the ensuing sections on the urban western and action hero sequential films of the 1970s and beyond. They serve as apt examples of how certain conceptions of knighthood were useful for addressing the conflict between community and the individual, between codified law and that of the solitary figure who remains outside of it. Like many Hollywood films, *Casablanca* and *Shane* show how these conflicting codes can be reconciled in the face of a common enemy.

Saloons, Shoot-Outs and Sad Goodbyes: *Casablanca* (1942)

Casablanca premiered on November 25, 1942, and was released on January 23, 1943. An immediate success, it was nominated for eight Oscars for the 1943 Academy Awards, winning three: Outstanding Motion Picture (Warner Brothers Studio), Best Director (Michael Curtiz), and Best Screenplay (Julius Epstein, Philip Epstein, and Howard Koch). Moreover, *Casablanca* has become arguably the most significant film of all time, in terms of the degree to which it has permeated American culture. In 2007, the film occupied the number three position in the *10th Anniversary Edition of the American Film Institute's*

100 Greatest Movies, behind *Citizen Kane* and *The Godfather*, having dropped only one place from the original ratings in 1997. Reasons for the film's continued appeal have been the subject of several studies. Robert Ray sees *Casablanca* as a work that best represents the films of the classic Hollywood studio system, and the legacy of that period (*A Certain Tendency of the Hollywood Cinema, 1930–1980* 4). Critic Umberto Eco, in his 1985 article "*Casablanca:* Cult Films and Intertextual Collage," maintains that the film has achieved its cult status because of the many memorable moments that can be "unhinged," arguing that its incoherence, or collage effect that references many cultural archetypes, is its strength. "*Casablanca* became a cult movie because it is not one movie. It is movies" (*SubStance* 14, no. 2, issue 47, 3–12). Howard Koch, one of the writers for the script, supports Eco's assertion that the film functions as a collage, "On close examination, we can find a number of inconsistencies and illogicalities" (*Casablanca: Script and Legend* 20), but considering the many talents that contributed to it, and the several tensions it had to contend with, this is understandable.

Casablanca revolves around an expatriated American, Rick Blaine (Humphrey Bogart), who flees Paris with his faithful companion, Sam (Dooley Wilson), when it falls to the Nazis in the spring of 1940. Rick settles in the city of Casablanca, in the neutral French Morocco, and becomes the proprietor of the *Café Americain*. Complications arise in December 1941 when Ilsa (Ingrid Bergman), the woman he loved who had jilted him the day he left Paris, arrives at Rick's café with her husband, Victor Laszlo (Paul Henreid), a famous and hunted resistance leader. Casablanca is a hub for refugees from Europe who are attempting to emigrate via a daily flight from Casablanca to Lisbon—and freedom—and the *Café Americain* is where many gather while they attempt to negotiate their passage out. The Nazis wish to detain Laszlo in Casablanca, or even silence him permanently, and only Rick has the means for him to leave Morocco for America—having been entrusted by a patron, Ugarte (Peter Lorre), with letters of transit that would guarantee a safe flight to freedom—but his prior relationship with Ilsa, the bitterness of lost love and a rekindled passion, makes the decision a difficult one. The conflict between the law and true justice is presented in the film, as we shall see, by the fact that Morocco is technically unoccupied, and should therefore be a place where the law will protect Laszlo and others who have sought asylum from fascism of the Axis powers; it is, however, under the control of the corrupt French Vichy government, and so it is not a guarantor of Laszlo's safety. The dramatic tension in the story, then, hinges on whether Rick will sacrifice his personal happiness in the name of a larger cause, represented by Victor Laszlo.

Although set in Northern Africa in the war-torn years of the early 1940s,

3. True Knighthood and the Outlaw Hero in Classic Hollywood

Casablanca (Warner Bros., 1942). Rick Blaine (Humphrey Bogart) in a "showdown" with Major Heinrich Strasser (Conrad Veidt) as the outbound plane for Lisbon carrying Victor Laszlo (Paul Henreid) and Rick's love interest, Ilsa Lund (Ingrid Bergman), is about to depart. This scene activates the standard western frame of the climactic shootout (Jerry Ohlinger's Movie Materials Store).

Casablanca employs many of the motifs of the western, overtly referencing what Eco calls "archetypal frames" that we encounter in the western genre. First, Rick's café is alluded to as a "saloon." Early on, an indignant German whom Rick refuses to allow into his clandestine gambling room in the back of his establishment exclaims, "If you think I am going to be kept out of a saloon like this, you're very much mistaken." Rick himself refers to his café in this way, "You'll excuse me, gentlemen. Your business is politics. Mine is running a saloon," and later he tells Ilsa, "I'm settled now, above a saloon." The film also includes in its concluding moments the classic "showdown," with the shootout between the Nazi, Major Heinrich Strasser (Conrad Veidt), and Rick, who proves faster on the draw. In this discussion of the mythic figure of the Westerner, Robert Warshow asserts that the climactic action he engages in is "thoroughly an expression of his being…. The westerner could not fulfill himself if the moment did not finally come when he can shoot an enemy down" (*Movie Chronicle: The Westerner* 438), an idea that also rings true for Rick Blaine. Finally, as Robert Ray emphasizes, it is a disguised western because "as in all westerns, the crucial issue in *Casablanca* turned on the woman" (110).

The history of the film's production helps to explain why its success remains a subject of interest. In her detailed study, *The Making of Casablanca: Bogart, Bergman, and World War II*, Aljean Harmetz provides the circumstances under which the film was conceived and completed. It began as a play, *Everybody Comes to Rick's*, composed by Murray Burnett and Joan Alison, after Burnett was shaken by the anti–Semitism he witnessed when he visited Vienna and Paris in 1938. Failing to find a Broadway producer for it, the two sold the play to Warner Bros. in December 1941 (Harmetz 39). About the film's indebtedness to the play, Harmetz asserts, "The central myth about the writing of *Casablanca* is that all that remains of the original play was the setting and the character of Rick. But *Casablanca* also contains much of the plot of *Everybody Comes to Rick's*, in which an embittered American who owns a café in Morocco redeems himself after a reunion with the woman who has broken his heart, by arranging for her and the anti–Nazi newspaper editor who accompanies her to escape to Lisbon" (36). She further points out that several of the more famous lines of dialogue in the film originate in the play (35–36; 38–39). During its development and production, several writers were assigned to work on the script, which was not yet finished when filming began in the late spring of 1942.

Harmetz traces the evolution of the film script in detail, pointing out that the earliest change was to the character of Rick and his relationship with the woman, Lois Meredith, in the play. In *Everybody Comes to Rick's* Rick Blaine is "a self-pitying lawyer who has cheated on his wife" (46), and Lois is portrayed as a loose woman who sleeps around (47). Moreover, how to resolve the love triangle had become so problematic when *Casablanca* was being shot that another writer, Casey Robinson, was called in to work on this angle of the story (Harmetz 47). Some of the issues were resolved, however, not by the genius of a script doctor, but simply because the film had to conform to the rigid Production Code, to which all Hollywood cinema was subjected at the time. Harmetz notes that this code insisted on "the sanctity of the institution of marriage" and that "impure love must not be presented as attractive and beautiful" (163). This meant that an alibi, or excuse, had to be invented for the adultery in the film between Rick and Ilsa; it also limited the options for the film's conclusion. When Ilsa explains to Rick why she did not leave Paris with him, the audience understands that she believed her husband to be dead when she met Rick, and therefore, she believed herself to be a widow. The larger problem of whether the sexual affair resumes when she comes to Rick's to plead for the

3. True Knighthood and the Outlaw Hero in Classic Hollywood 37

letters of transit is resolved by the cut when Ilsa collapses in Rick's arms after her feeble attempt to get the letters from him at gunpoint, a cut that leaves the rest to the audience's imagination, and the euphemism in Rick's words to Ilsa in the scene at the airport, "We'll always have Paris.... We'd lost it ... but we got it back last night." Casey Robinson tried to strengthen the three characters and their relationships with one another, but there was agreement among the writers, the producer, Hal Wallis, and the director, Michael Curtiz, that the conclusion of the film should be what was called "the sacrifice ending," meaning Ilsa would end up with her husband, Victor (Harmetz 229). *How* to make this plausible was the dilemma that had to be resolved. As we shall see, the film activated a formula that has been employed for several centuries, in order to earn what has become perhaps the most famous conclusion in cinema.

Rick Blaine is presented as a man with a mysterious past. Other than his prior love affair with Ilsa when he ran a club in Paris, the only actual fact revealed about Rick's past is that he was a freedom fighter—"running guns"—in Ethiopia and fighting for the loyalists in Spain. While Major Strasser avers that Rick is also a *persona non grata* in the United States, "although the reasons are a little vague," the film fails to convince us that this information is even accurate—Rick's "expatriate" status seems to be more of a choice than a necessity, and no one can doubt his patriotism by the end of the film. The French official, Captain Renault (Claude Rains), tries to ascertain why Rick is an expatriate: "I have often wondered why you don't return to America. Did you abscond with the church funds? Did you run off with a senator's wife? I like to think you killed a man. It's the romantic in me," to which Rick replies, "It was a combination of all three." Renault does not say "can't" but rather "don't," suggesting that the exile is self-imposed; additionally, the scenarios he offers are all clichés, which also suggests that Rick has not really run afoul of the law or government, that Strasser has been misinformed. One of the scriptwriters, Julius Epstein, recalls, "My brother and I tried hard to come up with a reason why Rick couldn't return to America. But nothing seemed right. We finally decided not to give a reason at all" (*The Making of Casablanca* 49).

Rick's initial cynicism and his desire to remain uncommitted to any cause is revealed early in the film, when he stands by and watches the French authorities gun down the pleading Ugarte (Peter Lorre), who has dispatched the German couriers and stolen the letters of transport they were carrying—the ones he has entrusted to Rick. "*I'm* the only cause *I'm* interested in" and "I stick my neck out for nobody" are representative of his position when the film opens. However, as the story continues, Rick's idealistic side, and the integrity of his private code emerges, shown through his acts of kindness, such as helping the Bulgarian refugee newlywed couple acquire the means to attain visas to America and, finally, through his decision to rescue the official hero—Victor Laszlo—by renouncing his love for Ilsa, returning her, putatively for the greater good, to her husband. This magnanimous act mirrors Lancelot's return of the queen to Arthur at the Pope's command. Yet Lancelot recognizes that a knight cannot serve two masters, or rather a master and a mistress. He must either devote himself to a wife, or he must remain free of that in order to pursue the vocation of knighthood. Rick, in sending Ilsa with her husband, "You are a part of his work, the thing that keeps him going," is also avoiding the demands of matrimony. He urges upon her that he, too, "has a job to do," one in which Ilsa can have no part. Again, this utterance reflects Warshow's observation that the westerner, if asked, will reply that "he does what he 'has to do'" but "what he defends, at bottom, is the purity of his own image—in fact, his honor" (439), yet another way that Rick may be compared to the western outlaw hero. In a self-effacing manner, Rick continues, appearing to have embraced Laszlo's views: "I'm no good at being noble, but it doesn't take much to see that the problems of three little people don't amount to a hill of beans in this crazy world." What seems a selfless act is in fact also a liberating one, as a close scrutiny of the film's conclusion shows.

In addition to the clash between love and duty, or domestic entanglements and masculine freedom, represented by the triangle, *Casablanca* dramatizes the inadequacy of the law to protect the innocent and serve justice, a role that must be fulfilled by the liminal hero, Rick. Laszlo is a public hero of extraordinary courage in his defiance of the Gestapo police who arrive in Morocco in pursuit of him; he has survived torture in a concentration camp, earned the loyalty of the European underground resistance, and eluded his persecutors who have followed him to Casablanca. Even the cynical Rick expresses open admiration for Laszlo when he first meets Victor at his café. Rick congratulates Laszlo for his work, and when the modest Laszlo replies that he tries, Rick insists, "We all try. You succeed."

In contrast to Rick's initial fierce independence, Laszlo is the idealist who believes in "the cause," and places his trust in the rights he thinks unoccupied France afford him: protection from the Germans who want him silenced. He is first introduced to Major Strasser in Rick's café, and receives him very coldly: "I'm sure you'll excuse me if I am not gracious, but you see, Major Strasser, I am Czechoslovakian," to which Strasser replies, "You were a Czechoslovakian. Now you are a subject of the German Reich." Refusing to be intimidated, Lazslo retorts, "I've never accepted that privilege; and I'm now on French soil," suggesting that Laszlo believes he will be protected by the ostensible neutrality of Morocco, but learning immediately after that the reality is quite different when he is ordered to report to the police station the next morning by the French official, Captain Renault, whose authority, unlike that of Strasser, Laszlo must acknowledge. "They really mean to stop me this time," he tells Ilsa, as he begins to recognize the limits of the law in Casablanca. Nonetheless, Laszlo continues acting according to his ideals, leading a patriotic French song in the café as Strasser looks on with a frown of disapproval, and then attending an underground resistance meeting that is broken up by the authorities, and for which he is arrested. At the film's conclusion, Laszlo reaffirms his conviction that community, cooperation, and official channels of governance will, in the end, prevail over evil, telling Rick, "And welcome back to the fight. This time, I know our side will win." What Ray calls the "moral center" (103) of the film is the allied fight against the Nazis, represented by Laszlo and the others who resist the German regime; however, the "center of interest" (105) is the love between Ilsa and Rick, which holds the audience's attention. The tension between Rick's own desire to reclaim the happiness he enjoyed with Ilsa in Paris before the Nazis drove them out, and the conflicting desire to sacrifice that, is what creates the dramatic tension in the film.

There are two essential features of *Casablanca* that tie it to Beverly Kennedy's typologies of knighthood: the conflict between Laszlo, the figurehead of authority, champion of the law, and representative of community values and interests, much like the "worshipful knight," King Arthur, and Rick, the "true knight," who adheres to an individual ethical code that transcends community and law, and invokes the privileges of the elect, like Lancelot. The second is the insistence that true knighthood, or liminal hero status, can only be maintained through the avoidance of feminine entanglements. Perhaps the most striking feature of the love triangle in *Casablanca* is the fact that it depicts the passion between Rick and Ilsa as an autonomous force, and not a choice. This exonerates the lovers, and in so doing, hearkens back to a cultural model that originated in the Middle Ages. In his study, *Love in the Western World*, Denis de Rougemont traces the myth of romantic passion, which found its fullest expression in the fatal love story of Tristan and Iseult, to its inception in 12th century, in southern France. Here, he insists, three historical factors converged to form the myth that persists in our western ideas about romantic passion: the religious heresy of the Cathars, the rise of *cortezia* (courtly love) as a social system among the privileged classes, and the appearance of secular "love" poetry composed by the troubadour poets. The famous tale of fated love and divided loyalties found in the Tristan story embodies the myth of romantic passion, as Tristan, the brave knight and nephew of King Mark of Cornwall, woos and wins a bride for his uncle, Iseult of Ireland, but through the magic of a love potion that he drinks with her, Tristan falls in love with his uncle's bride, through no fault of his own, and she with him. Thus, Tristan is often the champion for the official hero, Mark, yet he and Iseult die of their illicit love for each other, invoking the *liebestod* motif; when Mark learns that the couple fell in love unwillingly, he forgives them, reinforcing the idea that passion is autonomous, and therefore the lovers are both guilty of adultery but blameless.[1] The conflict in the final section of Malory's *Le Morte D'Arthur*, as we have seen in the first chapter of this study, likewise embodies the idea that the illicit passion, in this case, between Lancelot and Guinevere, is autonomous. This is one compelling reason why Arthur, the worshipful knight and official hero, ignores the adultery until he is forced to acknowledge and pronounce judgment on it, although he is loath to be at enmity with his greatest ally and asset, Lancelot.

In the backstory of *Casablanca*, Rick falls in love with Ilsa not knowing she is married, and she reciprocates because she believes she is free to do so, having been informed that her husband, Victor, has been killed. This is analogous to the love potion, which de Rougemont calls the "alibi" or "excuse" that exonerates the lovers even though they are adulterous. Like King Mark and King Arthur, Victor Laszlo accepts also the pretext that the lovers are guiltless, and confides in Rick that he knows they love the same woman: "The first evening I came here in this café, I knew there was something between you and Ilsa. Since no one is to blame, I, I demand no explanation." Yet neither Rick nor Ilsa has told Victor the circumstances under which they fell in love, so Ilsa's older husband is taking on faith the autonomous nature of the passion, something the audience is likewise impelled to do. At the airport, Rick fabricates a rather elaborate lie, intended to preserve the dignity of Ilsa and Victor's marriage. He confides in Victor that when Ilsa had come to his café to procure the letters of transit, she had only "pretended" to be in love with Rick still, so that she might help her husband to safety. He solicits Ilsa's tacit complicity with this version of events, "Isn't that right, Ilsa?" a fabrication that she affirms. Laszlo himself seems to accept this official version of the story, nodding, with a barely perceptible smile, "I understand." This also obfuscates the fact that, in the scene the night before, and despite the lacuna provided by the cut, we are invited to write what Eco calls a "ghost chapter" in which we fill in the lacuna by imagining the lovers had rekindled their passion, this time with full knowledge that it is adulterous. Here, we must accept that they are overcome with an emotion that they cannot be held accountable for, the only excuse that can be offered. Finally, Renault tells Rick, "What you just did for Laszlo. And that fairytale you invented to send Ilsa away with him ... she went, but she knew you were lying," reinforcing the significance of this scene in delineating the problem of public and private interests.

Casablanca serves the propagandistic end of showing American audiences that the United States' policy of isolationism was negated by Pearl Harbor, that its entry into the war was justified; however, the conflict between the rights of community and those of the individual transcend that historical moment. "With their different origins, the American Rick and the European Laszlo embodied the contradictory sources of the American ideology. For while official heroes (e.g. Jefferson, Franklin) provided continuity with the manners, learning, and sophistication of the Old World, the outlaw hero represented the instinctive repudiation of Europe and its culture" (99). Ray traces Rick's heritage to Huck Finn, who lights out for "the Territory" at the end of Twain's novel (105). Even though Huck helps the runaway slave, Jim, he cannot bring about social change, though that might have been one of the aims of the novel itself. Only an earlier model of the true knight, Lancelot, fully accounts for the conflict and its resolution in *Casablanca*, as the film's conclusion makes apparent.

Casablanca has taken on a life of its own, as evinced by the legacy it continues to enjoy. Not only have the principle actors achieved an iconic status— in some cases almost solely on the basis of their performance in this film—but individual lines and images from the film have become commonplace. It has been the subject of two television series, a novel that has attempted to revise its conclusion, and the subject of critical studies as well, just to name a few ways in which it has retained its vitality.[2] Each generation discovers it anew, responding to its appeal aesthetically, ideologically, and as a timeless story of fated love, but it also retains its appeal because Rick Blaine, the liminal outlaw hero, represents the typology that audiences find endlessly rewarding to encounter.

"And all that makes a man": *Shane* (1953)

While *Casablanca* is a disguised western, employing many of that genre's thematic paradigms, *Shane* (1953), directed by George Stevens, and released a decade later, represents the culmination of the western genre: in its setting, conflict, and characters. But even more interesting is Ray's insistence that, despite the fact that it is a western, *Shane* also represents "an ideal recapitulation of Classic Hollywood's thematic paradigm," thus functioning as "to use Freud's term, a 'screen memory' [of Classic Hollywood]" (70). While *Casablanca* employs motifs of the western, as we have seen, *Shane* embodies paradigms of classic Hollywood that transcend the western genre. Will Wright, in his groundbreaking study of the importance of the western myth as embodied in the western film genre, identifies four categories of plots in them: the classical plot, the vengeance variation, the transition theme, and the professional plot (*Sixguns and Society: A Structural Study of the Western* 15). The classical plot features the lone gunfighter from outside who saves farmers or homesteaders from ranchers (15). Also acknowledging the significance of *Shane*, Wright asserts, "*Shane* is the classic of the classic Westerns" (34). For our purposes, it features very clear examples of the typologies examined in this study: the official hero and the liminal outlaw hero (descendants of the worshipful and true knight, respectively) and of the conflict the latter resolves, that of bringing justice to a community when the law is not capable of doing so.

Casablanca, as we have seen, shot well after the United States entered World War II, reflects the climate of its time in attempting to reconcile the country's conflicting impulses to retain its isolationism of previous decades (its individualism) or to support a larger cause (the community). As such, it is an instance of conservative or integrative propaganda specific to a particular historic moment, and yet the film incorporates typologies that transcend this moment as well. It is also worth noting that *Casablanca* is set in the then contemporary World War II period, in French-governed Morocco, while *Shane* is set in the American west of the not too distant past, but one that has already entered the annals of history and the American collective consciousness. *Shane*, shot in 1951, in the years immediately following World War II and during the Korean War (June 1950–July 1953), reflects the preoccupation with borders associated with that war, and the question of whether such a conflict can or cannot be resolved without force. The Korean War was a result, in large part, of the end of World War II, in that the 38th parallel was the demarcation of conflicting ideologies and world forces that emerged and were delineated after the war. The Korean Peninsula had been governed by Japan from 1910 until the end of the war; after World War II, the Republic of Korea (South Korea) was supported by the United Nations, while the Democratic People's Republic of Korea (North Korea) was backed by China and the Soviet Union. George Stevens had served in a film unit in World War II, and shot footage that chronicled several of its important events (the D–Day invasion and scenes from the Dachau concentration camp) for which he was eventually recognized. This is the climate in which *Shane* was shot and released.

Shane is based on a novel of the same title, written by Jack Schaefer, a journalist-turned-fiction writer. The first version of Schaefer's novel appeared serially in 1946 under the title "Rider from Nowhere," as a three-part story in *Argosy* magazine. In 1949 it was published as a complete short novel, Schaefer's first (*Shane: The Critical Edition* 23). When he wrote the work, Schaefer, born in Cleveland, had never been west of Ohio, but he saw a need to write fiction about the west, historically important for the American identity, but underrepresented in historical studies and in fiction, so he set out to show that "there is no reason why an attempt cannot be made to create literature about the west as about the east or the south or any place anywhere" (*Shane: The Critical Edition* 16). Scharefer's novel portrays with accuracy the state of tumult in Wyoming leading up to the famed 1892 Johnson County War, also known as the Wyoming Range War (between ranchers and homesteaders). *Shane* also transcends this historical moment to explore the lasting question of the relationship between the individual and the community, an issue that, as we have seen in our discussion of *Casablanca*, is central to American values as they are portrayed in Hollywood film, but with roots in the distant past of medieval romance. *Shane* features two individuals who represent contrastive, yet at some point convergent, models of manhood for the young boy, Bobby, to learn from and emulate. It focuses on the issue of how disputes can be settled when the law is absent or ineffective. Thus, Schaefer's novel is also concerned with defining ideal manhood as it can be understood in its service to community but also as it draws on an innate sense of right. Much of Schaefer's novel addresses "all that makes a man," a phrase taken from Victorian poet laureate Alfred, Lord Tennyson's King Arthur in *Idylls of the King*, as he recounts the chivalric code by which he asks his knights to live, as discussed in chapter 2.

The *story* of Schaefer's novel—and the film that adapts it to the screen—is about examining the moral codes by which individuals and communities find it best to live, as well as when and how the two converge. Thus, it is a timeless story. The *plot* is specific to a particular historic moment in which ownership and use of the western lands, especially in Wyoming, was in dispute, as well as how statehood and the drafting of laws to curtail violence affected the outcome of this conflict between cattle barons, whose ranching style required extensive use of the land, and the homesteaders who pushed west to establish farms and build communities. The struggle between ranchers and farmers is a common plot in the western film genre, treated variously, but most often siding with the homesteaders.[3] In *Shane* Fletcher is the greedy, unscrupulous cattleman who will even resort to murder in order to retain his hold on the land, and our sympathies are enlisted for the homesteaders, earnest workers of the land who wish to raise families as well as crops and value community over their own self-gain. Although the settlers have legitimate claims on the land they work, Fletcher refuses to recognize their rights, and the law that should enforce them. The novel establishes that there is no sheriff in the budding town, but even if there had been, "he would have been Fletcher's man" (143), meaning that the representative of the law would have been corrupted by Fletcher's power and money. When one of the farmers is shot by Fletcher's hired gun, the others maintain that even if they could enlist the help of a United States marshal, the law would be inadequate, as the slain farmer was provoked into drawing on the gunman, with several witnesses present; therefore, through a technicality, the act of murder would be deemed self-defense (216). This points out the inadequacy of the law to dispense true justice. As we shall see, in Schaefer's novel and in the film, the law is either absent, potentially corrupt, or inadequate as an upholder of what is just.

In the novel, then, Joe Starrett is the acknowledged leader of the homesteaders, who refuse to buckle under to Fletcher's continued harassment and efforts to drive them off the land, but when an enigmatic stranger, Shane, rides up to the Starretts' farmstead, things are in a bad way, the community of farmers about to fall apart. Shane makes an impression on Joe, his son Bobby, and his wife Marion, and agrees to stay on as a farmhand. A sub-plot and complication to the range war is the love triangle established, comprised of Joe, Marion, and Shane, even as the young Bobby begins to engage in a kind of hero-worship of the newcomer, whose attire and manners, though cultured and polite, also suggest that he brings danger with him, or knows it intimately. For a time, Shane tries and succeeds in integrating into the life of the farmer, but there are physical altercations that force him into violence. As the conflict escalates, Fletcher sends for a hired gunslinger, Stark Wilson, to drive the farmers from the land. This is where Shane must step up, buckle on his guns, and use force to put an end to the threat to the community and to the family of which he has become so fond. Moreover, Shane must leave that family in order to avoid the domestic entanglement and the disruption resulting from the mutual attraction between him and Marion. He enters the community, defends it, but must leave it at the end. Like the knight errant of medieval romance, Shane recognizes and strives to uphold a code of behavior that shows reverence for service to a community, but he himself must remain outside of the group for whom he is the savior.

The novel is told retrospectively through the eyes of Bobby, the son of Joe Starrett, but as a boy his hero worship for the mysterious Shane rivaled his admiration for his father. As a grown man, Bobby recounts the arrival and departure of the enigmatic stranger, remembering Shane's impact on his family and on the community. When Shane first arrives, Joe's wife, Marion, expresses concern about whether the itinerant stranger, whom they have offered a job, can adapt to farm life as a hired hand. Joe reassures her: "What a man knows isn't important. It's what he is that counts…. He knows I'm in a spot and he's not the man to leave me there. Nobody'll push him around or scare him away. He's my kind of a man" (119). Later, when Bobby discovers Shane's magnificent gun, he asks his father why the former keeps it hidden, whether there is something wrong with Shane, but Joe again reassures Bobby: "There is more right about him than most any man you're likely to meet" (129). Joe and Marion, as well as the larger community, suspect that Shane is a professional gunman, whose business is to kill or be killed, but otherwise, he has no recognizable occupation, unless called upon to engage in violence. The space Shane occupies is liminal: he can function in the community and is not a wanted man who is at odds with the law, but he is looked upon by the community at large with suspicion and an amount of fear. Joe, however, understands that what a man *is* matters more than what he *knows*, as we see in his defense of Shane to Marion in the quote above. Shane adheres to his own code of conduct, and possesses the character qualities that make him superior to other men. Shane is a true knight, whose inner ideals are both fixed and laudable.

Joe's admiration of Shane's character—his inner moral certitude and his physical talent with a gun—is explored in the novel also by the young Bobby. Having witnessed a fist fight in which Shane reluctantly, but decisively, defeats a cowboy who insults him, Bobby asks Shane if he will teach him how to fight, too, but Shane's reply, slow and considered, reinforces the fact that what he *does* is what he *is*, something instinctive, and not something he can acquire: "A man doesn't learn things like that ... you know them, and that's all" (174). Instead, Shane wishes to impress upon Bobby his own ethical code, explaining when one can walk away from a fight with honor, and when one must face the challenge to one's dignity and character. His final words to Bobby, before he leaves the valley, underscore his desire to impart to the boy the importance of knowing who you are, and being true to yourself, when he tells Bobby that he tried to change, but was unable to be anything other than what he is, a gunfighter, something that Bobby seems to have grasped earlier: when, at last, Shane straps on his gun to protect the Starrett family and the community of farmers, Bobby understands that his weapons were "part of the man, of the full sum of the integrate force that was Shane," and that, for the first time since his arrival, he was seeing him "complete" (241). Finally, having witnessed Shane's ultimate stand against evil, Bobby subsequently describes him to Joe as having been "beautiful" (266) to watch, an image etched in his memory, and later recalled many times: "I would see again the power and grace of a force beautiful beyond comprehension" (273). "Force," as it is expressed in Shane's final defense against Fletcher and Wilson, is rendered aesthetically pleasing: harmony of spirit and body, clarity of perception, and a singular sense of purpose.

Shane is held up to be an ideal man in his rectitude and innate sense of right, living by his own ethical code, but one that requires him to remain a loner. However, both Shane and Bobby recognize the same quality of character in Joe, the leader of the community. Shane says to the other farmers that Joe is "the one real man in this valley" and that "once in awhile this country turns out a man like Joe Starrett" (217), a man of principle who will take on any odds with extraordinary valor, especially to help his family and community. His reputation for courage, honesty, hard work, and high ethical principles have earned Joe "worship" among his peers; his public role in the community and his faith in social justice also show him as a descendent of the worshipful, or social knight. He is the "official hero" who nonetheless needs the help of the liminal hero, Shane. Joe is the acknowledged leader of the farmers who are threatened by the powerful rancher, Fletcher, but Joe puts faith in the social cohesion of the community, and in the emerging laws that he believes should protect them. Though the time is premature for the law's ability to curtail violence as a means of settling disputes, and in upholding justice, Joe believes in it, but must at times, resort to retaliatory violence himself. Still, Starrett and Shane, very different in vocation, physicality, and in their relation to community, are nonetheless, in Schaefer's novel, bound by an awareness of themselves and their role in relation to others at a moment of destiny. They represent for Bobby two models of manhood, but with this essential feature that binds them together. Bobby can admire Shane and come to understand his importance as a hero, even though, in the end, he will emulate his father and retain the values of the community.

The success of Schaefer's novel would be augmented even more when it was made into a motion picture; the screenplay, written by A. B. Guthrie, Jr., himself a Pulitzer Prize novelist for *The Way West* in 1950, remains, in many ways, faithful in all of its essentials of plot and character to Schaefer's novel, but with some very interesting changes. *Shane* was shot in 1951, and directed by George Stevens, the same year that he won the Academy Award as Best Director for *A Place in the Sun*, although Stevens' insistence on heavy editing delayed the release of the film until 1953. It debuted at the Radio City Music Hall, the first effort to provide audiences with a panoramic vision.[4] Well-received critically and at the box office, *Shane* garnered six Academy Award nominations in 1954: two Best Supporting Actor nominations (Jack Palance and Brandon de Wilde), Best Director and Best Picture (George Stevens), Best Screenplay (A.B. Guthrie, Jr.), and winning the Oscar for Best Cinematography (Loyal Griggs). It has proved to be an enduring film in popularity. For instance, the *10th Anniversary Edition of the American Film Institute's 100 Greatest Movies* lists *Shane* as number 45 of the 100 best films of all time, and third in the western category, behind *The Searchers* and *High Noon*. It is frequently referenced in film and popular culture, and other films have paid homage to it, most notably, perhaps, Clint Eastwood's *Pale Rider* (1985), which follows *Shane* so closely in plot and structure as to qualify as a remake.

The titular figure, Shane (Alan Ladd), resembles *Casablanca's* Rick Blaine, in that his shadowy past is so mysterious; in this case, he even has no last name, which also emphasizes his individuality. As Robert Warshow points out, "The

Westerner is *par excellence* a man of leisure.... We see him standing at a bar, or playing poker—a game which expresses perfectly his talent for remaining relaxed in the midst of tension—or perhaps camping out on the plains on some extraordinary errand" (*The Immediate Experience* 138). Rick runs a saloon, but someone else manages the books; dressed in a white tuxedo he surveys his business, aloof from the day-to-day operations. Shane has no particular occupation or source of income; in fact, the viewer, along with the Starretts, are astonished when Shane rolls up his sleeves and undertakes, with a determination and skill, the physical labor of the farm: helping Joe remove a stubborn stump, for example, and the routine maintenance of a farm. Shane remains the solitary figure who lives outside the law, and yet, paradoxically, it is he who must come to the aid of the official hero, Joe Starrett (Van Heflen), and the community of homesteaders who are threatened by the ruthless rancher, Rufus Ryker (Emile Meyer), whose film name has been changed from the novel's Fletcher, (perhaps as a homonym for "reich") in a dispute over the use of the land.

In the Wyoming territory in 1889, Shane rides into the community and out of it unattached, and yet he is the only figure who can make the land safe when Ryker hires a professional gunman, Wilson (Jack Palance). The binary oppositions in the film are not only between the official hero, his family and the community of homesteaders as they contrast with the liminal outlaw hero, Shane, the itinerant drifter and gunfighter, but also between the ranchers and homesteaders, and the North and South. The rupture between north and south, twenty-five years after the end of the Civil War, is a feature unique to the film: in Schaefer's novel, Shane acknowledges his southern roots, telling Marion that his family moved from Mississippi to Arkansas, yet this fact bears no real significance, as it does in the film. In it, Shane manifests often his southern sensibility and heritage, an *antebellum* elegance in manners and elocution, often a metonymy for the Europe of the feudal past. Marion is immediately charmed by Shane's demeanor, for instance, and Shane later provokes Wilson, the hired gun, by calling him "a lowdown Yankee liar." The homesteader, the "Reb" Stonewall Torrey (Elisha Cook, Jr.), is associated with the song "Dixie" throughout the film, and boasts, "Alabama is the greatest state in the union." Torrey is provoked into drawing on Wilson in a rash act that will forfeit his life, when the latter insults Torrey's southern heritage and heroes: "I'm saying that Stonewall Jackson himself was trash. Him and Lee and all the rest of them Rebs. You too." By contrast, Torrey's counterpart in the novel, a homesteader named Ernie Wright, is provoked by Wilson when he calls Wright a "crossbred squatter" (214) showing that the film has substituted a southern heritage for the Native American heritage of Wright in the novel. The north/south conflict of the Civil War is evocative of the Korean War, in which two ideologies struggled for precedence, and this is one likely reason for the shift in emphasis from the racial issue of the Native American half-breed to that of a divided country, the other being the idea that the old south shares affinities with the feudal structure of medieval Europe, and therefore contrasts old world values with those of American progress and democracy. Finally, the film presents the violent ends of the frontier past, when disputes were settled with weapons, as this stands in opposition to the pacifism of the settled future, brought about by the imposition of laws and statehood as alternative ways to establish justice.

Shane attempts to abandon his past, settle down, and work as a hired hand for Starrett, his wife Marion (Jean Arthur) and son Joey (Brandon de Wilde). He exchanges his buckskin clothing for the proletarian attire of a farm worker, and soon becomes the object of hero worship for Joey, whom he teaches to shoot, another innovation introduced in the film that is not in the novel. It is noteworthy that the buckskin attire in the film differs from Shane's initial clothing in the novel. In Schaefer's work, what Bobby first notices about the approaching stranger is his clothing, elegant and costly, yet worn with time and travel; still, the clothes retain their "magnificence" and a "hint of men and manners alien" to Bobby's experience (*Shane: The Critical Edition* 63). The film's substitution of the distinctive buckskin for the elegant, yet

Shane (Paramount, 1953). "Galahad on the Range," says critic Pauline Kael (*5001 Nights at the Movies* 671). Shane (Alan Ladd) is clad in mythic buckskin rather than the clichéd black attire of the gunfighter, that clothing reserved for the other gunslinger in the film, Jack Wilson (Jack Palance) (Jerry Ohlinger's Movie Materials Store).

ominous black tailored suit of the gunfighter shifts the identity of Shane to the mythic rather than the clichéd: buckskin is evocative of the individual grit of American heroes such as James Fennimore Cooper's Natty Bumpo, as well as the famed Davy Crockett and Daniel Boone. Buckskin also suggests the primitive, self-reliant, and individualized code of the frontier man, as opposed to the urban, cultured, more uniform attire in the novel.[5]

When Shane agrees to stay on at the Starrett farm, an ever-growing attraction between himself and Marion creates a certain tension in the film, but this understated love triangle is only resolved when Shane is compelled to defend the community using violence. The love triangle augments Shane's function as a "true knight," or liminal outlaw hero, because it underscores the importance of his individualism and need to retain his independence, steering clear of domestic ties. Marion objects to Shane's profession as a gunfighter, becoming nearly hysterical when he instructs Joey in how to handle a weapon. Interfering with the lesson, she vows, "Guns aren't going to be my boy's life," to which Shane replies that a gun is just a tool, "as good or bad as the man using it. Remember that," but an indignant, protective Marion snaps, "We'd all be much better off if there wasn't a single gun left in this valley—including yours," an ominous pronouncement that foreshadows the story's inevitable end.

It is significant that the pacifism in the film is associated with the feminine, expressed by Marion—wife, mother, and center of family—a view that stands in opposition to the masculine drive necessary to survive in the west. As we have seen, the encumbering influence of the domestic and feminine accounts for Lancelot's avoidance of matrimony as a duty that would distract him from his dedication to the vocation of knighthood. For the Victorians, we will remember, woman, at the center of the domestic circle, was seen as the guardian of the society's moral fabric; the image of the now clichéd 19th-century "angel in the house," popularized by the Coventry Patmore's 1854 poem of that title, places the woman on a pedestal, but there emerged from that model of virtue a darker side. In Tennyson's poems "The Marriage of Geraint" and "Geraint and Enid," from his Arthurian epic *Idylls of the King*, the knight Geraint, succumbing to a uxoriousness for his perfect "angel" wife, Enid, neglects his masculine duties of governance and defense of his lands, and must work hard, once the fault is acknowledged, to restore his worshipfulness, his masculinity. Inadvertently, the perfect, idealized feminine has threatened Geraint's identity, and his service to the king as a knight. In Tennyson's *Idylls*, it is also Guinevere's infidelity to Arthur, more than any feuding factions among knights, that causes Camelot to come crashing down.[6]

The Victorian fear of the emasculating feminine continued into the twentieth century. As women entered the work force with the advent of World War

II and the continued shift from an agrarian to an urban, industrialized society, her role in American culture came under closer scrutiny and debate. Popular fiction writer and cultural critic Philip Wylie composed a controversial work titled *Generation of Vipers* (1942), a bestseller that sparked a great deal of debate, in which he addressed a number of issues that American society faced in the decade of the 1940s. In it, he coined the term "Momism," by which he meant the emasculating influence of a certain type of the feminine, and the cult of motherhood that both emasculated the spouse and impeded the normal development and independence of the son. Wylie's invective against the middle-class housewife is focused primarily on her conspicuous consumerism and self-serving frivolity, hence her pernicious influence on family and the larger community. It is tinged with misogyny and is much indebted to Freud, but what is important is the debate that it sparked and the notoriety it received. In his "Introduction" to the 1955 Pocket edition of the work (its twentieth printing), Wylie points out the many indicators of his book's popularity, including the fact that "in 1950 it was selected by The American Library Association as one of the major non-fiction books of the first half century. It was used, during the war, as an instrument for 'briefing' those British officers who were to have contact with our troops ... and it no longer seems possible for any author, lay or scientific, to discuss motherhood and mom without noting that the dark side of that estate was defined earlier by me" (*Generation of Vipers* x). To understand the context of the Momism, as at least a latent expression of the same concern articulated by Lancelot, is to understand why Shane must, in the end, leave Marion and the controlling domestic sphere over which she reigns, which is oppositional to Shane's very identity, the thing that makes him unlike all others, including her husband. It is worth noting that in Schaefer's novel the Momism does not take the form of pacifism, and an aversion to guns, but it still has a pronounced presence.

The self-abnegation in which this decision is cast—that Shane denies his personal happiness to protect the family unit of Joe, Marion, and Joey—is, in fact, also an act of self-preservation, or a way that Shane protects his own individuality, the same way that Rick sends Ilsa away with Victor, despite his strong feelings for her. More important, all three characters acknowledge the existence of the love triangle, but treat it as something for which no one is to blame, an attitude found in *Casablanca* but rooted in the courtly ideal. Joe, believing he must confront Ryker and meet his death at Wilson's hands in order to preserve his ideals and his reputation, confides in Marion that he has seen the feelings she has for Shane and he for her, and he takes solace in the fact that, should he die, she and Joey would be in good hands with Shane: "I know I'm kinda slow sometimes, but I see things ... and if anything ever happened to me you'd be took care of better than I could do it myself." He displays no jealousy, and seems to find no blame in the situation, like his forerunners, King Mark of the Tristan legend, King Arthur, and Victor Laszlo. The tacit understanding reached between Marion and Shane in the last scene they share before he rides off to fight Wilson also reinforces the idea that the passion they feel is blameless, though acting on it would be adulterous unless she were widowed.

For instance, when Joe and Shane spend an afternoon of what would now be called "male bonding," engaged in the determination and hard work of removing a tree stump that has been an insurmountable obstacle for Joe (a very Lawrencian moment, or one reminiscent of Sherwood Anderson's sublime story "The Untold Lie"), Marion is at work in her kitchen rivaling their efforts with her own culinary endeavors; she emerges once to show the men that she has altered her hat to match the current style in Cheyenne—having quizzed Shane on his observance of the ladies' latest fashions there—and is chagrined when she is virtually ignored by both Joe and Shane. When she returns a second time to the working men, who have triumphed over the stubborn stump, Marion leaves her pie unattended and it burns; angered, and over-reacting, she refuses to eat the dinner she has put on the table and sets out to bake another pie. Understanding this as a rivalry for his attention, and a contest between the masculine and feminine, Shane pronounces, with humor but with a disarming candor when he tastes the pie: "That's the best bit of stump I ever tasted" (*Shane: The Critical Edition* 111). Indeed, Gerald Haslam, contemplating the love triangle in the novel, has remarked, "Joe Starrett's dogged acceptance of his wife's feelings [for Shane] suggests the possibility that the odd triangle might have Shane rather than Marion at its apex" (28). Though expressed differently in the novel and the film, the feminine contends with the masculine, an essential feature that ties the story of *Shane* to that of the errant knight.

Shane's function as the liminal outlaw hero who must dispense justice with his gun, contrasts with Joe Starrett's faith in the law, and his role as official hero. In the opening sequence, when Shane has first arrived at the Starrett's farm, for instance, Ryker rides up and issues what is evidently one of many threats of violence to Joe and his fellow homesteaders. Joe responds, "The time for gun-blastin' a man off his place is passed. They're building a penitentiary." Later, in another verbal showdown with Ryker, Joe observes, "You think you've got the right to say nobody else has got any [rights to the land]. That ain't the way the government looks at it." Ryker himself acknowledges to the storekeeper, Grafton, that the "new law" exists, but he refuses to adhere to it. After Wilson murders Torrey, the farmers meet at the Starrett farm to decide what to do. Again, Joe expresses his belief that justice can be sought through legal channels, "There's a law against killing," but the others realize that the law is remote, and therefore ineffective: "The law is three days' ride from here," Ed Howells (Martin Mason) reminds them. Even Joe at last recognizes that, in order to keep his status as the leader in the community, he will have to sacrifice his own life by going into town to meet the challenge issued to him by Ryker, who has procured Wilson as his instrument of execution. Shane, however, is then prepared to take matters into his own hands, and has to fight Joe for the right to stand in as his proxy. Violence is the only way to win justice for the community.

As the film reaches its inevitable climax, then, it is apparent that only Shane can stand against the hired gunfighter, Wilson, but the mythology of the true knight, and that of this type of liminal outlaw hero, demands that he must then abandon his hope of integrating into society, as his departing words to Joey express: "A man has to be what he is Joey, you can't break the mold. I tried it and it didn't work for me." This utterance is, of course, not universally true: Chris Calloway (Ben Johnson) abandons his unscrupulous rancher boss, Ryker, and becomes an ally of the homesteaders; Fred (Edgar Buchanan) is a reticent homesteader who finally stands up for his rights after Joe's moving oration at Torrey's funeral. But Shane's point is true for him: his destiny is determined by his role as the elect savior who achieves justice for the community that he cannot or will not join.

In his review of the film, Roger Ebert, observing of Shane that "there is a little of the samurai in him, and the medieval knight,"[7] also asserts that while he has a code, like that of a samurai warrior or a knight, there is an enigma about Shane's actions: "He has a code. And yet—there's *something else* suggested by his behavior, a series of questions that probe deeper into Shane's motives than to attribute them only to altruism and self-sacrifice: a 'fear of women,' and a violence that can be controlled but not eradicated, leading to 'ritual reenactments of the pattern he's trapped in'" (www.rogerebert.com/reiew/great-movie-shane-1953). Ideology, and not psychology, however, can explain why Shane rides on in the end: a liminal outlaw hero must remain on the border, outside the circle of community to be a fully realized character.

Shane, like Rick Blaine, becomes heroic himself in aiding the cause of the official hero and the communal values he espouses, but in order to preserve his individual identity, living by his own private code, he must avoid the lure of the domestic entanglement—the feminine. Wounded after the showdown with Wilson, and slumped over his saddle, he rides alone out of town, vanishing into the mythic past. Thus, the film embodies the two typologies of knighthood: Starrett, the worshipful knight who espouses community and law; Shane the true knight who, despite that fact that he upholds the law, must remain outside of the community it benefits, the liminal outlaw hero whose internal moral code finally must dictate his decisions.

Shane, like Rick and Lancelot before him, remains free of the fetters of the feminine. Lancelot's avoidance of the marital couch, Rick's stroll into the sunset with Renault, and Shane's lonely exit on horseback, are examples of the tension between two paradigmatic codes of behavior. Yet their solitude authenticates them as true knights—the elect called upon to serve a higher calling—a saintly death for Lancelot, a newfound patriotic future for Rick and his sidekick, Captain Renault, and for Shane an escape into the vanishing west, a belated image of a past that no longer exists.

CHAPTER 4

Remediation: The Rise of Television and the Liminal Outlaw Hero

Switching Screens, Changing Channels: The Rise of a New Medium

Vestiges of the true knight are detectable in films other than those of the western genre (real or disguised), particularly the related genre of the action film. However, the solitary figure, representative of individualism while serving both a higher justice and the social ends of the official hero, comprises the heart of the western. In a letter dated March 1, 1958, while he was writing *The Acts of King Arthur and His Noble Knights,* published posthumously in 1976, novelist John Steinbeck made the striking assertion of Malory's text that "these stories form, with the New Testament, the basis of most modern English literature" (338). Steinbeck researched Malory's life and time in order to write his own version of the Arthurian cycle; he acquired considerable expertise on the subject of Malory and the *Morte,* corresponding and meeting with Eugene Vinaver, the editor of the Winchester manuscript, one of the definitive Malory texts. Researching and writing his Arthurian novel, begun in 1956, Steinbeck makes the astute observation that the western film genre is often a medieval romance in disguise, and insists that he will be able to demonstrate this in his work:

> And it can be shown and will be shown that the myth of King Arthur continues even into the present day and is an inherent part of the so-called "Western" with which television is filled at the present time—same characters, same methods, same stories, only slightly different weapons and certainly a different topography. But if you change Indians or outlaws for Saxons and Picts and Danes, you have exactly the same story. You have the cult of the horse, and the cult of the knight. The application with the present is very close, and also the present day with its uncertainties very closely parallels the uncertainties of the fifteenth century [338].

What Steinbeck understood, having witnessed the zenith of the Hollywood western, and its continued dispersion through a number of popular television series (two of which will be discussed below), is that it shared very close affinities with the medieval romance. We can see from this quotation also that he recognized that the appeal of the true knight, who answers the needs of a culture in a time of crisis, was true for Malory's own era—that of the War of the Roses—and for post World War II American culture as well.

It is worth noting, too, that Steinbeck grasped the problem that Lancelot in Malory's work poses for the reader: he becomes a tragic figure who should have achieved his destined quest, and yet he fails to do so, through the combination of his own virtuous code, his love for the queen, and the social circumstances that all conspire against him. Steinbeck arrives at the conclusion that Lancelot, the most complexly drawn character in Malory's text, is the "self character," Malory's self-inscription: "Now it is nearly always true that a novelist, perhaps unconsciously, identifies himself with one chief or central character" (326). In Malory's case, that figure is Lancelot: "Lancelot could not see the Grail because of the faults and sins of Malory himself" (327). Steinbeck concludes that Malory, himself an outlaw knight, yet one capable of composing a work as complex and accomplished as the *Morte D'Arthur*, would have identified with the character of Lancelot. Steinbeck sees, and tries to account for, the prevailing influence of the type of knight Lancelot represents in Malory's late medieval romance as it is expressed in modern literature and film.

Interestingly, at the same time Steinbeck was focusing on the central importance of Lancelot's character in Malory's text, his contemporary, T.H. White also recognized and attempted to account for Malory's portrayal of this problematic knight. In "The Ill-Made Knight" (1940), the third book of T.H. White's novel *The Once and Future King* (1958),[1] the author observes that Lancelot's conflict did not stem from the stereotypical love triangle, but rather from a "quadrangle" comprised of Arthur, Guinevere, himself, and God:

> The Ill-Made Knight was not involved in an Eternal Triangle. It was an Eternal Quadrangle, which was eternal as well as quadrangular. He had not given up his mistress because he was afraid of being punished by some Holy Bogy, but he had been confronted by two people whom he loved. The one was Arthur's Queen, the other a wordless presence who had celebrated Mass at Castle Carbonek. Unfortunately, as so often happens in love affairs, the two objects of his affection were contradictory [483].

White, like Steinbeck, recognized both Malory's genius, the manner in which the *Morte* could be adapted to speak to contemporary audiences, and the central tension of conflicting values embodied in the figure of Lancelot. It is no surprise that his work *The Once and Future King* has enjoyed success not only as a novel, but as a popular Broadway musical, *Camelot* (1960), and then as a feature film of the same name (1967). The Lerner and Lowe musical ran for 873 performances; the film, directed by Joshua Logan and starring Richard Harris (Arthur), Franco Nero (Lancelot) and Vanessa Redgrave (Guenevere), was nominated for five Academy Awards in 1968, and won three, as well as winning three of six nominations for the Golden Globe Awards of the same year. White's novel was also the source for an animated Disney classic, *The Sword in the Stone* (1963). From this, we can see that White's devotion to the *Matter of Britain* represents perhaps the most significant contribution to the revitalization of the legend in the first half of the twentieth century.

Both Steinbeck and White recognize in the conflicted figure of Malory's Lancelot, the same tension that Robert Ray labels the moral center/center of interest split in a film (66). The moral center is often represented by the values and goals of the official hero, which in the Malorian world are those of Arthur in his role as king and wronged husband. The center of interest, however, is that of the conflicted figure of Lancelot, who must try to reconcile his duty to God, his king, and his illicit love. Lancelot may fail, but he alone attempts to resolve these tensions. Audiences never tire, it seems, of entertainment that expresses, in dramatic form, the dilemma of the marginal hero who wishes to retain his individuality and at the same time rescue a community in need of a savior. This formula, as Steinbeck recognized in the excerpt above, endured from the time of medieval romance to that of what he identifies as "the so-called 'Western' with which TV is filled at the present time" (in the 1950s) when he wrote this astute observation.

The introduction of a new technology always affects complex changes in a culture's expectations and actions. The invention of the printing press in the fifteenth century, as we have observed in an earlier discussion of Malory's *Morte D'Arthur*, guaranteed its availability to future generations, not only by making it a "fixed" work of art, but also by providing the means for its immediate wider distribution and influence. In the modern era, motion pictures were designed for mass consumption, as was radio programming, but it was the development of commercial television that completed the triad of revolutionary public entertainment in the first half of the twentieth century. When a new medium is introduced, it pays homage to earlier media by refashioning or subsuming it, what critics like Jay David Bolter and Richard Grusin, for instance, identify as the process of "remediation" in their study *Remediation: Understanding New Media* (2000). Television functioned in this manner for both film and radio, as film had previously remediated live theater stage performances and photography. In *One Nation Under Television* (1990), J. Fred MacDonald chronicles the rise of this new technology. Efforts to develop it began in the 1920s; according to MacDonald "the first television drama, *The Queen's Messenger*," was broadcast in September 1929 in Schenectady, New York, followed by the cartoon character Felix the Cat in February of 1930 (9). A decade later, MacDonald notes, "regularly scheduled programming was born on April 30 [1939], when NBC cameras televised Franklin D. Roosevelt officially opening the [World's] fair" (13). Yet another decade and the momentous event of World War II brought an additional milestone: "Television became an acceptable, attractive and affordable national utility in 1948–49" (MacDonald 43). MacDonald points out, for example, that production of sets went from 6,476 in 1946 to 1.7 million in 1949; stations increased from 18 in 12 cities in January 1948 to 98 operating in 58 areas the following year (43), a phenomenal increase in availability and interest, setting the stage for the development of regular programming and sponsorship. It is not surprising that many radio shows—from quiz shows (*Break the Bank*) to variety shows (*Jack Benny*) and situation comedies (*The Life of Riley*)—quickly transitioned to television. *The Lone Ranger* also made its debut in 1949 (MacDonald 49).

The manner in which "Classic Hollywood" responded and adapted to the "Golden Age of Television" of the 1950s continues to be a subject of considerable discussion. MacDonald notes that the advent of television had a decided impact on the way Americans spent their leisure time: "By 1949 government statistics suggested that TV was the cause of major declines in movie attendance" as well as radio listening, ticket sales at live sports events, theatre and opera (69). No doubt, the convenience of living room entertainment took its toll on other forms such as these, but in *Fifties Television: The Industry and Its Critics* (1993), William Boddy insists:

> Traditional historical accounts need to be revised that suggest a mutual lack of interest and collaboration between the film industry and the television networks in the early years of the TV industry. Despite doubts about the viability of either feature films or original film programming in the early years of the medium, the major Hollywood studios followed events in the television industry very closely. Beginning in the late 1930s, motion picture studios became active in television research and manufacturing and made significant investments in television production companies, broadcasting stations, and networks [67].

Boddy points out that television studios owned sometimes controlling interests in broadcast stations (Warner Bros., for instance, owned 65 percent of a production firm in 1936), were eager to develop theater programs for television and "by 1951, Paramount was syndicating film and live programs from its Los Angeles station to forty-three stations" (67). MacDonald also recognizes the Hollywood interest in broadcasting, "the marriage of film to television was consummated in 1955," evinced by the fact that "by 1961 there were 12,209 feature films available to television" (121). It is also no coincidence that 1955 marked the debut of the "adult western" series, with the premier of *Gunsmoke*, followed that same year with shows like *Cheyenne* and *The Life and Legend of Wyatt Earp*. Hollywood was clearly prepared to adapt to the future that television initiated, and its B western, in turn, influenced the television adult western.[2]

One issue that came to the fore quickly was what type of programming would appeal to the vast audiences that were rapidly tuning in to the new technology, and what purpose it should serve in the lives of its viewers.[3] As mentioned above, several crossover programs from radio were the first to be featured regularly, but the prevailing *genre* of 1950s television was the western. MacDonald claims that the popularity of the western during this decade was in large part a result of the relationship between the Hollywood film industry and television networks (128). Leo Braudy notes that of the top fifty grossing feature films between 1949 and 1951, half of them were westerns (*From Chivalry to Terrorism* 497). *The Lone Ranger*, which now enjoys a permanent place in the American collective consciousness, aired in 1949, but its appeal was primarily to juvenile audiences; *Gunsmoke*, which debuted on CBS in 1955, introduced the "adult western" (MacDonald 67), the *genre* which dominated evening primetime programming. By the end of the decade, westerns comprised one-fourth of the nighttime programming, and eight of the top ten shows were Westerns (MacDonald 126; Braudy 479). Studios began to cast an eye for potential westerns. Richard Boone's biographer, David Rothel, includes interviews with professionals affiliated with *Have Gun–Will Travel*, discussed in more detail below. The idea of the show was first introduced to CBS as a private detective program set in contemporary New York; the studio asked instead for a western, so the premise was changed by the writers, Sam Rolfe and Herb Meadow, to feature a gunfighter for hire in late 19th-century San Francisco (*Richard Boone: A Knight Without Armor in a Savage Land* 18, 104). According to Rolfe, the two intended *Have Gun–Will Travel* to be "a modern day action/adventure series. We had no idea of doing a period western" (quoted in Martin Grams, Jr., and Les Rayburn, *The Have Gun–Will Travel Companion* 34). This easy conversion from an action/adventure story to a period western demonstrates that conventions of the western genre itself, which had become so successful in Hollywood productions, were conducive to the importation of the liminal outlaw hero in television broadcasts as well.

Casablanca and *Shane* serve as models of films that portray the liminal outlaw hero who maintains a balance between serving the needs of the community and retaining his own integrity, as we have seen in the previous chapter.

Two examples, then, that offered very wide cultural exposure of this type of hero on television are the titular figure in *The Lone Ranger*, which began as a radio show in 1933 but became a famous television series (1949–1957) at the time when Steinbeck noted that such westerns were romances in disguise, and *Have Gun–Will Travel* (1957–1963), which featured "Paladin" (Richard Boone), a knightly gun for hire. In his insightful article from 2007, "Political Outlaws: Beat Cowboys," Kurt Hemmer remarks that "the outlaw mask on the Lone Ranger set him apart from traditional virtuous cowboys…. *The Lone Ranger* is arguably the most influential radio show in the history of American pop culture. Playing at times to twelve million listeners a week, *The Lone Ranger* aired from 1933–1955" (*American Studies Journal* 50, 10–11). A large part of the Lone Ranger's appeal, as we shall see, resides in the fact that he operates in a liminal space outside the law, yet he adheres to a strict moral code; despite this, we must remember that he is also motivated by a highly personal vendetta against the villainous Cavendish Gang who left him for dead, having ambushed the group of Texas Rangers, of whom he and his brother (a victim) were members. He does not reside in one community, and remains free of domestic entanglements of any kind. He adheres to a very high standard of conduct, which became known as "The Lone Ranger Creed." *The Lone Ranger*, while possessing a wide audience appeal, was conceived as a show especially designed for young viewers, like other early shows, such as *The Gene Autry Show* (1950–1956), *Hopalong Cassidy* (1952–1954) and *The Roy Rogers Show* (1951–1957).

Research and ratings soon revealed that evening programming needed to accommodate mature audiences, and this is one reason why the "adult western," initiated by *Gunsmoke*, soon began to dominate the prime-time evening line up. In his chapter "The Adult Western: The Flourishing," J. Fred McDonald offers a detailed explanation of the inception of the adult western and how it differed from the juvenile western that targeted young audiences. While the latter group continued to enjoy shows like *The Lone Ranger*, the introduction of its adult counterpart meant "a break with the past," so that "no longer would the central characters of TV Westerns be those flawlessly moral, one-dimensional types spawned by the B film tradition. Brave and tough they would remain, but heroes in the newer series were sketched with more believability and depth of character" (*Who Shot the Sheriff? The Rise and Fall of the Television Western* 47). According to MacDonald, it was characterized by "dramatic conflict, human insight, outdoor beauty and subtle moralizing," while still retaining an action storyline (50), and featuring a morally complex hero, prompting critic Cleveland Armory to remark, "Nowadays on TV Westerns there are not only good guys and bad guys, but also in-between guys" (quoted in *Who Shot the Sheriff?* 51). In *Have Gun–Will Travel*, the profession of Paladin, unlike the main characters in many other adult westerns of the late 1950s, marks him as just such an "in-between guy," who occupies a liminal space, despite his erudition and high principles. Unlike Matt Dillon (James Arness), the Dodge City Marshal of *Gunsmoke*, *Have Gun—Will Travel* follows *Shane* in portraying a well-mannered outsider with a mysterious past, whose courtly gestures and erudite, polished character co-exists with their status as professional killers.[4] An ex-Texas Ranger and a Union Civil War veteran who has become a gun for hire would seem to have little in common but, as we shall see, they share a few essential features that place them together in a long-standing tradition of a particular typology of hero.

Television westerns of this period provided a venue for addressing pressing social issues and concerns of middle-class America. The genre leant itself to an exploration of gender roles: issues of masculinity and its importance, and the expanding roles of women in contemporary life are reflected in many of these series. In addition, westerns asked the audience to consider its position on minorities, politics, and criminal justice.[5] Although these two series are rich in providing insights into the role of early television in both reflecting and shaping cultural attitudes about important social issues of the 1950s, I will focus on two features that position each character in the role of the liminal outlaw hero, and discuss how this derives from the medieval concept of the true knight. First, both the Lone Ranger and Paladin remain *errant*, solitary figures, free of entanglements that might prevent them from their ardent pursuit of a higher ideal. The Lone Ranger is accompanied on his adventures by his loyal sidekick, Tonto, but he has no romantic interest, and no permanent address. The adjective in the title—"lone"—emphasizes his individuality, despite the fact that he has a constant companion. Paladin's permanent residence is not a home but a suite at the *chic* Hotel Carlton in San Francisco; several episodes feature old acquaintances (some friendly) and recurring characters, but when he sets out as a gun for hire, he works alone. More important, Paladin is often featured in the company of attractive females, but he always remains unattached, even when he falls in love, as we shall see, suggesting that his profession, like Lancelot's, Rick Blaine's, or Shane's, requires a dedication that cannot allow for domestic entanglements, even if that is what the characters, in part, would wish to enjoy.

Second, both the Lone Ranger and Paladin rescue, sometimes through force, the official hero and/or the legal system that figure represents, when inadequacy or corruption of the law, or other factions in the community, prevent it from serving justice. What the law will allow, and what the foibles of human nature dictate, on occasion, is not always what these heroes deem to be right, so they rely on their own inner sense of justice as a guide to action.

The Lone Ranger, in his quest to avenge himself on those who ambushed and killed his brother, also assists, along the way, those whom the law cannot protect. Paladin, too, is haunted by his past, which serves as a powerful motive for his choice of profession, but remarkably the audience does not learn this reason until the opening episode of the final season, suggesting that his actions themselves, and the reasons why he makes his decisions when confronted with ethical/legal choices, created enough interest to hold viewers' attention for five seasons. His services are enlisted by those who are unwilling or cannot turn to the law, for various reasons, or sometimes by the law or the government itself, in which case Paladin becomes a covert agent, or operative. But his role is to achieve justice; to do so, he must adjudicate between opposing positions, sometimes through his superior intellect and charismatic personality, but other times through violence. I will first provide an overview of each figure and his personal story, and then point to examples of particular episodes that dramatize their roles as liminal outlaw heroes.

The Lone Ranger (1949–1957) and the Mask of Justice

"Who is he, and what is his business?"
"His business is justice. You see, he's the Lone Ranger."
—*The Lone Ranger*, "Bullets for Ballots"

The inception of the masked man who won so many viewers when it premiered on television in September of 1949 was the established, enormously successful radio show that aired 2,956 individual episodes from January 1933 until September 1954, with some repeated episodes through 1956 (www.otr westerns.com/westerns/the-lone-ranger). The idea for the show was created by George Trendle, the owner of the Detroit radio station WXYZ, with the talent of writer Fran Striker who had scripted a number of successful programs for radio (*I Was That Masked Man* 2). Striker's initial conception of the Lone Ranger's character was more violent than Trendle had envisioned; in the first script he submitted, the character shot and killed seven villains (*I Was That Masked Man* 4). Trendle, however, rejected this and established a set of rules to protect the virtue and integrity of the character, with young audiences in mind: the Lone Ranger should not smoke, drink, or use profanity, he must espouse the founding principles of America, revere God, use precise speech, and never shoot to kill (*I Was That Masked Man* 14). The perfect leading man for the role was found in the athletic actor Clayton Moore; when offered the part, Moore replied, "Mr. Trendle, I *am* the Lone Ranger" (*I Was That Masked Man* 115), and with the exception of the 1952–1953 season, when he was replaced by John Hart, Moore starred in the show and the two feature films (130–131). When he made public appearances, Moore always wore his trademark mask, and frequently recited his motto, written for radio by Fran Striker as the central informing ideology of the show. It espouses the values that each individual in a free society should embrace, from the viewpoint of conservative propaganda: love of God, country, truth and fellow man. Moore embraced as his own "The Lone Ranger Creed" (*I Was That Masked Man* 129–130). The basic story of the Lone Ranger, particularly that of his origin, remains consistent in the radio show and the 221 episodes that comprise the television series, the two feature films, *The Lone Ranger* (1956) and *The Lone Ranger and the Lost City of Gold* (1958), as well as the many novelizations, comic strips, and the animated cartoon series that capitalized on the popularity of the television program.

The origin story, presented in the first three episodes of the television series ("Enter the Lone Ranger," "The Lone Ranger Fights On," and "The Lone Ranger's Triumph") begins in the untamed west of the Texas territory. Interestingly, the explanation of the Lone Ranger's genesis was not even mentioned on the radio program, according to Dave Holland, until October 13, 1941, but the television debut introduced the narrative beginning of the legend and all of its important lore, which had evolved gradually from several versions and writers (*From Out of the Past: A Pictorial History of The Lone Ranger* 351). The first television episode begins with a ruthless band of outlaws, known as the Cavendish Gang, who have been terrorizing honest citizens. Six Texas Rangers, one of whom is a brother to the leader, Captain Daniel Reid (Tristram Coffin), set out to capture the gang. They are betrayed by Collins (George J. Lewis), who pretends to be a victim of the Cavendish Gang and avers he can lead the Rangers to their hideout, but instead lures them into a trap at Bryant's Gap, where Butch Cavendish (Glenn Strange) and his henchmen open fire. All six are left for dead, and Butch also shoots Collins in the back, leaving him behind. A Native American, Tonto (Jay Silverheels), who has come to the canyon to hunt, discovers that Dan Reid's brother, the soon-to-be Lone Ranger (Clayton Moore) is not dead but is rather only badly wounded. Tonto recognizes a token that he had given to this man years before; his tribe had been attacked by "renegade Indians" who killed his mother and sister and left Tonto, then a boy, for dead. The young future Ranger had nursed him back to health, for which Tonto named him "Kemo Sabe" ("trusty scout"). He further insisted on giving Tonto a horse so that he could go in search of his father. Tonto accepted, but only on the condition that Reid would take his ring as a pledge of gratitude and friendship. It is this token that Tonto sees on a chain around the wounded Ranger's neck; the tables are now turned, and Tonto works devotedly to restore Reid to health. This version of their past history, and the forging of the new partnership between Tonto and the Lone Ranger, also underwent a complicated series of changes from its radio inception. Tonto was originally a "half-breed," and an old Indian when an adult future Lone Ranger rescues him under different circumstances than those recalled by Tonto in this premiere television episode (Holland 373–375).

While nursing the victim back to health, Tonto buries the other Rangers, and gives their personal belongings back to Reid. Now the Ranger Reid must decide upon a course of action. He fears the Cavendish Gang can recognize him, and will hunt him down and finish the job they started. Tonto and Reid decide to make a sixth grave, leading the gang to believe that Reid, too, is dead—the perfect cover. This idea was modified for *High Plains Drifter* (1973), starring and directed by Clint Eastwood as a "stranger" (a dead sheriff) who returns to avenge his wrongful death by a gang of bullies, and also a cowardly town that would lend him no aid when the outlaw gang fatally bullwhipped him. In *The Lone Ranger* the grave is a ruse, of course, while in *High Plains Drifter* the supernatural enters in, and the character is actually dead, but death as a camouflage works effectively in each case.

The misleading grave is a good cover, but for the fact that Reid decides he must avenge the deaths of his brother and the other Rangers, for which he needs a disguise in order not to be recognized. Tonto then fashions for him a domino mask, made from the vest of Reid's dead brother, Dan. Interestingly, in the radio show version of the origin story, the voiceover observes that this resolve can be seen in the hero's eyes, and likens it to the mission of a spiritual, crusader knight of old: "there is a light that must have burned in the eyes of knights in armor. A light that through the ages lifted the souls of strong men who fought for justice, for God" (quoted in Rothel, *Who Was That Masked Man?* 56). In the television version, Reid also vows that, in avenging the deaths of the Rangers, he will initiate a crusade against the lawless, bringing to justice 100 men for every Ranger who fell to this gang: "I'm going to devote my life to establishing law and order in this new frontier—to make the West a decent place to live" ("Enter the Lone Ranger"). He declares he will use his gun only to wound, and not to kill, as that should be left to the law.

The mask, which becomes the central iconic signifier, both conceals and reveals his identity, an encoded but palpable sign of his pledge. In the opening episode, in order to complete Reid's new identity, Tonto had made Reid's hat even whiter than it was by washing it in a stream and letting it bleach in the sun, a convention of the western genre that distinguishes the hero from the

The Lone Ranger's (Clayton Moore) signature items: the "domino mask," fashioned from the shirt of his murdered brother, a reminder of his pledge for vengeance, his gun that fires silver bullets, his horse, Silver, and his companion, Tonto (Jay Silverheels). *The Lone Ranger* aired from 1949 to 1957 (Jerry Ohlinger's Movie Materials Store).

villain, and had also bequeathed to Reid his new name—the Lone Ranger. Tonto then expressed his wish to join the Lone Ranger in his vow to bring law and order to the region. "Don't you have a family?" the Lone Ranger asked, but Tonto replied that he is "lone" also, in search of new adventures that will help them fulfill their quest for justice. Interestingly, according to Fran Striker,

4. Remediation: Television and the Outlaw Hero

Jr., the son of the radio series' scriptwriter, in the first ten episodes of the radio show the masked man rode alone, and the figure of Tonto was introduced "solely because it was necessary for the Lone Ranger to have someone to talk to."[6]

In the second episode, viewers learn how the Lone Ranger attains his memorable mount, Silver, and also how he acquires his trademark silver bullets to accompany his mask. He and Tonto travel to Wild Horse Valley, a little known place that harbors a particularly hardy herd of wild horses. When they arrive, they witness a magnificent stallion locked in a deadly struggle with a bison; wounded, the horse is helpless to defend itself from the bison's final charge. The Lone Ranger kills the bison, saving the stallion's life, and then nurses the horse back to health. Although he wants to tame the horse, the Lone Ranger respects it and offers it freedom but, surprisingly, it chooses to stay with him. The voiceover remarks that horse and rider "accept each other as equals." When Tonto observes that he is "a beauty, like mountain with snow, silver white," the Lone Ranger settles on the stallion's name—Silver. As the origin story continues, the Lone Ranger also decides in this episode to use the trademark silver bullets, which will be crafted for him by his partner, a retired Ranger named Jim Blaine (Ralph Littlefield), with whom Reid owns a secret silver mine. Holland notes that Fran Striker, in composing the radio scripts, had borrowed the idea of silver bullets from "another of his own stories in which Robin Hood shot silver-tipped arrows as an identifying symbol," but Holland concludes that they were introduced into the story not only to identify the Lone Ranger as the one who fired them, a kind of signature, but also "as expensive as they were, they quickly reminded you how expensive human life was, and therefore: Never waste one wasting the other" (*From Out of the Past* 403). Indeed, in the television show, the main character never kills, though he often wounds and is himself wounded. All of the hero's emblems of election are complete at the end of the second episode of the television genesis story: his mask, his companion, his silver bullets, his horse—and his avowed mission in life.

"The Lone Ranger's Triumph," the third episode, presents the model for future programs when the Lone Ranger and Tonto accomplish the dual task of bringing to justice the Cavendish Gang (which is the vengeance the Lone Ranger had sought for the murder of his brother and companions), but also aiding the town of Colby, whose sheriff (Walter Sande) has been unable to protect it from a hostile Cavendish take over. Thus this triad of opening episodes establishes that both the Lone Ranger and Tonto are free to pursue villains because they are not hindered by domestic obligations as they ride off in search of adventures that will help them fulfill their quest for justice, and creates the lore for each of the items that will become an inherent part of the Lone

Ranger's signature. The emphasis on his weapon, with the unique use of hand-crafted silver bullets, resembles that of the individuality of ancient and medieval weaponry that denote the election of the hero, (discussed in more detail when we scrutinize *Have Gun–Will Travel*). The importance placed on his horse, given intelligence and an equal status in their partnership, suggests the Lone Ranger needs Silver to complete his identity, and this also hearkens back to the most basic definition of a medieval knight, whose power lay in the strength of his weapon and his role as a mounted warrior, which gave him the advantage over foot soldiers.

Perhaps the most intriguing question about the Lone Ranger, called so even though he has a loyal companion, is why he chooses to work independently of both the Texas Rangers and the law, even though his cause is the same. Once the Cavendish Gang is brought to justice—the ostensible reason for the disguise of the mask—there is no further threat of being recognized and overwhelmed by their superior numbers, the initial reason given for adopting the mask. On National Public Radio's newsmagazine, *All Things Considered*, its senior host, Robert Siegel, explored the character and popularity of this hero in a January 2008 program titled aptly, for the purposes of this study, "The Lone Ranger: Justice from Outside the Law."[7] Siegel interviewed Professor Gary Hoppenstand who specializes in American studies and popular culture. He observes that the Lone Ranger's mask represents "the very symbol of the outlaws" he brings to justice. Indeed, it is part of the formula for these episodes that the Lone Ranger *is* mistaken for an outlaw because of the mask he wears. For instance, in "Sheep Thieves" (season 1, episode 22), an elderly sheep rancher whom the Lone Ranger wishes to help is at first suspicious of his offer because of the mask. A few episodes later (season 1, episode 27), in "Gold Train," the Lone Ranger is mistaken for a masked outlaw called "The Dude" and is jailed for a crime he obviously did not commit. Since it is unnecessary for him to remain incognito after he sees the Cavendish Gang disbanded and incarcerated, it seems clear that the Lone Ranger continues to wear his mask precisely because it functions as an equivocal sign of the liminal space he occupies—between the official hero of the law and that of the outlaws he has vowed to pursue. Hoppenstand describes the masked man as "a vigilante lawman who protects the criminal justice system by working outside it" and asserts that such a "masked vigilante who operated outside the bounds of government—but in the interests of the law-abiding public" was appealing to radio listeners, and later, of course, to television audiences as well. Hoppenstand's identification of the Lone Ranger as a "vigilante lawman" shows that he is an apt model for the liminal outlaw hero: he makes up his own mind about what is right, acts independently, but with interests of the community in mind. Although the term "vigilante" has negative connotations associated with wild-eyed lynch mobs, the Ku Klux Klan, and other types of irrational behaviors, it can include less nefarious representatives, like the Lone Ranger, who acts in the interests of justice, even when the law does not authorize or condone his actions. (American vigilante justice was not uncommon in the Old West, as we will see in the opening discussion of Chapter 5.)

The original aim of the radio show, as conceived by George Trendle, was to provide a role model for young listeners and, as discussed above, Trendle insisted on strict adherence to his own guidelines regarding the character and plot of *The Lone Ranger*. Even though it was necessary for the main character to remain unattached, free of domestic obligations in order for him to act on his resolve to travel the west dispensing justice, the traditional values that Trendle had in mind for the program to promote would include the conservative cornerstone of the family unit. One way that this was addressed in the radio program was to give the Lone Ranger a responsibility for the welfare of a family member. This is introduced in a scene just before the Cavendish ambush; Dan Reid, feeling apprehensive about the future, entrusts the safety of his wife and infant son, who are travelling west in a wagon train, to his brother (the future masked man), should anything happen to him (*Who Was That Masked Man?* 55). The development of the story about Dan Reid's son, Danny, was then pursued, according to David Rothel, with the aim of appealing to a juvenile audience: "To give 'The Lone Ranger' adventures even more self-identification for young listeners, the character of teenage Dan Reid, the Lone Ranger's nephew, was developed. With the same thoroughness of the origin story of the Lone Ranger, Fran Striker now set about writing 'The Legend of Dan Reid'—the story of how the Lone Ranger found his only living relative" (*Who Was That Masked Man?* 77).

The radio episode recounts how, by an apparent act of providence, the Lone Ranger and Tonto find the long lost nephew. Although they had earlier uncovered evidence that suggested Captain Reid's wife and son had both been killed in an Indian attack, the Lone Ranger holds out hope that they are alive. Years later, when they rescue from bandits a defenseless old woman and her adopted grandson, the dying woman, Grandma Frisby, recounts the story of how she came to raise Dan. She had been in a wagon train attacked by Indians; all were massacred, but she saved herself and an infant boy, escaping during the mayhem. She then shows the Lone Ranger a locket that she had taken from the scene, one worn by the infant. When he sees the picture inside the necklace, the Lone Ranger recognizes that it is a likeness of his brother and wife, Dan's parents. Thus, the Lone Ranger and his nephew are united, and the masked man can now honor his promise he had made to his brother years before. The

Lone Ranger tells Dan of his "heritage," not only his share of the silver mine that they now co-own, but also a lesson in civics, in that he has inherited the rights of all Americans (*Who Was That Masked Man?* 79).

In the television series, this background is not portrayed, perhaps because it was assumed that audiences were already familiar with the story. Instead, Danny Reid (Chuck Courtney) is introduced in "Sheep Thieves" (season 1, episode 22), and appears in a total of fourteen episodes from 1950 to 1955. What is interesting is the way the Lone Ranger's familial responsibility is managed. On the one hand, an orphaned nephew who has already reached his teenage years does not demand the same commitment of time and place that a spousal one would. This allows for the Lone Ranger to remain free to pursue his quest, but still to be perceived as a responsible "family man." In the television series, Danny is either attending school back east or he is accompanying his uncle and Tonto on their adventures. His horse, Victor, is even Silver's son. In this way, one important feature of the liminal outlaw hero is shown to be adhered to in *The Lone Ranger*—he remains itinerant, an errant figure in constant movement, searching for an adventure that will validate his own innate sense of himself as an ardent defender of justice, something that he can achieve only if he remains outside of domestic obligations. In fact, on one occasion, when his silver pistols for the show were stolen and recovered, Moore confesses: "I never kissed a girl on the *Lone Ranger* show—I only kissed Silver—but when they handed my revolvers back to me, I kissed the guns" (*I Was That Masked Man* 226). The monastic purity of the character is not far removed from the Lancelot who descended from the Grail family in the medieval Arthurian tradition; save for the latter's fatal love of the queen, he himself would have fulfilled the function of Galahad as the pure grail knight.

Despite his respect for the law, and his past as a Texas Ranger, the masked man remains a free agent, accomplishing a justice that the law is not always able to deliver. Sometimes the representative of the law is corrupt, other times the law is unable, on its own, to fight crime and accomplish justice because the force of evil is too powerful. "Outlaw of the Plains" (season 1, episode 43) features a crooked lawman, who has been appointed as acting sheriff in the permanent sheriff's absence. Sheriff Shattuck (Jack Lee) runs a cattle-rustling ring, hiding behind his badge to fool the locals into believing their stolen cattle are wandering off because of a drought. The ranchers are at first suspicious of the Lone Ranger because of his mask, and they must decide whose advice to follow: the sheriff's or the masked stranger's, this choice representing the manner in which the law is not always in accord with the Ranger's principles. "The Masked Deputy" (season 2, episode 10), alternately, centers on an inept older sheriff Higgins (Eddie Cobb) who has been intimidated by Will Bradly (Stuart

Randall), a cattle rustler who fronts as a railroad man; the Lone Ranger exposes Bradly's crime, and turns the sheriff back into an honest lawman. In "The Old Cowboy" (season 3, episode 42), the crooked legal representative is not the sheriff, but a lawyer. The Lone Ranger (played during this season by John Hart rather than Clayton Moore) has to protect a nearly blind old rancher, Jack Brewster (Russell Simpson), from a corrupt lawyer, Rafe Paulson (Steve Brodie). When the representatives of the law are themselves the criminals, the Lone Ranger's righteousness, and his position outside of the law, is what saves the day.

Other times, the law is unable to stand up against powerful individuals or gangs, either because the forces of evil physically overpower the law by numbers, are outwitted by the guile and disguise of evil, or are subject to blackmail, as in "Double Jeopardy" (season 1, episode 52) in which Judge Henry Brady (James Kirkwood) who is a star witness in a case, is being blackmailed into changing his testimony because his daughter, Molly (Christine Larsen), has been kidnapped by Ma Hinshaw (Marin Sais) and her boys in order to prevent her other son, Clyde (Ric Roman), from being convicted of murder. Even the Texas Rangers require the assistance of the Lone Ranger and Tonto in "The Outcast" (season 2, episode 19), when they attempt to capture an elusive band of outlaws by having one Ranger, Randy Tyler (Robert Rockwell), go under cover to infiltrate the gang. In "Bullets For Ballots" (season 1, episode 35), the town of Waynesville is holding a mayoral election that is being undermined by a corrupt banker Jeb Wesson (Frederic Tozere), who keeps his own man as mayor by framing Mayor Knox's (Frank Jaquet) opponents. The Lone Ranger helps the current challenger, an honest attorney named Robert McQueen (Craig Stevens), to win the election fairly. At the end of the episode, in response to the question about the masked man's identity and mission, McQueen is told, "His business is justice. You see, he's the Lone Ranger."

In "Behind the Law" (season 2, episode 21), justice cannot be dispensed against the Big Jim Folsom (Gene Roth) and his gang, who take over the town of San Carlo, outside of the county where they commit crimes. Sheriff Maloney (Bob Carson) is the "good" sheriff who would like to arrest the gang, but they flee to San Carlo, outside the law's jurisdiction. The weak lawman of San Carlo, Sheriff Gray (Marshall Bradford), and the inhabitants of the town, have allowed the gang to live there, so the Lone Ranger has to devise a plan that will see that the Folsom Gang is brought to justice. These types of episodes augment the discrepancy between justice and law that the liminal outlaw hero is designed to address, and tend to be more original than the many episodes that feature the standard stagecoach robbery, the dispute over the use of land, and the Indian uprising episodes that are conventional western plots. The title of the episode "Behind the Law" operates on several levels: geographically, the gang establishes its headquarters in the next county so that it cannot be arrested for the crimes it commits in another; behind also suggests that it is important for all citizens to back or support the law, so that justice can be achieved. It is the neglected civic duty of everyone in San Carlo, even its sheriff.

The character of the Lone Ranger, from its inception in its radio days, was conceived and controlled with care by its originator, George Trendle. Because of the decidedly patriotic emphasis Trendle insisted on in the scripts, and because he considered the Lone Ranger a model for juvenile audiences, the factors that define him as a liminal outlaw hero may not be, at first, readily discernible. The darker side of his character and mission in life, despite the overt signifier of his mask, remains latent. But it is important to remember that vengeance is his initial motivation in adopting the mask—he never considers asking the law or the Texas Rangers to do what he himself, for personal reasons, has determined he will do alone. He is defined by his mask and his mission, remains a loner who answers, finally, to his own code, and lingers outside the constraints of a community or family. The iconic status of the Lone Ranger has continued, long after the demise of the western television genre, perpetuating the idea that the devotee of justice can earn the approbation of a grateful community without relinquishing his freedom.

Have Gun–Will Travel: The Chess Knight and the Sacrifice of the Queen (1957–1963)

MADAM L: Check. Your move, sir.
PALADIN: If you'll permit me. Check. Sacrifice the queen, naturally. Checkmate.
—*Have Gun–Will Travel*, "The Prophet"

The opening sequence of *Have Gun–Will Travel* introduces the complexly drawn figure of Paladin, and the equivocal nature of his relationship with the law. Originally, the camera provided a close-up of Paladin's right side, with only his mid-section in the frame, privileging his gun and holster. The now iconic image of the traditional chess piece for the knight—the side profile of a silver horse's head with a ruby eye—mounted in relief on the black leather holster itself, establishes the relationship between the gunslinger and knighthood, and indicates, with its focus on the weapon, the potential for violent resolution of conflict. The gun is then drawn and confronts the audience, as a voiceover proclaims its accuracy; it is then placed back in its holster, still showing only the character's torso, but clearly revealing that he is clad almost exclusively in black. This sequence is accompanied by an ominous series of minor chords, composed by CBS' Bernard Herrmann (Grams and Rayburn 41).[8] A paladin is a legendary medieval knight of rare talent, likened to the Twelve Peers of Charlemagne, and especially to his nephew, Roland, who was martyred at the Battle of Roncevaux Pass in 778. But despite the adoption of this romantic pseudonym, the hero of the series is clad in black, except for a white tie, discarded during the first season because Boone disliked it (Grams and Rayburn 41), an attire that in conventional westerns signals the villain. Moreover, Paladin sports a moustache, yet forms a sharp contrast to his alter ego, the sophisticated, erudite, man of culture with the infectious laugh who seems to lead a life of leisure when he is not on a job. The mixed signals of the opening sequence augment the fact that the hero of *Have Gun—Will Travel* is not cast from the same mold as that of most other western television heroes, "official heroes" (e.g., Marshal Dillon). Instead, he defies stereotypes and prescribed codes, and will answer to his own conscience in matters of conduct.

Paladin's gun, as the voiceover (each week, excerpted from the dialogue of the episode itself) insists, is unique: "I want you to take a look at this gun. The balance is excellent. This trigger responds to the pressure of one ounce. This gun was handcrafted to my specifications, and I rarely draw it unless I mean to use it." That the gun is one of a kind, responding to its wielder, invokes a time-honored tradition of individual weapons that testify to the election of the hero, an indication he should be heeded by others. Throughout the Biblical book of *Exodus*, Moses' powerful staff works miracles, such as parting the Red Sea so the Israelites can escape the Egyptian army; only Odysseus (or his son, Telemachus) can string the bow with which he unleashes his wrath on the evil suitors in *The Odyssey*. King Arthur's sword, Excalibur, given to him by the Lady of the Lake, and the earlier sword that only he is able to pull from the stone, verify he is the rightful ruler of Britain, and Roland's unbreakable sword Durendal, which contains holy relics, was given to him by Charlemagne, who in turn received it from an angel (*The Song of Roland* 88–89). The uniqueness of the weapon, and the emphasis placed on it, underscores the individuality of the hero himself, hearkening back to a pre-industrial time before items could be mass produced, and in which weapon and wielder formed a single unit. A knight depended on his weapon and horse, and no two were alike; so it is with Paladin and his gun for hire. Often, weapons are part of the liminal outlaw hero's origin story—as we saw in *The Lone Ranger*—and an indicator of his election. This is the case with Paladin, and later with Dirty Harry, Rambo, and Batman, as we shall see in ensuing chapters.

The opening sequence of the series raises questions that *Have Gun—Will Travel* does not immediately answer. Unlike the first three episodes of *The Lone Ranger*, which provide the essential backstory that both establishes the creation of the hero's identity and supplies his motive, viewers of *Have Gun—Will Travel* must wait until the opening episode of the final season (season six), aptly titled "Genesis," to discover how and why Paladin became a gunfighter. Through the first five seasons—those of Richard Boone's original contract—the audience can glean some facts about the hero's past, but these do not reveal the enigmatic origin of this exceptional gunfighter.[9] For instance, Paladin served in the Union Army during the Civil War, and had formal military training. In the opening episode of the series, "Three Bells to Perdido" (written by Herb Meadow and Sam Rolfe), Paladin discourses on the ancient military practice of the phalanx, which prompts Jesse Reade (Harry Shannon) the man who hires him (reluctantly) to observe, "Ex-army officer," affirmed by Paladin. When Reade speculates further that his training must have been at West Point, Paladin remains evasive, but in ensuing episodes his knowledge of military tactics—both ancient and modern—becomes prominent. For instance, in "The Unforgiven" (season 3, episode 8), written by Jay Simms,

"A knight without armor in a savage land"? Paladin (Richard Boone) is clad in the black attire of the gunfighter, but with the figure of the chess knight on his holster. The most erudite gun for hire in the west, Paladin is an expert on chess, the law—and women. He recites the words of famous philosophers and poets, from Aristotle to Keats, and once saved the life of Oscar Wilde, but he is prone to violence. *Have Gun—Will Travel* aired from 1957 to 1963 (Jerry Ohlinger's Movie Materials Store).

Paladin meets up with a general he had served under in the Civil War, and in "The Prophet" (season 3, episode 16), he mentions having been a participant in the Comanche Expedition headed by General Ranald Slidell MacKenzie (1840–1889), a Civil War general who headed a number of campaigns against Native Americans during the 1870s and 1880s.[10] It is notable, too, that Paladin is well-versed in the law. Several episodes establish this, either by Paladin defending himself or another in the court room. For example, in "The Unforgiven," mentioned above, Paladin's former commanding officer, General Crommer (David White), remembers that, when he had tried to have Paladin court marshaled for disobeying his orders (even though in doing so Paladin saved the general's life), Paladin defended himself so well that, not only did he exonerate himself, but turned the tables on the general, who was subsequently "court marshaled and cashiered," the reason for his grudge against Paladin.

The gunfighter's alter ego exudes the natural eloquence of a medieval social knight. In "The Bostonian" (season 1, episode 21), Paladin claims to be the president of the San Francisco branch of the stock exchange, suggesting that he enjoys a comfortable lifestyle through his business skills as well has his talent with a gun. His erudition is a trademark of the show, with quotations from learned sources such as scripture, ancient Sanskrit, Aristotle, Shakespeare, Donne, and Keats. He is an accomplished chess player, another link with the romantic past of a medieval knight. He appreciates fine wine and gourmet food, and choice cigars, but also engages in daring flirtations with cultured beautiful women, with whom he exchanges the niceties of a ritualized *amour courtois*. At the beginning of "The Return of Dr. Thackeray," when offered a fee of $2000, Paladin rejects this, stating flatly that he spends $2000 a year in cigars, a small fortune at the time. Several episodes open with Paladin in the lobby of the Hotel Carlton playing chess.[11] All of these details are metonyms for his class and taste. What remains an enigma is his personal past, and why he lives two widely divergent lifestyles.

"Genesis," the opening episode for the sixth and final season, provides the backstory of Paladin's identity, how and why he became a gunfighter. Richard Boone's son, Peter Boone, reveals that this "was the episode Dad was the most proud of. He thought it was very good" (quoted in Rothel 78). "Genesis" was written by Sam Rolfe, the co-creator of *Have Gun—Will Travel*. William Conrad, who also starred as Norge, the villain of this episode, directed it. In "Genesis," Paladin, returning to his room one night, is jumped by a young man, Roderick Jefferson (James Mitchum), who confesses that his murder attempt was nothing "personal," but that he was forced to try to kill Paladin to pay back a gambling debt he was unable to honor. The man who ordered him to kill Paladin is the latter's gambling adversary. Once he has overpowered

Jefferson and learns of these circumstances, Paladin tells him that he, too, had found himself in a similar situation years before, and the episode then recalls, in flashback form, the origin of the gunfighter he has become. What is remarkable about "Genesis" is that it presents Paladin in three allegorical incarnations. He relates to Jefferson that, after the war, his parents sent him a remittance every month if he would stay away from home (for reasons that are not made clear). Young and irresponsible, Paladin routinely gambled away his income, and found himself on one fateful occasion indebted to a man named Norge. Paladin lost a card game to Norge and could not pay his debt, so Norge offered the same choice to Paladin as that which was given to Jefferson: kill an adversary and the debt would be forgiven. Norge, who earlier had been run out of Delta Valley by a notorious gunslinger named Smoke (also played by Boone), orders Paladin to kill him, but suggests it is only because Smoke is a killer and a wanted man.

Good at squandering his allowance on gambling, but not yet particularly savvy with a gun, the soon-to-be named Paladin tracks down Smoke, but is knocked out by his more experienced adversary, who accepts the challenge offered him, but not until he has taught his younger would-be assassin how to prepare for the duel, thus displaying his sense of honor. This begins a full initiation ritual: the elderly Smoke, who has claimed the literal and moral "high ground" in the episode, teaches his adversary how to draw the gun faster from the holster, and insists that he practice his draw, all the while watching and waiting. Smoke is well spoken, wise, mocking, and also already near death, with an unmistakable cough of someone whose time on earth is coming to an end. Having learned why he is a target, he ironically labels his adversary "a paladin. A gentleman knight in shiny armor, all armed with a cause and righteousness and a fine pointed lance, and yet a mercenary—a man who hires out for gold." Nonetheless, when he deems Paladin is ready to face him, Smoke fulfills his promise to duel, and is mortally wounded by his "younger self." His dying words represent a full initiation into the profession of gunfighter, but Smoke is unusual in that his code is closer to one of knighthood than that of the mercenary that he himself once was, and that of which he has earlier accused Paladin.

With his dying breath, Smoke cautions Paladin that although he believes he has rid the world of an evil gunfighter, he has in fact accomplished the opposite: "You think you've slain the dragon. You know what you've done? You've turned the dragon loose. The one decent thing I ever did in my life was to chain him away from these people. Who's going to stop Norge now?" He then admonishes Paladin: "Remember, there's always a dragon loose somewhere." Paladins, shiny armor, righteous causes, and dragons all suggest that the "genesis" of

Boone's memorable character resides in the knightly ideal of the Middle Ages. It is significant that Smoke should instruct the novice Paladin first in the more primitive skills of knighthood—weaponry and combat—and then initiate him into its higher, more spiritual form—that of the true knight, in which knighthood is a calling, a vocation and service to a higher ideal and to others. In this way, the story follows the structural pattern of the first Grail Knight, Perceval, who is initiated into various stages of knighthood by mentors commensurate with his own growing spiritual understanding. This is a transformative moment for Paladin, but he only fully understands what Smoke has told him when he observes his funeral in Delta Valley, learning then the particulars of Smoke's own story of redemption.

Smoke had been a gunfighter with no particular purpose when he arrived wounded in Delta Valley and was nurtured by the town. He witnessed Norge's tyranny over the citizens, and out of gratitude for their kindness, he vanquished Norge, becoming the town's hero and finding a purpose in his own life. This is the reason Norge wishes to have Smoke eradicated—so he can return to the Valley and resume his control. Paladin feels cursed, and is filled with remorse; the flashback concludes with a shot that reveals him to be standing in Smoke's position, wearing Smoke's clothing and his holster with the emblem of the chess knight for which he himself will become famous. Transformed by this newfound knowledge and purpose, Paladin awaits the return of Norge, the first true "dragon" he will, presumably, defeat.

When the story resumes in the present, it has served as a cautionary tale for the young Jefferson who is now contrite. Paladin gives him encouragement, articulating the moral of the story he has just recounted: "If a man's mistakes determine who he was, then what he does about those mistakes should determine what he is." Paladin has spent his life trying to live up to the highest standards for himself, an effort to redeem himself from his own earlier error. If Smoke, when Boone's character first meets him, is a figuration of his own future, then the young man who has just attempted to slay Paladin, represents his former self, and Paladin is able to prevent him from taking the same difficult path he has been destined to follow. It is with Smoke that his life has taken its decisive turn, one he hopes Jefferson can avoid. Boone does an admirable job of portraying both Smoke and his younger self in the flashback, and also his role in the present time of the series. From the purposelessness of his early life as a gambler and meanderer, he has become the solitary knight with a higher calling, albeit one that frequently enlists a violent solution.

The liminal outlaw hero, for reasons discussed earlier in this study, remains free of domestic entanglements, void of contractual marriage arrangements, and finally of any lasting relationship with a woman. For Lancelot, a marital commitment would mean having to devote his energies to his wife, rather than to the duties of knighthood exclusively, and his ideal is tinged also with a monastic overtone of chastity: a lecherous knight is a failed knight. As we saw in chapter 3, both Rick Blaine and Shane dodge the permanence of a romantic love. Their passion for a woman remains sublimated: Rick renounces his emotional hold on Ilsa, ostensibly placing a larger social cause over his personal happiness, as does Shane. Paladin, a lady's man like his predecessors, also avoids settling down, even when he falls in love. Guinevere, Ilsa, and Marion are all wed to others, so the obstacle for Lancelot, Rick and Shane is considerable, but when Paladin falls in love, the refusal to marry is not because such an impediment exists. It is a conscious decision of free will.

His many flirtations and implied secret assignations aside, Paladin is not immune to genuine feelings for a woman. In "Ella West" (season 1 episode 17), written by Gene Roddenberry, Paladin is hired by his old friend, Tomahawk Carter (Earle Hodgins), to transform his new female sharp shooter star, Ella West (Norma Crane), from a tomboy into a more attractive female. Tomahawk is worried that if Ella remains wild and unpolished, she will become a subject of ridicule and fail to remain an attraction for his traveling Wild West Show. Paladin agrees, for a price, but Ella is, initially, extremely hostile to the lessons he has to offer. The archetypal roots of the domestication and molding of the female in this episode are *The Taming of the Shrew*, especially in that it concludes, like the Shakespearean comedy, with the promise of wedded bliss, but also, because Paladin strives to transform Ella into an image of a model woman, invoking the Pygmalion myth, especially as popularized by George Bernard Shaw's play.

Paladin initially approaches his task in a professional manner, with a series of "lessons." Once he gains her confidence, Paladin learns of Ella's tragic life of poverty and neglect. He also learns that Ella has only joined Tomahawk's show because of Tracey Calvert (William Swan), her childhood love, who is also part of the troupe of entertainers. Ella avers that she wishes "to show that Tracey Calvert a thing or two" but she still loves him, and her unfeminine, boisterous behavior is a cover for her fear of being rejected by Tracey. Thus, there are two reasons for Paladin to help her: to save Ella's career and her role in Tomahawk's show as he has agreed to do for a fee, and to enable her to find happiness through Tracey's acceptance of her as an attractive woman. What begins for Paladin as a job, and perhaps a challenge, soon becomes a passion—he feels sympathy and admiration for Ella, charmed by her rare spirit and independence.

The complication in the story occurs when Paladin begins to feel a genuine attraction for Ella, proportionate with his success in transforming her into a lady. His initial amusement and sympathy for Ella grows into admiration, even passion. The intertextual references in the episode are designed to show viewers that Paladin finds himself truly enthralled by Ella's refreshing honesty and natural beauty, a contrast to the usual sophisticated socialite with whom he is so frequently seen cavorting. First, he recites to Ella, announcing its title and author, a stanza from the English romantic ballad "La Belle Dame Sans Merci" (1820) written by John Keats: "I met a lady in the meads / Full beautiful—a faery's child, / Her hair was long, her foot was light, / And her eyes were wild" (ll. 16–20). The knight in the poem speaks these lines in reply to a query: "Oh what can ail thee, knight-at-arms?" The *femme fatale* of the title is the alluring damsel who has enthralled this knight, and many others before him, with her wild beauty. If Paladin identifies with the knight in the poem, he is expressing the fact that he finds Ella enchanting, but also, of course, dangerous. The naïve Ella, obviously unaware of her own charm, responds that his recitation makes her feel "all tingly." Later, when Ella arrives at Paladin's room, bathed and in a dress, he admires her transformation into a lovely young woman. Ella asks if he will help her arrange her hair, the only part of her appearance she has been unable to improve on her own, averring that Paladin must have seen many women "put their hair up—and took it down, too." This elicits from Paladin another poetic excerpt, this time from Goethe's tragic play *Faust*, published in two parts (1808, 1832): "Beware of her fair hair, for she excels / All women in the magic of her locks, / And when she twines them round a young man's neck / she will not ever set him free." In his passage that Paladin recites, Mephistopheles is warning Faust about the wiles of Lilith, the archetype of the *femme fatale*, and, in some traditions, Adam's first wife. Again, Paladin uses his literary knowledge to express his awareness of Ella's enticements. Paladin finds himself under Ella's spell, but her peculiar power, unlike the belle dame sans merci and Lilith, is that she is guileless. He employs these literary references to express the spell of beauty, and his vulnerability to it. He then likens Ella to the desert flowers cultivated in a garden by missionaries he once visited, remarking on the pure white beauty and intoxicating fragrance of the mesquite bush. The comparison of Ella with the natural loveliness of the wild white cactus flower again emphasizes her virginal and therefore potent charm.

Ella then asks Paladin about "that silver thing on your holster. It's a knight, ain't it?" Paladin acknowledges that it is a "chess knight," and Ella posits, "Knights are real courteous fellas. They're got up so pretty and they talk so fancy that a girl might think they really mean what they say. I figure they're just being kindly." Paladin understands that Ella is questioning the sincerity of his compliments, so he answers her: "You'd only need kindness if you had no virtues, and you have many," citing her courage and honesty. Still unconvinced, Ella pleads with him not to flatter her out of pity, to which Paladin replies, "Pity is not included in the course," as he leans down to kiss her lips. This is the rhetoric of courtliness; this is the ritual of an impassioned knight.

The camera cuts away as they begin to kiss, and it is for the viewer to construct the lacuna between this scene and the next. The suggestive cut and the ensuing scene are used to convey what the television code of the period would not allow to be more explicit.[12] In the next scene, Ella, clad in a revealing dress (low cut, short sleeves), is shown in Paladin's room, pouring two glasses of champagne. A knock on the door, which Ella expects to be Paladin, is, to her surprise, Tracey. Paladin has sent Tracey a note to come to the room. In his absence, Tracey and Ella finally have an honest conversation about their youthful love for each other, and Tracey expresses his admiration for Ella's transformation into a woman. Ella admits she was wrong in being so stubborn about shedding her tomboy defense mechanism. She makes elliptical allusions to the events of the previous night when she says to Tracey, "Too bad we didn't talk before," and "Too late now, I reckon," an encoded admission that she and Paladin consummated their love. This is further underscored when, once Paladin arrives, Ella believes she is going away with him. Paladin gruffly announces that his business is concluded, and he is leaving alone, but he provokes Tracey into fighting him for Ella's sake, proving to them both that she belongs with her first love. When he departs, Paladin leaves a note saying that Tracey "had first claim" on her, but he also includes in the note a private token of his sincere feelings for Ella—a silver chess piece of a knight. Practically, there is no reason why Paladin could not take the girl away with him, as earlier she had asked him to do; she might well have believed that the consummation of their love was the pledge that he would do so, but he knows that he cannot be encumbered by such a relationship and continue his vocation. He sacrifices the woman to retain his individuality, but absolves himself of the responsibility of caring for Ella after the elided scene by providing a substitute in the form of Tracey. This closure is conciliatory, meeting the obligations of community, but avoiding the "magic of her locks," and thus preserving his individual freedom.

Another episode that features a true love affair is "The Princess and the Gunfighter" (season 4, episode 19), written by Robert E. Thompson, but this time the lady is of a very high class in society, and not from a poor and impoverished background, like Ella. Paladin is hired by officials from the small country of Montenegro to retrieve its heir apparent, the Princess Serafina (Arline Sax), who has gone missing during her grand tour of the west. As Paladin soon discovers, the princess has not been kidnapped, as was first feared; she has run away in order to taste freedom for the first time in her life.[13] Paladin pays off her escorts—two men hired as guides on the tour—and takes their place, pretending not to know who this proud princess is. Paladin is amused by Serafina's spirit, and during the few days it takes to return to San Francisco, the two share more than cooking duties. Paladin imparts his usual wisdom to the girl, who does not wish to face the life of heavy responsibility that lies ahead for her; she wishes to be "free." To counter this, Paladin tells her that freedom is an illusion: "We're none of us truly free. Once in awhile, we reach through the bars of our dungeon and touch, but none of us is free." He then cites Marcus Aurelius, who said, "The noble acceptance of the prison of oneself is the ultimate and only duty of man." The princess retorts to this sermon about duty, asking, "What about wishes? Desires? Needs?" The two have fallen deeply in love and the princess asks whether they really must return to San Francisco. Smitten, but still resolute, Paladin responds, "If there were no such thing as duty, if there were only wishes, I would wish away every kingdom in the world but this one, and I would never go back." This discussion ends in a passionate kiss, enfolded in each other's arms; there is then a cut to the Carlton Hotel, where the two, over a glass of champagne, have a mutual confession to make about their identities.

The princess begins to tell Paladin who she is when he confesses that he already knows, and then shows her his business card. Serafina is shocked, and believes that Paladin has not been sincere in his feelings for her. In fact, she asserts, "You are a gigolo!" At its best, a "gigolo" is a hired escort, but more commonly a paid sexual partner, and this is quite a curious word to use, considering the fact that they have shared some very intimate moments during their desert trek. Paladin is quick to deny this accusation: "No. Whatever happened between us was part of no bargain. But being what you are, a promise of fulfillment, and beauty, and peace, you made my job more difficult." The princess, still feeling betrayed, retorts, "I'm surprised you've not used up your store of pretty speeches," but Paladin insists that what he said, he meant, and as proof of his sincerity, he gives the princess a choice: he will take her wherever she wishes to go, as long as it is what she truly wants. He reminds her of their earlier discussions of duty, but also observes that, should she reject hers, many others will suffer at the cost of her "freedom." Sadder but wiser, the princess makes the choice of duty over personal happiness, taking comfort in their experience together: "But we did reach for a moment beyond the dungeon bars, didn't we? And we touched," which Paladin affirms. The obstacle to love presented in this case is class: the Princess Serafina will, apparently, be required to make a marital match commensurate with her royal responsibility. But it is Paladin himself who makes the princess sacrifice him and accept her fate. Once again, the woman is sacrificed so that the hero may remain unencumbered.

The princess, a future queen, is sacrificed so that Paladin may continue as an errant knight like the game of chess he so expertly plays.

Ella and Princess Serafina, although very different in their personalities and positions in life, are nonetheless presented as authentic love interests in the series, and not casual flirtations. The woman who poses the greatest challenge to Paladin's "freedom," however, is a physician, Dr. Phyllis Thackeray (June Lockhart), who appears in two episodes of the first season, "No Visitors," written by Don Brinkley (season 1, episode 12) and "The Return of Dr. Thackeray" (season 1, episode 35), co-written by Stanley Silverman and Sam Rolfe. Phyllis Thackeray and Paladin become acquainted in "No Visitors" when Paladin enlists her services in helping a woman and her baby, who have been abandoned by a wagon train, ostensibly because the child shows signs of typhoid. The inhabitants of the town do not take kindly to either its new female doctor or the prospect of letting Paladin bring the ailing woman and child into its midst. As Dr. Thackeray and Paladin team up to help the abandoned widow and her young daughter, Paladin is curious about his companion, asking her about her choice of profession, and her chosen location in the untamed west. He learns that she was the second woman to graduate from her medical school, as the idle life of a socialite, ensconced on "a velvet settee," holds no appeal for her. In reply to why she has come west, Phyllis responds, "I guess I am more missionary than physician."

Dr. Thackeray and Paladin are compatible souls: both like independence, learning, challenges, and helping others. In this episode, they must combat the religious fanaticism of the wagon master who has abandoned the woman and child, but also the fear the town members feel when they learn of the typhoid threat, and their unwillingness to extend compassion to the victims. Paladin forces them to allow the doctor and her patients to enter the town, where she can give them the medical treatment they require, and it turns out that the child was not afflicted with typhoid, but only measles. Both Paladin and Dr. Thackeray, however, have become afflicted by love. As he prepares to depart, she asks, "Must you leave?" and Paladin urges, "Come with me." Happily, his departure is delayed by a few days when Dr. Thackeray diagnoses Paladin with measles. She is a mature woman, intelligent, attractive, and unique in her independent lifestyle.

In "The Return of Dr. Thackeray," their relationship heats up. A cowhand comes down with smallpox, and Dr. Thackeray summons Paladin to keep the other members of the cattle drive quarantined in the town to prevent the spread of this deadly disease until a vaccine can arrive to eradicate the threat, a job that Paladin claims "has nothing to do with money." When he arrives, it is clear that the two enjoy an established, close relationship, one of mutual admiration and caring. For instance, preparing her a cup of coffee, Paladin remembers that she takes a half-teaspoon of sugar; when he insists she lie down and rest for awhile, he kisses her, saying, "By the way, hello." Waiting for the smallpox patient to improve, Paladin helps Dr. Thackeray tend to him, and she asks him to talk to her in order to stay awake. The usually articulate Paladin struggles here for words, saying that while it is easy enough to find "common words that men exchange with women," finding the right words at this moment is difficult, as the two "have grown too close for that." He then asks her, "We're neither one us ready for marriage, are we? You have to go on with your work. It's important to you, and to the people who need you," and she replies in assent, "And you have to go on with your work because of the kind of man you are." Paladin avers that people can change, but only if they are ready, "and we aren't ready to change." Finally, he says that he isn't proposing marriage, but explaining to her why he is not proposing, and says that this is the first time in life in which he felt even that explanation was needed. Dr. Thackeray then tells him, "We understand each other. We both want it that way." As Johnny Western observes, "Right at that stage in their lives, it would have been a mistake, but, obviously, the intimacy was there" (quoted in Rothel 105).

What all of this conversation amounts to is that both of these characters believe that marriage would impinge upon their freedom to pursue their professions, without really offering an explanation as to why this might be so. "We aren't ready to change" means that both make a conscious choice to avoid a commitment they would not value as much as the one to which they are currently bound. That June Lockhart should be cast as Dr. Thackeray—nurturing, mature, and wholesome, attractive but not especially alluring like Ella and Serafina—is presageful of two memorable television parts she would play: as Ruth Martin, mother of Timmy on *Lassie* (1958–1964) and as Dr. Maureen Robinson in *Lost in Space* (1965–1968), both maternal roles.

One wonders at first why this scene was even necessary, considering the fact that the western genre itself rarely features a married hero, and for the liminal outlaw hero matrimony would an even less likely occurrence, in part due to the itinerant lifestyle of such a figure.[14] Once again, however, one is reminded of Robert Ray's observance, discussed earlier, that the outlaw hero's role is conciliatory. He defends and upholds community values, of which the domestic life is such a central part, yet he evades the beguilement of the enticing feminine in order to preserve his own independence. Paladin can seem to endorse marriage while in fact rejecting it, a central defining quality of this type of hero.

The second defining feature of the liminal outlaw hero is his relationship with the law, or its official representatives, and how he comes to the rescue when the social and legal codes of a culture do not promote or render true justice. *Have Gun—Will Travel*, much more frequently than most other westerns, is concerned with this issue of justice, posing difficult questions about conformity and conscience, about the need to reverence legal institutions while also suggesting that there are times when the demands of justice require a disregard for the letter of the law. One reason why the series is preoccupied with the shortcomings of the law and its representatives is because of its premise— a gunfighter who works alone but acts in the service of the right. Kathleen Spencer calculates that of the 225 episodes, almost one-fourth of them, 58 by her count, portray Paladin's encounters with lawmen of various types: those who are competent but outnumbered, those who are inept and/or unwilling to take their duties seriously, and those who are corrupt, serving other causes than that of their sworn duty. In addition, as Spencer also points out, another score of episodes feature a trial, or turn on some other question of the law, so that *Have Gun—Will Travel* may be seen as "a sustained meditation on frontier justice, exploring the nature and limits of the law in these thinly civilized regions" (*Art and Politics* 107).

Frequently, Paladin finds himself entangled in the conflict between the sheriff and the members of the community who are either apathetic or hostile to the law; in the standard western struggle between ranchers and homesteaders, and other disputes over the land (e.g. the railroad, gold and silver mines); or between vigilante justice and due process of the law. In such cases, Paladin strives to uphold the law and assist its representatives. Other times, he displays his familiarity with the law in an actual court room—sometimes as a prosecutor or defense attorney (as in season 5, episode 18, "Justice in Hell" and season 4, episode 25, "The Last Judgment") and, as mentioned earlier, once defended himself successfully against a court martial, turning the tables on his accuser, General Crommer, who holds a grudge against Paladin until his dying day ("The Unforgiven"). In these instances, the "right" of a matter is usually clear, and Paladin needs to determine how best to serve justice by enforcing or assisting the law, either in the community or the courtroom.

Two other scenarios that address the issue of justice and the law do not rely on these standard types of conflicts, but offer a richer exploration of those circumstances under which the law and justice cannot or do not necessarily work in tandem. The first occurs when Paladin is charged with accomplishing justice in certain political situations where law or government cannot operate in an official capacity. In such cases, Paladin functions as an operative or covert agent, traversing boundaries that cannot be violated by the law. In "The Hatchet Man" (season 3, episode 25), written by Shimon Wincelberg, Paladin is hired by the San Francisco police to save the life of its first Chinese police detective, Joe Tsin (Benson Fong), who has been targeted by criminals in

Chinatown. The police cannot interfere because of cultural boundaries: a sense of honor prevents Joe Tsin from enlisting their help, and to leave town would dishonor him. Paladin is called upon to assist Joe Tsin, but must do so in such a way that the detective will not lose face in his own community.

On another occasion, Paladin is called upon by the State Department of the United States to ward off an international incident. In an episode written by Peggy and Lou Shaw, "Invasion" (season 5, episode 33), a charismatic Irishman, Gavin O'Shea (Robert Gist), travels from town to town to raise funds and an army for the Fenian Brotherhood, an organization founded in the United States in 1858, designed to support Irish independence from British rule. In this episode, Paladin has to prevent O'Shea from his plot to raise an army that will invade Canada; it is an election year, and the State Department wishes to avoid an international incident by having Paladin thwart O'Shea's plot without calling public attention to it. In Shimon Wincelberg's "The Prophet" (season 3, episode 16), Paladin is recruited by army intelligence to investigate their suspicions that a former colonel, Benjamin Nunez (Shepperd Strudwick), who married an Apache woman, is spearheading an Apache uprising. One officer who was sent to investigate the rumors of this was murdered, and the army wants to avoid an uprising, which would mean the loss of many lives. Before sending an officer to kill Nunez, the army wants Paladin to discern whether Nunez is, indeed, the "white war-chief" of the rumors. Paladin is called upon in this and other episodes because of his extensive knowledge of various Native American tribes, and because of his military experience. Again, his role is that of agent or operative. Such a role is, by definition, a liminal one, in that he traverses boundaries which the law or government (in the last two cases) is constrained to respect. The individual can do what an organization cannot. Paladin brings Joe Tsin's story to happy closure, but he is forced to kill O'Shea, diplomacy not being effective against the latter's blind fanaticism. Nunez, Paladin learns, is guilty of inciting an uprising, as the army suspected; Paladin's efforts to make him see that an Apache war would be devastating and futile are only partially successful, and Nunez' own fanaticism, like O'Shea's, is his undoing.

The second type of scenario that augments Paladin's liminal space presents situations in which he consciously invokes his own ethical or moral judgment, even if it runs counter to the legal system. In "The Hanging of Roy Carter" (season 2, episode 4), scripted by Gene Roddenberry, Paladin learns that an innocent man, Roy Carter (Scott Marlowe), is about to be executed for a crime to which another has just confessed in writing. To complicate matters, the warden's son was killed in the stagecoach robbery for which Carter has been falsely accused, so Warden Bullock (Paul Birch) is eager to carry out the execution orders, for personal vengeance. The only way to prevent this miscarriage of justice is through a gubernatorial stay of execution, and time is running out. Paladin sees that he will have to delay the execution by three hours, until the governor can be reached, but the warden is unwilling to bend the rules, "I have my orders to hang him. I'm legally bound to obey them," but Paladin retorts that saving a human life is more important than "strict adherence to a court's execution order." Paladin pleads with the chaplain (John Larch) to help him save Roy's life, but the latter asks, "What do you want me to do? Break the law myself?" In answer to this question, Paladin articulates exactly what is at stake—justice, and the service to a higher morality is here at odds with the law: "That depends on whose law you're talking about." The chaplain counters, "My duties are prescribed by statute," to which Paladin replies, "Well I guess that answers my question. I just wondered who you worked for."

As a last resort to save Roy's life, Paladin sabotages the gallows, wedging a piece of wood in the trapdoor so that, when the warden pulls the lever, the execution is thwarted; this causes a distraction, and Paladin, with Roy, retreats to Roy's cell. Here, he locks himself and Roy inside and destroys the key, breaking it in half with his boot. When a guard begins using a saw, the chaplain (John Larch), who had previously refused to help Paladin, is now shamed into action, pricked by Paladin's words and his own conscience; he grabs the saw, getting cut in the process, and destroys the blade. This is enough of a deterrent to win the day, and avoid killing a wrongly condemned man. It also prevents the warden from using his position to exact personal vengeance, lashing out at the most convenient target to assuage his grief over his own son's death. In this episode, Paladin acts in direct defiance of the law, which would not have served justice. The legal system was too slow to prevent this impending act of injustice, and Paladin makes clear that he is serving a higher cause than the law.

A second episode that reveals Paladin's dedication to justice, even when it means acting in defiance of the law, written by Harry Julian Fink, is "Fandango" (season 4, episode 24) in which Paladin acts decisively, using his conscience as a guide, in an unusual case about two juveniles sentenced to hang for a brutal murder.[15] Paladin reads about two youth, Bobby Ulsen (Andrew Prine) and James Horton (Jerry Summers), who have escaped the courtroom in which they have been sentenced to hang for beating to death a man named Tom Petty. Sheriff Ernie Backwater (Robert Gist), with whom Paladin served at Shiloh and Bull Run, has signed the notice that appears in the paper; he is responsible for retrieving the escapees and carrying out the sentence. Paladin captures Bobby, and meets up with Ernie, who has taken James back into custody. When Paladin asks Bobby his age, he learns the boy is only 16 years old, and Bobby seems as worried about his dog, Lucky, as he does about his own life. Likewise,

James asks whether he will be able to have ice cream as a last request, both of these indicators of how young the two are—too young to be facing the gallows.

An honest lawman, Ernie is determined to carry out the sentence, even though he dislikes it. But the complication comes in the form of a vengeful gunfighter, Lloyd Petty (Karl Swenson), whose brother the boys have killed. His arrival is imminent; he wishes to take the lives of the two who slew Tom, rather than letting the law do it. Paladin is reluctant to help his old friend, Ernie, in carrying out this "justice," confessing, "I usually know what I'm doing. I don't move until I can see," but this time Paladin is uncertain. He continues, "I'm starting to feel sick of the whole thing," a sentiment Ernie shares. Paladin asks Bobby and James why they killed Tom Petty. Bobby had claimed it was just a "fandango" (hence the title of the episode) gone awry, a foolish act, meant only to frighten or tease. James responds differently, "Maybe it was a fandango, but I meant to kill him," words that weigh heavily in Paladin's considered judgment of each boy. Troubled by their youth, Paladin asks Ernie whether there is any hope for a reprieve for the boys, but Ernie tells him that he must carry out the sentence the next morning; no pardon is possible, and the legislature had recently rejected a law introduced to prevent treating juveniles like adult criminals. Out of friendship and duty, Paladin agrees to help Ernie return the boys to jail and stay until their sentence is carried out, but he remains uneasy about whether justice is being served.

Lloyd Petty arrives and asks the sheriff to turn the boys over to him. He intends to put a bullet through their heads, adhering to the ancient cultural code of the heroic knight, for whom justice is equated with an exacting personal vengeance, swift and immediate. When asked why he is not satisfied with the prospect of their hanging, his reply is that his father taught him "there is nothin' stronger than blood." The clan mentality ingrained in him dictates that he should avenge his brother's death at any cost, but this also reveals his disdain for the law. Disgusted, Paladin observes, "He wants to cut the heart out of those boys, just like an Apache Indian," showing his own distaste for a model of retributive justice he considers uncivilized and crude, even though he often resorts to violence himself.

The whole town hides, cowering behind walls, as Paladin and Ernie stand guard over the prisoners. James voraciously consumes all the ice cream Paladin can procure for him (indicating how little he really understands about his impending doom), but Bobby knows the gravity of their plight and requests nothing. Ernie then reads to Paladin the opening address given by the county prosecutor during their trial, dated August 23, 1876, which claimed that the two showed "malice and forethought" and then went on to recount the very brutal nature of the beating and subsequent death of Tom Petty. The document negated the validity of what the prosecutor knew the defense would say about the mitigating circumstances—that one defendant (James) possesses a "low mentality and is of doubtful parentage," while the other, Bobby, is the only son of an "honest widow" and has therefore been "lacking a father's firm hand." (Both scenarios that are offered as mitigating circumstances are suggestive of juvenile delinquent films so popular in the 1950s.) Ernie apologizes to Paladin for having read the writ, stating he is "just trying to think it out."

Morning arrives, along with Lloyd Petty and few of his men. Ernie claims the jail is as strong as a fort, but Petty uses dynamite to blow open a wall. Ernie is wounded as he and Paladin shoot Petty's companions. Paladin then faces off with Lloyd Petty, reputed to be so fast that Paladin had earlier admitted that he was unsure of who would win, should they fight. However, Paladin easily outdraws him, killing him. The dynamite freed Bobby of his chains, but left James still incarcerated. When Paladin sees this, he tells Bobby to "Freeze," pointing his gun at him. Bobby does so, but in a tense moment, Paladin uncocks his gun and places it back in his holster, allowing Bobby to flee. "You made a mistake," Ernie insists, to which Paladin replies emphatically, "No, I made a *judgment*." But Ernie persists: "He'll kill another man tomorrow, and another the day after, and another the day after that." Paladin is not convinced of this. Ernie is resolved to carry out the sentence: "Well, I still got a prisoner, and I'm gonna do what the law prescribes." Paladin has no objection.

This episode dramatizes how Paladin acts in accordance his own higher spiritual code when the law does not dispense true justice. Bobby is 16 years old; his intent, unlike that of James, was not to commit murder when they planned the fandango against Tom Petty. Bobby sticks by James, even though he is more of an accessory than a co-murderer, and thus is slated to share the same fate. The law offers no reprieve, no middle ground—Paladin must decide, at that propitious moment, whether to side with the law or listen to his own conscience. He takes a chance on Bobby, that this was an anomaly in his character and not the indication of a future, habitual murderer. James, on the other hand, admitted that, no matter what the initial motive, he intended to kill Tom Petty, for no other reason than that he disliked Petty's demeanor. He will pay the heavy price for his crime, something that also weighs heavily on Paladin's conscience, but a hard truth he can live with, unlike the prospect of making Bobby share a similar fate. Paladin has read and discerned the text of Bobby, he has weighed his sense of justice against the hard, impersonal sentence of the law, and he has displayed the courage of Lancelot, who rescues a queen that is not guiltless, but who nevertheless is underserving of the harsh sentence of a law that hinders, rather than abets, true justice.

Have Gun—Will Travel enjoyed phenomenal success for a number of reasons. First, it cashed in on the popularity of the western genre, which was at its apex in the second half of the decade. It also tapped into the extraordinary talent of several skilled script writers such as Gene Roddenberry, who went on to create the *Star Trek* series (which has taken on a cultural life of its own) and Harry Julian Fink, who later scripted such important feature films as Sam Peckinpah's *Major Dundee* and served as the lead writer for *Dirty Harry*, which will be discussed in the next chapter.[16] Finally, the series benefited from its leading man, Richard Boone, whose personal and professional standards set the tone for the singularly high quality of storytelling it delivered week after week. Boone, a seventh generation descendent of Squire Boone, the brother of frontier legend Daniel Boone (Rothel 11–12), possessed a personal charisma and a professional devotion to acting that demanded excellence from everyone engaged in the show. As mentioned previously, several of his personal and professional acquaintances remarked that the qualities of character that make Paladin unique in the western genre are those that Boone drew upon from his own personality—his erudition, love of art and beauty, his fierce sense of justice and fair play. It is the latter quality that does, at last, serve as the impetus for Paladin to adhere to a higher standard of the knightly code to which he has sworn himself.

The advent of television and the flourishing of the western genre cemented the role of the liminal outlaw hero in the popular imagination. When the western declined in both feature films and on television, for reasons that remain the discussion of considerable scholarly debate, the liminal outlaw hero did not enjoy a similar fate.[17] Although the popularity of the western genre waned, the role of the liminal outlaw hero, who could negotiate between his individual freedom and service to a community, did not. Instead, he enjoyed a new incarnation in the urban western and the modern action film, as the ensuing chapters will attempt to show.

PART II

The Liminal Outlaw Hero and the Rise of the Urban Western

The Urban Western and the New American Cinema

As J. Fred McDonald asserts, the decline of the Hollywood and television western occurred in large part because of the rapid social change and political unrest of the 1960s, which altered the way audiences thought about violence, war and politics: "The undermining of self-perceptions fundamental to a century of American sociopolitical life has meant the death of the principle genre of romanticized, quasi-historical entertainment in the United States" (*Who Shot the Sheriff?* 118). In addition, the demise of the American western inevitably resulted from over exposure—brought about by the glut of western series on television and the formulaic conformity of western feature films. Included in her review of the Japanese Akira Kurosawa's film *Yojimbo* (1961), critic Pauline Kael wrote, "In recent years John Ford, particularly, has turned the Western into an almost static pictorial genre, a devitalized, dehydrated form which is 'enriched' with pastoral beauty and evocative nostalgia for a simple, heroic way of life" (*I Lost It at the Movies* 242).

In his 1985 study *A Certain Tendency of the Hollywood Cinema, 1930–1980*, Robert Ray traces the development of cinema after the apparent demise of the Western and the closing of the frontier in Hollywood film, so central to the formation and continuation of the American identity. In his chapter "The Left and Right Cycles," Ray avers that the films of the 1960s and 1970s, the period that ushered in the "New Hollywood" cinema and the rise of the modern action film, tended to be "superficially radical," but were "internally conservative," an ambivalence that reflected the larger culture's own divisiveness about its social and political environment during these transformative decades. Cinema of this period "concealed the obvious: the traditional American mythology" (of which the real and disguised westerns had served as a main ideological vehicle) "had survived as the generally accepted account of America's history and future" (296). That which the western promulgated continued in the new cinema of the period, its Left and Right cycles serving as "renovated versions of traditional genres and heroes," films of the Left expressing an ironic and films of the Right a nostalgic impulse (296). Ray shows that while the two cycles respond differently in one or two crucial ways to its past and present, the boundaries are often "blurred" and are similar more than disparate in their features.

Ray asserts that the Left cycle films respond to the passing of the frontier in four ways: first, through an expression of belatedness, by "relocating" westerns in a contemporary time; second, putting them in a confined space, as opposed to the open geography of the old west (often via the "urban western," as we shall see); third, by replacing the traditional villain with "relentless forces" that oppose the hero; and finally, by insisting that certain existing lifestyles are "anachronous" (306). Remarkably, Ray points out that Right cycle films also partake of the first two means, evinced by the rise of the urban western, discussed in the next two chapters of this study. On the third point, that of the portrayal of the opposition the hero encounters, Left cycle films (such as the iconic 1969 *Easy Rider*) presented a faceless villainous force to mirror the complexity of contemporary life. Right cycle films, reverting to the classic western formula, continued to reduce larger social problems to a concrete, localized situation in which direct action could resolve an issue (*Dirty Harry* and *Death Wish*, 1971 and 1974, respectively) without considering larger future consequences (307). According to Ray, *Dirty Harry* kept its "western references less explicit" than those overtly expressed in *Death Wish*, but both employed the western's values and assumptions (307–308). The last point, the Left's tendency to treat with irony certain lifestyles as "anachronous" or outdated in the modern world (notably in films such as *Butch Cassidy and the Sundance Kid* and *The Wild Bunch*, both 1969) is often countered in Right films by its tendency to acknowledge the pastness of the past while still hedging its response, to express a nostalgic, rather than ironic sentiment (*Coogan's Bluff* and *Walking Tall*, 1968 and 1973, respectively). Harry tossing away his badge at the end of *Dirty Harry* indicates this awareness of his own anachronistic position in the modern world (310–311). Because they perpetuate frontier values, Ray concludes, "far from being polarized opposites ... the heroes of the Left and Right both reincarnated the same mythic hero—the westerner" (317). Finally, and most important is Ray's assertion that both cycles manifest a lack of faith in institutions, espousing instead the individual, looking to the hero's "intuition" and "personal virtue" to solve problems, even those generated from an increasingly urban, complex world (317).

One transition between the western and the urban western was the Spaghetti (Italian) Western, which began as a type of low budget film shot on location in Spain. Not the first, but certainly the most famous director of the Spaghetti Western is Sergio Leone, who directed Clint Eastwood in the epoch-making trilogy, *A Fistful of Dollars* (1964), *For a Few Dollars More* (1965), and *The Good, the Bad, and the Ugly* (1966). Leone agreed with Kael's assessment of the traditional western, averring that it "had been killed off by those who had maltreated the genre"; the portrayal of the frontier as idyllic in the American western presented an inaccurate, simplistic picture that ignored its violent, harsh historical reality, the very quality that, for Leone, made the American west compelling (quoted in *Clint Eastwood: A Biography* 137). The Spaghetti Western acted as a corrective to the idea of the western past promulgated by the American film genre, presenting instead a world that was violent, immediate, and existential, unencumbered by overt propaganda and ideology. The characters act instinctively, prompted by straightforward motives: revenge, money, and self-preservation. If this was not in itself more accurate than the image of the west it was trying to dispel, it nonetheless offered a refreshing revision of a worn formula, and perhaps reflected, more accurately, the volatile decade of the 1960s itself, catering to the audience's changing tastes. Leone went on to direct another important work, *Once Upon a Time in the West* (1968), that debunked older images of the west as it was presented in the earlier film tradition, casting Henry Fonda as the villain, opposite his traditional heroic role. The Spaghetti Western served to transform the traditional genre into a form that resonated with an audience that had departed significantly from the sensibilities of 1950s viewers.

The urban western, which employs the conventions of the western genre in a contemporary setting, was, in some ways, the next logical step in the development of a type of hero who acted alone, sometimes placing him at odds with the law, when the interests of justice were hindered by legal shortcomings and/or bureaucratic red tape. Richard Schickel discusses reasons for the rise in popularity of cop shows during the late 1960s and early 1970s as being due in part to what he calls "'the law-and-order furor' of the Nixon years," but such programs also served as successful replacements for earlier types: "the westerner and the private eye had all but disappeared from the screen.... There was a need to find a contemporary place for hard losers—traditional males, if you will—to live plausibly. And the most readily available wilderness, the concrete wilderness, suddenly seemed more interesting and dangerous than ever" (*Clint Eastwood: A Biography* 258). The type of hero the urban western presented was one that enjoyed considerable audience appeal. The *Dirty Harry* and *Death Wish* films (1971–1988 and 1974–1994, respectively) along with the modern action film represented in this study by *Rambo* (1982–2008) and *Batman: The Dark Knight* series (2005–2012) all resulted in highly successful franchises that span several years, and in some cases decades. *Dirty Harry*, in the vanguard of the urban western, was prompted by the fact that Warner Bros. was eager to cash in on the surge of interest in growing street crime and the cops who had to face this every day. Clint Eastwood was not the first choice for the leading man, but his life experiences provided him with powerful inner resources that made his portrayal of Inspector Harry Callahan so compelling.

CHAPTER 5

Poetic Justice and the *Dirty Harry* Franchise (1971–1988)

Eastwood in the West and the Rise of a Star

Clint Eastwood was born in San Francisco on May 31st, 1930, just as the Great Depression hit. His parents were hard working, positive in their thinking, and happily married, but like many others, they struggled financially during these years, and were forced to move often in order to find employment. This itinerant lifestyle was difficult for a child, who had to learn a certain resiliency to overcome the problems inherent in always having to readjust to a new community, always feeling like an outsider. Schickel writes that while Clint Eastwood had a good rapport with his parents, and knew something of the financial pressures with which they had to contend during the decade of the Great Depression: "he hated the loneliness their travels imposed upon him" (*Clint Eastwood: A Biography* 15). According to Schickel, it is this early formative experience of separateness that contributes to the particular type of character so uniquely associated with Eastwood's performances. "His great theme has been the difficulty men have in making connections with any sort of community," nor are the characters he plays usually engaged in a lasting romantic relationship with a woman (16). This sense of separation from community corresponds to that of the liminal outlaw hero, the subject of this study, which will find full expression for Eastwood in the figure of Dirty Harry.

Like many others, Clint Eastwood drifted into acting and began his career with small parts in B movies during the 1950s, such as *Revenge of the Creature* (1955) and *Tarantula* (1955). A more stable, but not perhaps a very challenging role was that of Rowdy Yates on the television series *Rawhide* that aired from 1959 to 1965. His lasting onscreen identity began to emerge with the now iconic trilogy of Sergio Leone Spaghetti Westerns alluded to above (1964, 1965, and 1966), soon followed by *Hang 'Em High* (1968) and the important precursor to the *Dirty Harry* films, *Coogan's Bluff* (1968), which also marked the beginning of a very productive professional relationship with director Don Siegel. Eastwood worked with Don Siegel often after this, and it was Siegel who directed the first *Dirty Harry* film. Leone and Siegel, very different in their directing styles, were both significant influences on Eastwood's own approach to directing later in his career.

In *Coogan's Bluff* Eastwood plays an Arizona deputy sheriff, Walter Coogan, who is sent to New York City to extradite a fugitive, James Ringerman (Don Stroud). Coogan is very much a fish out of water in this urban environment; he is hindered by bureaucratic red tape, has violent encounters with Ringerman's constituents, and is exposed to a psychedelic counter-culture in the teeming life of the city. When he finally tracks the criminal to his hideout on the promontory of Coogan's Bluff, the deputy sheriff captures his charge and prepares to return him to Arizona, as ordered. The film's title is an actual place in New York City, but also a pun on the main character's name. What marks this as a precursor to *Dirty Harry* is its urban setting, which is a hostile environment; the explosive violence that Coogan alternately experiences and delivers; and Coogan's role as a law enforcement officer who has to combat more than a criminal, but also a corrupt and inept judicial system that grants criminals opportunities for evading incarceration. Coogan's clash with the officious Lt. McElroy (Lee J. Cobb), whose quip "A man's gotta do what a man's gotta do. That it, Wyatt?" prompts Eric Patterson to observe in his article "Every Which Way But Lucid: The Critique of Authority in Clint Eastwood's Police Movies" that McElroy's "sarcastic references to the heroic ideal of the traditional Western highlight the real nature of the conflict around which the action is structured: Coogan, an independent, self-reliant man, the embodiment of the simpler, freer social order of frontier America, is forced to confront a complex bureaucracy apparently concerned only with the enforcement of its own rigid system of rules" (*The Journal of Popular Film and Television* 94). In the end, in order to extradite Ringerman, Coogan capitulates to McElroy's procedures that he had ignored earlier, yet it is clear that his own determination is what finally leads to the capture of the fugitive in the first place. Coogan is a forerunner of Dirty Harry, despite some superficial differences. Stuart M. Kaminsky, one of Eastwood's early biographers, notes that both Coogan and Harry are assigned "every dirty job in the book," both also lose their collars (Ringerman in *Coogan's Bluff* and Scorpio in the first *Dirty Harry*) and feel pressure to recapture them (*Clint Eastwood* 103). Both are also individuals who prefer to work alone and according to their own methods.

It was the year 1971, however, that yielded three films which cemented Eastwood's career: *The Beguiled*, *Play Misty for Me*, and *Dirty Harry*. The first two films offered parts that were overtly risky for the actor to play, in large part because of his character's relationship with women. In *The Beguiled*, a Southern Gothic set during the Civil War, Eastwood plays a wounded Union soldier, John McBurney, who is trying to evade Confederate troops. He is rescued and nursed back to health by seven female inhabitants of a Louisiana boarding school. Discord breaks out when the women compete for his sexual favors and he rejects the advances of the headmistress, Martha Farnsworth (Geraldine Page), for a younger woman. He is held virtually as a prisoner, and the tension that results from their repressed sexuality, along with McBurney's manipulation of the women, soon leads to dramatic upheaval. When he injures his leg by falling down a flight of stairs, the vengeful headmistress, under the pretense of saving him from gangrene, amputates the leg, a rather transparent symbolic castration. The enraged McBurney responds violently, and the women finally murder him by serving him poisoned mushrooms. Directed by Don Siegel, *The Beguiled* presents Eastwood in the role of a vulnerable male, but one who is also in part responsible for his misfortune because he does not consider the consequences of his own unbridled sexual urges and manipulates the women while he is incarcerated. His response to this ensuing conflict is violence, but the women use guile. Both McBurney and the women are motivated by vengeance and the unhealthy, claustrophobic atmosphere augments its terrible consequences.

Play Misty for Me is a psychological thriller that marks Eastwood's debut as a director. In it, he plays a radio disc jockey, Dave Garver, whose successful career and gratifying bachelor's life is soon turned upside down when he picks up a woman, Evelyn Draper (Jessica Walter), at a bar, for what he clearly believes to be only a casual sexual encounter. Although she appears to be normal, Evelyn is deeply disturbed. Soon, she displays very possessive tendencies, intrudes in his life, and eventually begins to stalk Garver. When Evelyn takes his steady girlfriend, Tobie (Donna Mills), as a hostage, the climactic confrontation occurs. Garver arrives at her apartment to rescue Tobie, but Evelyn attacks him with a butcher knife. In an intense physical struggle, Garver punches her and knocks her through a glass door, where she falls from the balcony to her death. This shocking conclusion and explicitly violent treatment of a female was risky for any actor's career. Sixteen years later, the same plot would be exploited in *Fatal Attraction* (1987), which owed a clear debt to *Play Misty For Me*. In fact, as Schickel observes, when critics pointed this out upon the release of *Fatal Attraction*, *Play Misty for Me* was "the *only* source they could cite," proving how original the 1971 film was (255).

The third film of 1971 would provide Eastwood with his most enduring character. As fate would have it, Eastwood found himself available to star in *Dirty Harry*, the right film and the right character at the right time to propel him into a liminal space that would yield a large professional premium in spite of the risks the film took and the critical debate about it that ensued when it hit the theaters. Upon its release in December 1971, *Dirty Harry* drew nearly universal critical condemnation. Pauline Kael's now famous invective against the film, in her initial published review titled "Saint Cop," recognized Harry as a descendant of an earlier knightly ideal: "He's the best there is—a Camelot cop, courageous and incorruptible" (*For Keeps* 419), and comments also on his name: "The dirtiness on Harry is the moral stain of recognition that evil must be dealt with; he is our martyr—stained on our behalf," and this treats crime in a "medieval way, without specific causes or background" (420). Kael's main objection to the film was that it reduces the criminal to a simple embodiment of evil, without developing causation, making the "basic contest between good and evil ... as simple as you can get" (420). As a result, "it makes this genre piece more archetypal than most movies, more primitive and dreamlike; fascist medievalism has a fairy-tale appeal" (420). Kael reiterates this erroneous charge in her conclusion, stating, "This action genre has always had a fascist potential, and it has finally surfaced" (421). Clearly Keal read the film as being a conflict between traditional "conservative" and "liberal" lines, but the term "fascism" can hardly be applied to an individual who wishes to operate under less government rather than more. Part of Kael's dislike for the film, as is evident from her uninspired reviews of the sequels, is her dislike for Eastwood and his acting style. According to Richard Schickel, only one major critic, Jay Cocks of *Time*, viewed it positively upon its debut, and included it on his ten best films list for 1971 (*Clint Eastwood: A Biography* 272).

Conversely, as is often the case, *Dirty Harry* enjoyed remarkable popularity among moviegoers, its success exceeding the expectations of both the studio executives and the cast and crew. When the film premiered at Graumann's Chinese Theatre on December 23, 1971, a studio representative contacted Eastwood to report that audiences were wildly cheering Harry on as they viewed the film (Schickel 272), an indication of the manner in which it immediately resonated with middle-class America. *Dirty Harry* (and its sequels) has since taken on a life of its own in the American cultural psyche, winning its wager with the future despite its unfriendly critical reception. In 2012, *Dirty Harry* won the honor of being placed (with a very select group of films to keep it company) on the prestigious Library of Congress National Film Preservation Board List, time having vindicated it (www.loc.gov/programs/national-film-preservation-board/film-registry/complete-national-film-registry-listing). It is this incarnation of the liminal outlaw hero that created one of the more memorable urban westerns of all time, propelling the titular character—and the actor who played him—to international iconic status.

Enter *Dirty Harry* (1971)

> "When a naked man is chasing a woman through an alley with a butcher knife and a hard-on, I figure he isn't out collecting for the Red Cross."
> —Inspector Harry Callahan, *Dirty Harry*

The original screenplay of this most iconic of police films was composed by Harry Julian Fink and his wife R. M. Fink when they were writers under contract at Universal Studios, and it was their version that Eastwood first read with enthusiasm. Fink was a seasoned writer; based on his contribution to *Have Gun–Will Travel*, Richard Boone named him one the best television writers in Hollywood, as cited in the previous chapter. The script was sold to Warner Bros., and had meanwhile undergone a number of changes—most of them not for the better, as is often the case with manuscripts that float around Hollywood—so the various versions that existed when Clint Eastwood was available to make the film were not close to the original story as he had earlier seen it. He consulted Don Siegel, who agreed to direct the film and work on revisions of the script, and Siegel in turn suggested that veteran writer Dean Riesner, who had scripted *Rawhide* episodes for television, be brought on board to help with the final revision of the script (Schickel 257–259). Riesner was also one of the writers for both *Coogan's Bluff* and *Play Misty for Me*, so he was a logical choice for a script doctor in this case. He later contributed to the third film also, *The Enforcer*. On board as executive producer was Robert Daley, who was also either executive producer or producer for all of Eastwood's films during the lucrative period from 1971 to 1980 beginning with *Play Misty for Me* and *Dirty Harry* (both 1971) up through *Any Which Way You Can*, fifteen feature films in all.

Dirty Harry (1971) is an urban western set in San Francisco in 1971. To establish this, the film opens with a close up of a monument inscribed "In Tribute to the Police Officers who gave their lives in the Call of Duty, presented by a Special Citizens Committee," followed by a long list of the names of the fallen and the year they met their demise (which goes up to 1970). It then cuts to a view through a riflescope of a woman in a yellow bathing suit, swimming in a pool atop a San Francisco high rise. A single shot kills her, and a note to the mayor (John Vernon) follows this murder; it claims responsibility for the death of the woman, demands $100,000, and threatens to kill either a Catholic priest or a black person if the city fails to comply. The killer identifies himself as "Scorpio" (Andy Robinson), modeled loosely, as we shall see, on the notorious Zodiac serial killer who terrorized northern California in the late 1960s and early 1970s.[1] The mayor, in consultation with Harry's superiors, ignores Harry's advice to reject this demand, and chooses to pay the ransom for which the city is being held in terror of another murder. Harry is assigned to the Scorpio case, but the mayor then recalls how he remembers Harry, and cautions that he wishes to have no trouble like that which had earlier occurred in the Fillmore District, stating authoritatively, "That's my policy." Harry retorts that when he sees a man acting with the intent to commit rape, he reacts appropriately: "I shoot the bastard. That's *my* policy." In defense of his shooting of a suspect in the incident to which the mayor alludes, Harry insists: "When a naked man is chasing a woman through an alley with a butcher knife and a hard-on, I figure he isn't out collecting for the Red Cross." This exchange sets the tone for the rest of the film, with its conflict between authority, the legal bureaucracy, and the street-wise justice represented by Harry's approach to crime.

Harry is next shown at a lunch counter he frequents, which happens to be situated across from a bank where a robbery is taking place. Since he is off duty, he asks the owner of the luncheonette to call the police and inform them that Inspector Callahan thinks there is a 2–11 in progress. He settles in to eat his meal, saying, "Now, if they'll just wait for the cavalry to come." This reference to a standard scenario in the western film genre (the cavalry rushing in to the rescue at the last minute) serves as the first of several examples of what Umberto Eco calls "intertextual frames" in this film: "stereotyped situations derived from preceding textual tradition and recorded by our encyclopedia, such as, for example, the standard duel between the sheriff and the bad guy or the narrative situation in which the hero fights the villain and wins" (*Casablanca: Cult Movies and Intertextual Collage* 5). Just then, however, the criminals exit the bank and enter the getaway car. Still eating his hotdog, Harry foils their escape with some well-aimed bullets that stop the car and deter the thieves.

The continuation of this scene, in which Harry then approaches one of the robbers he has wounded, contains some of the more iconic lines in all of the *Dirty Harry* films. The criminal is in reach of his own gun, and Harry has no bullets left in his own, as he realizes when he nears the man, points his weapon at him, and relies instead on his own wit: "I know what you're thinkin'—did he fire six shots or only five? Well, to tell you the truth, in all this excitement, I've kinda lost track myself. But being as this is a .44 Magnum, the most powerful handgun in the world, and would blow your head clean off, you gotta ask yourself one question: 'Do I feel lucky?' Well, do ya, punk?" This bluff, delivered with a slight smile, causes the thief to surrender, but as he is about to be taken into custody by the police, he says to Harry, "I gots to know," so Harry points the gun at him, pulls the trigger, and reveals that the gun had no more bullets, again with a slight ironic smile. This scenario represents what Eco identifies as a "magic frame," a particular type of intertextual frame that transforms a film into a cult movie: "Let me define as "magic" those frames that, when they appear in a movie and can be separated from the whole, transform this movie into a cult object" (*Casablanca: Cult Movies and Intertextual Collage* 5). This scene activates an easily recognizable stereotypical intertextual frame from classic westerns in which one party in a shoot-out seems to have run out of "lead," while another is left to speculate on whether his adversary in fact has any bullets left. Here, it is used as a bluff and a test of wits: Harry is the victor because he wins the test of audacity, risk, and courage, and this moment in the film, even if removed from the whole, immortalizes *Dirty Harry*, one of several such instances.

Soon after, Harry reluctantly acquires a partner, Chico Gonzales (Reni Santoni), a rookie with a degree in sociology from San Jose State. Harry likes to work alone, and especially frowns on having "a college boy" for a partner, but he and Chico soon develop camaraderie, as they pursue the serial killer. Scorpio's attempt to make good on his threat to murder again is thwarted when he is discovered by helicopter surveillance while stalking a young black couple, whose mannerisms suggest a homosexual relationship. Instead, soon after, Scorpio takes the life of a ten-year-old black male child. He then sends another note to the authorities, along with a box that contains a bloody molar, a hair sample, and a red bra—he has abducted a young teenaged girl, whom he claims he has buried alive with enough oxygen to live only for 48 hours, and wants $200,000 for her life. Once again, the spineless Mayor wishes to comply with this demand, but Harry asks, "You know she's dead, don't you?" Still, he agrees to be the bagman for the money drop again (taping a switchblade to his leg in case he needs it), and as he races around the city, following the killer's instructions about where to meet up for the ransom exchange, Chico is wired to shadow Harry and assist as backup.

When Harry comes face to face with Scorpio, the latter disarms and then brutally beats him, stomping on his face and yanking his hair repeatedly (repetition of speech and gesture is one of his idiosyncrasies), as he insults the inspector, calling him a "rotten oinker." He then taunts Harry in the most sadistic manner, claiming of the girl that he is "going to let her die" now that he has the ransom money, proclaiming he wanted Harry to know this before he kills him as well, which is obviously what Scorpio intends to do. At this point, Chico opens fire, Harry implores him not to shoot to kill the criminal, and Chico is

Dirty Harry (Warner Bros., 1971). From left: Lt. Al Bressler (Harry Guardino) and the police chief (John Larch) watch as Harry Callahan (Clint Eastwood) prepares the ransom money for the serial killer, Scorpio (Andy Robinson), at the insistence of the mayor (John Vernon). Later, Harry takes the law into his own hands to save innocent victims (Jerry Ohlinger's Movie Materials Store).

himself wounded in the exchange of gunfire; Harry then stabs Scorpio in the leg with the switchblade he had managed to conceal. Harry wants Scorpio alive because he is trying to save the girl. He had thought her dead, but Scorpio's remark, that he "is going to let her die," leads Harry to believe she might still be saved, and this is why he orders Chico not to kill Scorpio. Eric Patterson's assertion that Scorpio here tells Harry "that he has already killed the girl" and that therefore Harry's motive for ordering Chico not to kill Scorpio is in deference to "the mayor's order against police violence" ("Every Which Way But Lucid" 95) is an implausible reading of the scene, as is clear from the killer's manic boast to Harry that he is "going to let her die." Moreover, Harry believes what Scorpio says here, as his later defense of his actions to the district attorney show: in explaining his actions in the abandoned stadium, he says he ignored procedures like obtaining a search warrant because he felt the urgent need to save the girl before time ran out.

The wounded Scorpio flees the scene with the knife in his leg, howling in pain, and escaping only because the two officers are themselves wounded. Scorpio then seeks treatment at the park's emergency hospital, and the doctor, having recognized him, directs Harry to the now abandoned football field, Kezar Stadium, across the street from the park hospital. The doctor recalls having seen Scorpio before because Scorpio used to work at the stadium.[2] Harry finds the quarters where Scorpio has been living inside the stadium, and chases him onto the football field. A police officer who has accompanied Harry turns on the floodlights as Harry shoots and wounds Scorpio, who then grovels and whines about his "rights" to medical and legal counsel. Harry repays the earlier brutality that Scorpio had visited on him, pushing on the latter's wounded leg with his foot, which apparently persuades the killer to divulge the location of the girl. In the next scene, she is pulled out of a well, naked and dead.

Instead of being incarcerated, Scorpio is treated and released. Harry is both incredulous and angered when the district attorney, William Rothko (Josef Sommer), informs him that, because Harry violated Scorpio's rights, he intends not to prosecute him, and that Harry is lucky he himself is not being indicted "for assault and intent to commit murder." He then invokes the Fourth Amendment (which addresses reasonable search and seizure and the need for a warrant), and the Escobedo and Miranda cases (1964 and 1966, respectively) about the right to legal counsel for criminal suspects. Rothko has called in a consultant, Judge Bannerman (William Patterson), who teaches classes in constitutional law at Berkeley; the judge confirms that Harry has violated Scorpio's fourth and fifth, and "probably his sixth and fourteenth amendment" rights. This climactic struggle with legal and bureaucratic authority prompts Harry's assertion "Well, then, the law is crazy!" This is clearly what motivates Harry to begin trailing Scorpio on his own time. Scorpio stalks children on a playground, and then strippers in a sleazy club, but with Harry on his trail, he cannot easily strike again.

Scorpio knows how to manipulate the law. He pays a thug to beat him very badly, then claims police brutality, using the media attention to accuse Harry of the beating. When Harry goes to the hospital to visit his injured partner, Chico, he learns that the latter does not intend to return to the force. On the way out of the hospital, Chico's wife tells Harry she feels responsible for this decision, as she was always worried about her husband's welfare, and did not think she could adjust to being a cop's wife. She then asks Harry how his wife copes with his profession, and Harry informs her that his wife is dead. "She was driving home late one night and a drunk crossed the center line. There was no reason for it, really." This is an important detail in the configuration of Harry's character as a liminal outlaw hero, as will be discussed below. Harry has been married, suggesting he is committed to the values of domesticity and community, yet the death of his wife allows, through no fault of his own, the freedom to pursue his profession without the usual obligations of family life.

The psychopathic Scorpio continues his acts of brutality, robbing and viciously assaulting an elderly liquor storeowner, and then finally hijacking a school bus with seven children on it. The high-pitched mania with which he insists they sing songs ("Old MacDonald" and "Row, Row, Row Your Boat") initially masks his cruel intentions, but as the tension rises he slaps one child who whines for his mother, and threatens, "Sing, or I'll go home and kill all your mommies!" He calls the mayor and demands not only the $200,000 but also a jet plane to escape. This time, a disgusted Harry refuses to act as bagman for the drop, stating, "Well, you can just get yourself another delivery boy." He knows the time has come for decisive, independent action.

The final showdown occurs when Harry jumps on top of the bus as it emerges from a trestle bridge (a stunt Eastwood performed himself), and a chase scene on foot ensues at a quarry. Scorpio sees a boy fishing and grabs him as a hostage, invoking another western intertextual frame. Between mad, sadistic laughs that border on hysteria, he orders Harry to drop his weapon, believing he has outwitted the detective; Harry lowers his gun but then, in a decisive moment, with deadly quickness and accuracy, shoots to wound him, allowing the frightened boy to escape quickly. As Harry approaches the bleeding Scorpio, the latter sees his own gun and considers reaching for it. Harry's litany to the bank robber he had subdued earlier he repeats now, *verbatim*, but he speaks the lines this time with a deadly anger that was lacking in the previous scene, much different in tone than the earlier character contest ("I know what you're thinking. Did he fire six bullets or only five?"). But Scorpio, unlike the earlier criminal, goes for his gun—this time, unlike in the prior scene, Harry has a bullet left, and he knows it. When Scorpio "draws" (completing yet another intertextual frame borrowed from the western) Harry is justified, killing him in self-defense (technically), but realizing that the legal system will, no doubt, entangle him in inquests and red tape, he tosses his badge into the quarry, in what would seem to be a definitive act of self-realization about his own values and convictions.

This is a clear statement of the individual who understands Thoreau's imperative of civil disobedience. Harry does what he does because it is right, in disregard of whether the law sanctions or condemns it. It is the action of the true knight, who answers to a higher moral imperative than the legal community allows. Interestingly, Siegel and Eastwood had a disagreement about whether Harry should toss the badge into the quarry at the end. Siegel directed him to do so in a gesture evocative of Gary Cooper's final action in the memorable western shot in virtual time, *High Noon* (1952), even though it is the cowardice of the town's citizens, and not the legal system itself, as in *Dirty Harry*, that causes the disdain for the badge Cooper's character expresses as he discards it at the end. Eastwood thought initially that Harry would not relinquish his job, as it is all he knows how to do, so he insisted that Harry should only contemplate discarding the badge. The day of the shoot, however, Eastwood had a change of heart, believing that throwing the badge away offered a closure and a stronger statement of Harry's position (Schickel 271). This ending, which does not invite an audience to think immediately of a sequel, suggests also that no one among the cast and crew imagined how wildly successful the film would be, and that it would be the beginning of an epoch-making series in the Hollywood urban western.[3]

What do we learn in this first film about Inspector Harry Callahan that establishes him as a compelling liminal outlaw hero? First, we witness the conflict between justice and the law, and this necessarily also pits the individual (Harry) against the establishment (the legal bureaucracy that interprets the law and upholds it). Throughout the film, Harry expresses his concern for the victims of crime, his pledge to protect the community, and his ardent desire to see that criminals pay for their transgressions. The authorities, on the other hand—the police chief, the mayor, the district attorney and his consultant, Judge Bannerman—are more concerned with a blind adherence to written law, of going "by the book," which in this instance means focusing on the rights of the criminal, even when this continues to pose dangers to the community. Harry, then, accomplishes what the average citizen is powerless to achieve; he alone occupies the liminal space (by virtue of his position on the police force and his own private code of common sense justice) that rids a community of a known psychopathic killer, even at great personal cost in the end. Several scenes in the film are designed to establish Harry's rapport with honest, working-class members of the community his badge authorizes him to serve, and to underscore the thankless risks he must take day after day to protect them. Harry can't eat a hotdog off-duty without having to make a collar; he is called upon to thwart a potential suicide, placing himself in danger by being elevated several stories to talk to a man poised to jump. After this incident he tells Chico, who has asked about his name, "Now you know why they call me Dirty Harry"—he points out that he is called upon to do "every dirty job that comes along." When Harry is continually asked to be the bagman for the serial killer's demands, Chico echoes this sentiment, telling their superior, "No wonder they call him Dirty Harry. He always gets the shit end of the stick."

For Harry, moral choices are simple and clear. If a naked man with a butcher knife is chasing a woman, he does not hesitate to deter him, even with force. If a bank robbery is in progress, he brandishes his .44 Magnum to prevent it. If a girl's life is in danger and time is running out, he uses any means necessary (including retributive brutality) to learn where she is. What surely instigated audiences to cheer while viewing *Dirty Harry* during its theatrical debut was the sense that, in eliminating Scorpio for good in the final scene, Harry was rendering a poetic justice in that the bad guy, who had both consciously manipulated the law and been protected by it, was finally getting his just desserts, something that would either not have happened at all, or would have been endlessly delayed had he been taken into custody. This solution serves as an apt example of Ray's "Right Cycle," in offering a concrete solution to a specific problem, a simplification of a complex social issue.

Although this would seem to be a topical issue, related to the introduction of the enactment of the Miranda rights in 1966, and the socio-political climate of this time period, the essential conflict between justice and the law is a transcendent one. When Paul Newman rejected the part of Dirty Harry because he objected to its tough attitude toward crime, Eastwood immediately expressed his interest in the script, averring, "Well, I don't have any political affiliations, so send it over" (quoted in Schickel 257). There is no doubt that *Dirty Harry* takes a definite attitude toward crime and justice in the face of the political and social unrest of the period. In an insightful article, "Conservatism in American Crime Films," Timothy O. Lenz discusses the *Dirty Harry* and *Death Wish* films as examples of the "new conservatism." He argues that although the debate between justice and the law dates to antiquity, it became a very pointed issue in the United States in the 1960s, and film, as a popular medium, was a way for the masses to think through the issues of crime, laws, and governance. In the 1968 presidential campaign, independent candidate George Wallace's speeches on crime were so popular they made his opponents follow suit. Both Nixon, the Republican Party candidate, and Hubert Humphrey, the Democratic hopeful, "parroted" Wallace's rhetoric "until the presidential election sounded like three sheriffs running for office" (*Journal of Criminal Justice and Popular Culture* 12, no. 2, 118).

Lenz establishes in his discussion a set of binary oppositions that are very helpful in understanding the *Dirty Harry* films in the context of their release. One fundamental difference between 1960s Liberalism and the new or Modern Conservatism, was the way each understood "law and order." Liberals privileged the idea of due process, and therefore viewed the law as an end in itself, while the new conservatives valued order, even when it meant going beyond the law. In other words, for them, the law was a means to an end, but order itself was the final objective. For liberals, the law was designed to protect individual rights, while conservatives viewed it as a means of crime control, so that, in order to maintain social order, the executives of the law needed to have "broad discretion" in interpreting it. Liberals focused on the rehabilitation of criminals, while conservatives tended to seek their punishment as a deterrent against future crime (119). Finally, while liberals pondered the "legal technicalities of the adversarial system of justice, which are elements of procedural justice," the new conservatism, which appealed to the average American citizen, thought more about "a suspect's guilt or innocence, which is a common sense matter of substantive justice" (120). Liberals tended to appeal to the intellectual classes, but the new conservatism (unlike traditional conservatism that wanted to maintain the *status quo* and its own privileges) won support from the middle, working classes (120). The Escobedo and Miranda rights alluded to in the *Dirty Harry* films (1964 and 1966, respectively) focused on the fourth, fifth and sixth amendment rights as they pertain to the individual crime suspect, and underscored due process. These are the impediments to Harry's pursuit of Scorpio, in bringing him to justice through legal channels. The fact that the arrogant character Judge Bannerman (called in to condemn Harry's treatment of Scorpio) teaches classes in constitutional law at the most liberal ideological institution of higher learning in the United States—the University of California Berkeley—makes clear the left's interest in the philosophical underpinnings of the law, instead of the pragmatic goal of fighting crime.

Dirty Harry also presents us with other topical issues. General social unrest, which prompted the new plea for law and order, was evident in the continued protest (sometimes violent) against the United States' involvement in Vietnam, the "Kent State Massacre" on May 4, 1970 (only a year before the film was shot), serving as the most notorious example. Evidence of this protest of the war as it worked its way into the culture, and indirectly, at least, into the film is seen by Scorpio's counter-culture appearance and attire (long hair, paisley necktie, and peace sign on his belt buckle). Finally, the looming fear of the infamous Zodiac killer served as a model for the villain in the film. Like Zodiac, who taunted police with his encrypted letters that he sent to various newspapers, Scorpio communicates this way and is equally arrogant in his taunts and demands. Both also send to the authorities objects from their victims' clothing: in October and again in December of 1969, the killer sent to the San Francisco *Chronicle* a remnant from the shirt of one of his victims, Paul Stine, to prove he was indeed Zodiac, as Scorpio sends the bra, hair, and tooth from one of his victims to the police. What makes the comparison more explicit is the fact that the Zodiac killer threatened to murder children disembarking from a school bus, and later to plant a bomb on it. Scorpio haunts a playground as Harry stalks him, and eventually does hijack a bus with children in it. Finally, the sadistic pleasure of the Zodiac killer, as expressed in the one communication that has been definitely decoded, in which he boasts that killing people is much more "fun" than killing animals and that he finds murder "thrilling" is mirrored in Harry's prediction to the district attorney that Scorpio will kill again "because he likes it." The unpredictability of a psychopathic killer on the loose drove home, in real life and film, the daunting problem of crime and the difficulty of protecting citizens, especially in populated urban areas that provide camouflage for killers.

Finally, the same conflict with which Lancelot is confronted at the end of the *Morte D'Arthur*, for instance, and which Paladin is so often asked to resolve is also Harry's. The specific *circumstances* that create the strife between justice and the law may differ, but the philosophical question remains the same. The hero must listen to and act upon his own innate sense of right (his conscience), even when it runs counter to the laws that govern a community. Harry negotiates between justice and the law, and ultimately he performs an act of service to a city held hostage by a psychopathic criminal, but at a cost: discarding his badge expresses the degree to which he feels his separateness from the legal structure and the community he has just helped. The position Harry occupies at the film's conclusion, and through much of its action, is that of the figure who has a tenuous relationship with the community that only he, apparently, can rescue. He may not be an *errant* knight with no specific home base, but the end of this first film raises the question of whether he will stay in the community, having relinquished his job by tossing his badge away after killing Scorpio. Moreover, he is and remains a solitary hero who prefers to work alone rather than with a partner, one of the recurring motifs in the film series. Most of his partners end up wounded or dead, so this offers an acceptable explanation about why he prefers to work alone; it seems not as anti-social.[4]

Another way in which Harry conforms to the typology of the liminal outlaw hero is his lack of family obligations. Because his wife was killed by a drunk driver, the widowed Harry is free to endanger his own life with reckless disregard, in contrast, for instance, to the district attorney, who says of Scorpio, "I've got a wife and three kids. I don't want him on the streets anymore than you do." Gonzales has to think about his wife, and for this reason announces he will resign as Harry's partner, and teach Sociology instead. Harry can spend his off-duty time trailing a killer, and not fulfilling marital or domestic duties. When we consider Ray's idea that the function of the outlaw hero is to reconcile for American audiences the contradictory desires of freedom and independence on the one hand, and the need to serve community and uphold its values, on the other, it becomes clear that the deceased wife is a very effective solution. Having been married, Harry is shown to ascribe to the value of domesticity and community; he is an ordinary guy. However, the death of his wife absolved him of the obligations of marriage, leaving him free to pursue justice—at any cost. This is a universal feature of the liminal outlaw hero: Lancelot, Rick Blaine, Shane, the Lone Ranger, and Paladin. They revere and defend the feminine and domestic values espoused by a community, but their freedom from such entanglements is a necessary part of their liminal outlaw hero status, as is their role as negotiator between true justice and the law.

We must not forget Harry's emblem of election: his .44 Magnum is his trademark. He is a skilled warrior in an urban jungle. When he is first assigned to try to trap Scorpio by baiting him with the opportunity to carry out his threat to kill a Catholic priest, Harry chooses to use a .458 Winchester Magnum rifle. When he acts as a bagman in his second delivery attempt to Scorpio and conceals a switchblade on his person, his superior remarks, "You know, it's disgusting that a police officer should know how to use a weapon like that," registering his disapproval of the use of a weapon associated with thugs and criminals. The concealed switchblade, although déclassé, is not unlike Paladin's habit of carrying a small derringer hidden in his belt, which saves him several times, as Harry's knife does when he wounds Scorpio with it and forces him to flee. In fact, Harry's handgun is such an integral part of his identity that the second film in the sequence, *Magnum Force*, refers to it in the title.

Magnum Force (1973) and the Limits of the Law

"Well, you're a good man, Lieutenant. A good man always knows his limitations."
—Harry Callahan to Lieutenant Briggs in *Magnum Force*

The sequel to the first *Dirty Harry* film has a somewhat surprising genesis because it had little to do with internal American political and social issues; instead, the idea for *Magnum Force* derived from the advent and proliferation of the South American death squads that were making the news in the 1960s and 1970s. The film's first and primary screenwriter, John Milius, became fascinated with the formation of secret, vigilante police groups in Brazil who began as idealists and soon became as corrupt as the criminals to whom they dispensed brutal torture and murder. In a chapter from a collection of essays, *Fear at the Edge: State Terror and Resistance in Latin America* (1992), Patricia Weiss Fagen provides a detailed discussion of the inception of death squads that in Brazil actually preceded the military coup of 1964: "Prior to the 1964 military coup, retired and off-duty police founded the Esquadrao da Morte (death squads) which undertook to kill petty criminals among the so-called *marginais*.

Sectors of the middle class at first welcomed the death squads, viewing them as more effective than the regular police" (Chapter 3: "Repression and State Security" 57).

Fagen states that the death squad was founded by Detective Mariel Mariscot, who was one of the "Twelve Golden Men of Rio de Janeiro's Police" (58). Even though their initial targets were habitual street criminals, Fagen observes, "in the late 1960s and early 1970s, without changing their methods (torture murders), the death-squad members devoted their major energies to killing political enemies" (57). Finally, in the 1970s, the death-squads were replaced by the military police, who had developed "an elaborate repressive apparatus" for dealing with perceived enemies of the state (Fagen 58). This issue was international news, and Milius thought that transposing the death squad idea onto an urban police force in the United States would be a compelling story for a Dirty Harry film. Although the San Francisco police force group in *Magnum Force* does not resort to torture and the punishment of political enemies, in several essential ways, as we shall see, they are modeled on the Latin American death squads that were receiving so much attention in the news. Eastwood liked the idea of a secretive police squad that developed into self-appointed judge, jury and executioner; this time, his character would not clash with an inept bureaucracy, but with corruption from within the law enforcement itself, an idea not unusual for a western, but one that could easily translate to the contemporary urban western setting. Harry's opposition to such a dictatorial group of elitists would provide a means for this sequel to serve as a sort of rebuttal to the fascism charges leveled at the first film.

Two other factors influenced the finished story. First, after having composed about sixty pages of the script, Milius was offered the chance to direct *Dillinger*, based on his own script, so he wanted someone else to finish *Magnum Force*. Eastwood was interested in another film that was in development, *Thunderbolt and Lightfoot*, and so he recruited its scriptwriter, Michael Cimino, to complete the *Magnum Force* script (Schickel 299–300). Cimino wrote and directed *Thunderbolt and Lightfoot* (1974), which was very successful; later, he went on to co-write and direct *The Deer Hunter* (1978), which won five Academy Awards, and which garnered for him both Best Picture and Best Director, followed by a film which nearly brought about the demise of United Artists studio, the financially disastrous *Heaven's Gate* (1980), an epic western about the Johnson County Wars. Veteran Ted Post was chosen as director for *Magnum Force*; he had worked with Eastwood in the early days on *Rawhide* and had also directed him in *Hang 'Em High* (1968).

Magnum Force included details of plot and character that served as a smooth transition from the first film, providing a continuity and also solidifying

Harry's identity by affirming his ethical code when tested against a new set of challenges and circumstances. For instance, when the story opens, we soon learn that Harry has been relegated to a routine stakeout of a convenience store, presumably as a punishment for his prior actions: that of the Fillmore District the mayor alludes to in *Dirty Harry*, in which Harry had shot a would-be rapist, and the fatal shooting of the serial killer at the conclusion of the first film. A homicide detective assigned to a rookie detective job places Harry in an antagonistic position to the law he represents. Another feature established at the start that hearkens back to the first film occurs in a conversation with his partner, Early Smith (Felton Perry), about the unhappy fate of previous partners. Harry tells Early that the police force is giving out odds on how long Early will stay alive being his partner. When Early asks how long the previous one lasted, Harry replies, "A couple of weeks," but adds that Gonzales is still alive, "teaching college," referencing Gonzales' decision in the first film to leave the force and teach Sociology because his wife could not adjust to the dangers of her husband being a cop. We know from *Dirty Harry*, however, that Gonzales is one of the lucky ones to serve as Harry's partner—he was wounded but recovered, as did Gonzales' predecessor, Fred Dietrich. However, the partner mentioned before Dietrich, Tom Fanducci, was killed, and this will be the fate of several other partners including, sadly, Early himself. The misfortune of Harry's partners underscores his loner status. A final motif that links the first and second films is the comic relief provided by the fact that Harry frequents eating establishments with all-American fast foods—hotdogs and hamburgers—but never manages to finish his meal before he is thrust into an unexpected crime scene. As in the first film, he has to consume his hotdog as he pursues the fleeing robbers of a bank, so in *Magnum Force* he has to finish on the run his hamburger that Bill McKenzie "an ex-homicide man" turned short-order chef, has prepared for Harry at an airport diner, because there is a hijacking in progress that Harry has to thwart by posing as a pilot. This incident, peripheral to the main plot, resembles that of the bank robbery and of Harry's rescue of a potential suicide in *Dirty Harry*. Such episodes are designed to establish the sudden dangers of a teeming urban setting, and Harry's ability to step up when called upon unexpectedly to prevent a disaster. Hence, the reason for his name, "Dirty Harry," referring to the fact established in the first film, that he is called upon to do every "dirty" job—the sordid, threatening, and unexpected—is reinforced here.

As the plot unfolds, so too do we see the reaffirmation of Harry's own ethical code as it conflicts with established authority, but in this case it is not so much a cumbersome bureaucracy (although we see the failure of the court system again) with which he must contend, but a corruption within the police force itself. After the opening voiceover that reminds us of the power of Harry's .44 Magnum (another reference to the first film), we see exiting the courthouse a crime boss, Carmine Ricca (Richard Devon), who has just been exonerated—because of a "technicality"—of the murders of a labor reformer and his family. Outside the courthouse is a deeply divided and angry crowd, some with signs that assert Ricca's guilt, and others that claim his innocence. The smug, triumphant Ricca climbs into his private car with his attorney and two henchmen, and the scene cuts to the torso of a police officer watching the proceedings on television as he prepares for work. Soon this yet unidentified motorcycle patrolman stops Ricca's vehicle and executes all four men inside. When Harry and Early, who "happen" to be close by, come to the crime scene, Harry exchanges quips with the investigating officer, Lt. Neil Briggs (Hal Holbrook), who clearly doesn't want Harry around. Briggs alludes to Harry's current assignment, a stakeout, insulting Harry by claiming that every time Harry goes out on the street the public cries police brutality, to which Harry replies flatly, "I just work for the city." Briggs answers, "So do I, longer than you, and I never had to take my gun out of its holster once. I'm proud of that." "Well, you're a good man, Lieutenant. A good man always knows his limitations," is Harry's wry, cutting reply, one that is echoed in the final line of the film. Harry learns the men were killed with a Magnum, and his detective instincts kick in. When Early asks him what is between Harry and Briggs, Harry identifies the source of antagonism as "jealousy," something he will have to revise later. He takes Early to an airport diner where a retired homicide detective flips hamburgers, and this is where Harry has to foil a hijacking attempt, slaying both of the criminals and saving the day.

In addition to the strange murder of Ricca and his entourage, other things begin to bother Harry. A fellow policeman and friend, Charlie McCoy (Mitch Ryan), nearly runs Harry over (accidentally) in the station parking lot. Charlie and Harry had served in the Marines together; Charlie has been on the force for ten years, but he is about ready to crack. Separated from his third wife, Carol, Charlie expresses his frustration and anger also with the system: "These days a cop kills a hoodlum on the streets" and "Those snot-nosed bastards [lawyers] will crucify him one way or another. A hood can kill a cop, but can a cop kill a hood?" Harry suggests in the course of this conversation that Charlie take some time off, or even retire. "I'll never retire! I'm goin' out fightin'!" is Charlie's reply. Although this is a reminder of a system that privileges criminal rights (as in *Dirty Harry*), in this case it is not Harry who is the main antagonist of the system, and he sees the dangers of what Charlie is experiencing. Harry next encounters at the force's firing range four new rookie cops who happen to be expert shots, a fact that impresses the seasoned detective. He soon learns from them that they were "Air Borne Rangers, Special Forces," before joining the force. Harry's expertise with a gun is legendary on the force, and the four admire him, mentioning that he wins the department's shooting contest every year, but Harry also compliments them: "When I get back on homicide, I hope you guys will come see me."

Execution style murders continue to occur in rapid succession. A wild afternoon pool party attended by criminals and their female companions ends in a blood bath when another faceless motorcycle cop launches an explosive and opens fire with a machine gun. A well-known pimp (Albert Popwell) who knows how to bribe traffic police is nonetheless pulled over by a uniformed cyclist and riddled with bullets, after having killed one of his prostitutes (Margaret Avery) by pouring drain opener down her throat. Questioned by the press about these violent slayings and being reminded there were 200 murders in San Francisco the previous year, the investigating officer, Briggs, declares, "There will be no bombs in pools. This town belongs to the people. We're going to have law and order here."

Harry and Early enjoy success on their stakeout, catching the robbers of the convenience store. Harry compliments Early for his performance on the stakeout, and returns to his apartment that night. We see a photograph of Harry and his deceased wife (which we know about from the previous film), but a knock on the door introduces the Asian girl, Sunny (Adele Yoskioka), who lives downstairs, and who expresses that she wants to go to bed with Harry. This tryst is interrupted, however, when Harry receives a phone call from Briggs that summons him to the morgue and reinstates him as a homicide detective, as the executions are getting out of hand, and he intends to assign surveillance teams to known criminals. Briggs assigns Harry and Early to tail Frank Palancio (Tony Giorgio), but Harry understands that the known criminals are the victims, not the suspects. During their surveillance of Palancio, Harry engages in one of his unorthodox techniques, which prompts Early to state, "You always have to do things your own way, don't you?" Harry replies, "You do something someone else's way, and you take your life in your own hands," reinforcing his common sense, self-reliance, and independence, which is a main reason for his resiliency. Harry doesn't go by the book, but he achieves results and avoids becoming a statistic.

Harry begins to suspect that the executions are being conducted by a police officer. The bullets come from a .357 Magnum, an unusual, custom gun and ammunition used by one of the Rookie cops on the firing range. Some of the victims (Ricca and the Pimp) allowed their murderer close access to their cars, suggesting a figure of authority was the killer. When another criminal who is under surveillance by a police team is murdered under the very noses of the detective on the stakeout, Charlie McCoy, who happened to be in the area at the time, runs into the executioner, the Rookie cop, Davis (David Soul), who murders Charlie in cold blood, so that the latter cannot identify him. Davis then reports the murder, averring he just happened to be in the neighborhood at the time of the shooting, but Harry is suspicious and contrives to get possession of one of Davis' bullets to run a ballistic test, which he does by borrowing the gun at the annual police contest and shooting a bullet into a structure, returning at night to retrieve it. Harry shares with Briggs, whom he believes to be a mediocre detective and a staunch advocate of the system, his evidence that suggests Davis' bullet matches those found at the latest crime scene. When Briggs tells Harry to serve an arrest warrant to Palancio, he requests two of the Rookie cops he now suspects, Davis and Sweet (Tim Matheson), and tells Early to "keep an eye on them" during the arrest. Palancio is tipped off at his hideout before the cops arrive, Sweet is killed, and Harry realizes he was "sacrificed" by whoever is killing the city's criminals. Briggs asks Harry for the incriminating evidence of the bullet he has tested, but a wary Harry gives him a phony bullet and entrusts Early with the authentic one, instructing the latter to give the real one to Briggs if anything should happen to him. At this point, Harry suspects the Rookie cops, but he believes that Briggs can still be persuaded that his suspicions are correct. He then confides in Early further, positing that the killers might be a "sub-organization in the police force," and "sort of a death squad like those in Brazil" a few years back—an overt reference to the source of the film's plot as Milius conceived of it. Aware of the dangers in exposing such a group, Harry cautions Early to take care of himself.

When he arrives at his apartment garage, the three remaining Rookies, astride their motorcycles, looking both somber and sinister in their appearance, confront Harry. They ask Harry to join them in their vigilante crusade against San Francisco's criminals: "We're the first generation that's learned to fight. We are simply ridding society of the killers that would be caught and sentenced anyway if our courts worked properly," an indictment of a corrupt or faulty judicial system that fails to dispense justice. Moreover, they see themselves as folk heroes, believing they have the approbation of the public: "We began with the criminals that people know, so that our actions would be understood." That they believe they represent the interests of the common people suggests the first Brazilian death squad that, according to Patricia Weiss Fagen, had widespread initial support by the middle class (*Fear at the Edge* 57). After confessing to their roles in the recent slayings, and reaffirming their commitment to continue, they give Harry a choice, "Either you're for us or you're against us," to which Harry, narrowing his eyes, replies, "I'm afraid you've misjudged me," dismissing them.

Immediately after, Harry saves Sunny when he realizes in the nick of time that their apartment mailboxes have been rigged with a plastic explosive. He hurriedly telephones Early to warn him; hearing his phone ringing as he arrives home, Early makes the unfortunate choice of first retrieving his mail, and meets his end that way. Harry calls Briggs, who comes to his apartment and claims they should take the plastic device to headquarters to show their chief. He asks Harry to drive, and the climactic ideological showdown, no longer one of professional jealousy, as Harry had believed, begins. Briggs is the mastermind behind the killings. He justifies the actions of the group, invoking the vigilantism of the Old West as a model for dealing with urban crime: "A hundred years ago in this city people did the same thing. History justified the vigilantes. Anyone who threatens the security of the people will be executed. Evil for evil, Harry. Retribution." Like the Rookies, Briggs believes he is a champion of the public good. Harry challenges Briggs' position, asking him, "How does murder fit in? When police start becoming their own executioners, where's it gonna end?" Briggs expresses surprise that Harry, who seems always to be at odds with the official channels of the law, should find himself defending the system, but Harry vehemently insists, "I hate the goddamn system. But 'til someone comes along with some changes that make sense, I'll stick with it," to which Briggs replies, indicating Harry ascribes to a now antiquated code, "You're about to become extinct."

This rather lengthy dialogue establishes once again Harry's position as liminal outlaw hero. Although he often sees the need to think and act according to his own internal code of conduct, sometimes for his own self-preservation, but also for the good of others, as he asserted in his conversation with his partner, Early ("You do something someone else's way, and you take your life in your own hands"), Harry cannot endorse the vendetta of the vigilantes. His motive is always to serve true justice, even when he is at odds with the legal system, but turning into a systematic murderer in order to rid the streets of criminals is beyond what his conscience will allow, its arrogance at odds with his own natural working class humility and common sense decency.

In order to escape Briggs' death sentence, Harry swerves the car and smashes Briggs' face into the dashboard, rendering him unconscious, after which a chase ensues when the Rookie vigilantes pursue him. After killing Grimes (Robert Urich) the two remaining cops follow Harry to a site used for old military vessels, industrial ruins similar to the abandoned quarry of the first film, and underscoring the urban sprawl of the city in each case. Inside an abandoned ship, Harry brutally beats to death Red Astrachan (Kip Niven) and is then pursued while riding Red's motorcycle by the only remaining cop, Davis. At the last minute, Harry ditches his bike, but Davis is unable to jump before he reaches the end of the deck, and falls to his death into the water. Harry throws Davis' helmet in after him, a gesture with a vague resemblance to his tossing the badge, another official emblem of the law, into the water at the end of the first film. Making his way back to the car, Harry starts to climb in but is stopped by Briggs (bleeding profusely from the head), who has regained consciousness; he intends to finger Harry for the murder of the three cops. He taunts Harry, "Who's gonna believe you? You're a killer, a maniac." Harry has furtively activated the plastic explosive that still lay on the seat, and as Briggs drives away, the bomb detonates. "A man's got to know his limitations," is Harry's final, sage pronouncement, with the irony he had employed when he told Briggs the same thing earlier. The repetition of a memorable earlier utterance at the end of the film was employed also in *Dirty Harry*, a signature of the series that ties them together.

Harry Callahan's position in relation to the law as it is portrayed in *Magnum Force* reaffirms his liminal outlaw hero status. As in *Dirty Harry*, he has little tolerance for red tape and bureaucratic nonsense, stating this explicitly to Briggs ("I hate the goddamn system"), but he attempts to work within the limits of the law even as he tries to accomplish true justice. Harry knows that the vigilantes are no better than the criminals they judge and execute. His position in this film is the middle, common sense ground, as it was in the first film. Moreover, only Harry, with his astute observation and keen insight, can solve the crime spree. A very good detective, Harry sees through the accusation that the murders are a result of a dispute among members of organized crime. Although at first Harry does not suspect Briggs as the ringleader of the vigilantes, believing only that Briggs harbors jealousy toward him and that he is a "by the book" officer, in the end he renders Briggs ineffective—permanently. The only way to uncover corruption from within the system in this case is through the efforts of Harry, another operative from within it. He alone disperses this menacing band of secret vigilantes, whose skewed sense of "justice," as Harry points out to Briggs, will eventually escalate and know no bounds.

The other feature of *Magnum Force* that conforms to the idea of the liminal outlaw hero is that he retains his solitary status and therefore remains on the fringes of community and domesticity, even though he upholds the values that community and family represent. First, after Harry's conversation with his old Marine buddy and fellow officer, Charlie McCoy, his concern for Charlie's psychological stress, brought on by his job but also by the dissolution of his third marriage, leads him to visit Charlie's ex-wife, Carol. Harry is shown on the couch watching TV in Carol's home, complimenting her on her "home-cooked meal" and receiving affectionate embraces from Carol and Charlie's children. He learns from Carol that Charlie had become suicidal and had waved his gun in front of the children; he had also been living with a nude dancer. Harry's temporary role as surrogate father/family man (a needed masculine presence) is extended when Carol overtly propositions him. This is an awkward moment for Harry (and the audience), who wants to be polite but who feels, presumably, it would be dishonorable to sleep with his friend's ex-wife. Harry is saved by a telephone call from Early. This scene shows us two things: Harry's loyalty and concern for his friend, Charlie (who will be murdered in the course of events by Davis), and that he appreciates the comforts of hearth and home, even though he himself remains unattached.

The other feminine enticement in the film is that of Sunny, who lives in the same apartment building as Harry. Sunny, too, openly and abruptly propositions Harry when she introduces herself to him: "What does a girl need to do to go to bed with you?" to which Harry replies, "Try knocking on my door." In only minutes, that is what happens. Later, we learn that Sunny has a key to Harry's mailbox, so we assume they are in a relationship, but after their initial romantic interlude, we are never shown any intimate scenes between them, nor does this character reprise her role in ensuing films. Moreover, before he sleeps with Sunny, Harry is shown gazing wistfully at a framed photograph of himself and his dead wife, which is the only personal effect on prominent display in his apartment, suggesting that his domestic entanglements have been relegated to the past. The inclusion of two women who proposition Harry is, no doubt, intended to reaffirm Eastwood's status as an actor with sex appeal, and not because either female character factors significantly—or even at all—into the story itself. Harry is honorable, protective, and chivalric to both of these sexually "liberated" women, but neither can attain a significant hold on his emotions. That privilege is reserved for Harry's next police partner in *The Enforcer*, the sequel to *Magnum Force*.

The Enforcer (1976) and the Sacrifice of the Woman

> HARRY: "Why aren't you married and having kids like everybody else?"
> KATE: "Why aren't you?"
> HARRY: "'Cause nobody in their right mind's asking."
> —Inspectors Harry Callahan and Kate Moore, *The Enforcer*

The Enforcer began when two aspiring writers, Gail Morgan Hickman and S. W. Schurr (Scott Shroers), delivered to Eastwood's restaurant, The Hog's Breath, a screenplay they had written, *Moving Target*, which they hoped would be developed into the next Dirty Harry film.⁵ Eastwood liked its idea of radical political groups and of a militant priest. Warner Bros. purchased the script, and it was then turned over to veteran writer Stirling Silliphant, who had recently composed two blockbusters, *The Poseidon Adventure* (1972) and *The Towering Inferno* (1974). Eventually, one of Eastwood's favorite script doctors, Dean Riesner, was also called in to revise the screenplay (Schickel 340). The topical issue of 1960s and early 1970s radical militant groups is eclipsed, somewhat, by the biggest innovation in this installment of *Dirty Harry* films—that of a woman partner for Harry, complicated by a tacit budding romance with her. Warner Bros. had hired Silliphant to write the next Dirty Harry screenplay prior to Eastwood receiving the aspiring writers' script, and his angle was to create a story that gave Harry a female Asian American partner. Eastwood liked the idea of a female partner, but thought it was important to remain true to the formula of an action film, and not on character development. As a result, the two separate screenplay ideas—that of the radical militant group that kidnaps a hostage, and of a female partner for Harry—were incorporated into one script, which became *The Enforcer*. Directed by James Fargo, who later directed *Every Which Way But Loose* (1978), and who had served as assistant producer/assistant director on *The Eiger Sanction* and *The Outlaw Josie Wales* (1975 and 1976, respectively), this was a reward for his loyalty to Eastwood projects.

The Enforcer opens when two male employees for Western Gas and Electric Company in Marin County are lured to a remote cabin by the obvious advances of a female hitchhiker, Miki (Jocelyn Jones), where the leader of a radical militant group called the People's Revolutionary Strike Force (PRSF) of which Miki is a member, murders them in order to use their truck to pull off a munitions heist. Their leader, Bobby Maxwell (DeVeren Bookwalter), puts on a veneer of having a political agenda, but is really more interested in extorting ransom money from the city, which leads eventually to the kidnapping of the loathsome San Francisco mayor. In typical *Dirty Harry* movie fashion, we first see the titular figure when we cut to Harry on patrol with Frank Giorgio (John Mitchum) who was present in the earlier films and is now named as Harry's partner. Harry first foils the efforts of a flim-flam artist whom he knows to habitually stage heart attacks in posh restaurants, and then they respond to an "all units, 406," a liquor store holdup in which the robbers are holding hostages in exchange for a getaway car. When Harry enters the store to negotiate with the thieves, they insult him by calling him "pig," spitting on him, and making him lie on his back to frisk him, soiling his new jacket. They reiterate their demand for a car, which a very angry Harry meets, with great ironic flair, by driving his police car straight into the store, shooting the suspects, and effectively ending the crisis, but this action serves as the now formulaic impetus for Harry's run-in with his bureaucratic superiors.

In the next scene, Captain Jerome McKay (Bradford Dillman), Harry's police force adversary in this film, reads him the riot act, accusing him of "excessive use of force" in the incident, and chiding him for the $14,379 in damages that resulted from smashing the police car into the store. "This little wild west show of yours yesterday is exactly the kind of thing this department will not tolerate," he tells Harry, and then reassigns Harry to "Personnel" as a punitive measure, similar to his stake-out assignment in *Magnum Force*. This elicits from Harry a strong protest: "Personnel! That's for assholes!"

When Harry reports to the personnel board the next day, he is informed that he is part of a panel that is interviewing applicants for eight positions as Inspector on the force, and that affirmative action has dictated that three of the eight must be women. To assure that this happens, a representative of the very politically conscious mayor sits in on the proceedings. Ms. Grey (Jan Stratton) intends to bring the department into "the mainstream of 20th century thought" and, with a pointed quip at Harry, announces the further intention of "winnowing the Neanderthals out of the department." Naturally, Harry is indignant about this dictate to hire on the basis of gender and is antagonistic toward the female applicant they interview, Kate Moore (Tyne Daly), who has no street experience, even though Harry is mildly impressed that she is well acquainted with the law. Moore is destined to be Harry's partner as unfortunate circumstances unfold. While Harry is serving his demotion in the personnel department, Frank and Harry's replacement, Tony, stumble upon a dead guard and a burglary in progress at the Pacific Overseas Shipping Company that the PRSF is conducting to gain arms for their terrorist activities. Frank is stabbed by Maxwell, incurring what will be a fatal wound, but before he dies, he relays to Harry, who rushes to the hospital to see Frank, that he had recognized the murderer as a pimp and possible homicide suspect of an old prostitute in the Fillmore District, whose case they had been assigned a few years before.

The PRSF sends tapes to the city demanding cash payment, and Harry is reinstated to investigate who is behind the burglary/murders—with his new partner, Kate Moore. Harry is chilly toward Moore. The film introduces in their initial conversation a reminder of the body count of Harry's prior partners when Moore, having researched her new partner, mentions the deaths of "Fanducci in '68 and Smith in '72, but it wasn't your fault." While reading files on the prior suspect in the Fillmore District prostitute's murder at the San Francisco Hall of Justice, a bomb is detonated in the restroom, Harry recognizes the black suspect (who is affiliated with the PRSF), and he and Moore give chase, finally collaring him in a church where a hostile priest, Father John (M.G.

Kelly), who sympathizes with the radicals, exclaims to Harry, "I think you're a disgrace to this city." This incident leads Harry to the headquarters of a known black radical political organization known as Uhuru, with whom the bomber, Henry Caldwell, was once affiliated. Its leader, Big Ed Mustapha (Albert Popwell, who had roles in the prior *Dirty Harry* films as a robber and a pimp, and who will appear as Horace King in the next film, *Sudden Impact*), denies having anything to do with the munitions theft and threat to the city. "We don't deal in violence," but he knows who might be responsible when Harry shows him a list of suspects, and Mustapha fingers Bobby Maxwell as "the main man."[6]

Mustapha avers that Maxwell's *entourage* is a group of "dudes he met in Vietnam," and says that the PRSF are not really radical thinkers, but are only on a crime spree "for the bread." Mustapha agrees to be an informant if Harry can get one of his constituents off of a possessions charge, and the two strike a friendly deal. Mustapha says to Harry, "You're on the wrong side. You get out and put your ass on the line for a bunch of dudes who wouldn't let you in the front door, anymore than they would me." Harry replies, "I'm not doing it for them," and when Mustapha asks, "Who then?" Harry, with a slight smile, says, "You wouldn't believe me if I told you," a rare moment in which his altruism is allowed to be expressed. This exchange between the two also underscores Harry's working class, man on the street appeal, and suggests that divisiveness in a culture can be prompted more by the gap between haves and have nots (class) rather than race.

The Mayor (John Crawford) and Captain McKay are more interested in image than justice, and wish to pin the crime on Mustapha and his Uhuru group. With all the fanfare of a S.W.A.T. team, they arrive and make an arrest, so that Harry's source for finding information about Maxwell's whereabouts is undermined. The Mayor contrives to boost his re-election chances by orchestrating—with McKay's help—a public commendation for Harry and Moore, which would falsely credit them for the raid and arrest of Mustapha at Uhuru headquarters. Furious, Harry clashes again with dishonest officials, refuses the "commendation" and leaves. Moore joins him, offering help, and the two establish a genuine bond.

Walking in a park near the Colt Tower, Harry asks Moore why she isn't married and having children, why she wants to be a cop. When she turns the question around to Harry, he demures, "'Cause no one in their right mind's asking," which is obviously a dodge of the real issue: that he is a loner by choice. What develops between the two in this scene is respect and also the hint of a mutual sexual attraction. Schickel observes rightly that this love is only "chastely suggested" but credits it as the feature that distinguishes it from the other films (342). Moore begins to flirt with Harry with a series of sexual innuendoes

5. Poetic Justice and Dirty Harry (1971–1988)

Rookie cop Kate Moore (Tyne Daly) and Harry Callahan (Clint Eastwood) cement their partnership on a stroll near Colt Tower. Eastwood wanted Daly in the role because he thought her all-American looks were in accord with Harry's values, making their understated romance more believable in *The Enforcer* (Warner Bros., 1976) (Jerry Ohlinger's Movie Materials Store).

(referring to the imposing structure of the Colt Tower as "phallic" and telling Harry, "You are Cold Bold Callahan with his great big .44" that offers "penetration"). Harry pays Moore a compliment: "Whoever draws you as a partner could do a hell of a lot worse." Harry suggests the two go and have a few beers, but that scene—an improvised one between Moore and Harry—was deleted from the final cut, so that the two are shown on the waterfront drinking apple juice instead (Schickel 343). Apparently, the improvisation, while producing some great dialogue, was too difficult to coordinate technically, but this does suggest that Daly, despite initial hesitations about taking the role, was comfortable working with Eastwood, and in the part itself. Eastwood was enthusiastic about Daly in the part, not wanting a glamorous Hollywood type, which would be counter to Harry's values and tastes (Schickel 342–43). Daly had the appeal of an all-American girl, a believability that Eastwood thought brought a lot to the role.

Next, the mayor is kidnapped by the PRSF, who demands $5 million for his release. Harry gets hot on the trail of the organization, primarily motivated by his anger over their murders of his ex-partner Frank, an elderly guard, and a bridge operator. He visits a brothel disguised, humorously as a stupid redneck named Larry Dickman, searching for a woman named Wanda, whom Mustapha has learned is a member of the PRSF. Harry revisits the militant priest, having learned that he knew Maxwell when the latter was incarcerated, but the priest refuses to cooperate, even though Maxwell has committed murder, arguing, "Sacrifices have to be made." Moore saves Harry's life by shooting Wanda, who is disguised as a nun and is preparing to shoot Harry while he is interrogating the priest. Father John relents at last and says they have taken the mayor to Alcatraz, where the final showdown will occur. Daly took the part under the condition that she could have input on the script; she insisted that her role as a female cop be treated seriously and argued for scenes that show her actually killing "a bad guy," or in this case, a woman (Schickel 343).

On Alcatraz, Moore works her way to the interior while Harry picks off some of the remaining PRSF members, now all male, as the two women of the group have been killed previously, one in the warehouse heist and the other in the church. Moore frees the mayor and orders one of the two surviving members to drop his gun. He looks at her, sneers because of her gender, and says, "You've got to be kidding me," and aims at her, forcing Moore to shoot him dead. Only Maxwell is left alive, and as Moore is guiding the mayor to safety, Harry prepares to converge with them, his back to Maxwell. Moore turns and sees that he is about to be shot in the back, and shouts to warn Harry, who steps aside quickly, Moore taking the bullets that would have slain Harry, the second time she has saved him. As she dies in Harry's arms, Moore repeats what she often said to him: "Don't concern yourself, Harry. Get him!" Harry blows up Maxwell with one of the LAW Rockets the group had stolen, and then looks down in disgust at the sniveling, grateful mayor whom he loathes, but whom he has saved. Wordless, he returns to Moore's lifeless body, cradling it as a helicopter with McKay, announcing they will pay the ransom (ironically) circles above, underscoring the inept law enforcement system and the mayor's own lack of character, even though he is the "official hero" in need of rescue.

The Enforcer ends in typical fashion with the demise of the criminal through the swift, retributive justice rendered by Harry. It also concludes with the sacrifice of the woman, a phrase that has to be understood in this context in two ways. In the immediate context of the film's action, Moore *makes* a sacrifice, ransoming her own life for Harry's, and apparently, quite willingly and heroically so, as is evinced by her final words to him. But the liminal outlaw hero also must remain detached from the considerable enticements of even a genuine romantic partnership, and so, as Robert Ray insists, the woman is sacrificed in the story so that the hero can continue to enjoy his freedom from this kind of life-changing responsibility. Through no choice of his own—ostensibly—the liminal outlaw hero is both the champion of traditional values and yet remains aloof from them.

Sudden Impact (1983) and "the .38 caliber vasectomy"

> "What are *my* rights? There is a thing called 'justice,' and was it justice they should all just walk away?"
> —Jennifer Spencer to Harry Callahan, *Sudden Impact*

Six years after the third successful *Dirty Harry* film, Eastwood reprised his role, once again featuring his attraction to a woman, but this time it was on the opposite side of the law. Based on the story by Earl E. Smith and Charles B. Pierce and a screenplay by Joseph C. Stinson (who is later credited for his work on *City Heat* as well), this is also the only *Dirty Harry* film that Eastwood both produced and directed. While it retains the formulaic features that define the *Dirty Harry* experience, this film also departs from its predecessors in some interesting ways, particularly in its use of the *film noir* style.[7] In *Sudden Impact*, Inspector Harry Callahan becomes involved with a female serial killer, Jennifer Spencer (played by Eastwood's off-screen romantic interest, Sondra Locke), who is hunting down and killing, one by one, a group of males who had, a decade earlier, gang raped her and her now catatonic, traumatized sister, Elizabeth (Lisa Britt). Spencer, now a successful painter, is shown in the opening scene of the film, exacting her revenge: she has lured her first victim, George Willburn (Michael Maurer), to a secluded place where, parked in a car and pretending to be sexually attracted to him, she pulls out a .38 handgun, shoots him first in the genitals, and then finishes the job with a bullet to his head. Willburn is a small-time criminal from the town of San Paulo, and Harry is sent there under the pretense that he should "investigate" his background for leads about the murder. In actuality, however, Harry is sent there as a punitive measure because of his recent actions on the police force, thus following the familiar formula of the prior *Dirty Harry* films.

We first see Harry as he enters a courtroom where one of his collars (Kevyn Major Howard) is set free because of his unorthodox methods in the arrest of the thug. A female judge (Lois De Banzie) curtly announces, to Harry's dismay and chagrin—though this is now a familiar scenario: "The case is dismissed because Mr. Callahan, and this is an old story, did not have sufficient probable cause for detaining Mr. Hawkins. Charges dismissed." The hood, though guilty, walks away (smugly) because of the charge of "illegal search and seizure." Angered, Harry leaves the courthouse and heads to the Acorn Café, an establishment he frequents, and orders his usual coffee to go. Preoccupied reading the newspaper, he does not see that the waitress, Loretta (Mara Corday), has poured an excessive amount of sugar in his coffee in order to attract his attention to the fact that he has interrupted a robbery, something Harry notices only when he has walked out the door. He enters through the back of the café and confronts the robbers, killing or wounding all but one, who has taken a hostage, pointing a gun at the waitress' head. Next, is the familiar showdown, the character contest Harry wins. Pointing his Smith and Wesson at the criminal, he pronounces one of the most famous lines in film history, "Go ahead. Make my day," causing the robber's surrender. But the final opening action that lands Harry in trouble with his superiors is when he crashes the wedding reception of a famous mobster's granddaughter. Threlkis (Michael V. Gazzo) is already being tailed by undercover policemen, but Harry confronts him for the torture and murder of a prostitute. He humiliates Threlkis in front of his family, accusing him of the homicide, and waving an envelope that he claims the dead woman has sent to the police, revealing Threlkis' crimes. This so enrages and frightens Threlkis that he suffers an apoplectic fit and expires, but Harry's superiors are angered by his interference in their surveillance of Threlkis. At police headquarters, Harry clashes with the smug Captain Briggs, played by Bradford Dillman, who had played a similar role as Captain McCay in *The Enforcer*. Oddly, the name "Briggs" was also that of Hal Holbrook's character, the crooked policeman who was the ringleader of the rookie vigilante cops in *Magnum Force*. At first, Harry is told to "take a vacation," and hit men from Threlkis' organization subsequently target Harry, but he is called back to duty when the authorities find the body of Willburn.

He investigates the homicide victim, "Some stiff's got himself a .38 caliber vasectomy," a cop at the scene informs Harry, and then asks Harry if he is tired of police work. Harry answers with an ironic "no," but then recites with disgust the crimes that show the audience what an urban detective is forced to address: "the shootings, the knifings, the beatings, old ladies being bashed in the head for their social security checks, teachers being thrown out of a fourth floor window because they don't give 'A's," and the usual "waves of corruption, apathy, and red tape." Harry Callahan is weary, angered by the failures of the judicial system, and disheartened by the inhumanity he has to face each day. He and Briggs exchange insults: "You're a dinosaur," Briggs tells him, "You're a legend in your own mind," is Harry's retort. Because Harry is now a target for the mob, and because there is also a homicide for him to investigate, a superior more sympathetic than Briggs, Lt. Donnelly (Michael Currie) sends Harry to San Paulo for his own good, while giving him a purpose, that of gathering information about the victim, Willburn. As soon as he arrives there, Harry witnesses and interrupts a robbery in progress, saving the life of a young police officer and collaring one of the criminals; however, instead of gratitude, the San Paulo police chief, Jannings (Patrick Hingle), is openly and inexplicably hostile to Harry's presence in the town.

In the meantime, Jennifer Spencer has also returned to San Paulo, having first visited her institutionalized, catatonic sister, where the brutal rape had occurred ten years before. She returns under the pretense of using her artistic training to renovate the carousel of the amusement park on the boardwalk there. "It must give you satisfaction to make old ugly things right again," says the woman who has rented Jennifer a house and shown her the carousel she is to renovate. This triggers the first flashback, which shows the brutal rape of Jennifer and her sister, all orchestrated by a sadistic female "friend," Ray Parkins (Audrie Neenan), who lures the two girls to the boardwalk and hands them over to the male gang. The androgynous name, "Ray," and the fact that she is later alluded to as a "dyke" underscores the vicarious pleasure she derives from witnessing the rape. But Jennifer soon sets about completing her revenge for the rape that shattered her sister and psychically wounded her. An attending physician in the institution where Elizabeth is cared for makes clear to Jennifer that her sister is not physically debilitated, that it is the trauma of the rape that keeps her catatonic and uncommunicative. Jennifer herself expresses the trauma this event had on her own emotional health, but she does so through the therapy of her art, producing dark paintings in an effort to exorcise the demon within her. It is important to recognize that Jennifer's main motive for the killings may be revenge and outrage at the injustice she and her sister have known, but she is also trying to "make old ugly things right again," for herself and Elizabeth.

Jennifer soon resumes her acts of vengeance, hunting down her second victim, Kruger (Jack Thibeau), as he fishes in an isolated spot on the beach, and dispensing with him in the same manner as she had Willburn. Harry realizes the similarity between the homicide in San Francisco and this one, but Chief Jannings, who clearly has something to hide, becomes irate when Harry tries to become involved in solving the case. Meanwhile, Harry has a few chance encounters with Jennifer, and clearly finds her attractive, her attitude toward crime being not the least of the charms. Over a beer, when Harry tells her that he is a San Francisco police detective who is in San Paulo investigating a homicide, he also states, "Everybody wants results but nobody wants to do what they have to do" for justice to be accomplished. Jennifer replies, "You know, you're an endangered species. This is the age of lapsed responsibilities and defeated justice. Today an eye for an eye is only when you are caught." The two share an affinity and continue. Harry then posits the motive for the homicide he is investigating, revenge: "the oldest motivation known to mankind." "You don't approve?" Jennifer asks him, but Harry nods and adds, "'Til it breaks the law." This is the liminal status he tries to occupy, and which will force a judgment for him at the film's conclusion.

Spencer continues with her revenge, killing her third victim, Tyrone (Wendell Wellman), now a local merchant in the town. He tries to plead for his life, saying he was young at the time, arguing that he was drunk, and asking her if it was really that bad—all of which only strengthens Jennifer's conviction that slaying him is just, and she executes him in the same fashion as the others. Unaware that she is the killer he is seeking, Harry tries to investigate the murders by interrogating the friends of the victims. When he arrives at Ray's house, he sees a car parked in front—Jennifer, who has come to finish the job is there before Harry—and calls in the license plate number to learn whose it is. The other rapist, Mick (Paul Drake), is at Ray's house; when Harry tries to question them, Mick attacks him but Harry overpowers him and takes him to the police station. In his absence, Jennifer, who has been hiding in the shadows, enters Ray's house. Ray hisses, "So the bitch is here. How's your slut sister?" which earns her bullets and death. Harry sees Jennifer afterwards on the boardwalk, where she claims she has walked to relax; Harry drives her home, and she propositions him: "Do you want to be alone tonight Callahan? Well neither do I." They sleep together, but when Harry walks outside, looks in her garage, and sees the car that was parked at Ray's, he understands that she is the killer.

He returns to his hotel room to find that his friend on the San Francisco force, Horace King (Albert Popwell), has come to see him and has been murdered. Mick has gotten out of jail and with two of his thug friends was waiting in Harry's room when Horace arrived. They then jump Harry on the boardwalk, beat him brutally, and believe he falls to his death in the murky water.

Jennifer is next seen entering the house of the police chief, and at last we learn why Jannings has been so hostile to Harry's presence. Jennifer confronts him and learns that Jannings' own son was one of the rapists, but he suffered from such guilt that he tried to commit suicide in a car wreck, which had left him in a similar catatonic state, ironically, as that of Jennifer's sister. Jannings, a widower, had covered up the crime to protect his only son, but now feels remorse. Jennifer tells Jannings there is one left (Mick) that she wants to kill, but Jannings avers he has Mick locked up, not knowing he has in fact been freed. Just then the sadistic, psychotic Mick, along with his two companions, enters Jannings's house, kills Jannings with Jennifer's gun and then takes her to the boardwalk where the crime had occurred years before. Jennifer fights for her life and escapes the thugs who chase her to the carousel at the amusement park.

Harry, meantime, has managed to return to his room, discovered Horace's murder, and retrieved his .44 Magnum "automag," about which he had earlier boasted to Horace that it "holds a 300 grain cartridge and if properly used, it can *remove* the fingerprints" from its victim. He arrives to save the day, to the disbelief of the criminals, who think they have earlier witnessed his death. Harry appears out of the darkness of night, a silhouette under the arc of the neon sign of the "Big Dipper" roller coaster ride. This scene is reminiscent of one in *A Fistful of Dollars* (1964) in which Eastwood's character, Joe (a.k.a. "The Man with No Name"), is believed dead by his enemies but later emerges out of the smoke, much to their terror, and to one in the last *Dirty Harry* film, *The Dead Pool*, in which Harry is first a voice and then emerges out of the fog to vanquish his adversary. Such scenes cast a larger than life aura on the character. Stuart Kaminsky identifies this as a quality of what he calls a "mystic antihero." Kaminsky avers of this type, "He is more interested in living according to a certain style, showing others that he knows how to ... face danger with amusement and without fear, and if necessary, how to die. In this sense he becomes an almost mystic survivor" and his sudden appearances from the presumption of his death is, in each case, "a mystical experience designed to unsettle the killer" (*Clint Eastwood* 32–33). When Harry emerges out of the blackness of night, unnerving his adversaries, he quickly dispenses with Mick's henchmen, and then shoots Mick as well. Already mortally wounded by the bullets, Mick is nonetheless impaled when he falls upon the horn of a carousel unicorn—a phallus—serving as an ironic commentary on his own impotence (established in an earlier scene with a prostitute he has hired), and the perverse nature of his crime against Jennifer and her sister. The sexual dysfunction of the two worst figures involved in the rape, Ray Parkins and Mick, adds a psychological dimension to *Sudden Impact* that is not present in the previous *Dirty Harry* films. Instead of concluding with the usual chase scene, *Sudden Impact* ends with the nocturnal setting of a dark murky boardwalk and abandoned amusement park, much more in the style of a *film noir* than that of an action film, although all of the films end at the site of some modern ruin, appropriate for an urban western: an industrial quarry (*Dirty Harry*), a scrapyard for outmoded ships (*Magnum Force*), the abandoned prison, Alcatraz (*The Enforcer*), an amusement park carousel in need of renovation (*Sudden Impact*), and, as we shall see, a pier in the final film, *The Dead Pool*.

Now the moment of decision comes for Harry, as the police arrive and he must decide about Jennifer, whose fate is in his hands. Evidently mindful of what Harry had said in their earlier conversation, that he approves of revenge "'til it breaks the law," Jennifer, still feeling justified in her actions, makes a hurried plea in her own defense. "What happens now? Do you read me my rights? What *are* my rights? There is a thing called 'justice,' and was it justice that they should all just walk away?" This is Harry's role as liminal outlaw hero: he must choose between justice and the law, posed in a way here that it has not been presented before. Harry knows Jennifer is guilty; she is the killer who has stalked each victim, and Harry's position as homicide detective investigating the murders would mean that he must arrest her. But here the criminal is the initial victim, more sinned against than sinning: the crime against Jennifer and her sister has gone unpunished, and would have remained so, had she not sought her own vengeance. The law itself, in the form of Chief Jannings, who placed his own personal interests above his obligation to bring the rapists to justice, forces on Harry the issue of moral rectitude residing outside of the legal system. Harry answers to a higher moral imperative in judging Jennifer, whose motive for killing has ended. He tells the policeman to run the gun and bullets through ballistics, pinning all of the murders on Mick. In a sense, Mick and Ray *are* the ones who are responsible for the crimes, having initiated the sequence of events that led to the death of every rapist. Harry turns to Jennifer as he pronounces to the police in attendance, "Yeah, it's over," and he and Jennifer walk away from the scene together, more in the fashion of kindred spirits or comrades in arms in the service of a higher ideal than two lovers who have just enjoyed a "one-night stand." The closure to the film does not suggest a continuation of a long meaningful romantic relationship between Jennifer and Harry, two fiercely independent individuals who are more like doubles in their ardent pursuit of accomplishing justice for those to whom the law has not rendered it. Indeed, some critics referred to Locke's character as "Dirty Harriet," although doubtless some of the linking between the two characters was a result of the affair between Eastwood and Locke that was by the time of the film a well-known fact despite efforts to keep up appearances to the contrary.[8]

Under Eastwood's watchful eye, *Sudden Impact* remained true to the successful formula of the *Dirty Harry* tradition in several essential ways. The punched-up one-liners, of which the phrase "Go ahead. Make my day" is the most famous, contributes to a longer list of iconic quotations generated by Inspector Harry Callahan. This one ranks number 6 on the *American Film Institute's Top 100 Movie Quotes*, only one behind "Here's looking at you kid" from *Casablanca*, and two ahead of "May the force be with you" of inter-galactic *Star Wars* fame. The institute lists as its three criteria for selection that it must be an *actual movie quotation*, a phrase or short, spoken dialogue from the film (not a song), that it must have a *cultural impact*, having become part of the "national lexicon," and establish a *legacy*, so that the quotation is used to "evoke a memory of a treasured film," and therefore "enlivens and ensures its historical legacy" (100 Movie Quotes.com). Also making the list at number 51 is the famous "Do I feel lucky?" quotation from the first *Dirty Harry* film.

Sudden Impact also introduces the conflict created by due process of the law as a deterrent to justice, which informs all of the films, in this case at the beginning in the courtroom scene, followed by Harry's crashing of the wedding reception thrown by the mobster Threlkis that results in his suspension (called a "vacation"). We also see Harry thwarting random acts of crime, even when he is off duty; in this case, when he prevents the robbery of the Acorn Café, and later the hold-up in San Paulo. Sadly, Harry's unofficial partner in this film, fellow police officer Horace King, meets the same end as so many of Harry's other partners—violent death. Some of the characters and actors made appearances in the previous films: Albert Popwell had a part in the prior three *Dirty Harry* films, and Bradford Dillman is recast here in the role he played in *The Enforcer* as an arrogant police superior with whom Harry clashes.

As always, Inspector Harry Callahan represents a form of justice that is swift and decisive, one that also contains his signature of irony. He answers to his own conscience in defiance of what the law says, and gains the audience's sympathy by seeing his way clear through the maize of legal and judicial obstacles he faces. Despite his romantic interlude with the woman, there is no suggestion of a permanent entanglement. In fact, this film prompted a series of critical responses that suggested Clint Eastwood was a "feminist filmmaker" because of the strong women presented in many of his films, something that seemed to have gone unnoticed until the advent of Jennifer Spencer, whom reviewers referred to as "Dirty Harriet" (Schickel 385) because of her affinity with Harry when it comes to the concept of retributive justice. It seems odd that a psychotic knife-wielding stalker (Jessica Walter in *Play Misty for Me*) and a serial killer (Sondra Locke in *Sudden Impact*) should be classified as "feminist" on par with Tyne Daly's character in *The Enforcer*, as though "strong" and "feminist" are interchangeable without any other character considerations, but it certainly did put a new spin on Eastwood's reputation.

This film departs from the pattern of presenting a particular politicized social issue as the others had done in the past, focusing instead on the relationship of justice and revenge, and whether revenge can be justified in a codified system that exists in the modern world. The ironic twist in this film is that it focuses on the victim's rights, something that would seem to be at opposite ends of the spectrum from the first *Dirty Harry* film and its references to the Escobedo and Miranda rules. Harry's character may have gained a certain complexity by his romantic interests in the opposite characters of Kate Moore and Jennifer Spencer, but he would remain the single, unattached liminal outlaw hero as long as the *Dirty Harry* mystique, and Eastwood's interest in keeping the character alive, endured. *Sudden Impact* grossed over $70 million domestically alone, the highest of any of the five *Dirty Harry* films, which proved that audiences still responded to Harry Callahan, a dozen years after his debut, and that there was room for stylistic innovation while still retaining the formulaic features that define a *Dirty Harry* film (Schickel 382, Eliot 208).

The Dead Pool (1988) and 15 Minutes of Fame

> "Whatever they're paying you, Harry, it couldn't be enough."
> —Samantha Walker, *The Dead Pool*

The fifth and final film in the *Dirty Harry* franchise was shot while Clint Eastwood was finishing a two-year term as the mayor of Carmel, California, a position that offered something of an ironic contrast to Harry Callahan's own run-ins with political officials in the series. Eastwood had little time to direct, so that responsibility went to Buddy Van Horn, who had directed him previously in *Any Which Way You Can* (1980) and who would go on to direct his project the next year, *Pink Cadillac*, in 1989. The story idea evolved in part by two nutritionists who had written a popular self-help book called *Life Extension* (1982). Durk Pearson, an MIT graduate, and Sandy Shaw, a UCLA alumna, wrote this book about how to live longer and healthier. According to Marc Eliot, Pearson and Shaw had been introduced to Eastwood by a mutual acquaintance, Merv Griffin; they developed a health program for Eastwood, consisting of a prescribed diet and exercise regimen, along with ample vitamin and mineral supplements (*American Rebel* 241). Also credited with the story, and receiving the sole credit for the screenplay was a collaborator of Pearson and Shaw, Steve Sharon. The same year, Eastwood made *Bird*, prompted by his life-long passion for jazz, but knew that project's box office success potential was uncertain, so he agreed to reprise his role as Harry one final time as a way of hedging his bets (Schickel 430).

When *The Dead Pool* opens, Harry Callahan has, for once, generated some positive publicity for the San Francisco police force by giving key testimony against a crime boss, Lou Janero (Anthony Charnota), who is convicted and sent to prison. The assistant district attorney, who prosecuted the case, remarks that Harry's was a crucial role in getting the conviction, so Harry's superiors wish to exploit this opportunity to build a positive image for the department.

Naturally, Janero's conviction also sends a series of hit men to exact their revenge on Harry. *The Dead Pool* probes the issue of how the media sensationalize violence, and the way its members, lacking ethics, will do anything to get the scoop on a story. This becomes evident with the introduction of the main plot, which begins when a rock star, Johnny Squares (Jim Carrey), dies of an apparent drug overdose while cast in a music video made by film director Peter Swan (Liam Neeson). When Harry and his new Asian-American partner, Al Quan (Evan C. Kim), investigate, they find the death turns out to be murder. Johnny's grief-stricken girlfriend, Suzanne Dayton (Victoria Bastel), appears on the scene and is hounded by aggressive reporters. Harry is scandalized by this, and destroys a television camera, for which news reporter Samantha Walker (Patricia Clarkson) seeks restitution from the police department. She offers to drop the lawsuit against the force if Harry will agree to take her to dinner, at which she proposes he let her write an exclusive story about his life. Samantha has compiled an impressive portfolio of Harry's career, including newspaper articles about Scorpio and some of his other now famous past exploits on the force. Harry, uncomfortable with his newfound celebrity status, refuses, in part also because he dislikes the media in general, and questions her motives in particular: "All you want is blood." Later, after Samantha seems to have taken Harry's advice to heart ("forget competition and start thinking about your responsibility to the public"), they enjoy a more agreeable relationship and conversation over yet another dinner. Upon leaving the restaurant, two men approach Harry; they want his autograph for having sent Janero to prison, and tell Harry, "We need more cops like you." Samantha then invokes the quotation attributed to Andy Warhol, variously cited, but referring to the fact that everyone will have fifteen minutes of fame.[9] This fame turns deadly, however, when two more hitmen riddle with bullets the exterior elevator while Harry and Samantha descend in it. Harry protects her, but shaken by the experience, Samantha begins to see how hazardous his job is: "Whatever they pay you Harry, it couldn't be enough." Harry, of course, is never in it for the money or the fame.

Soon after, Swan's production manager, Dean Madison, is gunned down in a restaurant hold-up in Chinatown that Harry and Quan happen upon. Harry quickly enters the restaurant while the crime is in progress; sitting at a table, he tells the leader of the criminals "You forgot your fortune cookie," and crumbles it to read the message: "It says, 'You're shit out of luck,'" after which Harry quickly shoots the robbers, while Quan uses his karate skills to collar the one who escaped the building. On Madison's body they find a list of celebrities, among them Johnny Squares and Harry Callahan, which leads to the discovery that Swan, Madison, and others associated with the production company have been playing the "Dead Pool Game." When questioned, Swan explains that this bizarre contest consists of each participant listing eight famous people whom they believe will be dead within a certain time frame, either because they are old, sick, or have high-risk professions. The player whose list has the most number of dead people on it by the specified time wins. Harry is on Swan's list because of the occupational hazards of being a police inspector, but especially now that he has testified against Janero, and is thus a "marked man."

Janero's hit men continue their attempts against Harry's life, so he takes his own steps to end this. He visits Janero in prison and, through a clever ruse, intimidates him. Harry brings a carton of cigarettes to enlist the unwitting cooperation of another prisoner, Butcher Hicks (Diego Chairs). Harry tells Hicks to simply stand in the hallway outside of Janero's cell. He then informs Janero that, should anything happen to him, Hicks will exact revenge on Janero: "See that gorilla down there? That's Butcher Hicks," who killed three people with his own teeth. Harry tells Janero he will write Hicks each week to report on Hicks' mother, and if Hicks does not get a letter from Harry, he will know Janero is responsible for interrupting Harry's "postal service" and will "cancel your ass like a stamp." Harry then returns to Hicks at the end of the hall and gives him the carton of cigarettes, telling Hicks that Janero has said "anyone who smokes as much as you do is one dumb son-of-a-bitch," resulting in Hicks glowering at and terrifying Janero. Harry's own game of wits saves him almost as often as his quick instincts, decisive action, and his personal weapons cache.

Harry doesn't like Swan's cavalier attitude toward violence and death—in both his film endeavors and in playing the dead pool game—and especially doesn't like being on the list, particularly when another person on it, movie critic Molly Fisher (Ronnie Claire Edwards) winds up murdered as well, by someone who, it turns out, is impersonating Swan in order to frame him for the murders. Although Harry first suspects Swan, whom he dislikes, he begins to think Swan is not the likely perpetrator of the crimes: "It just doesn't feel right," he tells Captain Donnelly (Michael Currie). Next, a third person on the list, Nolan Kennard (Bill Wattenburg), a talk show host (which again focuses on the role of media and high public profiles) is killed by a remote control operated toy racecar that has been rigged with a plastic explosive. From the murderer's point of view, we see when he stabs Harry's photo with a knife that Harry will be his next victim. Harry has established a romantic relationship with Samantha Walker and when he leaves her house, Quan is there to go to work with Harry. The killer has been stalking Harry, however, and a chase scene ensues with the deadly remote toy car in hot pursuit of Harry and Quan. Quan is injured, but not mortally so. Harry and Quan had interviewed Swan again and learned that a deranged fan, Harlan Rook (David Hunt), had become so obsessed that Swan's lawyer had to get a restraining order against him. At the hospital when Quan is injured, a psychiatrist, Dr. Friedman (John Frederic Jones), tells Harry he had evaluated Rook the year before, and diagnosed him as being afflicted with "process schizophrenia," explained as that from which the afflicted person's self-hatred becomes so pronounced he has no identity, and therefore searches for one through others. Psychiatrists differentiate between "process" and "acute" forms, the former developing gradually and lasting over a longer period of time. Certainly, the person becomes delusional, and Rook has apparently confused his own identity with that of Peter Swan. What matters to Rook, like so many others in the film, is his own fame. In one episode, Gus Wheeler (Louis Giambalvo) attracts the media attention he craves by claiming to be the dead pool killer, but he only wants the press to witness his suicide: he douses himself with gasoline and threatens to set himself on fire, just to receive the attention he believes he deserves in a world gone mad on media attention, a neurosis of modern life that Andy Warhol so aptly and humorously characterized in his fifteen minutes of fame observation.[10]

Rook's first attempt on Harry's life having been unsuccessful, he contrives a plot to lure Samantha into a trap with which to bait Harry. He calls her, impersonating Swan, and says he will give her an exclusive story. Meanwhile, the police arrive at Rook's apartment and find incriminating evidence to prove he is the killer, along with a receipt that shows he has been using an alias, Edward Butler, to pose as a security guard for Swan's film company. Rook takes Samantha to a shipyard on the docks, and Harry pursues him there, having found the address on the receipt in Rook's lodgings. Rook suffers from delusions that his former idol, Swan, had been stealing Rook's dreams and making them into films, so Rook set about to steal Swan's dead pool list by murdering the celebrities on it. When Harry arrives, he is forced to relinquish his gun to save Samantha, but outwits Rook by escaping the building and running to the edge of the docks, with Rook in pursuit, brandishing Harry's weapon. At the end of the dock, Harry's voice is heard in the fog: "You're out of bullets, and you know what that means. You're shit out of luck" (a line he had used earlier with the robber in the Chinese restaurant), at which point he emerges from the fog with a behemoth harpoon gun that had been used in a film scene Swan was shooting earlier, as Harry had looked on. Harry shoots the gun and impales Rook against the side of a shed; he reclaims his own gun, and reveals to the audience what he himself knew all along—the gun had one bullet left. The game of wits with the killer is vintage Dirty Harry material. With his wry wit, Harry informs police when they arrive that Rook "is hanging out back there," as he and Samantha leave the scene together, Harry having survived the "Dead Pool Game."

The Appeal of *Dirty Harry* Justice

The Dead Pool conforms to the formula of the previous films in several ways. The random crime that Harry encounters on the street in every movie is present here when he and Quan stumble upon the robbery in the restaurant. Harry clashes with his superiors also, unhappy about publicity in this case, as an impediment to doing his job. He employs unorthodox methods to protect himself, as we see when he visits Janero in prison, and he uses his wit to outsmart Rook in the end, hoodwinking him into believing he has used up all of his bullets. Finally, the misfortune that befalls Harry's partners is activated here, although Quan, aware of the dangers of being Harry's partner, sports a talisman against evil, at the request of his grandfather when he learned Quan would be Harry's partner. Harry had told Quan to get a bulletproof vest, something that saves Quan's life. The end of the film also follows the *Dirty Harry* formula in that it is set in a cold, abandoned industrial shipyard. Additionally, Harry uses a spectacular and unusual weapon to finish the villain off. The harpoon gun is as singular as past weapons, and Rook being impaled by it suggests something about his delusions of being martyred, treated unjustly, therefore providing a kind of poetic justice that is also a trademark of the *Dirty Harry* films.

Like *Sudden Impact*, which did the best of the five films at the box office, *The Dead Pool*, which was a success but grossed the least, employs a style that is evocative of the *film noir* genre. Nocturnal settings are as common as daylight chase scenes; Harry in both films confronts his nemesis by emerging from a cover of night or fog, and the pulsing nightlife of the city contributes to the urban dangers that inform the sensibilities of both films. In *The Dead Pool* we enter the arena of the increasing influence of the media, image, and the perpetuation of violence, but also the exploration of fame. Sex and violence in Swan's films, news reporters who want "blood" and a scoop on a story at any cost, and music videos that approach reality TV in casting drug addict rock stars as themselves, tell us that the film has its roots in contemporary issues quite different from those of the *Dirty Harry* films of the early 1970s.

Yet, Harry here is the same inspector who won the approval of moviegoers in his debut film. When he encounters a problem or personal threat, as he does with Janero's henchmen, he deals with it in his own way, often using his wit, grit, and cunning to outsmart the criminals. He dislikes and continually combats impediments to justice and strives to remain free of the fetters of bureaucracy, even when, as in this film, it wishes to give him a well-deserved "commendation." Harry does not want fame—a main theme of this film—but rather he wishes to impose his strong sense of what is right on the community of which he strives to remain a part, but one on which he also keeps a wary eye. For Harry, the way is always clear; his moral code and actions are almost always in alignment. In *The Dead Pool* Harry does what is right in testifying against Janero, not because he seeks a commendation or public adulation (fame) but because it is the right thing to do, even though it endangers his life to the extent that he makes Swan's "dead pool" list. And while he may have romantic interests, women are, in the end, there to be rescued—without exception—and not to serve as part of a permanent domestic arrangement.

The *Dirty Harry* films were released over a period of sixteen years, 1971–1988. They were created in a context of significant social change in America, and reflect some of the issues that define the two decades in which they are set: internal divisiveness over the war, race relations, affirmative action, political scandal, increasing urban violence, and issues associated with growing media and the complexities of individuality in a crowded world. Five different presidents served in the oval office during the period that the *Dirty Harry* films—one after the other—enjoyed phenomenal box office success and achieved iconic status. Despite the fact that the films are very much of their time, this does not account for their unexpected popularity upon release (defying the harsh reception by the majority of critics), nor can it explain why they continue to resonate with audiences, having taken on a life of their own and a permanent place in the collective cultural imagination.

The appeal of the *Dirty Harry* films rests in their consistent rendering of *poetic justice*, an enduring and universal concept that transcends the topical issues that precipitate it. The *idea* of poetic justice is an old one; it informs much of ancient Greek tragedy (Sophocles' *Oedipus Rex* serving as perhaps the best example) and can be found in literary texts throughout the ages (e.g., Dante's use of the *contrapasso*, in which the punishment of the sinners in his *Inferno* is a customized result of each particular sin) but the *term* itself was coined by the 17th century English lawyer turned literary critic Thomas Rymer (1641–1713), his two professions combined perfectly in the coinage. Following the precepts of Aristotle, about whose *Poetics* Rymer wrote an extended treatise, he maintained that literature should be illustrative of moral precepts. Then, as now, "poetic justice" is at work when a person receives what he or she deserves: virtue is rewarded and vice punished, but the latter in a particularly appropriate or ironic way. In his discussion of the conflict between modern notions of justice and revenge, critic Paul A. Cantor observes that we have been taught to place our faith in "civic justice," which means that "our very notion of being civilized has been bound up with the need to renounce revenge" and that we associate the idea of vengeance with primitivism (*The Invisible Hand in Popular Culture: Liberty vs. Authority in American Film and TV* 32). Yet, as Cantor so convincingly points out, our continued and enduring approval of revenge tragedies—like John Ford's iconic film *The Searchers* (1956)—and, as this chapter shows, the unexpected success of the *Dirty Harry* franchise also demonstrates, "our sophisticated legal system can provide us with *civic* justice, but it cannot provide us with *poetic* justice, and we sense the gap between the two" (33). Revenge tragedies, ancient and modern, fulfill a human longing for "swift, direct, and personal vengeance" (33). This "gap" that Cantor identifies is the liminal space in which Harry—and his predecessors—finds his vocation in life.

In the *Dirty Harry* films, poetic justice takes the form of retributive justice, which so frequently contrasts with the idea of due process (or, as Cantor puts it, "civic" justice): it is appropriate, swift, and final, providing its audience with a cathartic experience, a vicarious release of emotion and the satisfaction of knowing that the principle of justice exists in art, if not always in life. As Cantor asserts, "Poetry must make up for the deficiencies of politics" (Cantor 33). It reinforces the value of moral rectitude, at any cost. Harry discerns the right and dispenses justice, of a particularly poetic kind, turning violence back on its perpetrators with razor-sharp irony: in *Magnum Force*, Briggs is blown up by the very explosive device with which he and his rookie vigilantes intended to silence Harry; at the climactic end of *The Enforcer*, Harry slays Bobby Maxwell with the LAW Rocket Bobby had stolen in order to terrorize the city. Likewise, the heavy, Mick, is grotesquely impaled on the phallic horn of a carousel unicorn at the end of *Sudden Impact*, a purely symbolic gesture that signifies his monstrous sexual crime, and closes out his story by giving him his just desserts. Finally, in *The Dead Pool*, Rook meets his end impaled by a harpoon gun, a commentary on his delusions of martyrdom. Poetic justice legitimizes Harry's actions, but it is important also to notice that Harry's moral code, his own sense of what is right and just, transcends the boundaries of class, race, gender, profession, and politics. Crime is crime, no matter who commits it: in *The Enforcer*, female members of the terrorist People's Revolutionary Strike Force meet the same violent end as their male compeers, and Inspector Kate Moore earns more respect than any of her male counterparts in the *Dirty Harry* films, even at the price of her own life. "People thought I was a right-wing fanatic," says Eastwood of the films, but "all Harry was doing was obeying a higher moral law," one that was blind to race, gender, and social position (quoted in *American Rebel: The Life of Clint Eastwood* 169). If Harry points his Magnum at a black bank robber, as he does in *Dirty Harry*, in *Magnum Force*, he develops an affectionate relationship with his black partner, Early Smith, and in *The Enforcer* he makes a pact with the black leader of the political group, Uhuru. The service to a higher moral imperative, the preservation of his own individuality, and the fact that he remains clear of domestic ties, are the two traits that tie Harry to the typology of the true knight and provide him with the liminal outlaw hero status that has won him a permanent place in the collective cultural imagination.

Chapter 6

"Now cracks a noble heart": Revenge Fantasy in the *Death Wish* Series (1974–1994)

At the conclusion of Shakespeare's revenge tragedy, *Hamlet*, the stage is littered with dead bodies, including that of the titular character. Forced to alienate or kill almost everyone close to him because both the ghost of his murdered father and tradition dictate that he must avenge this wrong, Hamlet accomplishes his objective and forfeits his own life. His loyal friend, Horatio, wishes to follow Hamlet in death, but Hamlet rejects this, insisting that Horatio remain alive to tell the story that will justify his actions and restore social order. Upon the death of the tragic hero, Horatio speaks movingly: "Now cracks a noble heart. Goodnight, sweet prince" (5.2.397). How to reconcile one's conscience to avenge the death of a loved one when there seems to be no other recourse is the problem Hamlet faces, resulting in retributive justice. *Hamlet* is a revenge tragedy because in it he is compelled to act based on a tradition of vengeance, but he must think for himself before he is willing to accomplish this justice.

"Vigilante" has become a loaded term that conjures up almost exclusively negative images: hooded figures, burning crosses, and lynch mobs, common features of the classic western, but also evocative of real life organizations like the Ku Klux Klan. Vigilantism represents some of the darker chapters in American history—acts of terrorism and cowardice committed by faceless individuals in the stealth of night. Ultimately derived from the Latin verb, "vigilare" (to be watchful) or the noun *vigilia* (a "vigil" being a period of devoted wakefulness, often with religious overtones), the term "vigilante" originated in mid– 19th century Spain and had no such negative connotations as those associated with it today; it simply meant "watchman," but became used in the United States to identify groups of citizens in the Old West who felt they had to protect themselves from criminal activity in a time and place where laws were not adequate or its representatives were neither able to protect the public nor maintain order. As we saw in the previous chapter, Lt. Briggs in *Magnum Force* proudly traced for Harry Callahan the roots of the vigilante rookie cop organization of which Briggs himself is the ringleader, back to the movement in San Francisco known as the "Committee of Vigilance," founded in the early 1850s to protect the town from a gang called the "Sydney Ducks" and its criminal constituents. Consisting of immigrants from Australian prison colonies who had come to the area to capitalize on the gold rush, this group introduced an element of crime to the Bay area. In response to this, citizens in San Francisco organized their own defense against the onslaught of crime, taking the law into their own hands by judging and executing those they deemed a threat.[1]

In the 20th century, with growing crime statistics in American urban areas, vigilante groups and individuals began to emerge, garnering media attention that sparked debate about their motives and rights to act. In New York City, on February 13, 1979, Curtis Sliwa founded the "Guardian Angels," a group of unarmed citizens who patrolled the New York subways in an attempt to help prevent muggings. They are recognized by their red berets, and represent a more positive side of "vigilantism," with community volunteers involved in crime prevention.[2] The famous "Subway Vigilante," Bernhard Goetz, who shot four black youths on December 22, 1984, sparked much debate about private citizens standing up to defend themselves, in defiance of the law, but he managed to enlist the sympathy of the jury at his criminal trial, being found not guilty of the shootings because of self-defense, and being charged only with carrying an unlicensed weapon. Subsequently, Goetz became something of a celebrity—albeit, in part, as a self-parody—appearing on talk shows, running for mayor of New York City, and being cast as a criminologist in a 2002 film, *Every Move You Make*.[3]

Five years before the formation of the Guardian Angels and a full decade before the notoriety of the Goetz shootings (both occurring in New York City), an influential film, *Death Wish* (1974)—popular enough to inspire four sequels—addressed escalating urban street crime and raised the issue of vigilantism as a response to the threat of violent criminal activity in the city. The time was ripe to address the law's inadequacy to protect private citizens in the "urban jungle," compounded by what was sometimes seen as the obfuscation of justice and an over-emphasis on due process for criminal suspects. While the *Dirty Harry* films, through the 1970s and 1980s, portrayed a police inspector who walked the line between his own moral imperatives and those of the law he was appointed to represent, often clashing with legal authorities, another urban western sequence, *Death Wish*, presented a private citizen with liberal, even pacifist leanings, who is driven to become a vigilante, hunting predators on the street and ridding the public of their threat. He breaks the law by carrying a weapon he has not registered, provoking criminals to accost him and then shooting them. But what makes him a liminal hero, rather than an outlaw hero, is that the legal authorities, when they become aware of his identity, refuse to arrest him, fearing he will be martyred if they do, but also with the tacit recognition that he can achieve what they cannot—a radical decline in muggings. Moreover, this hero is motivated initially by revenge of a very personal nature, but with a growing understanding of the larger social problem, he also attempts to ignite the public into action by serving as an example of how average citizens must shake free of passive acceptance and apathy, and stand up for their own right to live without fear, even in the crowded landscapes of New York City and Los Angeles. Therefore, one is tempted to think that in the case of groups like the Guardian Angels, and the actions of an individual like Bernhard Goetz, life and art coincide, *Death Wish* serving as an *imagining of justice and order* accomplished through the actions of citizens as a response to an inadequate legal deterrent to crime.

Death Wish (1974): The War Zone in the Oneiric City

> PAUL: "Cut and run, huh? What about the old American social custom of self-defense?"
> JACK: "We're not pioneers anymore, dad."
> PAUL: "What are we, Jack?"
> JACK: "What do you mean?"
> PAUL: "I mean, if we're not pioneers, what have we become? What do you call people who, when they're faced with a condition of fear, do nothing about it, they just run and hide?
> JACK: "Civilized?"
> PAUL: "No."

Paul Kersey, at the beginning of the first *Death Wish* film, is a lucky man. He is happily married and vacationing with his wife in Hawaii, a luxury his career as an architect with a large New York City firm affords them. He lives in a spacious, upscale apartment, has an adult daughter who is wed to a successful lawyer, and is surrounded by affluent friends and associates. By the end of the film, Paul is loner and a cunning persecutor of crime. His character resonated with audiences and has continued to do so for decades. Like the first

Dirty Harry, *Death Wish* met with critical disdain and popular acclaim. To understand how and why Paul Kersey became an iconic figure in American culture, we must begin with a brief discussion of the genesis of the *Death Wish* series, a 1972 novel of the same name (promoted as a "thriller"), written by Brian Garfield.

The idea for the novel originated in two incidents from Garfield's own life experiences. First, his wife's purse was stolen on a subway; in addition, on a winter night in 1971, Garfield was at a party in New York City and upon leaving, discovered that the top of his convertible had been senselessly slashed, only one small item having been taken from the car. Garfield felt such anger in response to this latter episode that he began to think about "a man who enters that moment of rage and never emerges from it" (Paul Talbot, *Bronson's Loose: The Making of the 'Death Wish' Films* 1).

The resulting novel is about a middle-aged New York City accountant named Paul Benjamin who is forced into that state of bewildered rage when his wife Esther and daughter Carol are attacked in the Benjamin apartment by three hoods who have gained entrance under the pretense of delivering groceries, having been allowed in by Esther. The brutal beating leaves Esther dead and Carol in a traumatized catatonic state. The hoods apparently intended robbery but when they discovered that the women had very little cash they flew into a murderous rage, aggravated by probable drug abuse, evinced by Carol's later recollection of their manic behavior, and that "they never stopped laughing" (Garfield 32). The detective in charge of the case, Lieutenant Briggs (the same name that is used for two different officers in the *Dirty Harry* films), and Paul's son-in-law, Jack, acknowledge that there is very little chance the criminals will ever be caught. "They're never found, these animals, are they?" Paul asks of the policeman who was at the scene, to which he can only reply, "They're doing everything they can" (22). At the opening of the novel, in a conversation with his friend and professional associate, Sam, about crime and the suffocating atmosphere of urban life, Paul is shown to be a civic minded liberal; Sam even says to him, "You're a Goddamned bleeding heart, Paul" (9). Paul's liberalism, his belief that crimes are the result of inequitable social circumstances that can be improved to prevent them, and that they are things that only happen in the abstract—to someone else—is suddenly turned upside down. After Esther's funeral and Carol's slippage from shock into catatonia, Paul "had to get used to an entire new universe of reality" (47) and has to rethink all of his assumptions about the world and his role in it. Embittered, feeling helpless because the perpetrators will never be caught, and trying to live with pent-up rage, he tells Sam, "A liberal is a guy who walks out of the room when the fight starts" (63).

Trying to cope with this violent intrusion into his life, Paul becomes nocturnal, unable to sleep, unable to find any distraction that will allow him to pick up the pieces of his shattered life. One night, watching a western on TV, Paul comes to the realization that the reason why that genre enjoyed such success is because the western embodied a timeless, eternal truth. He understands that "the hero in every myth was the hero who defended the farmers against raiders on horseback, and the constant contradiction was that the hero himself was always on horseback" (87). This moment in the novel affords a two-fold *dianoia* for Paul. First, he sees a historical continuity: the hero can be a figure in the Old West, or a medieval Robin Hood, and the villains can be cattlemen who wish to drive off farmers, or they can be ancient Romans or Huns. Even more important is what he recognizes, established in this excerpt, about the nature of a mythic hero—he defends the innocent in part by taking on certain features of the villain. The hero that defends farmers against aggressive cattlemen on horseback is himself on horseback. This is the story of *Shane*, the gunfighter who drives out another gunfighter and frees the community of homesteading farmers from the menacing influence of the greedy cattle mogul. He is a liminal outlaw hero, with whom Paul sympathizes. As Paul thinks about this, he tells himself wryly that there have been no TV series about Gandhi, perhaps his earlier hero, but only about cowboys and detectives, concluding, "The only match for a gun was a gun of your own" (88). This realization occurs after he has already begun to arm himself, having warded off a would-be mugger by hitting him with a sock that contained two rolls of quarters, an empowering experience that left Paul exhilarated, but on reflection also frightened (82–83).

Paul acquires his weapon in a gun shop, .32-caliber Smith & Wesson revolver, when he is sent to Arizona by his firm to examine the books of a company for a business transaction. When he returns to New York and learns that Carol's condition has worsened and she must be institutionalized, Paul becomes a predator and begins to court danger, frequenting high crime areas in his nocturnal wanderings, in the hopes of encountering criminals. He first kills a junkie who tries to rob him (120), and soon after another criminal who is in the process of robbing a drunk asleep on a park bench (125–126). He continues his efforts to entrap criminals, baiting a group of hoods who vandalize cars by staging a scene in which he has to leave a vehicle—a rental—because he has run out of gas, and then waiting in the shadows to perform his swift and violent act of judgment on the them. Although they are described as "two thin boys," their dismantling of the car is "very professional," and Paul coolly shoots and kills both of them (131). Not long after, Paul kills a man climbing down a fire escape with a stolen television in his possession (132). This is when the media begin to notice the crimes and report on a street vigilante (133), which also attracts the attention of Deputy Inspector Frank Ochoa, who notices that all were shot with the same caliber gun. Ochoa surmises that the vigilante is seeking revenge; he also begins to form a more detailed profile of the street killer.

As the media and the police bring the case to higher visibility, Paul becomes more cunning, but also more jaded and more convinced that what he is doing is necessary and right. He does not think he will be caught, as his "campaign" is rational, not compulsive like a true psychotic's, and he holds the conviction that while what he is doing is extreme, it is also right, and only the "insane norms of society" make his actions appear abnormal. Paul begins to see himself as a role model, a hero who can affect change by challenging the apathy and evil in a world gone mad (135). When he attends an anniversary party at Sam's house, Paul is bored and disgusted with the behavior and small talk of the guests, and he retreats into the bathroom to escape the crowd. There, he reads a lengthy article in *New York* magazine, "The Vigilante: A Psychiatrist's Profile," about himself. The psychiatrist reasons that the vigilante they are seeking appeals to Americans because he fits the mythology of the "rugged individualist" who is "acting out fantasies" everyone shares, doing so because he is less inhibited than most people (142–143). He has tried the justice system and found it inadequate (146), and has a sincere desire to improve society by getting criminals off the streets (147). It may have begun with revenge and frustration, but because the vigilante probably was once both idealistic and liberal, his intentions have become, in a twisted way, altruistic. Paul realizes that this analysis is very close to the truth.

He begins to have hope that the example he has set is enough to effect improvement in the community of his native New York City, a city he loves and does not wish to abandon in favor of a less stressful suburban residence. Policemen begin to applaud the vigilante, and copycat acts of gunned-down criminals (one with a different caliber weapon than Paul's), make him think that others are following his example. Again, Paul compares himself to a hero in a western, wondering if he can finally hang up his guns, but he reasons that unlike a western movie, crime in real life has no end, and he can't retire from his nocturnal crusade (153). In the final episode of the novel, Paul sets out to put an end to "a vicious and dangerous" game (155) that he has heard about; he stalks and then attacks a group of youth who have positioned themselves on a rooftop waiting for a passenger train on which they drop heavy missiles of brick and chunks of cement. These crash on top of and into the windows of the train, injuring its passengers, a senseless and terrible act. Paul kills all three boys involved, while a girl escapes, but he is sure she has not seen his face. He begins to collect the cartridge cases from the scene, and suddenly sees a cop. Refusing to shoot a policeman, Paul stands frozen, waiting to be arrested. Instead, the cop removes his hat in an act of *homage*, turns his back to Paul, and stands still, a signal of approbation and a message for him to flee. As he leaves the scene, Paul looks back to see the policeman in the same frozen position (158–159), in complicity with this street justice the officer has just witnessed.

Brian Garfield sold the rights to his novel to two music and film producers who had worked with big names like the Mamas and the Papas, Steppenwolf, and Three Dog Night, and who had recently also produced Johnny Cash's *The Gospel Road* (1973). Garfield recalls that Hal Landers and Bobby Roberts purchased rights to *Death Wish* and another work of his, *Relentless*, and offered him the chance to write the screenplay for either of the two. Garfield chose the latter because he thought *Death Wish* would not adapt well to the film genre: "The whole book takes place inside the character's mind and emotions" (quoted in Talbot 3). Instead, veteran screenwriter Wendell Mayes composed the screenplay. Mayes had been nominated for an Oscar for his screenplay of *Anatomy of a Murder* (1959) for which he won the New York Film Critics Circle Award and had, more recently, co-written with Stirling Silliphant the screenplay for *The Poseidon Adventure* (1972). (Silliphant teamed up with Dean Riesner soon after to compose the script for *The Enforcer*, as discussed in the previous chapter.)

The most important production choice, however, was the selection of British director Michael Winner, because with him came the lead actor, Charles Bronson. Winner and Bronson had made three films together: *Chato's Land* (1972), *The Mechanic* (1972), and *The Stone Killer* (1973), so they were a compatible team, much like Clint Eastwood and Don Siegel, who launched the *Dirty Harry* franchise. Winner, born on October 30, 1935, enjoyed the advantages of an affluent British family. In his autobiography, Winner states that he entered Cambridge University at age 17 and graduated with an "Honors Degree in Law and Economics" at the age of 20 (*Winner Takes All: A Life of Sorts* 47), but he went on to pursue his true interests as a writer and eventually a film director. His privileged background could not have stood in greater contrast to that of Charles Bronson (born as Charles Dennis Buchinsky on November 3, 1921), the ninth child and seventh son of fifteen children, according to his wife, actress Jill Ireland (*Life Wish* 12). Bronson's father was a Lithuanian who immigrated to America in 1906 and worked as a coal miner in Ehrenfeld, Pennsylvania, until his death from the dreaded black lung disease in 1933. Growing up in poverty few can understand,[4] Bronson was the first in his family to graduate high school and also worked in the mines until he was drafted in 1943 (Michael R. Pitts, *Charles Bronson: The 95 Films and 156 Television Appearances* 1). In Guam, he was a tail-gunner on sixteen missions. After the war, according to Jerry Vermilye, he first attended Hussian Art School on the GI bill, then pursued his interest in theatre and acting in both Philadelphia and New York (he shared a room with Jack Klugman in Harlem), moving to Hollywood to start a career as a film actor in the early 1950s, beginning with minor television and film roles (*The Films of Charles Bronson* 14). According to an article in *The Lithuania Tribune*, it was in 1954 that he changed his surname from Buchinsky to Bronson apparently because it sounded too Russian during the witch-hunt years of the McCarthy Era in Hollywood (www.lithuaniatribune.com/27386/a-classic-migrant-success-story-charles-bronson-201327386). In the 1960s, Bronson's career advanced with supporting roles in important films like *The Magnificent Seven* (1960) and *The Dirty Dozen* (1967). A memorable part was in Sergio Leone's epoch-making western *Once Upon a Time in the West* (1968) in which Bronson was cast opposite Henry Fonda, who himself played the villain against type. Followed by his work with Winner in the early 1970s, Bronson achieved stardom from very humble origins.

When Winner read the script for *Death Wish*, he immediately wanted to make it, but United Artists objected on grounds that it was impossible to market a film that featured as its hero a vigilante, to which Winner replied, "It happens in westerns all the time." Studio heads thought a modern film in which "a citizen kills citizens" was doomed to failure, and that the role of a white-collar vigilante was "uncastable" (Talbot 4). Winner finally found an independent backer, Dino De Laurentiis (with whom he had also worked for *The Stone Killer*), who was willing to finance the film, and with some changes to make the main character more compatible with Bronson's image, persuaded Bronson to play the lead role, even though Bronson's agent also had doubts about whether the film would be a good career move for the actor because of its controversial content (Talbot 8). It was also Winner who brought on board Herbie Hancock to score and perform the music for the film. Winner was dating an actress from *Sesame Street*, Sonia Monzano (who also plays the supermarket check-out girl in *Death Wish*), and she urged Winner to listen to Hancock's recent release, *Headhunters* (1973), which had gone platinum. When Winner heard it, he knew he had the composer he wanted, even though De Laurentiis urged him to hire "a cheap band" (Winner 201).

When supporting cast and crew were in place, the film was shot on location in thirty-nine days in the winter of 1974, under budget and on schedule (Talbot 10) and premiered in front of cheering crowds on July 24, 1974, in New York City. Against all odds, a new icon had been born. Dino De Laurentiis said in an interview that making a successful film is like mixing a good drink— if you combine an able producer, a talented writer, a good director, appropriate cast and competent crew and let them do their jobs, the end result will be a hit, evinced by the approbation of an audience that feels it was entertained for the price of a ticket (Talbot 12). This formula explains how an unremarkable novel was transformed into a blockbuster film franchise that has earned a permanent place in American cinema.

First, some important changes in character and story were introduced in transforming the literary work into a screenplay. The most significant perhaps are those alterations to the novel's protagonist. Paul Benjamin, the middle-aged cerebral accountant, becomes Paul Kersey, an architect, with Bronson's rugged face and virile physique working in tandem with his white-collar profession and sophisticated liberal politics. In the novel, Paul served in World War II in non-combat, but in the film he is a veteran of the Korean War, having served as a conscientious objector. When Paul visits a prospective Tucson client, Ames Jainchill (Stuart Margolin), we learn that he has become a pacifist because his father, who loved guns, was killed in a deer-hunting accident; Paul's mother, like Marion Starett in *Shane*, believed the world would be better off without guns, and after his father's death, Paul ascribed also to that philosophy. The other characters are similar to those in the novel, although Paul's wife's name is changed from Esther to Joanna (Hope Lange).

Some key scenes have been added or altered as well, the most important being that of the attack in the Kersey apartment. In the novel, the two women are brutally beaten, but Carol (Kathleen Tolan) is not raped, or at least that is not explicitly stated (she does exhibit signs of rape victim trauma, however, retreating further into her own private thoughts, refusing to eat, and not wanting to be touched by anyone). The film version includes the violent gang rape of Carol by three "freaks" (Jeff Goldblum, Christopher Logan, and Gregory Rozakis) seen mostly from the point of view of her moribund mother, Joanna. The rape, along with the spray-painting of Carol's body, adds to the revolting nature of this scene, increasing the audience's sympathy for the victims and providing a stronger motive for Paul's eventual transformation. After the incident, he has the same difficulty adjusting to this sudden turn in his life and beliefs, as does his counterpart in the novel. One scene added to the film is when Paul looks out of his apartment window one night and sees a car being vandalized by hoods. He simply pulls down the shade and turns his back on it, indicative of his initial apathy, and in contrast to the active intervention he will soon adopt. Turning his back to crime serves as a contrastive prelude to the transformation of his character.[5]

Another altered and expanded scene adds a richer dimension also to Paul's character when he is sent by his firm to Arizona to develop a project for the wealthy landowner, Ames Jainchill. This episode in the novel is used only as a means by which Paul, in cruising a Tucson street, happens to spy a gun-shop where he procures his weapon, being able to do so with some anonymity and with greater ease than in New York. In the film, the likeable cowboy mogul, Jainchill, takes Paul to a famous movie set, "Old Tucson," where they witness a re-enactment from a classic western in which a marshal engages in a gunfight with three villains. Bystanders from the town look on, cheering as the lawman defeats each one. This counters the apathy toward crime that typifies that of contemporary New Yorkers, and good clearly overcomes evil. An announcer underscores the lesson of this mythic Old West scene—while outlaws thought they could escape justice, there were "honest men, with dreams, who would fight them—and would plant the roots that would grow into a nation." The ethos of the past, in which justice was direct, swift, and final, gaining the approval of citizens, deeply affects the still-grieving Paul. This scene also makes explicit the fact that *Death Wish*—an urban western—consciously invokes the intertextual frames of the classic western genre, here in the form of the showdown on main street between the representative defender of the town (the marshal) and the disruptive villains.[6]

In this expanded Arizona episode, the film also contains the important dialogue with Jainchill about how Paul became a pacifist, discussed above. This occurs when Jainchill takes Paul to a gun club for dinner. Showing Paul his impressive collection of antique weapons, Jainchill first asserts to Paul, "A gun is just a tool," echoing Shane's remark to Marion Starett. Jainchill continues, "This is gun country. Unlike your city we can walk our streets and through our parks at night and feel safe. Muggers operatin' out here just plain get their asses blown up." When Paul wields an antique gun that Jainchill claims "belonged to Candy Dan in 1890" and hits the target dead on, Jainchill is impressed, but Paul also begins to feel empowered. In a rare moment of genuine communication with another person in the film, Paul confides, "I grew up around guns," then continues to tell the story of his father's accidental death and his mother's understandable opposition to guns. But Paul likes the feel of the gun, and Jainchill likes Paul, who has faithfully designed Jainchill's vision of a development project that would respect his wishes for the preservation of the open spaces of the old west, so he gives Paul "a little goin' away present" that Paul does not unwrap until he arrives back in his apartment—the gun he will use in the future. Thus far, Paul has only experimented with self-defense by warding off a mugger with the two rolls of quarters in a sock (as in the novel), but this is about to change.

He returns to New York, learns that Carol's condition has worsened and the police have no leads about those responsible for the attack. Paul happens to view the photos of his wife that he took in Hawaii on their vacation in the opening sequence, and unwraps Jainchill's gift, an antique gun. This is the decisive moment in the film—Paul is ready to become the liminal outlaw hero in

"Read about Vigilantism this week" is the message on the billboard behind the mild-mannered "bleeding-heart liberal" Paul Kersey (Charles Bronson), who turned rogue after the murder of his wife and rape of his daughter. His nocturnal escapades attracted the attention of the media, public, and authorities in Paramount's *Death Wish* (1974) (Jerry Ohlinger's Movie Materials Store).

the form of a street vigilante. It is also the point at which, as Christopher Sorrentino argues, Paul Kersey and Charles Bronson become indistinguishable (*Death Wish* 53), the actor drawing heavily on his own personality and experiences for his onscreen persona. When asked how he prepared for the part of Paul Kersey, Bronson corroborates this assertion: "to play him, I draw upon my own feelings. I do believe I could perform this way myself."[7] The Arizona episode functions something like a reverse *Coogan's Bluff* (1968) in which the Arizona deputy sheriff Coogan (Clint Eastwood) is the "fish out of water" figure in New York City and comes into conflict with the prescribed due process of a legal system to which he must eventually adhere to complete his task of extraditing his prisoner. Here, the city slicker, Paul Kersey, when he visits Arizona, is exposed to a belief system that is evocative of the justice of the old west.

Two other significant changes of the film are shown in its second half, once Paul returns from his trip. In the novel, Paul's victims number eight: a junkie who tries to rob him, a thief who tries to rob a drunk asleep on a park bench, two youths stripping a car, a man on a fire escape absconding with a television set, and three youths dropping cement chunks onto the roof of a passenger train. In the film, the first kill is virtually identical to that in the novel: Paul is confronted by a junkie with a knife who demands money, and shoots him dead, after which he returns to his apartment and vomits. After that episode, the scenarios in the film are different than those in the novel. Paul's second vigilante encounter occurs when he sees three thugs attacking a helpless man in an alley. When they notice Paul watching, they approach him menacingly and Paul shoots all three. The man they were attacking, whom Paul has rescued, sees Paul clearly, but when the detective, Deputy Inspector Frank Ochoa (Vincent Gardenia), questions him, he refuses to provide any details about his rescuer's appearance, already suggesting public support for Paul's actions. The third episode occurs in a subway at night; Paul is alone in a car when two hoods approach him as he sits with a bag of groceries next to him, reading a newspaper, and waiting for an opportunity to use his gun. When one of the two pulls a knife on Paul, he shoots them both, but narrowly escapes authorities, having to leave his grocery bag behind. The location of the neighborhood supermarket, where Paul purchased the groceries, provides a clue for Frank Ochoa, who begins his hunt for the street vigilante. Ochoa surmises that Paul may have been riding the subway for hours to bait his victims.

The fourth episode makes clear that Paul has begun to actually lure criminals. He selects a diner populated with hookers and other unsavory characters, and then flashes a large roll of cash as he pays his bill. Two black men take the bait and follow Paul down into the subway station. They produce knives, face Paul, and say, "Let's see the money, man," to which Paul replies quietly but assertively, "You'll have to take it." He kills them both, but one of them wounds him on the shoulder, and lives long enough to tell police, "I cut that motherfucker." This provides Ochoa with more evidence about the vigilante's identity when he compares the blood on the knife with a bloody bandage that he later finds in Paul's apartment, but which he attained illegally, having entered without a search warrant. The fifth and final portrayal occurs when he is walking alone at night and is confronted by two hoods as he begins to descend a set of stairs. Behind him is another, Paul being surrounded and outnumbered. He shoots them, but one shoots Paul in the leg, wounding him. The police arrive at the scene and Paul is taken away in an ambulance, in preparation for the film's conclusion, which departs considerably from that of the novel. In the film, then, Paul's death count is ten, with one escaping in the final showdown, as opposed to eight in the novel, not a radical difference in number, but in the configuration of his victims and where he encounters them: in the novel, two incidents involve very young victims, the "two thin boys" who are only stripping a car, and the victims who are dropping debris on the passing passenger train are described as "teenage boys" and one girl (Garfield 155), but in the film all are at least of adult age, and in every case they pose an immediate threat to Paul, wielding weapons, which is not the case in the novel. Clearly, these changes are intended to eliminate negative views of Paul as someone who kills under-aged victims, or those who are vandalizing property but not directly threatening lives.

Another significant difference between the novel and film is their conclusion. In the final chapter of the novel, as discussed earlier, a cop who witnesses Paul's slaying of the teens who are dropping debris on a passing train removes his hat and turns his back, allowing Paul to escape the scene. This suggests not only police complicity but even that Paul has earned the respect of the street policemen, despite the fact that Deputy Inspector Frank Ochoa has been assigned the task of "the vigilante case" (133) and takes this seriously. The media have made Paul a celebrity, and a prominent psychiatrist has developed a lengthy (and even sympathetic) profile of the vigilante killer (Garfield 142–150). By contrast, the second half of the film consists of a cat-and-mouse game between Paul and Frank Ochoa, who himself is the one that develops the profile of the killer, using his sharp detective skills to do it. When he finally narrows the pool of suspects and zeros in on Paul, he takes his evidence to the district attorney (Fred Scollay) and the police commissioner (Stephen Elliott) who tell him flatly, "We don't want him." Earlier, during a press conference, they had publicly denied that muggings in the city had decreased since the vigilante killings started, but privately to Ochoa they admit that the statistics are dramatically lower, from "950 to 450" per week. Their reasoning is that they have to keep this information quiet because they fear it could create more vigilantes, and they instruct Frank to make the killer desist, and leave town. They do not want him arrested for fear of making a "martyr" of him. Frank says, "I'll try to scare him, but that's as far as I'll go," and the commissioner tells him, "That's right, Frank. Scare him off." Frank makes an anonymous phone call to Paul telling him he is being watched; he tries other dubious tactics to frighten Paul into fleeing the city as the second half of the film unfolds.

Paul easily eludes the surveillance he is placed under, and it is only when his fifth vigilante encounter goes awry, wounding him in the leg, that he is caught. Ochoa interviews the cop who had arrived first at the scene of Paul's injury, confiscating Paul's gun from the officer, and instructing him, "You never saw it." Ochoa tells the officer, Patrolman Reilly (Christopher Guest), not to enter the gun in his report; he then asks the patrolman his name, telling him he will remember it, obviously to repay the favor in the future. Next, Ochoa visits the hospital where Paul has been taken for treatment. He brings the gun, castigates Paul for his refusal to dispose of the weapon and desist from his vigilante activity, having been given the opportunity to do so. "Get a transfer, and I'll drop this gun in the river," he instructs Paul. "We want you to get out of New York permanently," which prompts Paul to respond using a western film cliché: "By sundown?" In the film's final scene, Paul has been transferred to Chicago and is greeted by a new colleague in Union Station. The first thing Paul notices is a young woman being harassed by three freaks, and he runs to her rescue. The three turn to taunt Paul from a distance, but the last shot shows a close-up of Paul, facing them, with his finger cocked as though he is pointing a gun at them. At the time of its release, no one could have anticipated how popular the film would be and therefore this could not have been for the purpose of setting up a sequel, although, as it worked out, it was a perfect way to do so; rather, it indicates Paul's conviction that what he is doing is right, and that he will continue his one-man fight against crime, no matter what city he calls home. What is audacious about the film is the gamble it takes, at Winner's insistence, in suggesting that Paul feels vindicated in his fight against crime, even that he enjoys it, as the smile on his face in the last shot suggests.[8]

The police never apprehend the three freaks that murder Joanna and traumatize Carol, nor does Paul ever encounter them in the film. Thus, when he begins his crusade against crime, the perpetrators who incur his wrath are surrogates. Paul starts from the very personal motive of revenge and the rage of helplessness against a senseless, faceless crime. It seems particularly significant that the crime occurs inside the Kersey apartment, the home being the archetypal place of both intimacy and security—a sacred and inviolate sanctuary, defiled by murder, rape, and vandalism. Paul returns to live there even after the crime occurs, although he paints the walls a wild, vibrant orange and begins to play jazz music in an effort to buoy himself up, but also as a reflection of his rejuvenation of spirit once he begins to take victims. The question implicitly posed to the audience is "What would you wish to do if you were Paul Kersey?" It would be natural to want to avenge the violent, unmotivated murder and rape of loved ones; at the very least, one would want to see "justice" done by having the criminals apprehended, tried, and incarcerated. But in this case—and others in a city teeming with crime—the police are often ineffective. Paul cannot continue to live with the tension between his pent-up rage and the recognition of the fact that this violation against his family will go unanswered if he doesn't act. *Death Wish* is not a distortion of reality, something that critics who savaged the film upon its release (and have continued to do) fail to recognize; instead, as Sorrentino maintains, it is a revenge fantasy.

From the date of its release many—although certainly not all—critics have descried *Death Wish* as a dangerous right-wing vigilante film, even though it struck a chord with audiences. One of the producers, Bobby Roberts, was in the theatre that offered a preview, and observed that viewers stood up and cheered when the first shooting occurred (Talbot 18). Winner also remembers this opening success (202). Its estimated budget was $3 million, but its domestic gross alone was $22 million (www.imdb.com).

Several critics did notice that *Death Wish* is an urban western, drawing on the tropes and motifs common to the classic western genre. In *Films in Review*, Ted Zehender calls the film "an eastern western," that is "decked out in modern trappings and set down, cozily, in the Tombstone Gulches of NYC" (quoted in Pitts 63). Rex Reed, in the *New York Daily News*, said *Death Wish* left him "rhapsodizing in its vicarious sense of urban justice" (quoted in Winner 203), and Judith Crist in *New York Magazine* observed that with "bristling topicality" the film provides "more Aristotelian purgation for the beleaguered city than a monthful of Lone Rangers or a legion of Shanes in our innocent Western-oriented past" (quoted in Pitts 63).

In his *New York Times* review, Vincent Canby wrote an invective against the film (followed by others) that condemned it for its violence and lack of realism. This issue is addressed by the best discussion of the discrepancy between critical and public reception of *Death Wish* in Christopher Sorrentino's study of the same title. In his first chapter, "*Death Wish* and the City," he maintains, "The premise that the film was a dangerous lie depended on its establishment as an attempted representation of reality" while in fact it is "a *fantasy*" a fiction (*Death Wish* 11). The director, Michael Winner, used location shots, but Sorrentino asserts that this does not mean the director was aiming at a "realistic" portrayal of crime and the city. He only uses it "as the sinister backdrop for a series of mythical confrontations" (16). Paul becomes convinced that he has a right, and even an obligation, to resort to violence because he is operating in accord with a higher moral imperative, a belief that we have identified as an essential feature of Kennedy's true knight, and that we have seen consistently in our exploration of the liminal outlaw hero in both disguised and classic westerns. Sorrentino avers that the city's administration, which wants to be rid of Paul without making a "martyr" of him, plays the role of Creon to Paul's Antigone, Sophocles' play exploring the conflict between an individual's "obligation to the state and its laws and the need to answer to a higher more 'natural' law" (24). The media, Sorrentino continues, acts like the Chorus in a Greek tragedy, voicing for the larger populace the approbation of Paul's vigilantism. Indeed, the film is saturated with media attention about Paul's actions: billboards such as an advertisement for an issue of *Harpers* which reads, "Frontier Justice in the Streets: Rising Vigilantism," live television broadcast interviews with those who have followed Paul's example, and the countless magazines and print articles on Paul's end table that feature his escapades.

The atmosphere of *Death Wish* has a decided oneiric quality, and is misjudged if viewed as an attempt to manipulate its audience by presenting a "realistic" but distorted picture of the city, a deliberate and therefore propagandistic lie (Sorrentino 10). Such a view, Sorrentino maintains, naturally diminishes its artistry. Further, the objections to Paul Kersey's vengeance are in large part due to this misreading of the film's intent in presenting urban crime. If the story had not been cast as a contemporary urban western, but had instead "explicitly foregrounded the fantasy elements," alternately setting it in a near dystopian future as a survival story, like *Escape From New York* (1981), or in the past in the "Hollywood West whose myth it expressly quotes," it would have been far more difficult to level charges that it should be dismissed as right-wing propaganda (Sorrentino 10).

If the New York of the film is presented with a disregard or deliberate distortion of the "real" city, the other two urban areas in *Death Wish* are treated the same way, each representing a mythology that helps us understand the story. For instance, the opening shot of the film is on a secluded beach in Hawaii, seen through the lens of Paul's camera as he snaps photos of Joanna, an idyllic second honeymoon. In fact the place is so beautiful and isolated that Paul suggests they have sex right on the beach, but Joanna avers they are too "civilized" for this. Paul responds, "I remember when we weren't," but he capitulates and they return to their hotel for their intimacy. Hawaii is paradise for these two city dwellers, evocative of an idealized past for them and the world, and it is little wonder that they do not wish to return to New York. The other urban scape is that of Tucson, Arizona. Paul is sent to negotiate plans for an ecologically innovative urban development that would respect open space and incorporate a vanishing way of life, the vision of Ames Jainchill, a cowboy millionaire. In the scene discussed at length earlier, we will remember that Jainchill characterizes Tucson as the epitome of law and order, a place where citizens "can walk our streets and through our parks at night and feel safe" because "this is gun country." Justice is swift and immediate to would-be criminals because, like the past represented by the "Old Tucson" movie set, guns are still used properly, as deterrents to crime.

Neither the idyllic serenity and under-populated beach of Hawaii nor the virtually crime-free Tucson streets and parks as depicted in *Death Wish* are rooted in the actual conditions of those urban areas. Crime rates in Hawaii and Tucson at the time the film was made were "roughly comparable per 100,000 population" to those of New York City, according to John Shelton Lawrence and Robert Jewett in their book *The Myth of the American Superhero* (114). Yet Hawaii is presented as an escape from an urban "war zone," and the fetters of "civilization," and is representative of a personal and cultural past. Likewise, Tucson embodies both an idealized past and a utopian future—the "Old Tucson" movie set portrays a moment in history when justice, law, and citizens worked together to deter crime, the present Tucson offers the security of a city governed by its lenient policies about guns, and the urban development Paul plans under Jainchill's vision presents a future that preserves the past, a blend of the urban and rural. These are important archetypal representations for understanding Paul's character in *Death Wish*, and how he becomes transformed in an equally mythic New York setting.

To understand fully the mythic confrontations that prompt the change in Paul's character but which also show how the film operates as a revenge *fantasy* (a "wish") it is important to understand that there are two New York cities that coexist in the story, one above ground and the other the subterranean realm that becomes Paul's hunting ground for criminals, a point that Sorrentino discusses in detail. In an ordinary routine day, it is almost certain that Joanna and Carol would have never encountered the freaks that shatter their lives, because they know and obey the tacit rules about safe borders. (As mentioned earlier, what is particularly nightmarish about the attack on the women is that it occurs inside their home.) The freaks have violated the implicit boundary of the quotidian life of New York's citizens, and Paul, likewise, has to enter into their subterranean, mostly nocturnal realm of subways, alleys, and abandoned park pathways in order to find his victims, a domain that Sorrentino calls "the cave into which predators can crawl" (26–27).

Since the freaks violate the tacit rules about both spatial and behavioral boundaries, crossing over into and violating a world where order is an ideal, so Paul also deliberately transgresses the imaginary boundary that separates these worlds, himself becoming a predator in the predator's terrain. Had Joanna and Carol been attacked because they wandered into this subterranean world, we would have a different film than one in which the freaks violate the implicit rules and Paul is then "obliged to track the cave-dwellers down where they live to restore order" (Sorrentino 27). But of course he does not track down the particular criminals responsible for his personal tragedy; instead, Paul has to settle the score by acting out a fiction that restores order in a world where the law is found incapable of doing so. When Paul enters the outlaw territory populated by street criminals, he acts as a liminal hero, accomplishing what the law cannot achieve, earning the approbation of the public, and even inspiring others to emulate him. He watches with interest television reports that imitate his fight against crime, and reads several newspapers and magazines for the same reason. To serve as a role model for others to emulate reinforces Paul's conviction that he has a right to pursue and punish those who would victimize him and others.

Despite the fact that the community enters into a "remote communion" with Paul Kersey (Sorrentino 24) one feature that identifies him as the liminal outlaw hero is his solitude. He converses with his colleagues, confides in Jainchill about his past, and argues about the politics of justice with his attorney son-in-law, Jack (Steven Keats), but Paul is seen almost always alone—and contentedly so—reading or watching television in his apartment, or in his solitary, nocturnal wanderings in search of a criminal. In addition to his statement "I don't have any friends, and I don't want any friends" (quoted in footnote 6), Bronson said in the same interview with Roger Ebert at the time *Death Wish* was being filmed, "I'm entertained more by my own thoughts than by the thoughts of others." Moreover, Paul's vigilantism is itself a type of disguise, like the vigilante prototype, the Lone Ranger (discussed in Chapter 4), who also began his crusade for justice motivated by revenge (Paul has no mask, but has to make sure he shoots to kill those victims who might identify him). Necessarily, this type of hero is nearly always a loner: the *errant* knight, the itinerant gunfighter, the police inspector who searches where no one else looks in order to apprehend to a criminal.

Most important, Paul is an independent thinker who answers to an authority that is his own, positioned in this case between a law enforcement that at best means well but cannot always, or even often, defend its citizens, and at its worst deliberately violates the law (Ochoa's illegal search of Paul's apartment and later his cover up of Paul's vigilantism, throwing his gun in the river instead of arresting him) and an urgent need to claim personal satisfaction by seeing that justice is served and order is restored, even through violence. Paul Kersey discovers in his vigilantism, first motivated by paralyzing anger and a need for revenge, a vocation. Through this act of violence against him and his family, Paul is forced to reassess all of his former assumptions about himself in relation to his world. He finds that he is not only capable of answering this violence, but that he is rejuvenated by it, and the end of the film makes clear that, although he has been "run out of Dodge," so to speak, he has no intention of relinquishing his new calling.

To that end, the other condition of the liminal outlaw hero is also a key feature of this and the ensuing *Death Wish* films, as we shall see: through Joanna's death, terrible as it is, and Carol's seemingly permanent trauma, Paul suddenly finds himself free of domestic obligations. At first he finds this, naturally, a difficult adjustment, but when he no longer needs to worry about the safety and well-being of his wife and daughter, Paul is transformed (indicated by the vibrant orange he paints his apartment, the jazz records that he plays loudly in his living room, and the freedom to make eclectic meals that consist of liver and spaghetti). When, some time long after the attack, he invites his son-in-law over for this meal and the downtrodden Jack introduces into the conversation the latest depressing news about Carol's mental condition, Paul continues to dance to the music on his stereo, and replies, "What am I supposed to do? Moan and groan?" Paul's loss is devastating but also liberating, freeing him to pursue what he feels has become his calling, a risk that now endangers no one but him. The liminal hero is capable of love and espouses traditional family values, but he always remains aloof or liberated from domestic ties.[9] As we shall see, the pattern of losing a loved one to violent crime is present in each of the ensuing *Death Wish* films. The scenarios and locations for the sequels to the first *Death Wish* changed, but the story and the character of Paul Kersey resonated with audiences for two decades and beyond.

Reprisal: *Death Wish II* (1982)

PAUL: "Do you believe in Jesus?"
STOMPER: "Yes, I do."
PAUL: "Well, you're gonna meet him."

Death Wish was a huge box office success that propelled Bronson to international stardom. Talbot states that it was named in the top ten list of films for 1974 by several magazines and newspapers, and had grossed $20 million in the United States by the end of that year (*Bronson's Loose* 27). As Michael R. Pitts observes, the role of Paul Kersey, more than any other, brought Bronson fame. In *Death Wish*, avers Pitts, "Bronson gives what is perhaps his greatest film performance, certainly one deserving of an Academy Award" (60). However, when *Death Wish* was made, and despite its ensuing success, no one involved had in mind a sequel. It was eight years before the next film in the *Death Wish* franchise was released. It included some cast and crew from the first film, but also a new production company, one that badly wanted a hit from a legitimate film enterprise.

Death Wish II came about because in 1979 two very successful and ambitious Israeli producers who wanted to break into the American film market purchased the controlling interest in Cannon Films (part of the Cannon Group, Inc.), a production company known for making minor B movies during the seventies. Menahem Golan and his cousin Yoram Globus were known for *Operation Thunderbolt*, which had garnered an Academy Award nomination in 1977 for Best Foreign Film. When they took control of Cannon Films, they wanted "a big movie with a big star" (Talbot 32). In addition to *Death Wish II*, they produced *Death Wish III*, another famous series that featured the iconic Chuck Norris in three action films, all produced between 1984 and 1986: *Missing in Action*, *The Delta Force*, and *Invasion U.S.A.*, and *Over the Top* (1987) starring Sylvester Stallone. As Patrick Runkle notes in "Cannon Films: The Rise and Fall, A Short History," they also produced Oscar-nominated films such as *Runaway Train* (1985), and in 1987 both the critically acclaimed *Barfly* (1987) directed by Barbet Schroeder, starring Faye Dunaway and Mickey Rourke, and Jean-Luc Godard's *King Lear*, among several other fine feature films (www.cannonfilms.com).

Golan and Globus purchased the rights to make a *Death Wish* sequel and, always mindful of budget, hired a little known writer, David Engelbach, to develop a script. Engelbach later was given co-credit for the story upon which *Over the Top* (1987) was based, although the screenplay was co-written by its star, Sylvester Stallone, and Sterling Silliphant (the latter of whom had worked on *The Enforcer*, several other hit films, and was famous for his work on the television series, *Route 66*). Jimmy Page, the legendary member of Led Zeppelin, was hired to compose and perform the soundtrack for the film. They needed Charles Bronson, however, or there would be no *Death Wish II*, but the star was not inclined to do another. He was persuaded because he needed another hit and was offered $1.5 million to reprise his role as Paul Kersey. He also insisted that Michael Winner direct, and Winner, too, was in need of a box office success, so he signed on as well (Talbot 34–35). Apparently, it was Winner who also heavily revised the screenplay that Engelbach composed, making it similar to the original film. Winner reasoned: "Times have changed a bit, but most sequels that are successful don't wander too far from the original" (quoted in Talbot 36). The other condition that Bronson imposed was that his wife, actress Jill Ireland, should also have a part in *Death Wish II*. They had acted together in twelve prior films, but Bronson had earlier refused to allow her to play the part of Joanna in the first *Death Wish* because of the character's brutal beating and death. Of all five films, Ireland's is the only female character whose relationship with Kersey does not end in a violent death—in fact, in *Death Wish II* she is never even placed in danger.

It was important for the second film to account for the time lapse and provide continuity for Paul Kersey's story, especially since eight years separated the first *Death Wish* and *Death Wish II*. The sequel had to remain true to the essential formula, as Winner understood, but it also had to provide a rationale for the Los Angeles setting, the first film having taken place in New York City and concluding with Paul's relocation to Chicago. *Death Wish II* is set in 1981, as we can tell from movie marquees that advertise *Any Which Way You Can* and *Excalibur*, and we learn that Paul has been living in Lost Angeles for two years.

The film opens with a skyline shot of downtown Los Angeles and a voiceover that consists of a radio interview with the city's police commissioner (Anthony Franciosa), one of two scenes that express his concern about growing crime. He states emphatically: "Fear of crime has brought about a deterioration in our community ... a number of citizens killed and maimed. It is almost as if we've been struck by enemy bombs. This is a war zone and the only way we are going to win it is by community intervention," an invitation for citizens to become active combatants against street crime. We soon learn that Paul has relocated from Chicago, bringing his emotionally disturbed daughter, Carol (Robin Sherwood), with him. She is still institutionalized, but she has begun to talk and even smile, signs of recovery. Paul, who has chosen Los Angeles because an old friend owns a radio station there, has his own architectural business, a stylish apartment with a Spanish maid, Rosario (Silvana Gallardo), and a girlfriend, Geri Nichols, played by Bronson's real spouse, Jill Ireland. Geri is a reporter who opposes capital punishment, which creates an ideological tension between the two, but also provides a means to interject discussions of crime and justice into the film. (It is Geri who is interviewing the police commissioner in the opening sequence.) It doesn't take long, however, for crime to disrupt Paul's life once again. One afternoon, he and Geri take Carol to a street carnival in the heart of old Los Angeles; while waiting in line to buy ice cream, Paul's wallet is stolen by five thugs, and he gives chase. He catches and assaults one of the perpetrators, but he is not the one in possession of the wallet.

When Paul drives Carol back to his place for a dinner that Rosario had been preparing, they enter to find the pickpockets who have learned his address from his driver's license. While Paul had been enjoying the rest of the afternoon with Carol, we see the creeps forcibly enter Paul's home, breaking in through the back door, because Rosario had refused to open the front door when they claimed they had a delivery. This scenario immediately reminds us of the first *Death Wish*, in which the three freaks, averring they were delivering groceries, were admitted into Paul's New York apartment by Carol. The five hoods gag, gang rape, and brutally beat Rosario, who is barely alive when Paul and Carol enter. When she tries to phone for help, they kill Rosario, knock Paul out with a crowbar, and abduct Carol. This is a replay of the first film, with Rosario as the surrogate mother whom Carol responds to very positively, and with whom Paul shares a very respectful domestic arrangement. The scenario of the motherless family, and surrogates to cope with this, is borrowed from the western.[10] Paul's home is once more violated; like Joanna, Rosario is beaten to her death, and Carol is raped by one of the thugs in an abandoned warehouse where they take her. However, Carol escapes, crashes through a second story window, and falls to her death, impaled on a fence.

Geri arrives at Paul's apartment as he regains consciousness. Ironically, when this horrific crime was occurring, Geri had been interviewing the liberal Senator McLean (Paul Comi) on the subject of capital punishment: "There is only one truth about the death penalty: Why do we kill people who kill people to show killing is wrong?" When the authorities arrive, Paul refuses to cooperate with police, giving only vague descriptions of them and later refusing to even look at mug shots. Paul tells the lieutenant that the same thing happened to him in New York City, where the police got a very good description but failed to find the murderers. Vengeance will be his—for the violation of both Rosario and Carol.

After Carol's funeral and a few days spent in a borrowed cabin to collect himself, Paul returns to work, but keeps his distance from Geri, claiming he is not yet ready to socialize. Instead, he starts his double life—that of hardworking architect Paul Kersey by day and by night that of street vigilante, using the alias "Kimble" (borrowing perhaps from Richard Kimble of the 1963–1967 television series *The Fugitive*, starring David Janssen). He rents a ratty room in that name from a Chinese landlord (Peter Pan) in the district where his wallet was stolen, wears working class clothes, and keeps his pair of Beretta 84 pistols hidden there. He walks the streets searching for the five punks who committed the crime. Amidst evangelical mission houses and activities ranging from revivalist meetings to the "Church on Wheels," to a group of Hare Krishna, Paul, always on the lookout for the guilty ones, encounters the seedy comingling of prostitutes, drug dealers, motorcycle gangs, thieves, and alcoholics, a defining feature of the urban western. Sometimes, Paul intervenes when he happens upon random crimes, as he does when he saves a tourist couple by shooting the men who try to rape the woman. Having been rescued, they refuse to describe Paul to the authorities: "That guy saved our lives. Where the hell were you guys? He was a very good citizen!" the rescued tourist tells the police, but the detective counters, "He was a killer." The woman then says, facetiously, "He was 21, blonde, with a club foot," and the male tourist says, "That's funny. From where I was it was a large black man with a red beard." The detective in charge, Inspector Lieutenant Mankiewicz (Ben Frank), says to another policeman, "You know what we got here, don't ya? A goddamn vigilante." The rescued tourists' refusal to identify Paul resembles the protective response of the man whom Paul had rescued from muggers in the first film.

The suspicion of a street vigilante places city officials in a dilemma. During a meeting, the Police Commissioner, who had been heard at the opening of the film calling for community activism against crime, again remarks to Mankiewicz, "My wife goes to mace class. A police commissioner's wife going to mace class," and then continues, "Now you tell me there's a vigilante out there." Not knowing how to manage this, one of them recalls the case of a vigilante back east five years earlier, and they decide to consult the New York City police detective who had been in charge of it. Frank Ochoa, who had run Paul out of New York, has been keeping tabs on Paul and knows of his move to Los Angeles. News that Paul may have resumed his vigilante activities puts the New York City trio—the police commissioner (Paul Lambert), Detective Ochoa (played again in this film by Vincent Gardenia) and the district attorney (J. D. Cannon) in a quandary: "What if word gets out we had him and didn't prosecute?" The D.A. continues by pointing out that he would be disbarred, the police commissioner's career would be over, and Ochoa, who plans on retiring this year, would receive no pension. To cover their tracks, Ochoa is dispatched to Los Angeles: "You get him before they get him" are his instructions. When he arrives in L.A. and meets with the police, Ochoa learns crime statistics are as bad as those in New York; in the past month, there were 96 deaths, 1,500 seriously injured, and 579 reported rapes, explaining why the commissioner is so concerned, and why a discussion of capital punishment permeates the film.

Ochoa's unorthodox methods continue from the first film when he breaks into Geri's apartment and awaits her return. He fills her in on Paul's background in New York, stating that he had killed nine people there. When asked whether he was charged, Ochoa admits that the police had not charged him, since he had killed muggers. But Ochoa tells Geri that Paul has resumed his vigilante activities in Los Angeles. When Geri confronts Paul, he lies, easily persuading her that he is innocent of Ochoa's charges, another example of his duplicitous existence.

Paul's night walking vigil pays off as he locates and dispatches each of the five criminals responsible for Rosario and Carol's deaths. He first spies Stomper (Kevin Major Howard) with two others who were not involved in the crime, and trails them as they meet up with drug dealers in the ruins of the old Hollywood Hotel, now infested with rats. Paul shoots the two drug dealers, but he dismisses the two companions of Stomper, leaving him alone with the first of the five he is pursuing. Seeing that Stomper is wearing a crucifix around his neck, Paul asks him, "Do you believe in Jesus?" to which Stomper replies, "Yes, I do." "Well, you're gonna meet him," Paul says decisively and swiftly shoots him twice. Not long after, patrolling the area by night, Paul hears a scream in a parking ramp, where he interrupts the crime against the two tourists. As it turns out, one of the men committing the crime, Jiver (Stuart Robinson), was also responsible for Carol's death (he is the one who raped Carol, and is in the process of raping another woman now). Paul shoots him in the leg, but Jiver escapes on foot; when Paul catches up to him, he simply utters, "Goodbye," and kills the second of the five.

Ochoa begins his dogged pursuit of Paul, tailing him by night, using the same guile he had employed in the previous film. One night, Paul finally finds the three remaining punks when he sees them dancing to a boom box, then boarding a bus. Paul follows, and keeps his face hidden in a newspaper, observing them as they harass a young woman who resembles Carol. One of the three vandalizes the bus with spray paint, reminiscent of the vandalizing of Paul's New York apartment in like fashion when Joanna and Carol were attacked. Finally, the three enter Point Fermin Park in San Pedro, followed by Paul, who has been followed by Ochoa. They meet gun dealers there and exchange drugs for weapons. When a sniper who has been posted in a tree as a lookout by the gun dealers uses a spotlight to scan the trees, Ochoa, realizing Paul is in danger, shouts a warning to him. Everyone opens fire: Paul shoots the sniper, both gun dealers, and two of the three remaining thugs he is after, Cutter (Laurence Fishburne III) and Punkcut (E. Lamont Johnson). The other hides behind a trash can and escapes, but Ochoa is fatally wounded. When he sees him, Paul exclaims, "I'll be damned! You, you stuck your neck out for me?" to which Ochoa replies, "It was you or them. Did you get them all?" When Paul tells him one was able to flee, Ochoa urges, "Get the motherfucker for me," and then, in his same dying breath, begins the Lord's Prayer. In some ways, Ochoa and Kersey are doubles, both using their own independent methods in the pursuit of justice, which helps to establish Paul as something other than just a crazed vigilante. When the cops arrive at the scene, one of the two thugs is still alive; before he dies the police make him reveal the name of the escapee who killed Ochoa.

Legal impediments create the obstacle for Paul's attempt to achieve his revenge, and also now Ochoa's, on the final thug, Charles Wilson, a.k.a. "Nirvana" (Thomas Duffy). The police, hunting him for Ochoa's murder, zero in on him and put a SWAT team in place. Paul, who has secured a police scanner from the radio station where Geri works, the same owned by Paul's friend, hears of the location and tries to get to Nirvana before he can be arrested; he shoots but misses. Later, in court, the judge (Frank Campanella) pronounces that the prosecution offered only circumstantial evidence that Nirvana was Ochoa's killer, and that his attack on police officers when he was arrested was due to the fact that he was on a "mind altering drug, PCP" maintaining that psychiatric evaluation is in order. A smirking Nirvana is committed to McLarren Hospital under the care of a psychiatrist, Dr. Clark (Steffen Zacharias), another liberal-minded acquaintance that Geri is interviewing for her magazine article on "Crime and Punishment in L.A." Trying to change Paul's conservatism, Geri takes him along to meet Dr. Clark, but Paul uses it as an excuse to gain access to the hospital. In this case, the legal system is the encumbrance to Paul's revenge, and he finds a way to dispense with Nirvana by impersonating a doctor. Having absconded with a lab coat and successfully forged an I.D., Paul enters the hospital at night and manages to have Nirvana brought to him in a patient's interrogation room that contains electric shock equipment. A violent struggle ensues, Nirvana stabs Paul repeatedly with a scalpel he had hidden in his shoe, and eventually, his fist breaks a glass door to a high voltage electric shock machine. Paul pulls the lever and executes Nirvana. The attendant (Charles Cyphers), having heard the row, enters to find a bleeding Paul sitting in a chair: "He raped and killed my daughter," is all Paul can say in his own defense. To his surprise, the guard replies, "I read about it. I'll give you three minutes until I ring the alarm." Paul picks up his unfired gun and flees, his last act of vengeance completed. Yet again, an ordinary citizen who is sympathetic to Paul's tragedy and his mission lets him go free.

Geri arrives at Paul's apartment in his absence, as the two had planned to fly to Acapulco to be married. She sees the forged I.D. attempts on the floor near a wastebasket and hears on the radio of Nirvana's slaying. Knowing now that Paul lied to her, she leaves the ring on top of the crumpled forgery and departs. The film cuts to the famous Hollywood sign, signaling a time lapse, and we hear a news broadcast voiceover that addresses the rumor of a vigilante killer being responsible for two new murders which, the newscaster states, is denied by Lieutenant Mankiewicz, who now finds himself the Los Angeles counterpart of the deceased New Yorker, Inspector Frank Ochoa, partaking in a cover up. This broadcast also suggests that Paul has continued his vigilante activities, even though he has hunted down the five who murdered his maid and daughter. To make this even more evident, the closing scene between Paul and his friend who owns the radio station, reveals that, far from being dejected that Geri has left him, Paul seems pleased that he has his freedom back. His friend marvels at Paul's high spirits and asks, "Have you been drinking?" He then queries Paul because he hasn't been able to reach him by phone: "Where the hell you been at night?" He then invites Paul to a party celebrating the opening of the new radio station building Paul has designed for him. When he asks Paul if he is free, Paul replies, with a knowing grin, "What else would I be doing?" The film then cuts to a Los Angeles street at night, and we hear a series of gunshots.

Essentially, *Death Wish II* is the same film as the original. Paul's home is violated, Rosario substitutes for Joanna, and Carol endures the same nightmare rape as before, this time taking her own life. This prompts the return of Paul's nocturnal vigilantism while he retains his role as respectable citizen by day. In both films, Paul is revitalized by his vigilante justice, which appears to be the only reparation for the terrible fate suffered by his loved ones. Once again, the authorities are uncertain about how to respond to a vigilante and engage in a corrupt cover-up, this time involving police on both coasts. Witnesses whom Paul has helped refuse to identify him to police, suggesting community support for his actions. One significant difference in the story is that this time Paul is successful in exacting his personal revenge on the actual perpetrators rather than settling for surrogates. The other departure from the original is the addition of a fiancée, Geri, but in the end she drives out of Paul's life, not suffering the same ill fate as every other woman in the *Death Wish* franchise who becomes close to him.

Death Wish II continues to portray Paul Kersey as a liminal outlaw hero. First, the inadequacy of law enforcement is apparent in the two scenes that feature the Los Angeles police commissioner's remarks about rampant crime and the need for citizens in the community to become actively involved in combating it—a restatement of the initial apathy on the part of New York City citizens in the first film, until Paul's actions start to galvanize the community there and deter muggers. The rescued tourists call Paul "a good citizen" and protect his identity. Second, legal authorities are corrupt, covering up the vigilantism rather than addressing it. Moreover, Inspector Frank Ochoa engages in both films in illegal entry. But at the end of his life in *Death Wish II*, Ochoa expresses the same strong desire for personal revenge that motivates Paul, demanding that Paul "get the motherfucker" responsible for his own death and that of Rosario and Carol. By this, Ochoa is shown to experience a *dianoia* that sanctions Paul's vigilante justice. Finally, in this film, the legal system is shown to harbor criminals, as in the case of the incarceration of Nirvana in a mental hospital rather than a prison.

Second, Paul remains a solitary figure, unencumbered once again by domestic responsibilities. His daughter Carol is not only institutionalized but removed from Paul's life permanently. He is shown to be a loving, caring father in the opening sequence of the film, but his obligation is cut short by her terrible death. The romantic relationship with Geri Nichols, which is suspect from the start, is also terminated. Geri and Paul will never see eye-to-eye on the issue of crime and punishment; ideologically, they are on opposite ends of the issue. Paul can declare his love for Geri and propose to her over an expensive bottle of Dom Pérignon champagne, but through most of the film he evades her, either to protect her from harm or because the operative premise of his life demands secrecy and solitude. In his interactions with Rosario, Carol and Geri, Paul is shown to be caring and kind, but in the end he is alone. This is the way the liminal outlaw hero negotiates for its audience the importance of domestic and community ties, while still preserving the need for individual freedom from those obligations, a formula for continued box office success.

Death Wish 3 (1985): "A new breed on the streets"

> "I admire you. I'm a fan. The truth is I hate creeps, too. But I can't do much about it—
> I'm a cop. But you, you shoot 'em, right?"
> —Inspector Richard Shriker, NYPD, to Paul

With the success of *Death Wish II*, Cannon was eager to release another film in the series, and began looking for a suitable script. Golan and Globus assigned the task of developing a screenplay to one of their writers, Don Jakoby, whose story returned Paul Kersey to New York City. Apparently Bronson initially rejected the script, but later recanted and signed on (Talbot 59–60). The writing credit for *Death Wish 3*, however, is attributed to Michael Edmonds, a pseudonym. For the titles of the last three *Death Wish* films, beginning with this one, the Roman numeral of the first sequel, *Death Wish II*, was replaced by Arabic numbers, because a survey revealed that many moviegoers had difficulty reading Roman numerals (Talbot 71). With Bronson and Winner on board, *Death Wish 3* was filmed quickly, edited by Winner under the pseudonym of Arnold Crust, and released in the United States on November 1, 1985, the year after the Bernhard Goetz subway shootings. Set in New York, only a few location shots were filmed there; for financial reasons the rest was shot in London, on a set built to look like a rundown neighborhood in New York, with the police station being filmed in an old historical structure known as the Lambeth Hospital, a workhouse and infirmary to which an eight-year-old Charlie Chaplin and his brother had been sent in 1898 when their mother was diagnosed with syphilis (www.workhouses.org.uk/Lambeth).

Paul Kersey, still using the alias "Kimble" introduced in *Death Wish II*, arrives on a bus in New York City, planning to meet up with his old friend and coworker from the first film, Charley (Francis Drake), now retired and living in a neighborhood that has been overrun by gangs. Paul arrives at Charley's apartment just in time to take the blame for his murder, which had in fact been committed by gang members terrorizing Charley because he refused to pay them to leave him alone. When Paul is brutally "interrogated" at the precinct, a veteran on the force, Inspector Richard Shriker (Ed Lauter), recognizes him as Paul Kersey, the New York vigilante from ten years before. When Paul asks for a lawyer, Shriker refuses; when Paul asks whether he always violates peoples' constitutional rights, Shriker fires back, "This is my jail, Kersey. And I'm the law. That means I get to violate your constitutional rights." He locks Paul up in a group cell that contains the murderous gang leader, Manny Fraker (Gavan O'Herlihy), with whom Paul has a fight. Fraker is freed by his lawyer, but tells Paul he will get him "next time" adding, "Center and Belmont—that's my turf."

This is a six-block area in New York where gangs terrorize citizens, where gang wars take place, and police are unable to contain the rapidly escalating crime rate. "This isn't a neighborhood," Shriker tells his men, "it's a war." Even though patrols have been increased, so has crime—up by 11 percent there. Shriker decides he needs Paul. He tells Paul that while they both hate creeps, "I can't do much about it—I'm a cop. But you, you shoot 'em, right?" We then learn that Shriker has been keeping tabs on Paul's activities since his banishment from New York at the conclusion of the first film. He has a "theory" that Paul "turned and went pro in L.A." and reads his list of suspected executions: "six creeps shot in 36 hours. Then four gang members in Kansas City, two mugger-rapists in Chicago," which maps the path of Paul's return to New York. Paul denies the charges, averring he is "done with all that" and that he has only returned to New York, his home, because he missed it. But Shriker knows better and strikes a deal with Paul—freedom for him if he will go after the gang that is perpetuating the violence in the neighborhood the police cannot protect. Shriker proposes, "I'll minimize the vigilante stuff to the press, tell them it's creeps killing creeps. It will be just like before, Mr. Vigilante, with one important difference. You're gonna work for me." Paul has *carte blanche* to deal with crime on the streets, so long as he keeps him informed about the gang activity and works with the image-conscious Shriker to allow the police some good publicity. Here, Paul's role as liminal hero becomes more explicit than in either of the previous two films—not only is his vigilantism tolerated, it is a pact with the legal authority of an ineffective force. When Shriker asks Paul, "You in?" Paul nods in agreement, with a slight grin. Shriker returns Paul's gun to him, claiming he never saw it, and offers a final bit of advice: "Kimble, watch it. There's a new breed on the streets." The public defender, Kathryn Davis (Deborah Raffin), arranges for Paul's release, urging him to file a suit against the department for violating his rights, which he refuses to do.

Paul returns to Charley's apartment and makes the acquaintance of another tenant, Bennett (Martin Balsam), with whom Charley fought in World War II. (Bennett recalls that Charley mentioned Paul had served in Korea, and Paul tells him he was a conscientious objector, tying this to the earlier films, now part of *Death Wish* lore.) Bennett explains small business owners in the neighborhood, like himself, and the other tenants in the building are being forced to pay the local gang for their own lives and livelihoods. The gangs routinely break into their apartments, rob and mug them on the street, and carry on their own war with other gangs in the area.

Paul decides to stay in Charley's apartment; to "thin the herd," he starts setting a series of traps for the gang by pounding nails into a board and placing it under his bathroom window, booby-trapping one of the tenant's windows with a board triggered to hit the intruder in the head, and baiting would-be thieves with a new car parked conspicuously in the open. While having dinner with an elderly Jewish couple in the apartment building, Paul hears that the car is being burglarized; he politely excuses himself, and walks outside to confront the thieves, part of Fraker's gang. When asked what the problem with the car is, the two reply arrogantly: "We're stealing this fuckin' car. What's it to you?" Paul replies: "It's *my* car." With a confident, malicious grin, one pulls a knife and exclaims, "Now you gonna die," but before the other can even spring his switchblade, Paul shoots and kills both, then returns to dinner, explaining, "I sent them a message." On another occasion Paul continues his habit of walking the streets at night to invite crime. As in *Death Wish II*, he enjoys the American pastime of going out for ice cream. He strolls to the neighborhood store, buys a frost stick, and exits, flaunting an expensive camera in order to bait another gang member, the "Giggler" (Kirk Taylor) known for his speed and that he murdered a woman in the neighborhood. When the Giggler sees what he believes to be a naive target, telling his friends as he smiles smugly—"Look at that fucker with the ice cream"—he takes the bait and snatches the camera on the run. Paul kills him with a special weapon he has ordered—a .475 Wildey Magnum that shoots a cartridge similar to one used on "African big game." This weapon was designed especially for the film by a Connecticut firearms manufacturer, Wildey J. Moore, who was hired to teach Bronson how to wield it; Moore likened it to "an elephant gun" (Talbot 67). When Paul drops the Giggler in his tracks the local residents and rival gang members who observed the shooting begin to cheer and applaud. Thus, as he begins to fight back against street crime, he sets an example that the heretofore passive citizens begin to emulate.

This challenge to the gang does not sit well with its psychopathic leader, Manny Fraker, who begins to make threatening telephone calls to Paul. Paul queries Shriker: "Fraker's the chief creep around here. Why don't you bust him?" "He's got a cleaner arrest record than you," Shriker replies, referring to Fraker, ironically, as a "perfect citizen," just because Fraker hires an attorney who can manipulate the law and keep him out of jail. This fact points to the problem of due process as it conflicts with justice, a familiar theme in urban westerns. It is reinforced by the frustration of Kathryn Davis, with whom Paul becomes romantically involved, when she confesses to him that, as a public defender, "Sometimes I feel I'm on the wrong side." Davis declares, "People should fight back!" and Paul observes with a wry, knowing smile, "Some people might call that an extreme position." Paul has told her that he is an "unemployed writer," so she has no idea she is speaking to a person that does just exactly what she has expressed. Sadly, Fraker attacks Davis as she waits in the car for Paul to retrieve his mail, knocking her out and sending the car down a hill where it collides with another, explodes, and kills her. She meets a violent death, like all the other females for whom Paul cares in the *Death Wish* series (except for that of Geri Nichols, who is sent away in *Death Wish II*), yet another feature of the liminal outlaw hero's identity.

Fraker makes unsuccessful retaliatory attempts on Paul's life. The gang then kidnaps, rapes, and kills Maria Roderiguez (Marina Sirtis), a tenant whom Paul had rescued once before. They kill the elderly wife of a local storeowner who had refused to pay them off, and then blow up Bennett's business when he too refuses to cooperate. This angers the older man so much that, with the intent of shooting the gang members in the street, he takes out one of two Browning machine guns that Charley had saved from World War II. Before he can do so, the gang throws him from a fire escape; Bennett is hospitalized, but survives, and asks to see Paul. Shriker had placed Paul in protective custody since there were witnesses who saw him kill the Giggler, but brings him to Bennett's room at the latter's request. Bennett tells Paul one of the machine guns is still in his apartment, with the exhortation to "blow the scum away." Paul escapes through the hospital window and heads back to the apartment to arm himself with all of his emblems of election: the .30 M1919 Browning machine gun owned by his decorated veteran friends (Charley and Bennett)—conveying the idea that it is patriotic to fight back—the potent .475 Wildey Magnum, his original gun (a Colt Cobra .38 Special), leaving behind an M72 LAW rocket launcher he has ordered. He is joined by Maria's husband (Joseph Gonzalez): "All I got is a zip gun," Rodriguez tells Paul, to which Paul, a walking arsenal, responds with his usual litotes: "Well, we should get a few of them." Meanwhile, Fraker has called on called on gangs from other territories for help in the impending showdown with Paul and the authorities.

The concluding moments of the film show the general destruction of the collective gang, who terrorize the neighborhood like the intrusion of lawless roughriders into a western town. Anarchy reigns: firebombs cause wholesale property destruction, citizens are burned alive and gunned down, bullets flying at a dizzying pace in this western shoot 'em up scenario. Paul answers with a counter attack, spraying bullets from the machine gun that mows the enemy down at a rapid rate. We see shots of citizens joining the fight, pulling a chain threaded across the road to flip motorcycle gang members from their bikes, a woman blasting a hood when he invades her apartment, and cops shooting it out on the street, as in a western movie. He is joined by Shriker, who saves his life: "I owed ya' that one, dude," the term "dude" serving as yet another nod to the western genre. When Paul runs out of ammunition and returns to the apartment to reload, Fraker sneaks up behind him, ready to shoot, when Shriker again arrives in the nick of time to save Paul, getting wounded in the process. Fraker has a bulletproof vest, however, and grabs his gun, ready to kill one of the two. Paul uses the LAW rocket launcher and blows Fraker away, causing the gang to disperse, defeated—at least for now.

The camaraderie between Shriker and Paul is apparent in their final exchange: "Better get goin.' I'll buy you a few minutes. Get outta here. They'll be after you," he tells Paul. Who "they" could be we can only surmise—other law enforcement officers or remnants of the retreating gang (less likely), but it is clear that Shriker knows he has to disinvest in Paul, now that Paul has accomplished what Shriker wanted, getting rid of the gang problem in his jurisdiction. Paul gathers his bags and walks away from the scene, the equivalent of riding into the sunset, an intertextual frame borrowed from the classic western—the outside gunfighter, having rendered an audacious justice, must then distance himself from the community he has saved.

As with the previous two films, the critical and box office reactions to *Death Wish 3*, were at odds. Critics repeated the usual litany against its violence (attributed to Winner's direction), Bronson's uninspired performance, and the equally repetitive accusation that it wasn't "realistic," something that the *Death Wish* series never set out to be, as Christopher Sorrentino has so ably pointed out. Walter Goodman of the *New York Times* wrote that there is not a "moment of credibility" and Roger Ebert averred that it followed the other *Death Wish* films in that it ignores "racial tension in big cities" in its portrayal of mixed-race gangs (quoted in Talbot 71). Despite the usual critical dismissal, the film pleased moviegoers. Like its two predecessors, *Death Wish 3* was number one at the box office its opening week and was Cannon's second highest grossing film of the year (Talbot 72). Audiences apparently enjoyed the now familiar portrayal of Paul Kersey's sense of justice against an inept or corrupt legal system, and against all odds as well. In *Death Wish 3*, Paul's role as liminal outlaw hero is made explicit by his pact with Shriker, who knowingly turns him loose to accomplish what the Inspector's entire force cannot succeed at doing. Shriker uses Paul as a weapon against crime, but Paul Kersey in this film is comfortable in the role of vigilante outlaw hero. *Death Wish 3* features many comic lines and scenarios lacking in the previous two films. Moreover, in *Death Wish 3*, Paul's activities are metonymically linked with patriotism. He lives in Charley's apartment, with the latter's medals and an American flag on display, along with an oil painting of a cavalry charge on the wall. He loves ice cream and home cooked meals of stuffed cabbage, pleasurable moments with neighborhood friends. Yet Paul remains a loner, and despite a romantic interlude and short-lived integration into a community in need, is forced to remain a solitary figure, thus negotiating the opposing ideals of service to a larger cause while maintaining his independent lifestyle, retreating at the end of the film into the liminal space he now calls home.

The Return of "Mr. Vigilante" in *Death Wish 4: The Crackdown* (1987)

DETECTIVE REINER: "Hold it, Kersey. Put down the gun. Stop right there, goddamn it, or I'll shoot."
PAUL KERSEY: "Do whatever you have to."

By now, it was apparent to the financially strapped Golan and Globus at Cannon that the *Death Wish* franchise would always turn a profit, especially with the added revenues brought in by video releases. After *Death Wish 3*, they were in rather urgent need of another script, which was ultimately supplied by Gail Morgan Hickman (*The Enforcer*), who had written the screenplay for the thriller *Murphy's Law* (1986) that starred Bronson as a Los Angeles police detective. *Murphy's Law* was produced by Pancho Kohner (who would also produce *Death Wish 4*) the son of Bronson's agent, Paul Kohner. It was directed by J. Lee Thompson, the sixth film Bronson made under his direction, including *St. Ives* (1976), *The White Buffalo* (1977), *Caboblanco* (1980), *10 to Midnight* (1983), and *The Evil That Men Do* (1984). After *Death Wish 4*, the seventh project, Bronson would go on to work with Thompson in *Messenger of Death* (1988) and *Kinjite: Forbidden Subjects* (1989), totaling nine films, three more than he made with director Michael Winner.

Hickman had supplied three different story ideas for *Death Wish 3* when Bronson rejected the first script, but none were used when the star changed his mind and decided he liked the original. Because he had just written *Murphy's Law*, Hickman was asked to develop a script for the next *Death Wish* film. The first idea was what he called "a very character, angst-driven story" in which Paul Kersey has a series of nightmares about his vigilantism and experiences remorse, so he tracks down his estranged fiancée, Geri Nichols (Jill Ireland), from *Death Wish II*, renounces his role as avenger and marries her. While in a

Los Angeles restaurant, robbers enter and shoot everyone in the place; only Kersey, who has a bullet in the head, survives. Having made a promise to his deceased wife not to kill, he sets about capturing the killers and turning them over to the police, who do not believe Paul's testimony, knowing his history, so they let the murderers go. This is when Paul reverts to his prior vigilante tactics, hunting down each murderer. Others liked this idea, but Bronson rejected it because Ireland, his wife, was in the middle of treatment for breast cancer, and he naturally did not want to act in a film in which she dies (Talbot 81–83).

How to avoid too much repetition had to be weighed against the need to provide some continuity with the previous films in the series. A script had to be developed and agreed upon quickly. Hickman struggled with the issue of Kersey's vigilantism in a fourth film and finally settled on the idea of making it "a kind of Italian western," a reprise of the Sergio Leone and Clint Eastwood hit, *A Fistful of Dollars* (1964), borrowing the plot of two gangs being placed at enmity and subsequently destroying each other (Talbot 84), but with a new twist. If Paul Kersey was called upon to eradicate an entire New York City neighborhood gang in *Death Wish 3*, his next task is even more formidable in *Death Wish 4: The Crackdown*, when, having relocated once again to Lost Angeles, he finds himself taking on drug moguls who control 90 percent of the illegal narcotics in southern California.

At the opening of the film, Paul is once again a successful architect in Los Angeles, apparently trying to curtail his vigilante activities, which have been giving him nightmares. Paul has even acquired a new family: for two years, he has been in a romantic relationship with a news writer, Karen Sheldon (Kay Lenz), and has a good rapport with her teenage daughter Erica (Dana Barron) as well. Things go awry when Erica's boyfriend Randy (Jesse Dabson) takes her to an arcade to meet a drug dealer, Jo Jo Ross (Hector Mercado), and she ends up dead from a crack overdose. Karen, a single mother, is both distraught and guilt-ridden over her daughter's death, so Paul urges her to write about the drug problem, bringing it to the public's attention. Meanwhile, he trails Randy, who is also filled with grief and guilt, as he confronts Jo Jo and threatens to go to the police. Paul sees this confrontation from a distance, and witnesses Jo Jo's fatal stabbing of Randy, which then prompts Paul to shoot and kill Jo Jo. A witness saw the make of Paul's car and the last three digits of his license plates. When Paul arrives home, a message in an envelope under his door reads enigmatically, "I know who you are," and Paul is summoned to a meeting with a wealthy, prominent citizen, Nathan White (John P. Ryan), who refers to him as "Mr. Vigilante."

White wants to hire Kersey to wage a war against drugs. His motivation, he avers, is that his own daughter, Lisa, had died of a drug overdose while at college; White has spent a fortune compiling information about the narcotics traffic in southern California, learning that 90 percent of it is controlled by two families. White offers to share the information with Paul and finance his crusade to wipe out these sources of illegal drug supplies. Paul hesitates but a few days later agrees, motivated by anger at Erica's death and wanting revenge. Karen sets out to ascertain information about the narcotics epidemic among the young so that she can write about it; her boss is initially reluctant to let her pursue the topic to report on, averring that "everyone is on drugs," and that "it's the new American way of life," but after cautioning her to be careful in her investigation, he allows Karen to pursue to the story. She visits the arcade where her daughter had purchased crack and retains Jo Jo's sidekick, Jesse (Tim Russ), as an informant.

Ed Zacharias (Perry Lopez) has an uneasy truce with rival suppliers, Jack and Toney Romero (Mike Morroff and Dan Ferro, respectively). These two factions import and supply dealers with virtually all of the narcotics in the area. Paul goes undercover in various guises, sometimes using his alias, "Jack Kimble" from the prior two films, in order to reignite the war between Zacharias and the Romero brothers, thus having the two operations cancel each other out. He does this by murdering key henchmen on each side, so that they think the other side is responsible. When White informs Paul that Zacharias uses an old fish cannery in San Pedro as a front for importing drugs from Columbia and converting the goods to street crack in a lab there, Paul goes in and wipes it out, single-handedly.

Meanwhile, two members of the LAPD, Detective Reiner (George Dickerson) and his partner, Detective Nozaki (Soon-Teck Oh), who have been investigating the shooting of Jo Jo at the arcade and the recent executions of the Zacharias and Romero cartels, begin to suspect Paul. Nozaki sees Paul leave the building where he has just killed a hit man for the Romero brothers, Frank Bauggs (David Fonteno). As Paul drives away, Nozaki notices the make of his car and the last three digits of his plates match those that the witness reported at the scene of Jo Jo's death. Nozaki and Reiner begin to gather evidence that Paul is the famed Los Angeles vigilante, and go to his office to question him. They report their suspicions to their superior, Lieutenant Higuera (Gerald Castillo), stating that in 1975 his wife was killed in New York and his daughter in Los Angeles in 1981—dates that show a careless disregard for those in the prior films. Higuera tells them to drop their pursuit of the vigilante and to concentrate instead on getting a handle on the drug war that is starting to leave a trail of bodies in the area, ironically not knowing that Paul is the one who is fueling the strife.

Nozaki, however, is a corrupt cop, in the employ of Zacharias. He tells

Zacharias that he suspects someone other than Jack and Tony Romero are behind the executions of his men, and Zacharias orders him to find out who the person works for, then to kill him. Nozaki confronts him about his identity at gunpoint in his office, where Paul is working late, trying to extract information about who has hired Paul. When Nozaki confesses he is on the take, and aims to kill Paul, "I can be very, very nasty, if I want to," Paul shoots Nozaki in self-defense, his concealed gun having been in his lap, and replies, "So can I."

Zacharias begins to suspect the plan to cause enmity between him and the rival drug suppliers, so he calls Jack and Tony to set up a meeting. Earlier, Paul had managed to bug Zacharias' telephone, so he hears when and where this will occur. He observes from a hill above the oil fields where the two sides, both suspicious of the other, have their confrontation, which ensues like a western showdown between warring factions. When Paul snipes and hits Jack in the arm, violence erupts and an all-out gun war wipes out everyone but Zacharias. Paul then shoots him in the leg, and approaches him, his moment of revenge at hand. "Who are you?" Zacharias queries, to which Paul replies, "I'm the guy that set you up." When asked why, Paul shows Zacharias Erica's picture. "I don't even know the girl," Zacharias claims, to which Paul answers, "I do," and kills him.

The two narcotics sides now having been virtually eliminated, it would seem Paul's mission to exact his personal revenge for Erica's death and that of serving the public by ridding it of the major sources of drugs peddled to the young, is complete. Two final twists await Paul, however, and converge at the end. White contacts Paul for a final meeting that turns out to be a trap—Paul is locked in a car and barely escapes before it blows up. Angered, he returns to the White mansion where they had their first meeting, only to find it occupied by the real Nathan White (Richard Nugent-Aherne) who has been in Europe for the past three months. The man who hired Paul was an imposter, with the aim of having Paul eliminate the drug cartels in southern California so he could take it over. When he departs White's mansion, Paul is stopped and incarcerated by two crooked cops; realizing this, he causes an accident and escapes.

He returns to his home to find Detective Reiner there, ready to kill Paul because of Nozaki's death. When Paul tells him that his partner was "dirty" and had been on the take, Reiner refuses to believe him. Just then Paul gets a call from a frightened Karen, who has been kidnapped by the imposter White, demanding that Paul meet him in the parking garage of the Sunset Roller Rink. Paul knocks Reiner out, opens his weapons arsenal hidden behind his refrigerator, and heads to the final showdown. Not fooled by the trap in the garage, Paul pursues the imposter, who uses Karen as a shield, killing his henchmen along the way. Karen wrenches free of her kidnapper's grasp and runs toward

6. "Now cracks...": Revenge in Death Wish (1974–1994)

Paul, but the imposter shoots her in the back. At this point, Paul uses an M203 grenade launcher that was incorporated into his M16 rifle, and incinerates Karen's murderer. He hears a click behind him; it is Detective Reiner, who has followed Paul to the scene, apparently still bent on avenging Nozaki's death. He issues the usual orders: "Hold it, Kersey. Put down the gun. Stop right there, goddamn it. I'll shoot." Paul keeps walking, his back to Reiner, and says wearily, "Do what ever you have to." Reiner lowers his gun, Paul having won the character contest.

Death Wish 4 premiered in over a thousand United States theaters on November 6, 1987. The film, while not as popular as its predecessors, was still a moneymaker for Cannon. It brought in extra profit from its overseas release, from home video releases ($2 million) and video rental sales of 100,000 copies (Talbot 99–100). While for the most part critical reviews remained negative, they lacked the usual hostility, perhaps because *Death Wish 4* contained little explicit sexual violence (except for an interrupted rape scene in the opening sequence that turns out to be a nightmare of Paul's), which might in turn be explained by the fact that the series had a new director, J. Lee Thompson having replaced Michael Winner.

By now, Paul Kersey and the *Death Wish* franchise had become so familiar to audiences and critics alike—iconic—if you will, that critic Kevin Thomas, writing his review for the *Los Angeles Times*, refers to *Death Wish 4* as a "good-looking comic book fantasy," and then observes, "By now Paul Kersey is an architect in the same way that Clark Kent is a reporter. His Vigilante has become as much an above-the-law mythological figure as Superman." This is an insightful commentary: one feature that makes the *Death Wish* series unusual, and that defines Paul Kersey as a liminal outlaw hero, is the fact that his vigilante activity is not very secretive, but is instead almost always either willingly ignored or even applauded by legal authorities and average citizens alike. Paul routinely hides this side of his character to his romantic interests and keeps it out of his domestic life, but the films always contain people who know of his crusade against street crime and take few or no steps to obstruct it.

Death Wish 4 addresses the topical issue of narcotics trafficking on the street and the growing problem of drug cartels operating in the United States in the 1980s, which elicited the public cry for a "war on drugs." In addressing a larger social problem with a formidable enemy, it followed *Death Wish 3*, departing from the first two films that focused on an isolated gang, with random street crimes being punished as Paul encountered its perpetrators. *Death Wish 3* and its sequel, *Death Wish 4: The Crackdown*, both portray Paul's fight against greater odds—an organized street gang and two powerful drug cartels—which is why critics, along with Gail Morgan Hickman, the screenwriter, comment on its "cartoon" or comic book quality. Hickman asserted, "If you are going to make it entertainment, then it has to be a cartoon" (Talbot 86). *Death Wish 4* remained true to its successful formula, however, in two essential ways that guaranteed its appeal to audiences, and that underscore Paul's role as liminal outlaw hero.

As in the other *Death Wish* films, Paul Kersey enjoys a good rapport with a community, and has a close relationship with family and friends. Here, he has returned (putatively) to his career as a successful architect, and in the opening scene, he is shown encouraging the young Erica as she shares with him some building blueprints she has designed. Paul is in a romantic relationship with Erica's mother, Karen, one so serious that she is about to propose marriage to him when the telephone call about Erica's overdose interrupts her. As in the first two *Death Wish* films, Paul's motive for his vigilante justice is a response to the death of a loved one; in this case, Erica is a surrogate for Paul's own deceased daughter, Carol. (In *Death Wish 3*, the murder of Paul's old friend and business associate, Charley, is the motive.) But here, as in the prior films, the death of Erica and, in the end, the murder of Karen, leave Paul free of domestic ties. By now, he is reluctant to make such commitments, knowing what happens to those he loves. His hesitance in proposing marriage to Karen, whom he has been seeing for over two years, is clear from the fact that, while Paul enjoys an intimate family dinner with Karen and Erica on the night the latter overdoses, Karen is poised to prompt him about the subject of marriage. This shows that Paul is capable of lasting domestic relationships, and values them, but the death of both Erica and Karen leave him, once again, free of the responsibility of this obligation.

Paul also renders a justice that the law is unable to achieve. He infiltrates and sabotages the two narcotics rings that dominate the importation and distribution of drugs in southern California, taking out a few corrupt law officers along the way. His presence is known and ignored, as is evident when Lieutenant Higuera, presented with evidence of Paul's identity by Detectives Reiner and his corrupt partner, Detective Nozaki, tells the two to forget about apprehending the vigilante and to focus instead on Zacharias. Moreover, late in the film, Paul admits to Reiner that he is the vigilante who caused the gang war at the oil fields. In the end, Reiner lowers his gun and lets Paul walk away from the scene in which he has just seen Paul incinerate the crooked imposter of the real Nathan White. Thus, *Death Wish 4* remains true to the liminal outlaw hero formula: Paul is shown to cherish traditional values of community and family, but remains free of them, in the end, to dedicate himself to the obliteration of an enemy the law cannot defeat. As in *Death Wish 3*, in which the neighborhood gang is dispersed but will, no doubt re-form and return to wreak havoc, so in this film the drug cartels are for the moment destroyed by Paul, but the problem of drug use and trafficking will continue. Both films emphasize the need for individuals to be "vigilant" in taking a stand against such social evils, even if not all have Paul Kersey's motivation for doing so—he represents a "wish," not a reality.

Final Reprisal—*Death Wish V: The Face of Death* (1994)

PAUL: "Tell me, how long have you been trying to take these guys down?"
LIEUTENANT KING: "Sixteen years. These guys are pros. It's not like some gang of doped up muggers."
PAUL: "Sixteen years. That's a long time to be failing."

Twenty years after the debut of *Death Wish* and seven years after the release of the fourth film in the series, Charles Bronson would play Paul Kersey for the fifth and final time. The Cannon team of Yoram Globus and Menahem Golan had split up when facing bankruptcy in 1989, although both continued to make films. Golan formed a company called 21st Century Pictures, and several Cannon films now belonged to MGM, through a purchase and merger with a group known as Pathe Communications (www.cannonfilms.com). Golan was struggling because of a series of recent flops, and he once again turned to the *Death Wish* franchise to bail him out of his immediate financial woes (Talbot 103). Charles Bronson's wife, Jill Ireland, had lost her long battle with breast cancer in 1990, and the grieving Bronson had done little work. In addition, he would be turning 72 years of age in 1993, the year the film would go into production, perhaps too old to play such an action-packed role; however, without Bronson there would be no new *Death Wish* film. Bronson was reportedly paid $5 million to return to the screen as Paul Kersey (Talbot 106).

Golan owned a script intended initially to be used for the fourth film, but decided it would cost too much to produce, so he hired a fledgling writer, Michael Colleary, to create a screenplay. The first director hired for the new *Death Wish V: The Face of Death* was Steve Carver, who had directed for Cannon *River of Death* (1989) and films for other companies—*Capone* (1975) and the Chuck Norris films *An Eye for an Eye* (1981) and *The Lone Wolf* (1983), so he had experience as an action film director (Talbot 104). Golan faced financing and budget issues, especially because of Bronson's salary. Although it is set in New York City, *Death Wish V* was shot in Toronto because the Canadian government offered tax incentives, but the film had to employ Canadian citizens to receive these breaks. Several actors cast in the film were Canadian, including Kenneth Welsh (who plays Lieutenant King), Robert Joy (Freddie Flakes) and Erica Lancaster (Chelsea). In addition, Allan A. Goldstein, who enjoyed American and Canadian dual citizenship, replaced Carver as director. Goldstein and Bronson had been working together at Warner Bros. on a film called *One Way Out*, which was described by Goldstein as an "anti-vigilante piece," but it was not made at the time. He and Bronson got along very well, so when offered the opportunity, they shared aspirations about making the next *Death Wish* film both true to the original formula but also adding some black comedy, "an absurdist element" to the story. According to Goldstein, Golan allowed him (in collaboration with Bronson) to write the screenplay (Talbot 107–108). *Death Wish V* was shot in March and April of 1993, and opened in theaters on January 14, 1994—less than ten months before Bronson would turn 73 years old. Although he starred in three made for TV movies after this (*Family of Cops, Breach of Faith: A Family of Cops II*, and *Family of Cops III: Under Suspicion*, 1995, 1997 and 1999, respectively) *Death Wish V: The Face of Death* was Bronson's final theatrical release, as well as his last Paul Kersey role.[11] While *Death Wish 4: The Crackdown* had opened in 1,030 theaters, its sequel opened only in 248: Golan was clearly more interested in the revenue the film would generate by selling its home video rights than in promoting it upon its theatrical release. In addition, there was an earthquake in Los Angeles the weekend *Death Wish V* debuted. Despite this, it still opened at number seven at the box office the first week (Talbot 113). Fans still felt enthusiasm for Bronson in his most memorable role.

The story of *Death Wish V: The Face of Death* follows closely the formula that audiences by now expected when they went to see Paul Kersey in his liminal outlaw hero role. Set in the clothing manufacturing district of New York City, the film opens with Paul in attendance at a fashion show featuring the designs of his soon-to-be fiancée, Olivia Regent (Lesley-Anne Down), sitting with her young daughter, Chelsea (Erica Lancaster). We learn that Paul now teaches architecture at a local university, and uses the name of Professor Paul Stewart, having participated in a witness protection program years before. Enter Tommy O'Shea (Michael Parks), Olivia's ex-husband, a mobster who extorts money from area shops and uses his half-ownership of Olivia's business to launder money, unbeknownst to her. When Paul learns that O'Shea has threatened Olivia and become physically abusive, primarily in a dispute over custody of Chelsea, he confronts O'Shea at the fashion show. Flanked by his armed thugs, brothers Chick and Sal Paconi (Keven Lund and Chuck Shamata), O'Shea asks Paul, "Do guns make you nervous?" but Paul, who is not intimidated, snipes, "Guns have their uses. Idiots with guns make me nervous." When the firm's bookkeeper, Big Al (Jefferson Mappin), refuses to cooperate with O'Shea's illegal operations, claiming, "We're moving more cash than clothes," O'Shea cuts into his stomach with an electric saw. Eventually, his hired guns kill Al when he is discovered having a wire on his person, cooperating with police in an attempt to get evidence to prosecute O'Shea, also slaying Detective Janice Omori (Lisa Inouye) as she tries to protect Al, and then killing Al's co-worker Reggie (Michael Dunston) who had tried earlier to intervene on Al's behalf.

Paul contacts the district attorney, Brian Hoyle (Saul Rubinek), who had helped him acquire a new identity in the witness protection program and tells him about O'Shea's threats to Olivia. Hoyle urges Paul to convince Olivia to testify against O'Shea's illegal business activities, which the cops have been trying to stop, promising to protect her if she agrees. It is clear that Paul has left his former vigilante life behind and wishes to continue to do so; he takes Olivia out for a romantic dinner, proposes marriage, and persuades her to turn state's evidence against O'Shea, who is watching the couple menacingly in the restaurant. When Olivia uses the restroom, she is brutally attacked by one of O'Shea's men, called Freddie "Flakes" (Robert Joy) because he has chronic dandruff. Flakes, dressed in drag, locks the door to the ladies room when Olivia enters and smashes her face repeatedly into a glass mirror, leaving her disfigured, and threatening Chelsea, in the event that Olivia should testify against O'Shea. It turns out that the deputy district attorney, Hector Vasquez (Miguel Sandoval), who had accompanied Hoyle when he met with Paul, is an informant for O'Shea, explaining how he knew of Olivia's intent, and also why O'Shea has eluded police for so long. When Olivia is rushed to the hospital and Paul learns that she will be permanently disfigured, the police try to show Paul photos to identify her attacker, whom Paul had had a glimpse of in the restaurant. Irritated, Paul says, "What about Tommy O'Shea? He's the one," but realizing that O'Shea has someone else perform such acts and therefore escapes persecution, sees that he is "wasting his time" by cooperating with authorities. Paul assumes temporary custody of Chelsea while Olivia is in the hospital, and he begins to tail the Paconi brothers, observing the illegal operation of O'Shea's organization. This is when he witnesses the murder of the detective who had been trying to protect Big Al, as she is mortally wounded in a hit-and-run by one of O'Shea's thugs.

The deceased Detective Janice Omori's partner, Lieutenant Mickey King (Kenneth Welsh) asks Paul, "What the hell were you doing there? You aren't thinking of going back to your old ways, are you?" This tells us that he recognizes Paul as a former vigilante. Paul replies, "Is that such a bad idea?" to which King responds, "Let the cops take these guys down. You know sometimes the law works." But Paul retorts, "And sometimes it doesn't. You know these people.

They steal, they murder, they destroy peoples' lives and get away with it. They have alibis, money, lawyers, power. They have everything. Tell me, how long have you been trying to take these guys down?" King admits, "Sixteen years. These guys are pros. It's not like some gang of doped up muggers." Before he walks away, Paul says, "Sixteen years? That's a long time to be failing." Although we see at this point Paul is still hoping to live a normal life, he is disgusted with how slow and ineffective the legal system is in apprehending and prosecuting the guilty and in protecting the innocent.

Paul brings Olivia home from the hospital with the plan that she will still testify, but telephones Hoyle to say that she will not, knowing that his phone is bugged. He then goes to Hoyle's house to tell him in person that Olivia still intends to cooperate, so Hoyle says he will send an agent to protect her immediately. Hector, who is at Hoyle's house when he learns this, tips off O'Shea; Paul recognizes Freddie Flakes when he arrives at Olivia's apartment impersonating the agent who has been sent to protect her. Paul quickly commands Olivia to exit via the fire escape and tries to draw Flakes and his henchmen off as Olivia ascends flights of stairs, but as she makes it to the roof, Flakes arrives and kills her, while Paul narrowly escapes. An ensuing inquest into Olivia's murder exonerates O'Shea, who then seeks and gains legal custody of Chelsea. Hoyle urges Paul to testify about the men who killed Olivia, maintaining that if he does so, one of the goons responsible will cave in and finger O'Shea as the one who ordered the hit on Olivia, but Paul refuses: "Every time I talk to you, someone gets hurt." When O'Shea comes to take Chelsea away soon after, he has to knock Paul out to leave with her. Paul's motive now is to avenge the death of Olivia and to protect his surrogate daughter, Chelsea, as he had promised his fiancée moments before her death. Like a retired gunfighter who has to resort to his weapons to defend what is right, Paul retrieves his weapon from a safe in his study, and sets out to resume his vigilante role in the name of justice.

In *Death Wish V*, arguably for the first time, the retribution itself takes on a dark humor in the form of poetic justice. Each of Paul's victims is killed in a different manner, reflective of the hideous nature of their own persons and crimes. The corpulent Chick Paconi is the first to taste Paul's justice, literally, when we see him in his sister's restaurant wolfing down cannoli pastries that Paul has furtively sprinkled with cyanide. When Chick begins to choke (an apt *contrapasso* for a glutton) and the sister runs out of the restaurant screaming for help, Paul, now left alone with him, approaches Chick and says, "You got a problem?" as he quietly exits the scene. O'Shea is perplexed about who is responsible for Chick's murder, so he summons his informant, Hector Vasquez, who tells him, "Well, you've got a problem. Ever heard of the name Paul Kersey, a vigilante killer a few years back? Well, that was your ex-wife's boyfriend. Kersey's no amateur and you pissed him off." When asked how to find Paul, Hector issues a warning: "You know, Kersey's going to be going down the list. Get it?" and points his gun finger at O'Shea.

Paul's next target is the paranoid and neurotic Freddie Flakes, whose house is grey compound with extra security. Paul purchases from a toy store a soccer ball with a remote control device, grinning as he tells the clerk (played by Director Allan Goldstein) that it is "a treat for someone special." When Freddie arrives home that night, he activates all of his security devices and settles into a luxurious bath with his bimbo girlfriend, who is treating his eczema and massaging anti-dandruff shampoo onto his scalp. When Paul arrives, he sends the wired soccer ball through the gate to trigger the alarm. Freddie is relieved when he runs out to investigate and sees it is only a ball, but when he picks it up, Paul calls out from the shadows, "Hey Freddie. I'm gonna take care of your dandruff problem for you," and detonates a bomb hidden inside, a disguised and guileful danger, similar to Freddie's own tactics.

By now, the mayor has become concerned about the body count and leans on the authorities to ascertain who is behind the eccentric killings that are causing grotesque headlines. Paul suspects that Hector Vasquez is the mole, so he sets a trap by calling Hoyle and telling him to meet Paul at Olivia's apartment. As Paul sits on Chelsea's bed with his back to the door, he sees in the mirror Hector enter the room and pull out a weapon. The over-confident deputy district attorney then says, "I didn't know this would be so easy" as he prepares to shoot. Paul quickly turns, replies, "Neither did I," and kills Hector first. Arriving just after, Hoyle sees that his assistant has been on the take. Hoyle says to Paul, "You're right. You can't trust the justice system," and agrees when Paul replies, "He would have killed you, Brian." Hoyle then realizes, "No judge, no jury, no appeals, and no deals." Paul then asks him what he intends to do about the fact that he has just seen Paul kill Hector, and Hoyle replies, "Paul, I'm not even here." In this case, the district attorney is willing to engage in a complete cover-up of Paul's slaying of a crooked authority, having come to the realization that it was justified, allowing Paul to continue his activities.

Paul issues his final challenge to Sal and O'Shea when he sends a "message" to Sal (next on his list) in the form of Hector's corpse, encased in a wooden crate. Sal, now visibly shaken, tells the worker who opened the crate to "ship him to Jersey" for disposal, and then insists to O'Shea, "This is a vendetta that we brought on ourselves." Unable to find Paul, O'Shea sets a trap to lure him to the warehouse, by having Sal bring Chelsea there, knowing Paul is trailing them. Three professional killers are supplied a small arsenal to kill Paul as he enters the warehouse, while O'Shea waits in the office with Sal and Chelsea.

Paul outwits and kills two of the three and wraps the third one in cellophane in order to get him to reveal where Chelsea is. Paul then uses a walky-talky of one of the thugs to issue his warning: "I'm coming for you, O'Shea." When they try to find Paul, he shoots Sal, who then lands on a conveyer built. Eventually, he trips O'Shea as the latter pursues a fleeing Chelsea inside the showroom, cutting his face with a broken beer bottle—an obvious retaliation of Olivia's disfigurement—and then corners O'Shea after the latter has wounded Lieutenant King, who has shown up at the warehouse. Paul then turns the tables on O'Shea, repeating what he had first said to Paul: "Guns make you nervous?" O'Shea tries to bribe Paul to save his own life, telling him he will give Paul anything he needs. "I don't need anything. But you, you need a bath," Paul quips, as he shoots and O'Shea lands in a pool of acid. Sal's body is shredded to bits on a conveyer built—payback for having used hot pressing irons on Reggie in the same warehouse earlier in the film, and Tommy O'Shea perishes in an acid vat there, retribution for the heinous act of sawing part of Al's stomach off there.

Lieutenant King has just witnessed the end of Paul's vengeful pursuit of Olivia's killers. Paul asks King if he is OK and the latter says he thinks so. "What are you going to do about me?" Paul then inquires. "Don't worry. I'll take care of it. The girl is outside. She's safe," is the Lieutenant's response. As Paul turns to exit the dim warehouse, he utters his final words as he vanishes into light and legend: "Thanks, Lieutenant. Hey, Lieutenant, if you need any help, give me a call." As District Attorney Hoyle had earlier overtly engaged in sanctioning Paul's actions, covering up his knowledge of Hector's slaying, so here a high-ranking police officer openly agrees to exonerate Paul. As in the third film, Paul and the police actually work together in the end to accomplish what the law—for sixteen years—has been unable to accomplish.

Death Wish V adheres to the formula that made the series a success, once again using a personal loss as a motive for Paul's revenge. When the film opens, Paul is perhaps closer to his early self as a gentle, law-abiding citizen and family man than he has been in any of the sequels. He has returned to the New York City area, and although we do not know the particulars, we do learn that he has entered the witness protection program (using the alias of Professor Paul Stewart) presumably as a result of having helped the authorities. He is on good and familiar terms with the current district attorney, and he is about to assume the role of husband (proposing to Olivia) and father (enjoying a close relationship with Olivia's young daughter, Chelsea). All of this is altered, as it is in the first *Death Wish*, as a result of Olivia's murder and Paul's frustration because the guilty remain unpunished—the police and the legal system itself are shown to be at best inadequate and at worst corrupt. This time, Paul does visit justice

6. *"Now cracks..."*: Revenge in *Death Wish (1974–1994)*   179

on the individuals who are actually responsible for the death of Olivia, and slayings of Big Al, Reggie, and Detective Omari as well, doing a service to the community as he also accomplishes his revenge. Moreover, the authorities in this case are openly supportive of Paul's actions, evinced by District Attorney Hoyle's admission that justice is not always best served by the legal system and by his cover up of Paul's fatal shootout with Hector, and by Lieutenant King's assurance that he will handle the matter of the final showdown at the warehouse—Paul having achieved in a short time what King could not accomplish in sixteen years.

Because of Bronson's age, and perhaps also because of Menahem Golan's marketing of the final film primarily through home video, the sense that *Death Wish V: The Face of Death* would be the last, affords the opportunity to deviate somewhat from the conclusion to the previous films. As long as another sequel seemed possible, Paul Kersey, or his alias, "Kimble," would remain at the end of the films a loner, unattached romantically, domestically, and apart from a community he has served. These two features—the detachment from domestic ties and the errant, quasi-itinerant existence—allow for his role as liminal outlaw hero in that he is free to pursue and render justice. In *Death Wish*, Paul starts out in New York and ends up in Chicago. When *Death Wish II* opens, Paul has been living in Los Angeles for a few years, where he remains until he begins to make his way back east, staying for at least some time in Kansas City and again in Chicago before arriving back in New York City, as we learn in *Death Wish 3*. He is back in Los Angeles for *Death Wish 4: The Crackdown*, and then finally returns to New York City for *Death Wish V: The Face of Death*. This time, Paul has lost his fiancée, but he still has the now-orphaned Chelsea at the end and can presumably honor his promise to Olivia, who had implored Paul to care for her daughter in the event of her own death. Unlike Paul's grown daughter Carol in the first two films, and his surrogate daughter Erica in the fourth—both of whom meet terrible premature deaths—Chelsea is allowed to survive, suggesting Paul might now assume a domestic obligation once again. Still, his final words to Lieutenant King, "If you need any help, give me a call," reaffirms Paul's conviction that what he has done is right, and that he would willingly do so again if the need were to arise.

As Paul Kersey vanishes into the light and into film history, he might well regret the turn his life has taken while still feeling vindicated in his actions. It is one thing to be sorry that he has found himself bereft *repeatedly* (since the films collectively insist on their oneiric, fantasy quality, a "death wish," without regard for "realism") of a quotidian existence comprised of career, community, and family, while still not feeling regret for having actively visited a poetic justice on his adversaries. Paul acts in accordance with his conscience, even when it is at odds with the law, even when it leaves him isolated, outside of community. This is the story of the liminal outlaw hero, especially in its American incarnation. It is the powerful mythology that informs the western genre—both classic and urban—the source of its perennial appeal to audiences. From the classic lonely exit of Alan Ladd in *Shane* to the demise of John Bernard Books—and of John Wayne, the dying icon who played him in the sublime film *The Shootist* (1976)—audiences see that these mythic figures accept their fate and adhere to their beliefs, even though they do so at a regrettable cost.[12] This, too, remains the appeal and strength of Paul Kersey.

The Legacy of *Death Wish* Justice

"The nightmare in *Dirty Harry* is the tolerance of bad laws; the nightmare in *Death Wish* is the tolerance of evil itself" (Sorrentino 35). Its peculiar power lies in its presentation of an ordinary citizen, rather than a law enforcement officer, who is confronted with an unspeakable violation—everyone's nightmare—that strikes at the very heart of his life. The murder and assault on his wife and daughter shocks him out of his comfort zone and into an urban war zone. Paul has nothing but his own inner voice and self-reliance that he listens to and acts upon. He knows satisfaction when he finds that the *vox populi* endorses and takes inspiration from his example. Harry Callahan's decision to allow a vigilante killer to go free after she exacts revenge years later for the gang rape of her sister and herself in *Sudden Impact*, released nine years after *Death Wish*, explores the same issue of justice and revenge, the conflict between the law and the right, as we saw in the previous chapter. That the character is a female vigilante avenging the wrong done against her as well as a loved one, shows a prevailing interest in the issue of justice and revenge.

Other films that feature retaliatory vigilante justice followed the influential *Death Wish* as well. *The Brave One* (2007) stars Jodie Foster as Erica Bain, a radio personality turned female vigilante very similar to the circumstances under which it happened to Paul Kersey. Walking their dog through Central Park, Erica and her fiancé, David (Naveen Andrews), are attacked by three thugs who kill David and abscond with the dog. After a period of depression and sense of helplessness, Bain begins her crusade against crime, killing first a robber in a convenience store, then hoods on a subway train, and finally a pimp. The media and the police notice her vigilantism, and she becomes friendly with the detective, Sean Mercer (Terrence Howard), assigned to the "vigilante case," very similar to the situation in *Sudden Impact* between Jennifer and Harry. Eventually, she does locate the thugs responsible for David's death—something the police are unable to do—and kills two of the three. Detective Mercer arrives just as she is struggling with the last thug, and intervenes, but his sympathies are with Bain. He covers up for her, the last thug being killed in the struggle, and allows her to go free, again, like the conclusion to *Sudden Impact*. *Death Wish* and the success of its sequels clearly inspired later films about vigilantism and personal revenge, *Sudden Impact* and *The Brave One* serving only as a few examples. Paul's shield—that which earns the approbation from his audience rather than its condemnation—is the terrible price he has paid that prompts his vigilantism. The brutal attacks and murders of those close to him are offered as the justification for his activities. The *extreme* suffering and sacrificial price that each vigilante has experienced—Jennifer Spencer, Paul Kersey, Erica Bain—is what earns the audience's sympathy. They must be ordinary, likeable characters until the calamitous clash with crime, and the inadequacy of the law to address it, prompts them to seek their own justice. Consider, for example, the low-budget *Ms. 45* (1981) in which an already deeply troubled young woman, Thana (Zoe Tamerlis Lund), is sexually assaulted by two separate rapists on the same night, once on her way home from work, once after she arrives at her apartment, which leads to a series of psychopathic murders and gruesome dismemberments of bodies that make the revenge motif unpalatable.

In life, as well as art, as mentioned at the beginning of the chapter, the much publicized case of Bernhard Goetz, the "Subway Vigilante," which occurred in December 1984 (ten years after *Death Wish*) created a flood of positive reactions to his case, from ordinary citizens to law enforcement officials, who openly applauded Goetz's actions (Sorrentino 35). Yet Goetz is one of very few to engage in a vigilante response to violent confrontation, just as Paul is one of only a few citizens in all of the *Death Wish* films, and even then not without provocation, who acts upon his wish to see justice done. Michael Winner, speaking of the success of *Death Wish*, insists, "It was the most imitated film in history. After *Death Wish* showed that you can have a citizen killing bad guys and be a hero, practically every American action film since took that theme. *Kill Bill* is *Death Wish* with Jap swords. Revenge films abound now. Before *Death Wish* it was only in Westerns that a citizen could gun down nasty people and be applauded" (*Winner Takes All* 198–199). The five films that comprise each *Dirty Harry* and *Death Wish* franchise are two urban westerns that feature heroes who have attained iconic status by being cast from an enduring mold—the independent loner who acts outside the constraints of the *status quo* to answer a higher calling, negotiating for audiences the need to balance conflicting impulses of obligation to community, the desire for individual freedom, and the sometimes terrible choice between justice and the law.

Part III

The Liminal Outlaw Hero in the Modern Action Film

The Warrior as Liminal Outlaw Hero

In his 2007 study *Action Speaks Louder Than Words: Violence, Spectacle and the American Action Movie*, Eric Lichtenfeld states, "The action genre, like any other, is a concoction of elements—some a matter of plot, some mythological, some purely cinematic—that creates for the audience a sense of ritual and a host of expectations" (1). A "synthesis of other genres," he maintains, it is "derived from the Western, *film noir*, and the police procedural (with special guest appearances made by the disaster film and others)" (5). It is true that the Western genre, so central to the shaping of an American identity, indisputably makes its *imprimatur* on later cinematic genres, including action films from the 1960s on. However, Ari Mattes, in his insightful 2013 article "Turning the Gun on America: *Cobra* and the Action Film as Cultural Critique," maintains that both popular and academic critics of the modern action film "continue to marginalize or dismiss it," failing to see its value as social commentary; he also observes that most approaches to 1980s action films have generated "readings of gender and political ideology" (*Australasian Journal of Popular Culture* 2, no. 3, 457). Mattes further asserts that Lichtenfeld and others who have written about 1980s action movies have tended to be "dismissive of the films as examples of propagandistic exceedingly 'Reaganite entertainments'" (457). In fact, however, their messages can be read "as simultaneously conservative and subversive; reactionary and radically liberal" (467), as he demonstrates in his discussion of *Cobra* (1986), an action film starring Sylvester Stallone. As discussed throughout this study, a recurring concern expressed in American cinema is that of the relationship between the individual and community, and the debate over more or less governance. These issues are reflected in movies because they are central to American identity, as both Paul Cantor, who identifies a persistent libertarian impulse in television and film, and Robert Ray, with his discussion of the official and outlaw hero figures, and his analysis of left and right cycle films, so ably show.

Robert Ray's chapter titled "The Left and Right Cycles" from his earlier study *A Certain Tendency of the Hollywood Cinema, 1930–1980* (1985) anticipates Mattes' conclusion that the conservative and liberal labels applied to certain films can be deceptive, and that the issue is a complex one. Discussing Hollywood's response to the demise of the western, this chapter discusses films of the 1960s and 1970s as responses to the closing of the frontier in American cinema. Ray concludes of what he calls Left and Right cycle films that "superficially ... their opposed attitudes toward the closing of the frontier and the validity of the values associated with it made the Left and Right films appear very different ... but in fact they were remarkably similar" (309). For instance, *Dirty Harry* (1971) is a Right cycle film, but when Harry tosses away his badge at the conclusion, he is displaying a Left cycle quality by acknowledging his own "out-of-datedness" (310). Left and Right cycles often blur their own boundaries; a dismissal of Right cycle films as simple conservative propaganda results in a superficial reading of them. Mattes' point about acknowledging the complexity and ambiguity of some modern action films also rings true.

The "action film" as defined by Litchenfeld and others, then, is a broad generic category that has been applied to crime drama, dystopian science fiction, martial arts movies, spy films, thrillers, urban westerns, and super-hero comic book pictures. Its development and characteristics continue to be discussed and debated. In the last four decades, however, in addition to the live-action super-hero who derives from comics (Spiderman, Superman, Batman) action heroes that first come to mind are those played by stars like Bruce Willis, Arnold Schwarzenegger, Chuck Norris, and Sylvester Stallone, who appear in films that share certain features of style rather than plot or setting. The modern action film arguably developed with the demise of the Hollywood studio system and the rise of "New Hollywood" in the late 1960s and is geared toward distribution that takes advantage of globalization, especially audiences in the Pacific Rim and Latin America. For the purposes of this study, it might best be characterized as internationalized cinema that can be identified by its distinct *style*—its editing and pace, its under reliance on dialogue (in part to minimize the need for sub-titles with the advent of growing overseas markets), the physical demands it places on its protagonist, its inclusion of violent exploits—rather than being recognized for its use of a particular theme, setting, or story.

The modern action film shares some of these features with other genres, for sure, but the examples of such films that employ the liminal outlaw hero exemplified in the two highly successful franchises discussed in the chapters which follow—Rambo and Batman, in his incarnation as the Dark Knight—are distinct, in one way, from those discussed in the previous chapters that focus on modern figurations of the knight as liminal outlaw hero. These two characters are members of a trained professional warrior class, hearkening back most directly in this way to the medieval knight. Both are shown to be of an elect, singled out for their potential and abilities. Beverly Kennedy asserts that, while there are other models in Malory's work, "it is Lancelot who best exemplifies the *military*, political, and judicial functioning of the True Knight" (*Knighthood* 93, emphasis added). A more extreme form of the knight who combines a physical and spiritual superiority above other men is the Templar knight—the warrior priest class who emerged during the Crusades. Rambo, especially, shares some affinities with this figure. As we have seen, the manner in which gunfighters learn their trade remains enigmatic, although sometimes they are shown to have acquired their trade from another, even though commonly they are Civil War veterans (Shane, Paladin). The Lone Ranger, a vigilante, is a former Texas Ranger, but he espouses nonviolence, using force only as a last resort, a creed his descendant, Batman, will also espouse, but not often be able to keep. Harry Callahan is a trained detective and an expert marksman, but he is not presented as a hero with highly specialized training in overcoming punishing physical odds, greatly outnumbered by an enemy, nor does he practice martial arts, another common feature of the modern action hero. Paul Kersey is a civilian whose father taught him to shoot, but Paul has lived all of his adult civilian life as a pacifist until he turns to violence after his wife's murder.

Rambo, on the other hand, belongs to an elite, highly trained class of professional killers; he is a decorated, battle wise Green Beret, a veteran of the Vietnam War. Bruce Wayne (a.k.a. Batman) begins as a civilian who seeks vengeance for his parents' murders and works toward the abolishment of crime; with the advent of his persona as the "Dark Knight" (the focus of the next chapter) in the series initiated by *Batman Begins*, he also seeks professional training to hone his combat expertise, acquiring elite warrior skills. He travels to Bhutan, in south Asia, and is trained by a group known as the "League of Shadows." (Neither Rambo nor Batman possess the traditional "superhero" status defined in the comic book tradition, in that they lack particular supernatural abilities or powers, despite their sometimes implausible feats.) Rambo comes from an impoverished background. The lore that emerges from the collective films in the franchise reveals that he is of Native American and German descent, raised in Arizona by a father who brutalized him until he ran away. By contrast, Batman

(Bruce Wayne), although orphaned early on when his parents were murdered, was born into a family of privilege and wealth. Nonetheless, Rambo and Batman both embody the ideal of the liminal outlaw hero, caught between justice and the law, intent on employing their specialized training in the service of a higher ideal, even though doing so exacts a heavy personal price.

This *askesis* often attributed to an elite warrior class is one distinctive feature of the liminal outlaw hero in his action hero incarnation. In his chapter, "The Solitude of the Wandering Knight," Leo Braudy reasons that the solitary knight on a quest in the Middle Ages represented an effort by the Christian community to "reshape the warrior heritage into a new system of values," because it recognized the dangers of "unfocused prowess," which, if left unchecked, could lead to the destruction of the knight's own community. This was best accomplished when the knight remained solitary, separated after battle from the elite warrior band, alone with his own chivalric code and God (*From Chivalry to Terrorism* 91). This separateness of the professional warrior served to cultivate the introspective, spiritual side of his nature, in turn designed to keep his violent training in check: "The artistic preoccupation in both Western and Japanese culture with the solitary adventurer ... in increasingly complex urban societies, owes a crucial debt to the chivalric model of the warrior, knight or samurai," which is why in earlier times Shane remained an *errant* figure, for instance, and why the modern Rambo, in *Rambo III*, is found in a Buddhist monastery when his warrior skills are called upon yet again by authorities (Braudy 92). This is perhaps also why Bruce Wayne travels to Bhutan (in south central Asia) to acquire additional training in the art of war. Warrior skills, however, must be balanced with spiritual refinement, cultivated in solitude; it is imperative for this type of trained warrior hero to heed his conscience and answer to a higher moral imperative dictated by his own conscience.

The particular training of this kind characterizes the liminal outlaw hero in these contemporary action films. Like the other incarnations we have seen, he is both above the law and outside of it, yet is called upon to serve it, but his professional training as a warrior, and how this is employed, is a distinguishing feature, one associated with the action film genre itself. Rambo and Batman come from widely divergent backgrounds and experiences, but they both fulfill the role of liminal outlaw hero, coming to the rescue of the "official" hero and/or community, and remaining loners devoid of permanent entanglements, like their predecessors. Their encounters with crime and the inept systems that fail to eradicate it pose central questions about law, order, individual and community rights, and what type of governance best promotes the ideal of justice. Both have learned to be skilled professional warriors, which necessarily dictates their continued existence in this liminal space.

CHAPTER 7

Reconciling Opposites in the *Rambo* Franchise (1982–2008)

> "and the minstrel sings
> Before them of the ten years' war in Troy,
> And our great deeds, as half-forgotten things.
> Is there confusion in the little isle?
> Let what is broken so remain."
> —Alfred, Lord Tennyson,
> "The Lotos-Eaters" (ll. 121–25)

The origin of the now iconic hero of four blockbuster action films was the publication of David Morrell's novel *First Blood* (1972), sometimes called "the father of the modern action novel" (David Morrell, "Rambo and Me: The Story Behind the Story"). It portrays an itinerant Vietnam War veteran and Green Beret known only as "Rambo," who, while passing through Madison, Kentucky, has a run-in with its sheriff, Will Teasle, himself a decorated veteran of the Korean War.[1] Teasle dislikes Rambo's looks—especially his long hair and beard—so he escorts Rambo to the edge of town, making clear his presence is unwanted. Rambo, however, who does not like being "run out of Dodge," repeatedly returns to Madison; he is charged with vagrancy and resisting arrest, for which he is sentenced to thirty-five days in the local jail.

This poses a serious dilemma for the unfortunate traveller. Rambo was trained in Special Forces and completed many missions, but we learn in a flashback that he was finally captured and tortured by the North Vietnamese. Near death, he managed to escape and made his way south 390 miles, evading his captors for weeks, and in a state of exhausted delirium arrives at an American military base. "They held him in the hospital for a month until his hysteria left him" (*First Blood* 49). Six months before Rambo finds himself under arrest in

Madison, we learn that he had been "convalescing in a hospital," yet was unable to control his urge to kill—he had broken a man's nose in a Philadelphia bar for pushing ahead of him to see a stripper, and he had slit the throat of a black man who had pulled a knife on Rambo as he slept on a park bench, also pursuing and killing the thug's companion—a vigilante activity, but also an incident that made clear to Rambo his difficulty adjusting to civilian life (29).[2] The strife between Teasle and Rambo escalates when, after humiliating the prisoner by strip-searching him and cutting his hair, the sheriff and his deputies attempt to shave his beard. Rambo bears the emotional but also the physical scars of war—slashes on his back, three deep gashes on his chest, a bullet hole scar on his leg. Because he was knifed and tortured as a prisoner in Vietnam, when the deputies try to put a straight razor near his face, Rambo loses control, kills a deputy and escapes town on a stolen motorcycle.

The ensuing battle of wits and will between the stubborn Teasle and Rambo brings about the death of several more deputies along with Teasle's adopted father, Orval, in the initial manhunt for Rambo, who has vanished into the rugged rural terrain. Only Teasle escapes Rambo's guerrilla tactics, at which point he unwillingly has to accept the help of the State Police and eventually the National Guard. When he still evades the authorities, Rambo's ex-commander, Sam Trautman, appears on the scene: "I've come about my boy," he tells Teasle, and then boasts that Rambo "was the best student we ever turned out" (159). Despite the manpower now deployed, Rambo relies upon his military survival tactics and manages to return to the town—even though he could have fled the area and headed to Mexico as he initially planned—bent on exacting his revenge, the struggle in the novel almost exclusively being that between himself and Teasle. Rambo uses his munitions knowledge to wreak havoc in the town, detonating explosives that result in massive fires. Finally, he and Teasle mutually and mortally wound each other; Trautman finds the moribund Rambo and shoots him in the head, after which Teasle also dies, completing the novel's pattern of alternating between the two characters' point of view. In his engaging essay "Rambo and Me: The Story Behind the Story," David Morrell explains, "I never favored one character over the other," and concludes, "It's an allegory of sorts," in which Sam Trautman represents "Uncle Sam," the official government position, while the opposition between Rambo and Teasle embodies "conflicted America," at a time when the country was in turmoil over U.S. involvement in the Vietnam War. Having completed this allegorical story, the novel provides a mystical, if not transcendent death for both Rambo and Teasle, locked in a personal vendetta against each other, but also bound together through their mutual end.

"There *are* no friendly civilians":
First Blood (1982)

"In town, you're the law. Out here, it's me. Don't push it. Let it go."
—John J. Rambo to Sheriff Will Teasle

When *First Blood* was published in 1972, this first novel for David Morrell met with favorable reviews, and Columbia Pictures soon after purchased the movie rights for it, intending Richard Brooks to write and direct it ("Rambo and Me"). Brooks was a seasoned film director and screenplay writer, whose director credits included *Blackboard Jungle* (1955), *Cat on a Hot Tin Roof* (1958) and *Looking for Mr. Goodbar* (1977). He wrote the film adaptation for Frank O'Rourke's novel *The Professionals* and for Truman Capote's *In Cold Blood*, both of which he also directed in 1966 and 1967, respectively. Columbia apparently disliked Brooks' script, which he reportedly had worked on for a year, and sold the rights to Warner Brothers, who intended it to be directed by Sydney Pollack, with Steve McQueen cast as Rambo. The story changed hands repeatedly: in all, according to Morrell, no less than 26 scripts were prepared ("Rambo and Me"). Finally, a full decade after the novel's publication, the film made its debut, released by a relatively new company, Carolco Pictures. Two independent international film distributors, Hungarian-born wigmaker and Hong Kong cinema owner Andrew Vajna and Beirut-born Mario Kassar, formed Carolco in 1976, having met at Cannes Film Festival the previous year. They purchased the film rights from Warner Bros. in 1980 for $385,000, hired Ted Kotcheff to direct, and Sylvester Stallone to play the lead role.

Born July 6, 1946, in New York City, Sylvester Stallone grew up in Philadelphia in the home of his mother and stepfather, his parents having divorced when he was young. After high school, Stallone studied dramatic art at American College in Switzerland and then the University of Miami, eventually moving to New York and finally to Hollywood in order to try to break into acting ("Sylvester Stallone," *Bio*, A&E Television Networks). While trying to launch an acting career, he also busied himself writing scripts, one about an underdog and aspiring boxer, Rocky Balboa. Stallone refused to sell the script unless he was cast as its star: "Several producers offered to buy the screenplay, wanting to cast a name star in the title role, which Stallone insisted on playing himself. Although his bank balance was barely $100, Stallone held fast with his perseverance" (www.sylvesterstallone.com/bio). *Rocky* (1976) earned ten Academy Award nominations and won best picture, launching an American iconic figure that would result in five sequels: *Rocky II* (1979), *Rocky III* (1982)—the same year he starred in *First Blood*—*Rocky IV* (1985), which coincided with *Rambo:*

First Blood Part II, *Rocky V* (1990), and *Rocky Balboa* (2006), released just two years before his fourth appearance as the hero of *Rambo* (2008). Rocky Balboa and John Rambo have both become mythic American heroes, down-and-outers who have fought their way through adversity, not unlike the actor who portrayed them.

Ryan Lambie writes in "The Rise and Fall of Carolco," that upon its release in October of 1982, *First Blood* was a huge hit, and made Carolco "a major Hollywood production company." The company went on to release not only the next two Rambo films in 1985 and 1988 (*Rambo: First Blood Part II* and *Rambo III*) but also, after aligning with TriStar, made such blockbusters as *Total Recall* (1990), *Terminator 2: Judgment Day* (1991) and *Basic Instinct* (1992), making a few pictures a year with big budgets, and relying on the increasing revenues from foreign markets to finance their films (Tino Balio, "A Major Presence in all the World's Important Markets" in *The Film Cultures Reader*, ed. Graeme Turner, 211).

Critics also generally viewed the film favorably. Janet Maslin's review in the *New York Times*, published on October 22, 1982 (the day of its release) praises Stallone's performance in this action film characterized by sparse dialogue, remarking, "As a tough, powerful, silent presence, he is unexpectedly commanding." Moreover, she praised the story's "energy and ingenuity" which, coupled with Stallone's portrayal of a "fierce, agile, hollow-eyed hero" provides the film with something of a "distinct" if not definitely a "universal appeal" (www.nytimes.com). Roger Ebert disliked the film's conclusion, but was impressed also with Stallone's performance, especially in the sequence when he is being pursued in the woods. Calling Stallone "one of the great physical actors in the movies," Ebert states that "although almost all of 'First Blood' is implausible, because it's Stallone on the screen, we'll buy it." It is "well-paced" and "well-acted" by Stallone, Richard Crenna and Brian Dennehy (www.roger ebert.com). *First Blood* grossed $47,212, 904 domestically, but its world-wide gross was much larger—$125, 212,904—demonstrating the appeal of modern action films for burgeoning international cinematic audiences (www.boxoffice mojo.com).

Set in Madison, Kentucky, because Morrell wanted "a slight southern flavor," the town in the novel is actually modeled on Bellefonte, Pennsylvania, the scene of a real 1966 manhunt known as the "Shade Gap Incident, "to capture a kidnapper and murderer, William Hollenbaugh. It involved dogs, helicopters, and the FBI traversing a mountainous terrain similar to that in the novel ("Rambo and Me"). The film, however, is set in the Pacific northwest, in a fictive town called Hope, Washington. Hope, British Columbia, is where the film was shot in order to take advantage of "Canadian financial incentives"

("Rambo and Me"), the same reason that *Death Wish V: The Face of Death* was later filmed in Toronto, although it is set in New York. Yet the theme of the American veteran who encounters hostility in his own country required that it be set in the United States, so Hope, British Columbia, became Hope, Washington. The Canadian film location is also the likely reason that Ted Kotcheff was selected to direct *First Blood*; he was a Canadian citizen and the government required some of its citizens be employed by the production.

The screenplay is credited to Michael Kozoll (known mostly as a television writer in the 1970s and 1980s for such series as *Quincy M. D.*, *Kolchak: The Night Stalker*, and *Hill Street Blues*), William Sackheim, whose writing credits date back to the 1940s and 1950s with films like *Homicide* (1949) and *Forbidden* (1953), and who also became a prolific television writer, and finally to Sylvester Stallone, the star. The most significant change introduced when the novel was adapted to a screenplay was that of shifting the sympathy to the main character, now called John J. Rambo. This was accomplished by making the sheriff a much less complex figure than he is in the novel, and also by both "softening the character" of Rambo and "making him a victim" ("Rambo and Me"), an alteration that also turned the character from an outlaw to a liminal outlaw hero. The change is accomplished in part by the opening sequence, discussed below, and by the fact that Rambo initially avoids killing. Morrell observes, "My Rambo is furious about the war experience ... not in the movie" ("Rambo and Me"). Perhaps most important of all is the altered ending in which Rambo is not killed by his mentor, Sam Trautman, but is instead taken into custody, after an emotional breakdown and a reconciliation with his former commander. His fate remains uncertain, but not without hope. Stallone insisted on this, a wise decision in that it allowed for a sequel. "Stallone was determined to make Rambo more sympathetic and less violent in the movie, according to Ryan Lambie in "The Rise and Fall of Carolco," (www.denofgeek.com).

First Blood establishes the character and background of Rambo, and the circumstances under which he will become a liminal outlaw hero in the three ensuing sequels. The film's opening, not found in the novel, immediately enlists the viewer's sympathies and establishes a melancholy mood that eventually erupts into violence. Instead of being set in the heat of the summer as in the novel, it is early winter (evinced by Christmas decorations around the town) and Rambo makes his way to a lakeside cabin, where a woman hangs clothes on the line while her children play nearby. He inquires after his Vietnam War buddy, Delmore Barry, only to learn from his widow that he died as a result of his exposure to Agent Orange during the war. When his former commander, Sam Trautman (Richard Crenna), catches up with Rambo in the climactic concluding scene, we learn that Barry was Rambo's last hope of finding a surviving member of his squadron, so this news of his demise means that Rambo is the only one left, further intensifying his sense of isolation.[3]

As David Morrell notes, additional changes made the figure of the sheriff more shallow and that of Rambo more sympathetic. Sheriff Teasle (Brian Dennehy) and his deputy, Galt (Jack Starrett), are as close to stereotypical southern redneck lawmen as one is likely to encounter. Teasle treats the town like it is his own possession, and judges Rambo solely by his appearance, assuming he is a hippy, with all of the requisite social and political baggage that goes along with the term. For instance, Rambo has a decal of an American flag sewn to his jacket, and Teasle snipes, "You know wearin' that flag on your jacket, lookin' like you do—you're askin' for trouble around here, friend.... We don't want guys like you here, a drifter," and then advises Rambo to take a bath and cut his hair. Rambo resents that he is denied the right to enter Hope, even for a meal: "Is there any law against me getting something here?" he asks Teasle, who responds dictatorially, "Yeah, me." Later, in the wild, Rambo remembers Teasle's arbitrary decision to declare himself the law and, on his own turf, replies in kind.

Teasle's stubborn refusal to heed anyone else's warnings about escalating the private war with a trained, angry ex–Green Beret, and his clash with Trautman, adds to the negative treatment of his character, which has little of the complexity and ambivalence toward Rambo present in the novel; the film omits the fact that Teasle is in the process of divorcing his wife to account for his stress, and scarcely touches on his distinguished military service in the Korean War. He does not die at the conclusion of the film, but is only wounded, suggesting he is merely foolish rather than tenaciously courageous. Although set in the northwest, Deputy Galt speaks with a southern accent and engages in sadistic acts when Rambo is incarcerated; he brutalizes him, humiliates Rambo by hosing him down instead of letting the prisoner take a shower, and places him in a strangulation hold with his Billy club when another deputy attempts to shave Rambo. Two short flashbacks that portray Rambo's capture and torture in Vietnam in this sequence augment the inhumane treatment of him in the jail cell, and explain the panic that makes him break free. In the novel, Rambo disembowels Galt during his escape, but here he practices only evasive tactics, killing no one as he flees.

This contrast with the novel continues when the authorities pursue Rambo. An enraged Galt rides in a helicopter and is intent on killing Rambo, firing at him repeatedly. In self-defense, Rambo hurls a rock at the hovering helicopter—one of many assaults against technology he launches in the films—and Galt falls out of it to his death. When the sheriff arrives at the scene, Rambo comes out of hiding with his hands up, trying to surrender: "There's one man dead. It's not my fault. I don't want any more hurt…. I didn't do anything." The posse opens fire on Rambo despite his effort to surrender peacefully, and the sheriff vows revenge for Galt's death. Our sympathies are enlisted further when, in their vengeful pursuit of Rambo, he uses improvised but effective means to ambush the sheriff and his men, setting guerrilla warfare traps, yet kills none of them. Trapping and disabling the others, Rambo, now quite transformed in his combat mode, then pins Teasle against a tree, holding a knife to his throat: "I could have killed them *all*. I could have killed *you*. In town, *you're* the law. Out here, it's *me*. Don't push it. Don't push it—or I'll give you a war you won't believe. Let it go." He then vanishes into the woods as suddenly as he had appeared. Obviously, the fact that Rambo wishes not to kill, although we see in this scene his seething anger that he controls only with difficulty, is designed to show that he is the wronged party, reluctant to engage in warfare, but dangerously close to being provoked into reverting to his survivalist and warrior training.

Rambo is the victim, not the criminal. He respects the law until its representatives prove unworthy and pose a threat to his existence. The villainous Galt deserves the end he meets, while the willful Teasle is driven first by a prejudice and finally by a vengeance for which there is no convincing motive in the film. The argument about law and justice becomes more explicit when the State Police join the manhunt. Its leader Kern (Bill McKinney), upon hearing from another of Teasle's deputies, Lester (Alf Humphreys), that Galt was "hard on Rambo" earlier at the station, disapproves of the brutality, calling the deputies "assholes." Teasle, however, defends Galt and the others who were cruel to Rambo, insisting, "It doesn't make one goddamn bit of difference. People start fuckin' around with the law and all hell breaks loose," expressing a conservative preoccupation that values *order* over the liberal position (Kern's) that sides with a prisoner's rights and *due process of the law*. Rambo's conflict is that of an American who knows his rights have been impinged upon by the narrow, biased thinking of the sheriff. The law in Teasle's hands is unjust, so much so that even the state policeman, Kern, finds the treatment of Rambo deplorable. In standing up for his rights, Rambo is trying to serve justice, even though it means clashing with the local lawman, not an uncommon theme in romances or westerns.

The corrupt local authorities, the State Police, and an inept National Guard unit all fail to capture or kill Rambo. The Army sends Colonel Sam Trautman to rescue them from his own former Green Beret. Trautman declares with pride, "God didn't make Rambo. I made him. I recruited him. I trained him. I commanded him in Vietnam for three years. I'd say that makes him mine."

The relationship between Trautman and Rambo is much more personal in the film than in the novel. Here, Trautman takes responsibility for Rambo, from his recruitment to serving as his commanding officer on missions for three years. In the novel, his counterpart says, "I didn't train him myself. My men did. But I trained the men who trained him" (Morrell 159). The bond between Rambo and Trautman is made much stronger, even becoming paternal at the end. This, too, works toward moving Rambo into the liminal outlaw hero space, as his background in Vietnam shows him to be patriotic, having completed extraordinary acts of heroism for his country, at great personal sacrifice and risk. Trautman reminds the sheriff that Rambo was "trained to ignore pain, weather, to live off the land. To eat things that would make a Billy goat puke. In Vietnam his job was to dispose of enemy personnel. To kill. Period. Win by attrition. Now, Rambo was the best." Knowing that Rambo is now in his combat survivalist mode, Trautman advises the local authorities to "let him go. Pick him up in a few weeks and no one else will get hurt."

When the relentless sheriff refuses to do this, Trautman speaks with Rambo on a walky-talky that Rambo has confiscated from his pursuers. Trautman lists the names of all the men in the former squadron, trying to re-establish his bond with Rambo, but Rambo's poignant answer is "They're all gone, sir. All dead, sir," and finally, "I'm the last one, sir." Trautman offers to come and get Rambo, but it seems that the commanding officer has been out of touch with his "boys." When Rambo says he had tried to contact Trautman, no one at Fort Bragg knew where he was; Trautman had in fact been in Washington D.C. Obviously, Rambo has been isolated and alienated, unable to reintegrate into the culture, and he tells Trautman of his wish to be back at Fort Bragg, too, the military life being the one he now knows. When Trautman says, "We'll talk about that when you come in," Rambo refuses: "I can't do that, sir." When Trautman counters that Rambo can't run around out there "wastin' friendly civilians," the full extent of Rambo's alienation from society becomes shockingly clear when he replies, "There *are* no friendly civilians." Rambo then tries to explain his current predicament: "There wouldn't be no trouble if it weren't for that king shit cop. All I wanted was something to eat. But the man kept pushing, sir.... They drew first blood, not me," and then Rambo disconnects, refusing to be co-opted by Trautman, but the exchange allowed the authorities to pinpoint Rambo's location.

Guardsmen are dispatched to the coordinates, a cave in which they believe they have trapped Rambo and blown him up with an M72 LAW Rocket. The sheriff gloats, "Special, my ass. He was just another drifter that broke the law," to which an angered Trautman retorts, "Vagrancy, wasn't it? That's gonna look real good on his gravestone at Arlington. 'Here lies John Rambo, winner of the

Congressional Medal of Honor. Survivor of countless incursions behind enemy lines. Killed for vagrancy in Jerkwater, USA,'" again driving home the point that Rambo has been served nothing but injustice by the law. Teasle confesses to Trautman that he felt "cheated out of his chance." "I wanted to kill that kid so bad I could taste it." Trautman observes that "doesn't sit well with that badge," reminding Teasle that his personal vendetta against Rambo is at odds with his duty. When the sheriff counters by asking, "What would you have done with him if he came in? Would you have wrapped your arms around him and gave him a big sloppy kiss, or would you have blown his brains out?" to which Trautman answers that he couldn't know that until he met Rambo face to face. In the novel, Trautman does indeed shoot Rambo in the head, ending his life, but instead he rescues him in the film.

Trautman suspects correctly that Rambo has escaped death. Rambo continues to avoid killing when he can, letting a boy in the forest run free, and when he hijacks a national guard truck to return to Hope, he lets the driver of the vehicle out by the side of the road, with the order to "go home." Rambo returns to Hope and sets off a series of explosions, direct insults to the sheriff's possessive jealousy of his town and his unwillingness to let Rambo into it, but also as a set of diversions so that he can hunt Teasle in the "private war" instigated and escalated by the sheriff. Trautman warns the sheriff, "You're gonna die, Teasle," proclaiming that, as his former commander, he is the only one who might be able to make Rambo desist. "God knows what damage he is prepared to do," Trautman warns. Teasle does not listen, and storms out of the office in search of Rambo.

Trautman recognizes the grave danger that has resulted from inciting Rambo's wrath. In his chapter "The Shape of Fury," Leo Braudy traces the very interesting tradition, dating back to the ancients, of the berserker warrior, citing Rambo as a rare modern fictional example that once had many representations (*From Chivalry to Terrorism* 43). When Rambo earlier had warned Teasle (at knife point, barely maintaining control) to "let it go," he was clearly trying to avoid what he eventually becomes in the film—the "enraged warrior" (Braudy 42)—a menace that Trautman tries in vain to warn Teasle about here. Rambo's tenuous connection with the "civilized" world has been severed by this confrontation with Teasle, and he reverts to the instinctive, natural world, becoming a predatory danger to community.[4]

In the showdown on a now decimated main street, Rambo wounds Teasle and is prepared to finish him off, but Trautman appears in time to talk him out of this, pleading with Rambo to return to Fort Bragg with him. He argues that Rambo also "did everything to make this private war happen" and, urging him to see that he is hopelessly outnumbered, Trautman insists, "the mission is over." Now, all of Rambo's pent up rage is released: "Nothing is over! You don't just turn it off! It wasn't *my* war. You asked *me*. I didn't ask *you!*" Emotionally overwrought, he reminds Trautman that in Vietnam he tried his best, but "somebody wouldn't let us win." Upon his return to the United States, Rambo resents that he was reviled by protesters of the war, to which Trautman responds, "It's all in the past now," but Rambo exclaims, "For *you!* For me, civilian life is nothing."

Touched by Rambo's grief and confusion, Trautman tells him, "You're the last of an elite group. Don't let it end like this." "Back there, I could fly a gunship. I could drive a tank. I was in charge of million-dollar equipment. But here I can't even hold a job," is Rambo's perplexed and sad response. Remembering the death of one of his fellow squadron members, Rambo breaks down entirely, and Trautman, who earlier boasts that he, and not God, had "made Rambo," takes responsibility for his warrior that he has abandoned. Like Victor Frankenstein, who creates and then abandons his monster, only to realize too late the consequences of having done so, Trautman sees the results of Rambo's isolation, and the toll it has taken. He tries to avert disaster with compassion, not the vengeance Victor Frankenstein showed to his creature: he kneels, places his hand on Rambo's back, as the latter weeps in his arms. As Teasle is taken off in an ambulance, Trautman and Rambo exit without incident the destroyed building, with a sequel hanging heavy in the air.

In *First Blood* the character of Rambo is poised to assume the role of liminal outlaw hero that he will fulfill in the ensuing sequels. First, he fights against injustice: he has a "right" to enter the town of Hope, Washington, enter a diner, and eat a meal. He has a "right" to expect that he will not be judged by his appearance, that he will not be harassed by corrupt lawmen, arrested on a flimsy pretext, or treated in an inhumane, humiliating manner when he is incarcerated. When Rambo relives the torture as a POW in Vietnam, his panic and need to escape that experience indicates the extent to which his transition to civilian life has been ignored. When he flees, still mindful of not harming others, Rambo becomes persecuted so that he slips back into a role of warrior/survivalist that has become "second nature" to him. He challenges the injustice he incurs from the local law, but also from the manner in which both the military and civilian segments of the population have abandoned or reviled him after the war. Rambo is a loner, the last of an elite squadron of fighters, and his sense of belatedness—of having lived beyond a time in which he was useful—haunts him in this film and its sequels.

Trained as a professional warrior, in the future Rambo will be called upon to use his expertise to rescue a collective "official" hero, to complete missions a larger systemic military, diplomatic, or government agency cannot. Rambo must undertake these "missions" alone, unfettered by domestic ties and unsupported by the earlier brotherhood he enjoyed in his squadron. He will fulfill the role of liminal outlaw hero, an individual called upon to rescue a collective official hero, sometimes an unworthy one, so that true justice can be achieved for innocent and/or worthy others. Rambo must also undertake a redemptive spiritual journey existing, as he does, in a liminal space between his past (as a military "killing machine") and his need to reconcile this past with the present. He is the hero who returns home to an alien existence, and must find a way to negotiate a future that can help him live with this past. Rambo is at once the most loyal of patriots and an ex-patriot who finds that he has no home after the war. His quest for spiritual healing becomes an ongoing undertaking in the three sequels, even as he continues to serve the country of which he no longer feels himself to be a part.

Rambo: First Blood Part II (1985): "The kind of war you don't win"

TRAUTMAN: "What is it you want?"
RAMBO: "For my country to love us as much as we love it."
TRAUTMAN: "How will you live, John?"
RAMBO: "Day by day."

After the box office success of *First Blood*, plans for a sequel began almost immediately, and *Rambo: First Blood Part II* was released on May 22, 1985, exactly two years and seven months after the first film. Directed by George P. Cosmatos, who went on to direct Stallone in *Cobra* (1986), released the following year, the story credit goes to Kevin Jarre, known also for the Wyatt Earp western *Tombstone* (1993), a film that Cosmatos also directed. The screenplay is credited to Sylvester Stallone and James Cameron. Cameron experienced a major breakthrough in the film industry with *The Terminator* (1984) which he directed and co-wrote with Gayle Anne Hurd (whom he married in 1985); however, before it was released, he had already written a screenplay for the second *First Blood* film, tentatively titled *First Blood II: The Mission*, and dated December 22, 1983 (www.jamescamerononline.com). Although *Rambo: First Blood Part II* follows the script in its overall plot, there are some significant changes that appear in the finished film when compared to Cameron's screenplay—these, then, one assumes, represent Stallone's writing contribution. The three most important changes are the elimination of a partner for Rambo on his mission (a character named Brewer is assigned as his partner in Cameron's version), deleted details about the background of Co, Rambo's female Vietnamese guide and love interest in the film, and the added coda at the end which features an important conversation between Rambo and Trautman.

The topical issue in the 1982 film *First Blood* is the disillusionment of a Vietnam war hero who returns to a country still divided over the United States' involvement in Southeast Asia, and the difficulty of adjusting to this divisiveness, having taken great risks to defend it. In this way—despite the differences between the novel and the film, discussed above—the latter reflects David Morrell's stated purpose in writing the novel, which he began to formulate shortly after he moved to Pennsylvania to attend graduate school at Penn State in 1966 and completed writing in June of 1971 ("Rambo and Me"). The topical issue addressed in *Rambo: First Blood Part II*—that of the MIA/POW—draws directly from concerns about soldiers unaccounted for and prisoners left behind in Southeast Asia after the war ended. James Cameron's script, dated December 22, 1983, employs the subject that preoccupied American politics and attitudes about Vietnam that lingered long after the official war was over. Films of the late 1970s and 1980s, such as *The Deer Hunter* (1978), the recipient of four Oscars, *Uncommon Valor* (1983) starring Gene Hackman and directed by Ted Kotcheff (who directed *Fist Blood* the year before), Carolco's 1984 *Missing in Action* (along with its two sequels in 1985 and 1988), starring Chuck Norris, and *First Blood Part II*, fuel the persistent myth of American POWs purportedly detained by North Vietnam after the war.

It was the story itself that garnered mostly negative critical reviews of the film. Michael Wilmington of the *Los Angeles Times* calls *Rambo: First Blood Part II* "an inane sequel to a fairly good melodrama," the former film showing audiences a "disconsolate Vietnam vet ... pushed too far" and battling a town, but here Rambo takes on "the combined Soviet and Vietnamese armies," an implausibility masked by explosive special effects, but reducing the audience's ability to sympathize with the main character (www.latimes.com). In his *New York Times* review, dated the day of the film's release, Vincent Canby, who had savaged *Death Wish*, includes in his review of *Rambo: First Blood Part II* his disdain for his perception of the film's attack on liberal politics, but he also rails against the self-obsession of Rambo and the actor who plays him, averring the camera "caresses Mr. Stallone's face and body with an abandon not seen on the screen since Josef von Sternberg made movies with Marlene Dietrich" (www.articles.latimes.com/1985-05-22/entertainment/ca-16965_1_john-rambo). Despite the generally negative critical reception, *Rambo: First Blood II* earned enormous dividends at the box office (the highest of the four films) with a domestic gross of $150,414,432 and a staggering $300,400,432 when it played to international audiences (www.boxofficemojo.com).

In his book *The Remains of War: Bodies, Politics, and the Search for American Soldiers Unaccounted for in Southeast Asia,* Thomas M. Hawley examines the reasons for and implications of the persistent myth of POWs and with repatriation of the dead, the latter an issue that did not exist in previous wars, in which unaccounted for bodies were seen as an inevitable result of modern warfare. Discrepancy cases, live-sightings, and the MIA/POW Activist Movement all worked toward creating a mythology that the United States was either being lied to by communist countries who retained American prisoners after the war, or that the government engaged in cover-ups in order to extend peace negotiations with North Vietnam (Hawley 64–67). This suspicion that fueled the burgeoning myth was related to the larger distrust of the government's handling of the war, and the United States' involvement in it. Hawley asserts that the absence of bodies "would become synonymous with the absence of principles that characterized the war itself" (68) and the continued belief in the MIA/POW mythology became "part of a continuous legacy of the Vietnam War" (3). Hawley's remark that "Hollywood apotheosized the warrior ethic in films in which a brawny hero rescued emaciated POWs, thereby finishing a job the effete American government had been unable to accomplish on its own" (67), suggests the connection between the lingering divisiveness in the country over America's involvement in the war itself, and the distrust of the government that spawned POW/MIA myths, all of which appear in the second *Rambo* film.

It is also important to remember that the construction of the Vietnam Memorial Wall was completed in October and dedicated in November 1982, and the symbolic "unknown solider" was interred in 1984, although the remains were exhumed, positively identified as those of First Lieutenant Michael J. Blassie (who had been MIA since 1972), and moved in 1998 (Hawley 1). Much publicized were the real and aborted "rescue" missions of ex-Green Beret Lieutenant Colonel James "Bo" Gritz. Gritz organized privately-funded missions (William Shatner and Clint Eastwood being two notable contributors) to return to Southeast Asia in an effort to locate POWs, one of which was aborted, while another ended in disaster. These escapades continued to fuel the controversy over the war and perpetuate the mythology of the MIA/POW.[5] In fact, H. Bruce Franklin so ably shows in his book, *M.I.A. or Mythmaking in America,* how the myth of American captives in southeast Asia was used as political propaganda by the Nixon administration: "The POW/MIA issues served two crucial functions in allowing Richard Nixon to continue the Vietnam War for four years.... It was both a booby trap for the anti-war movement and a wrench to be thrown into the works of the Paris peace talks" (74).[6]

Filmed in Mexico but set in Thailand and Vietnam, *Rambo: First Blood Part II* picks up five years after the first film's conclusion. Rambo has been placed in a military prison (in Cameron's script he is in lockdown in a military hospital in Fayetteville, North Carolina) and is shown working in a quarry there when Sam Trautman (Richard Crenna) arrives and offers him a reprieve in the form of a "covert operation in the Far East," which, if it results in success, may earn him a presidential pardon. Rambo is skeptical and reluctant to accept the offer, "In here at least I know where I stand," but when Trautman tells him the mission involves the rescue of POWs left behind in Vietnam, Rambo agrees, asking his former commander, "Sir, do we get to win this time?" to which Trautman responds, "This time, it's up to you." When Rambo travels to Thailand to meet with Trautman and the CIA operative, Marshall Murdock (Charles Napier), who is in charge, he is disappointed to learn that he is to parachute into an area where he was once held prisoner himself, in order to discover whether rumors of POWs being held in secrecy are true. The catch is that should he find such prisoners, Murdock orders that he is only to take photographs of them. Incredulous, Rambo queries, "Photographs?" Murdock states emphatically, "Just photographs. Under no circumstances are you to engage the enemy." He then avers that if POWs are located Trautman and an assault team will free them later. Rambo is told emphatically not to try "the blood and guts routine," and to "let the technology do the work," but his distrust of technology—and the mendacious, manipulative bureaucratic world of the CIA—prompts his retort: "I always thought the mind was the best weapon."

Trautman believes what Murdock says at this point, but Rambo has caught him in a lie: trying to impress Rambo, Murdock claimed that in 1966 he had served in the 2nd Battalion of the 3rd Marines at Kon Tum. Rambo tells Trautman that the 2nd Battalion was not at Kon Tum, but at Kud Sank, and that Trautman is the only one Rambo trusts, but he agrees to continue with the mission. He has 36 hours to investigate the POW rumor, take photos if he finds any of them, and then arrive at an agreed upon "extraction point" to return. After he parachutes out of the helicopter at his drop site (cutting away for his own safety most of the technology he has brought along), Rambo meets the contact that will help him negotiate his way downriver where the prison camp is supposed to exist. Co (Julia Nickson) is a young Vietnamese woman recruited for this mission. In Cameron's screenplay, her code name is "Night Orchid"; she is described as beautiful and about 28 years old, and has earned a Master's Degree from the University of Saigon. In his draft of the script, Co has agreed to work for the U.S. government in Vietnam in exchange for the safe passage to the states of her brother, who would have otherwise been executed by the North Vietnamese, and her now twelve-year-old son, Nguyen, who lives in Huntington Beach, California, and whom she has not seen for eight years.[7] In the film release, however, none of these details about her back-

7. Reconciling Opposites in Rambo (1982–2008)

ground are provided, and she instead shows very good combat and negotiation skills, two traits that help Rambo. We learn only that her father worked for an intelligence agency, that Co has seen "too much death," and that she wishes to live the "quiet life," maybe in the United States. En route, Rambo, feeling an affinity with her plight, confides in Co: "I came back to the states and found there was another war going on ... kind of like a quiet war ... against all the soldiers returning. The kind of war you don't win." In Cameron's script, another ex-soldier, Brewer, accompanies Rambo, but in the film version Co is his only companion.

When they arrive at the prison camp, it looks abandoned initially, but soon Rambo discovers that it is indeed occupied, and that there are American prisoners being held in it. Some are incarcerated in a filthy, rat infested cell, but one prisoner is tied cruelly to bamboo poles outside, obviously having been tortured. Rambo becomes the liminal outlaw hero when he answers a higher, compassionate calling and disregards his order to only take photographs: he frees the suffering prisoner and with Co they escape the camp. The pirates who gave them passage downriver are there to meet them the next morning, but this time they have sold out to the enemy, forcing Rambo to explode the patrol boat, escaping with Co and the rescued prisoner just in time. He then tells Co, "This is the end," that she should part from them, her duty being complete, and danger imminent. Rambo arrives at the extraction point with the prisoner. Trautman, who is in the approaching helicopter, sends a message to the headquarters, exclaiming, "Christ, he's found one!" Hearing this, Murdock immediately orders the mission to be aborted, leaving Rambo and the freed prisoner to be captured, and Trautman both disillusioned and furious at Murdock. When confronted, Murdock confesses that the mission was never meant to find prisoners, but only to go through the motions of investigating the rumors about POWs. Worse yet, Murdock admits that the CIA knows there are POWs that the North Vietnamese retained when the U.S. government reneged on an agreement to buy their freedom.[8]

Rambo is held captive with the other POWs; when a Soviet Army helicopter arrives at the camp, the other prisoners proclaim, "Damn Russian bastards. He's dead now," knowing that Rambo's fate is to be tortured and killed. After a prolonged torture session (a worthy rival to any masochistic Mel Gibson saga) at the command of the Russian, Lieutenant Colonel Podofsky (Steven Berkhoff), Rambo sees that Co has snuck into the camp disguised as a prostitute and with her help, he breaks out. Using a radio in the camp, Rambo sends a message to the CIA base in Thailand: "Murdock, I'm coming to get you!" On the run, Rambo tells Co, "What you did back there, I won't forget it. Thanks." Co softly asks, "Take me with you, to America," to which Rambo replies, "Yeah." The two kiss, but within fifteen seconds, Co is shot down by the pursuing soldiers and dies in Rambo's arms. "You not forget me?" she implores, to which he adamantly replies, "No no." In Cameron's script, Co persuades Rambo to agree to marry her so that she can enter the United States and join her child, something that he finds agreeable, but which clearly adds a pragmatic motive to the more overtly romantic scene in the film release. Rambo buries Co, but keeps her jade necklace, a knightly token and talisman (she had earlier told him it was "good luck") to help him now accomplish his revenge for her death as well as Murdock's betrayal. In a fast-paced action sequence, Rambo single-handedly wipes out the pursuing enemy and their Russian supporters, using all of his clever resourcefulness to do so. The technology offered him at the start of the mission he viewed with disdain, telling Murdock, "I always thought the *mind* was the best weapon"—certainly Rambo's ability to improvise and devise weapons out of the indigenous materials he finds in the rice patties and villages he traverses in his return to the camp shows this. He rescues the prisoners and they escape in a helicopter, Rambo sending a message to the CIA headquarters in Thailand that he is bringing back the freed POWs. Upon his return, his fury is turned on the wicked technocratic world of the CIA, as he sprays bullets to destroy the computer and communication equipment it employs. He then wields his huge knife and pins Murdock to a desk, but manages to control his rage, thrusting the weapon into the desktop with utter disdain: "Mission accomplished! You know there's more men out there. Find them, or I'll find *you*!"

In the film's final scene, one that must have been written by Stallone, as it is absent in Cameron's script (which ends with the return to the headquarters), Trautman tells Rambo, "You'll get a second Medal of Honor for this," but Rambo refuses to return to the United States. "You can't keep running, John. You're free now. Come back with us," Trautman urges, but Rambo replies, "My friends died here. Part of me died here." He has to remain in this threshold liminal space between his past and future until his redemptive journey is complete. Pressing the issue with convincing paternal concern, Trautman pleads, "What do you want?" "I want what they want—for our country to love *us* as much as we love *it*." Resigned to the fact that Rambo intends to stay in Thailand, an ex-patriot who loves his country, Trautman asks one final question: "How will you live, John?" to which Rambo replies, "Day by day."

At the end of the film, then, Rambo has his freedom, but he knows that he must remain aloof, unable to re-establish his life as a civilian in his native country, having also necessarily lost his chance for domestic happiness with the death of Co. It is impossible, considering the kind of heroism Rambo represents, to imagine a "Mrs. Rambo." His clash in this film with corrupt authorities, in this case the CIA cover-up of having knowingly abandoned POWs, places him in the liminal outlaw hero position: he rescues the deserving prisoners of war, but must reconcile himself to the fact that factions of the government representing the country he loves are manipulative and corrupt and that only hostility awaits him at home. This is the reason why earlier Rambo told Co about the domestic war, one that is "quiet," and one "you don't win." But another war rages within Rambo's own conscience—guilt over being the last survivor of his squadron, guilt perhaps also for "too much death" at his own hands (a warrior who yearns for the end of war), guilt that he cannot return to a country he loves but sees also as injured by a corrupt bureaucracy that lies to the general populace. Such would not be the case if he had no higher spiritual aspirations and moral dictates guiding him to serve an idea of justice greater than himself, greater even than his native land, beyond politics. In the end, he is armed with a principle, reliant on his solitary self, and void of ties to community and family.

A paradox of the warrior/knight is that he functions as a savior figure to a community from which he must remain distanced, as Braudy discusses at length in "The Solitude of the Wandering Knight," cited earlier in this chapter. In order to avoid unleashing his battle fury on the community he has sworn to protect, he lives an errant life of solitude, one designed also to cultivate a kind of spiritual refinement as he listens only to his own conscience. A modern incarnation of this ancient warrior/knight, Rambo's appeal to his audience resides in his ardent desire to rejoin and serve a collective democratic ideal, to partake also of a vision of an earlier, agrarian American past, while circumstances force him to retain a fierce independence from the confinement that family and community also necessarily impose, thus resolving, for the moment, opposing ideological positions. A devout patriot, Rambo nonetheless remains unfettered at the end of the film, awaiting the next opportunity to act as the liminal outlaw hero.

"Coming full circle": *Rambo III* (1988)

> "Wandering between two worlds, one dead,
> The other powerless to be born,
> With nowhere yet to rest my head,
> Like these, on earth I wait forlorn.
>
> • • •
>
> Oh, hide me in your gloom profound,
> Ye solemn seats of holy pain!
> Take me, cowl'd forms, and fence me round,
> Till I possess my soul again"
> —Matthew Arnold,
> "Stanzas from the Grande Chartreuse" (1855)

Carolco/TriStar Pictures released *Rambo III* on May 25, 1988, Memorial Day weekend, just as Soviet troops began their withdrawal from Afghanistan, where the film's action occurs. The opening credits list Sylvester Stallone and Sheldon Lettich as the writers. The latter was an ex-Marine who served a year in Vietnam and later enjoyed success as a playwright. The same year that *Rambo III* was released, Lettich's screenplay for a martial arts film, *Bloodsport*, starring Jean-Claude Van Damme, also debuted in theaters. Stallone hired Russell Mulcahy, who had directed several successful music videos and more recently the *Highlander* film (1986) to direct but when the two had a disagreement and Mulcahy departed two weeks into the production, he was replaced by the second unit director, Peter MacDonald. While he had a great deal of experience as a second unit director and cameraman, this marked MacDonald's directorial debut.[9] Much of the film was shot in Israel, with additional locations in Thailand (notably at the Chiang Mai temple) and Peshawar, Pakistan; the final scenes were filmed at the Yuma Indian Reservation in Yuma, Arizona.

In *Rambo III* Richard Crenna reprises his role for the third and last time (he died five years before the release of the fourth film) as Colonel Sam Trautman, sent to Thailand to recruit Rambo to team up for a dangerous mission in Afghanistan. The film's opening minutes feature a brutal stick-fighting match—observed by Trautman and an official, Robert Griggs (Kurtwood Smith), from the United States Embassy in Bangkok, Thailand—in which Rambo controls his battle fury only with great difficulty. Urged on by an admiring crowd chanting his name, Rambo overpowers his opponent, regains control of his instinct to annihilate the enemy, and spares the other's life. Yet after this violent victory, Rambo quickly departs the scene in a boat that takes him to his current home, a majestic monastery. Uneasy with his past, and uncertain of his future, Rambo's plight is that of the poet in "Stanzas from the Grand Chartreuse," quoted above. As he seeks refuge from a spiritual conflict he is unable to resolve—"wandering between two worlds, / one dead, / The other powerless to be born"—he finds solace and respite with the monks. The monastic solitude offers Rambo a way to avoid his warrior past through this contemplation; his stick-fighting matches allow him to curb his warrior impulse through sublimation. The monastery and the fighting ring represent the oppositional forces at war in Rambo's character, a continuation and development of his emotional plight in the two previous films.

The Soviet-Afghan war that lasted for nearly a decade from late 1979 until the withdrawal of Soviet troops in 1989 provides the topical issue of *Rambo III*. This armed conflict is also the third of the "proxy wars" fought in southeast Asia between the Soviet Union and the United States, following Korea and Vietnam. Although the Soviet invasion into Afghanistan incited the rebellion of native or ideologically sympathetic warriors known under the collective name, the Mujahedeen, the United States was one of the countries that supplied covert military and financial support for the Afghan rebels. A turning point in the war was when it provided Stinger anti-aircraft missiles, part of a larger CIA covert operation known as "Operation Cyclone," led by a Texas congressman, Charles Nesbitt Wilson, the subject of the film *Charlie Wilson's War* (2007) starring Tom Hanks. The fall of the Berlin Wall (erected in 1961 to divide East and West Germany) did not begin until late 1989, the year after the release of *Rambo III*, so the film reflects the last years of the Cold War before that momentous event occurred.

In an interview with Roger Ebert (who had seen a rough-cut of the film in Manhattan before its official release) dated May 15, 1988, Stallone remarked that Rambo's residence in the monastery at the opening of *Rambo III* should be seen as an atonement for the character's previous violent escapades: "Now he's in a little Catholic passion play, to purge himself." He continues, "I'm always taken aback by the way the character is misperceived. He is not a violent character per se. He is constantly questioning his own integrity—and the futility of war. Rambo is never blistering for action—not for war, per se." Stallone also points out that in this film Rambo only kills to protect the innocent (women and children) and out of loyalty to his friend and mentor, Colonel Trautman, whom he must rescue from a sadistic Russian commander. Ebert marveled that by his estimate Rambo speaks less than 200 words, but the audience at the preview chanted his name and, despite the paucity, applauded Rambo's "grim and apocalyptic speeches." Ebert also noted that the film's success, upon its imminent release, was guaranteed, as it was with the simultaneous *Rocky* films, because each installment acted as a "commercial" for the next (www.rogerebert.com/interviews). To the iconic Rocky and Rambo, Stallone added a third character, Cobra, a cop he had played in the 1986 film of the same title.[10] The excellent pace of *Rambo III*, along with the sparse dialogue (which to Ebert offers a striking contrast to Stallone's own ability and willingness to articulate his views in an interview) are two reasons why, as a modern action film, it enjoyed such wide appeal to international audiences with its under reliance on dialogue, requiring fewer subtitles, and its emphasis on well-arranged action sequences.

Janet Maslin, who had favorably reviewed *First Blood* in the *New York Times*, published an insightful review aptly titled "Stallone's 'Rambo III,' Globe-Trotting Cowboy for the 80's Audience." Echoing Stallone's assertion that at the opening of *Rambo III* the character is undergoing a "purgation" and that he is loath to kill, Maslin comments on the film's "messianic streak," noting that its hero is portrayed as "a long-suffering, deeply religious person who would much rather be repairing the roof of a Thai monastery" than taking lives. Despite the character's "tendency toward false modesty," Maslin avers that one must "acknowledge his very real accomplishments, along with those of Sylvester Stallone, who this time seems to know exactly what the global action-film audience would like to see." Finally, Maslin asserts that *Rambo III* and its hero cast in "a latter-day narcissist's version of a John Wayne role" has "forcefully reinvented the western to accommodate the character's munitions mad, avenging-angel style," in this way enabling the film to deliver "a wallop that no traditional western or war film could match" (www.nytimes.com). Box office revenues proved the anticipated appeal of *Rambo III* to its international targeted audiences—while it grossed $53,715,611 domestically, its total worldwide gross added up to $189,015,611 (www.boxofficemojo.com).

Returning to the monastery after his stick-fighting match, Rambo hands his winnings over to the monks, and engages in some quiet work. When he sees the arrival of Colonel Trautman and a stranger from the embassy, Rambo knows what lies ahead, muttering to himself, "I don't believe this." Trautman gets to the point, a propagandistic one—the Russians in Afghanistan have used unscrupulous methods such as chemical warfare and mine fields to slaughter more than two million people, many of them innocent women and children. While the Afghan rebel forces are holding their own, having been supplied Stinger antiaircraft missiles, there is one Soviet stronghold, 50 miles over the border, with an "exceptionally brutal commander," that needs to be wiped out. Trautman has agreed to go in, and asks Rambo to accompany him. "I put in my time ... *my* war's over," is Rambo's answer. Rambo expresses his doubt that Trautman's mission could really have any effect, even if he is successful, stating that "before" it made no difference. Rambo then tells his former commander: "I don't know what you think of this place, but I like it. I like being here.... I like belonging to something." Trautman responds that Rambo *does* belong to something, but not the world of the monastery: "When you gonna come full circle? You said your war is over ... but not the one inside you." He then insists that as much as Rambo would like to retreat into this contemplative life, he cannot escape what he really is, "a full-blooded combat soldier." Rambo avers, "Not anymore. I don't want it," but Trautman retorts, "That's too bad, 'cause you're stuck with it." He then launches into an analogy about a sculptor who avowed that he had in fact not created a statue others admired—it was always there, and he had merely cleared away the pieces that obstructed it. "We didn't make you this fighting machine. We just chipped away the rough edges. You're always going to be tearing away at yourself until you come to terms with what you are, until you come full circle." When Rambo insists, "I guess I'm not ready yet," Trautman desists, tells Rambo to look him up when he is next stateside, and departs.

The war within Rambo is exacerbated soon after when Griggs informs him that the Soviets have captured Trautman. What he won't do in response to propaganda or for ideological reasons, Rambo readily does for "a friend," and asks Griggs to help him launch his own covert operations rescue of his former commander. Griggs agrees, and Rambo is seen next in Peshawar, Pakistan (2,285 miles from Bangkok), where he meets his contact and guide, Mousa Gani (Sasson Gabai), an Afghan freedom fighter who supplies medical aid to the rebels. Mousa Gani knows that Trautman is being held in a Soviet fort, near the village of Khost, 30 miles over the border. He gives Rambo the supplies he has requested from Griggs, and the two set out on the journey west and north.

Meanwhile, Trautman is tortured by the sadistic commanding officer, Colonel Zaysen (Marc de Jonge), who wants to know the location of the Stinger missiles that are being imported to aid the Afghans. Defiant and courageous, Trautman proselytizes to his captor that the Soviets had "underestimated the competition. These people have never given up. They'd rather die than be slaves to an invading army. You can't defeat people like that. We tried. We already had *our* Vietnam. Now you're going to have *yours*." (Interestingly, journalist Richard Cohen's article about the Soviet withdrawal, published in the *Washington Post* on August 22, 1988, is titled "The Soviets' Vietnam" [www.highbeam.com].) In *Rambo III*, Trautman is not only Rambo's recruiter, but also another soldier who endures torture and faces death, abandoned by his government during a covert operation. When a spy reports to Zaysen that Rambo is en route to the fort, Zaysen is confident Rambo will pose no real threat, asking Trautman, "One man against thirty commandos? Who do you think this man is—God?" to which Trautman replies, "No, God would have mercy. He won't."

As they travel to their destination, the garrulous Mousa Gani discourses on the history of the Afghan people and their character, one that corroborates Trautman's claims about them to Zaysen. Gani reminds Rambo that Alexander the Great, Genghis Khan, and the British Empire all tried and failed to conquer his people. He then recites a prayer purportedly uttered by an ancient enemy: "May God deliver us from the venom of the cobra, the teeth of the tiger, and the vengeance of the Afghan." When he asks if Rambo understands the meaning, the latter replies in the modern vernacular, "That you guys don't take any shit." When they arrive at a Mujahedeen village, a hub for rebel soldiers, Rambo meets their leader, Masoud (Spiros Focas), and learns more of the Soviet horrors inflicted on the indigenous population—the children killed by exploding mines they mistake for toys, poison gas, and disease, while the women are raped and killed. Masoud even claims that the previous year in the Valley of Laghman (a province of Afghanistan) Soviet soldiers bayoneted pregnant women and threw their babies into fire, not unlike atrocities attributed to the Nazis in World War II. This is why, though sympathetic to Rambo's mission, Masoud initially refuses to lend him any men to help him—his troops must first defend their families. The Mujahedeen view themselves as "holy warriors" and their resistance a holy war. They have taken "last rites" and consider themselves "dead already," stopping at nothing to win the war. When Rambo says he will go alone and Masoud cautions that he will die, the undaunted Rambo says, "Then, I will die." Masoud, impressed by this courage, says he will reflect on the best way they can help Rambo free Trautman, and Rambo is made an honorary warrior when he participates in a rough-and-tumble 3,000-year-old "insane game" on horseback that the soldiers are playing, even though he says wryly, "I'll take football." Minutes later, a Soviet airstrike decimates the village. Masoud tells Rambo, "Now you see how it is. Somewhere in war there is supposed to be honor. Where is the honor here?"

Gani asks Rambo why he insists on undertaking what he believes is a suicide mission, and Rambo replies: "Because he'd do it for me." Gani leads Rambo across the border to the Soviet fort, followed furtively by a young boy, Hamid (Doudi Shoua), who admires Rambo. Both the boy and Rambo are wounded during the rescue attempt, but eventually Rambo frees Trautman and several other prisoners as well, escaping with them in a hijacked helicopter, pursued at Zaysen's command by a Spetznaz team. The copter crashes and the Afghans know where to flee to safety, but Trautman and Rambo are forced to head to the border on foot. Pursued by Soviet special forces soldiers as they take refuge in a cave from an air attack, Rambo uses his signature crossbow to destroy most of the enemy. Just as they near the border and think they are home free, more Soviet troops, led by Zaysen, surround them with heavy artillery. They open fire on the Soviet troops even though, hopelessly outnumbered, the two believe they will meet their end. However, just then the Mujahedeen warriors show up on horseback, invoking an intertextual frame borrowed from the western— that of the cavalry to the rescue. With renewed battle fury, Rambo charges on horseback and commandeers a tank, felling the enemy, then exploding the helicopter that carries the sadistic Zaysen, which collides with Rambo's tank, allowing him to make the narrowest of escapes.

Both Trautman and Rambo incur wounds, but the film's coda includes their departure from the Afghans in an Army jeep. Rambo had earlier given Hamid, his young admirer, the jade pendant he is shown wearing in the first part of the film—a reminder of Co, his deceased love interest in *Rambo: First Blood Part II*, telling the boy the pendant is "for luck." When Hamid offers to return it, Rambo tells him to keep it, suggesting that he is able to put the terrible loss of Co behind him, now that he has embarked on a new chapter of his life,

7. Reconciling Opposites in Rambo *(1982–2008)* 209

Green Beret Colonel Sam Trautman (Richard Crenna) teams up with his protégé John Rambo (Sylvester Stallone) against Soviet forces in Afghanistan in *Rambo III*. The scars on Rambo's body from his torture in Vietnam reflect his psychic wounds. This third *Rambo* film, released by TriStar in 1988, was the last in the series Crenna appeared in before his death (Jerry Ohlinger's Movie Materials Store).

having undergone a "purgation" in the rescue of Trautman and in aiding the Afghan cause for freedom. Hamid pleads, "Can you not stay?" "I've got to go," Rambo answers, slowly but resolutely, giving Hamid a wistful look. As they drive off, Trautman muses, "I hate to admit it, but I think we're getting soft," to which Rambo replies, "Maybe just a little, sir. Maybe just a little." For someone who is a "fighting machine," and "full-blooded combat solider," "getting soft" can only mean one thing—becoming a civilian, vulnerable to its attractions. If there is no definite resolution to Rambo's inner struggle, there is also no sense of concern expressed by Trautman, as in the prior two films. Moreover, their departure signals the severing of any community ties—brief and tenuous as those have been—to remain free for another mission. This scene is evocative of *Casablanca's* end (discussed in Chapter 3), in which Rick Blaine and Captain Renault stroll into the fog, having sent off to Lisbon—and by extension, the civilized world—Ilsa and Victor Laszlo (the official hero), while they plan to join "a Free French Garrison over in Brazzaville," aiding the cause of the resistance. Like Rick, Rambo is a patriot who can't return to his own country and remains free of familial obligations.

When he visited the monastery to recruit Rambo, Trautman argued that Rambo would have to "come full circle," and accept what he really is—"a full-blooded combat soldier." In the first film, Trautman boasted, "God didn't make Rambo. I did," but in *Rambo III* he argues that it is an innate quality of Rambo's own character—his destiny—that is responsible for making him the warrior he wishes in vain to renounce. It is a vocation, an elect calling. Lancelot was to be the original grail knight until his sin with Guinevere necessitated the need for his illegitimate son to replace him, though Lancelot later dies in a monastery as a saint. In *Casablanca*, Laszlo tells Rick, "Each of us has a destiny, for good or evil," and Shane's last words, "A man has to be what he is, Joey. You can't break the mold," pointing to the belief in an elect hero, even a reluctant one, whose path is foreordained for him.

The liminal outlaw hero role that Rambo plays in this film can be discerned, then, by two factors. First, although there is no woman in the final version of the story to represent family and or community ties, there is the importance of the monastery, the home that Rambo has found and which he is loath to leave (he even acts the part of the domestic "breadwinner," surrendering to the monks his winnings from the stick-fighting match).[11] When Trautman visits, Rambo rejects the call to war, forsaking his peaceful life and prompted to action only when his friend is in danger of losing his life. Later, his attachment to the adoring orphaned boy, Hamid, is one that he reluctantly but decisively relinquishes. The liminal outlaw hero remains an errant figure, void of domestic commitments and free to act.

Second, Rambo refuses to act when the official from the American Embassy in Thailand accompanies Trautman to recruit him for another covert operation. He views all government officials with suspicion, based on his experience in Vietnam, the war that he and his fellow Green Berets were "not allowed to win," and also on his encounter with the corrupt CIA operative, Murdock, in the previous film. But he does answer the call to action when it involves loyalty to a friend, and to fight the cruelty inflicted on the innocent in Afghanistan—that is, when his sense of justice demands that he engage an enemy for a right cause. He can accomplish what official forces, hindered by the politics of the Cold War, cannot. As Stallone told Roger Ebert in the interview cited earlier: "If you had four people like Rambo, you wouldn't need a Star Wars project." Though tongue-in-cheek, this is in fact a very insightful observation—Rambo is hostile to technology that is part of the modern, impersonal, faceless form of warfare. He nearly always reverts to an earlier warrior *ethos* and method, preferring his emblems of election: the Lile knife (crafted

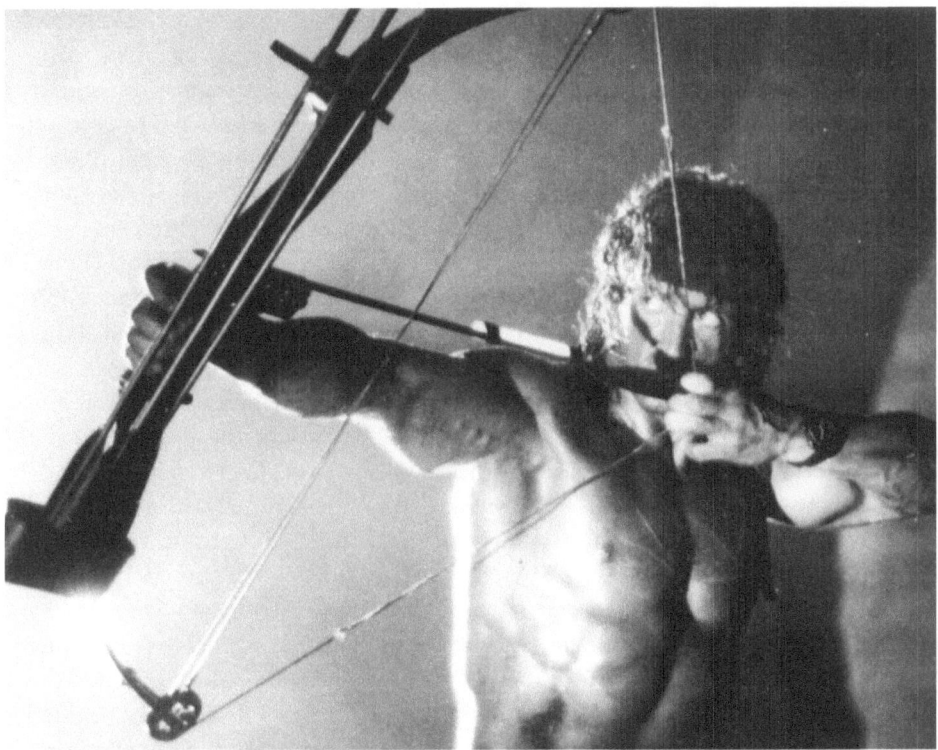

One of Rambo's emblems of election is his compound bow, which in *Rambo III* he employs to kill by stealth the Soviet troops stalking Trautman and Rambo. Especially iconic weapons are his compound bow and Lile knife, the latter crafted by a famous Arkansas knife-maker, James Lile (Jerry Ohlinger's Movie Materials Store).

by an Arkansas knife-maker, James Lile), Browning compound crossbow, quick thinking, and his hand-to-hand combat skills, engaging in close-up combat with individuals or small groups of adversaries. It would be two decades before Stallone would reprise his role as the incarnation of the warrior hero, but that day did come, demonstrating that Rambo was not a forgotten hero, but an icon that continued to resonate with American and international audiences alike.[12]

Rambo (2008): Healing Wounds

"Any of you boys want to shoot, now's the time. And there isn't one of us that doesn't want to be somewhere else. But this is what we do, who we are. Live for nothing, or die for something."
—John Rambo to the mercenaries

Released in 2,757 theaters on January 25, 2008, *Rambo* featured the return of the still troubled hero. In "It's A Long Road: Resurrection of an Icon," included on the extended cut, Stallone and his producers discuss the history of the fourth film. The long lacuna was a result of searching for and finding the right story for Rambo's return to the screen. One version they considered posited that Rambo, having returned to Arizona after his Afghanistan experience, investigates the disappearance of his housekeeper's daughter, who fails to return from a trip to Mexico. He finds himself immersed in yet another mission, much larger than that of retrieving the girl. Stallone averred that while the story had promise, calling it "more of a modern day western," it didn't "touch on the essence of Rambo," a figure he envisioned to be "still a lost man, wandering the world"—in other words, an *errant* warrior knight, isolated in the same liminal space he has occupied in the prior films.

The idea of focusing on the political unrest in Burma (Myanmar) made perfect sense; it continued to show Rambo as a champion of the oppressed and persecuted, begun in the previous film when he fought on the side of the Afghan rebels against a Soviet invasion. A BBC "Myanmar Profile—Overview," of March 2015, states that Burma (a.k.a. Myanmar) was ruled by a corrupt military dictatorship from 1962 to 2011, noting also its "appalling human rights record." In addition to this, the profile observes that the "junta," or ruling military group, "suppressed almost all dissent and wielded absolute power in the face of international condemnation and sanctions" (www.bbc.com). According to the BBC article, in 1990 a general election resulted in a landslide victory for the National League for Democracy, the main opposition party to the junta, but the latter ignored the results and placed its leader, Aung San Suu Kyi, under house arrest from 1989 to 2010. She was released when "a nominally civilian government"—but one led by former junta military leader and prime minister Thein Seinn—was installed as president in March 2011. Since that election, the newly-formed parliament continues to operate under strong military influence, and ethnic tension remains an issue. The majority of Burmese are Buddhist, but two of several groups who have been systematically persecuted are the Christian Karen (featured in *Rambo*) and the Muslim Rohingya (www.bbc.com). One of the poorest countries in Asia, Burma's economy is under-developed, even though its soil is rich, it has off-shore oil holdings, and is a main exporter of teak, jade, pearls and other gems: the corrupt military has largely controlled the economy, resulting in an inequitable distribution of wealth. In addition, according to the BBC article, the military "has been accused of large scale trafficking of heroin, of which Myanmar [Burma] is a main exporter," an issue that also appears in the film. This hotbed of military corruption, political oppression, and ethnic persecution provided an appropriate setting for Rambo's much anticipated return to the screen.

Carolco Pictures was defunct by 1996. Miramax Films purchased the *Rambo* franchise, but sold it in 2005 to Avi Lerner's Millennium/Nu Image Films, which produced the fourth film, distributed by Lionsgate. The opening credits list as writers Stallone and Art Monterastelli, the latter of whom had written for various television series (*Simon and Simon, Total Recall 2070*) and recently had scripted a horror feature film, *Buried Alive* (2007). However, an "unspecified draft" of a script titled *Pearl of the Cobra (Rambo 4)* and dated November 6, 2006, written solo by Sylvester Stallone is close to that of the theatrical release; since the filming began in January of 2007 and concluded in May of that year, there was little time for a radically different screenplay to have been developed in this two month period. With the exception of a few explicit alterations, *Pearl of the Cobra (Rambo 4)* is the story of the finished film.[13] For the first time, Stallone stepped in as director of a *Rambo* film when another (unnamed) bowed out, but members of the cast and crew averred that because of the "prowling camera" and tense energy that characterizes the film, "Rambo directed the movie" ("It's a Long Road: Resurrection of an Icon"). The conclusion of *Rambo* was shot in Arizona, where the story ends, but most of it was filmed on location in Thailand, on or near the Salween River, which constitutes the border with Burma.

In an extra that consists of the director's production diary titled "Rambo: To Hell and Back" included on the extended cut, Stallone discusses the obstacles incurred in making *Rambo*—the Burmese actors, who were extremely difficult to recruit because they feared government reprisals for themselves and their families, being shadowed by the Burmese secret police in Thailand, and Stallone himself receiving phone threats warning him not to complete the film. Although it was banned in Burma upon its release, bootleg copies of *Rambo* were in demand, and parts of the dialogue became a rallying cry for the oppositional forces to the government, especially Rambo's line "Live for nothing, or die for something." When he learned of this, Stallone is quoted in a February 18, 2008, article in the British newspaper *The Telegraph*: "These incredibly brave people have found a kind of voice, in a very odd way, in American cinema." The article mentions repercussions in the form of alleged arrests of some of the supporting actors' relatives (www.telegraph.com). This corroborates Stallone's claim about the fear the Burmese actors expressed and their reluctance to be in the film, and exemplifies the power of cinema to raise awareness about important political and human rights issues.

In theaters alone (not including later DVD sales that added revenue to the franchise), the total domestic gross for *Rambo* was $42,754,105, and its worldwide gross was $113,244,290 (www.boxofficemojo.com). Although some critics, oddly, found the dialogue awkward (a strange observation, since its lines actually served as a rallying cry for Burmese rebels), other reviews of *Rambo* were favorable. For instance, A. O. Scott's review in the *New York Times*, printed January 26, 2008, while frowning on the film's violence, nonetheless observes that it has "its own kind of blockheaded poetry," and comments that the earlier "films were better than polite opinion might lead you to believe. At the time their politics made some people nervous, but to dwell on Rambo's ideological significance was (and still is) to miss his kinship with the samurais and gunslingers of older movies." He praises Stallone's intelligence in presenting the "mythic dimensions of the character without apology or irony.... Welcome back" (www.nytimes.com).

Rambo opens with actual footage from television reports about the contemporary political strife in Burma, recounting also a brief history of the persecuted Karen people, "poor Christian farmers" who have been singled out in the "longest running civil war in the world." The film immediately cuts to an aged but still virile and embittered John Rambo, who resides in the neighboring country of Thailand on the Salween River. His retreat into nature from the modern world is almost a complete immersion—even his contact with the monks is tenuous. He makes his living, apparently, by hunting and maintaining deadly snakes (cobras and pythons) for a tourist show and, occasionally, by operating a water taxi on the Salween River with the boat he owns. Having bagged a few dangerous reptiles, Rambo is shown spearing fish, which he gives to local monks as they pass his boat, suggesting that he continued respect for the contemplative life, established at the beginning of *Rambo III*, but he no longer resides in a monastery.

Spiritually, Rambo may find some solace in his proximity to the monks, but the metaphoric images at the outset point to the complex liminal space in which he resides in his attempt to reconcile the inner conflict that still plagues him, evinced by his mythic retreat into nature. Others allude to him as "The Boatman" who lives on a river of death (which houses Burmese pirates, deadly snakes, and is the gateway to the oppressive Burma); the Salween can be likened to the River Styx, with Rambo as the mythical Charon, who ferries the souls of the dead, himself existing in a purgatorial death-like state, also a reason why he has no fear of the snakes he captures.[14] Like the Styx, it serves as the border, or liminal space, that divides the living from the dead, Burma being a deathtrap for many who enter or reside there. But as the fisherman, Rambo is associated with life, spearing fish to provide sustenance for the monks, the river also freeing him from the constraints of "civilization" as it does the archetypal Huck Finn. Finding solace as a fisherman is also evocative of the Rich Fisher, or Fisher King of medieval Arthurian legend, the suffering figure whose fishing expeditions provide the only distraction for alleviating the chronic pain inflicted from his thigh wound. As David Morrell points out, and as the opening moments make abundantly clear, the years between the third and fourth film have made Rambo even more "angry and disillusioned" than he was when he made his screen debut, thus hearkening back to the spirit and tone of his origin in the novel ("Rambo and Me"). When spoken to, his reply is as much of a growl as an answer. Cynicism like his—which nearly always masks a disappointed but not entirely obliterated idealism—has become so acute as to affect a kind of spiritual paralysis.

Rambo is approached by Michael Burnett (Paul Schulze), the leader of a group of Christian missionaries from Colorado, who wish to hire him as a water taxi to take them to a village in Burma inhabited by Karen farmers persecuted by the government for their Christian faith. The missionaries want to deliver Bibles, medical supplies, and food, in the hopes of "changing peoples' lives." Rambo refuses flatly, "Burma is a war zone," and asserts cynically that since they are bringing no weapons to the Karen, "you're not changing anything." "Well, it's thinking like that that keeps the world the way it is," Burnett insists, with more than a hint of arrogance in his idealism, to which Rambo snarls in reply, "Fuck the world," and dismisses them. What changes his mind is the group's only woman, Sarah Miller (Julie Benz). When she implores Rambo to accommodate them, he repeatedly refuses, telling her gruffly to "go home." "Maybe you lost your faith in people. But you must have faith in something. You must still care about something. But trying to *save* a life isn't wasting *your* life, is it?" Sarah's physical beauty, her inquisitiveness about the reasons for Rambo's refusal to help, and her idealism, manage to charm him despite his savage defensive exterior.[15]

On the boat the next day, Rambo tells her, "It's because of *you* we're going up river. Anytime you want to turn around, it's done." He has nothing but disdain for Burnett, who is more than a little jealous of Sarah's attention to Rambo, establishing an under-stated but decided love triangle. Rambo treats Sarah with gruff courtesy, honoring her wishes and protecting her from rape and certain death on more than one occasion in the film, even at great personal risk. When Burmese pirates demand that Rambo turn "the whore" over to them, Rambo tries to bargain but at last has to kill them all in rapid succession. Burnett is shocked and sanctimoniously outraged by this, but Rambo, his battle fury still in full throttle, grabs him by the throat and snarls in reply: "They would have raped her 50 times and cut your fucking heads off! We're going back." Once again, Sarah intercedes, pleading with Rambo to continue the journey to the village, "Please. Please, John," she implores, touching his arm. "Go sit down," says Rambo, and he delivers them to their destination. As the group prepares to continue on foot inland to the Klaw Kbe Lo Village where the Karen reside, Sarah entrusts Rambo with the wooden cross pendant she had been wearing, a token of their unspoken bond, but also of her faith and hope that has in some way broken through Rambo's seemingly impenetrable defenses. On the way back down river, Rambo disposes of the bodies of the Burmese pirates he had slain the night before; the missionaries are shown to have arrived safely at the Karen village and begin dispensing medical assistance and Bibles, but soon after the village is attacked and obliterated by the Burmese military (in a shockingly brutal, violent scene), commanded by the sadistic Major Pa Tee Tint (Maung Maung Khin), who takes the missionaries captive.

Having returned to his quarters in Thailand, Rambo is shown in contemplation, fingering Sarah's pendant reverently, like a devotee with rosary beads, or a courtly lover with a cherished fetish object.[16] A nightmare designed to show Rambo's inner torment presents a montage consisting of flashbacks from each of the previous three films, and from conversations with Sarah: "Aren't you curious to see how things might have changed back home?" Sam Trautman haunts Rambo: "You're a full-blooded combat soldier. You're always going to be tearing away at yourself until you come full circle." As Trautman in the dream sequence utters Rambo's first name, he is awakened by a real voice, urgently inquiring, "John Rambo?" that of the pastor, Arthur Marsh (Ken Howard), who has come from the American Embassy with news that the missionaries have been captured. Marsh has hired a band of mercenaries to try to rescue them, but he needs Rambo to guide them to the place where he dropped them off many days before. Knowing Sarah is in danger and that the official hero (the U.S. Embassy) is powerless to rescue her, Rambo agrees to taxi the hired guns to the drop-off point, planning to retrieve her himself, and thus assuming the liminal outlaw hero role.

Preparing for departure, Rambo forges a new special weapon to add to his unique collection—half machete and half knife, for hand-to-hand combat—using ancient smithing techniques. As he does so, his conscience wars with his propensity for violence: "War is in your blood. Don't fight it. You didn't kill for your country. You killed for yourself. The gods are never gonna make that go away. When you're pushed ... killing is as easy as breathing." This sentiment echoes the dying Rambo's self-reckoning in Morrell's novel: "He had killed a great many people, and he could pretend their deaths were necessary because they were all part of what was pushing him.... But he did not totally believe it. He had enjoyed the fight too much" (*First Blood* 249). These opposite impulses—those of the skilled warrior who is called upon to kill for a larger cause and those of the contemplative, alone in a spiritual world of his own—are what Rambo has not yet been able to reconcile for himself, and by extension for his audience. Interestingly, in the extended cut, this self-reproach just after Marsh's visit, as Rambo makes his weapon, is deleted and replaced by his request that the pastor say a prayer—not for himself (feeling cursed), but for the captives. Marsh obliges, reciting what is known as the "Prayer of St. Francis," an overtly pacifist sentiment.[17]

The five mercenaries Rambo shuttles to the drop site only know him as "the boatman." Along the way, we learn from their conversation that corrupt Burmese generals are in league with drug lords, exporting methamphetamine in order to fund their ongoing war against insurgents. Heroin, and not meth, is in reality the drug that is commonly exported from Burma, as David Morrell points out (davidmorrell.net). When they arrive, with the help of a young Burmese guide, Myint (Supakorn Kijsuwan), at the site of the devastated village, the leader of the mercenaries, an Australian named Lewis (Graham McTavish) and his four followers, School Boy (Matthew Marsden), Diaz (Rey Gallegos), Reese (Jake La Botz), and En-Joo (Tim Kang), see the slaughtered bodies of the villagers and animals. Soon, they take cover when a military vehicle appears with insurgents; the soldiers force the captives to race across a rice patty that has been mined, taking bets on who will win, and preparing to kill them after, as the concealed mercenaries look on with helpless horror. But Rambo stops this with his crossbow, much to their surprise, since Lewis had ordered him to remain behind with the boat. Believing the missionaries to be dead, and seeing that any effort to investigate further is almost certain death, Lewis insists they abandon the rescue mission. This is when Rambo steps up and usurps the role of leader. Pointing an arrow at Lewis' head while the others have their weapons leveled at Rambo, he states firmly, "Any of you boys want to shoot, now's the time. And there isn't one of us that doesn't want to be somewhere else. But this is what we do, who we are. Live for nothing, or die for something. Your call." This wins the day, and they work together to complete the mission.

They enter the camp by stealth at night, using as camouflage the truck of the slain Burmese soldiers. Depicted as depraved psychopaths, the Burmese troops are found indulging in a drunken bacchanal, abusing and sexually assaulting female entertainers and rebel captives. They manage to rescue the male missionaries (except one who has been tortured and killed earlier) and some of the mistreated Burmese women, while Rambo frees Sarah. In two separate parties, they make their way southeast toward the river, with General Tint and his men in pursuit. Tint's forces, which greatly outnumber the mercenaries and missionaries, collide. A long and violent battle ensues that unleashes Rambo's fury, but the Karen rebels, brought by Myint, appear and turn the tide (another intertextual western frame with the cavalry to the rescue, like the Afghan rebels in *Rambo III*). Rambo is wounded but still disembowels a fleeing Tint with his newly forged weapon. Among the carnage, Sarah searches frantically for her fiancé, Michael, who has been seen during battle crushing the head of a soldier, and thus betraying all of his nonviolent convictions—a scene that vindicates Rambo by showing the capacity for killing exists even in earnest missionaries. As Rambo looks on pensively from a distance, Sarah collapses in Michael's arms. Pulled suddenly back into his civilized role of betrothed missionary medical doctor, Michael then salutes Rambo, perhaps in recognition of his own capacity for violence as well as showing an expression of gratitude. Rambo realizes that Sarah represents and belongs to a domesticated world, very different from his own.[18]

This parting from the woman is, of course, a necessary part of his role as warrior/knight and liminal outlaw hero. In the final shot, Rambo arrives at his father's ranch outside of Bowie, Arizona—significantly, a border town named after the legendary frontiersman, Jim Bowie, owner of the knife that bears his name as well. (Bowie's fame stemmed in large part from this knife named after him—one with a blade over nine inches long, with which he disemboweled Norris Wright, in the culmination of a long-standing feud between the two. Bowie met a patriotic end at the Alamo.) Rambo approaches the rusty mailbox with "R. Rambo" on it and traverses down a long lane, with horses in pastures on either side, still a solitary figure clad in a military garb, until he vanishes as the credits roll.

At the opening of this film, Rambo embodies opposites: the boatman of death, the life-giving fisherman; he lives a quasi-monastic life of solitude but is ever cognizant of his warrior past. Unlike the previous two films, in which agents of the United States government recruit him for a covert operation, here, the role of "official hero" is filled by civilians, the Christian missionaries (who happen to be American) and, by extension, the persecuted Karen rebels. Rambo rescues private citizens because he wants to, relying on his own inner resources and warrior skills to do so. What is it about this experience that earns him his passage home after such a long exile?

First, the motive for the rescue is the woman, whom Rambo cannot resist. When, after Michael fails to do so, Sarah tries to persuade Rambo to taxi the group upriver, he responds to her idealism and candor, even though he rejects her belief that she and the other missionaries can make the fallen world a better place. He is vulnerable to her goodness (what the medieval troubadour tradition called *notatio*) as well as her physical beauty (*effictio*), despite his hardened veneer of cynicism. His pledge of service to her, against his reason and better judgment, invokes a courtly model, where the lady commands a knight, whose role it is to obey her without question, and in turn prove his worth and virtue for having done so. In her article "Undercutting the Fabric of Courtly Love with 'Tokens of Love' in Wolfram von Eschenbach's *Parzival*," Evelyn Meyer explicates the courtly ritual and its significance. The lady, having attracted a knight through her reputation "as a noble and beautiful woman" (the *notatio* and *effictio* mentioned above, in this case) could "take action only after the expression of masculine desire by demanding a specific service of him and thus control the lover" (9–10). The knight, taken with her beauty and goodness, "had to submit himself to the beloved as an expression of his courtliness, love and service commitment to her" for which she would give him "a token of love in recognition of his service" (9).[19] On the boat, we will remember, Rambo tells Sarah that he has only agreed to taxi them on the dangerous Salween River because of his regard for her; should she wish to abort the mission, he would comply. After he slays the pirates who had demanded that he turn her over to them, he is determined to abort the journey when the touch of her hand on his arm urges him forward. His reason is over-ruled again by his affection for her.

When they reach their destination and they are ready to part ways, Sarah gives Rambo a love token, the wooden cross on a leather string. This later exerts a power over Rambo—he is seen with his head bowed in contemplation, holding it reverently, and when he undertakes the mission to rescue Sarah, it is wound tightly around his wrist. It operates as a talisman, much the way the jade pendant from Co served as a token of his commitment to her after her death in *Rambo II*, a good luck charm that he bestows on the Afghan boy, Hamid, in *Rambo III*. It is important to remember, however, that Rambo and the mercenaries hired by the pastor can only redeem the missionaries through violence. Moreover, their actions in this case offer immediate help, but solve nothing of the larger political strife in Burma. The only hope for change resides in the impact of the film itself, bringing to the world's attention conditions there, and rallying the rebels, as it apparently managed to do. Sarah's influence on Rambo does not include adhering to her pacifism, which cannot save her or the others. Violence, Rambo's *modus operandi*, is the only salvation, as the liminal outlaw hero uses his guerrilla tactics to rescue the official heroes.

An unspoken, but unmistakable love triangle comprised of Michael Burnett, Sarah, and Rambo develops, but she is already betrothed to Michael. In the end, Rambo honors this bond that he witnesses between Michael and Sarah, and this is the way in which he retains his liminal outlaw hero status by remaining unattached. However, Sarah has exerted her influence on Rambo—during the nightmare in which he experiences flashbacks from the previous films, the only exception in that sequence is Sarah's earlier statement to him: "Don't you want to see how things might have changed back home?" Rambo returns home to the United States, but unencumbered by a lasting commitment to a woman or community, that of the Arizona ranch and his father serving only as the most tenuous of ties. There is no finality in his return. In fact, a fifth *Rambo* film, evidently the one that will bring closure to Rambo's saga, is imminent.[20]

The legend of the cobra pearl included in the draft of the script dated November 6, 2006, bearing that title (see note 13), serves as a particularly striking metaphor for the Rambo of the final film. The luminous amber-colored gem, found only on rare occasions in the hood of very old Naga Mani cobras, is said to bring to its possessor piety, wealth, health, victory over enemies—all forms of good luck—but only if it is obtained by fortune. Killing the cobra to extract the pearl negates its talismanic power.[21] A pearl is, of course, an ulcer produced naturally in a living animal by some form of irritant. An aged reptilian predator, wise and battle-scarred, contains within its own body the crystalized story of its life experiences—which makes it what it is, finally yielding the parabolic "pearl of great price." The gem, then, is a metaphor for the character of the cobra itself. It is Rambo's good fortune to have found one—or for it to have found him—an emblem of his election, and a worthy tender for his passage home. In this earlier version of the screenplay, the cobra pearl that Rambo wears around his neck (and the old Naga Mani that produced it), is a reflection of himself—angry and scarred from his experience, but also capable of and responsive to goodness and beauty. Sarah's wooden cross in the final version replaces the cobra pearl of the earlier imagining, a more conventional and quotidian, but less interesting inscription of Rambo's warrior and pacifist division.

Home at Last?

The success of the *Rambo* franchise is dependent on the fact that the hero faces conflicting values and works to reconcile competing ideological stances. Rambo is a veteran of an unpopular war who returns to a culture that has become alien to him and which he finds corrupt, yet he is later recruited to serve the very nation in which he no longer feels at home. As a liminal outlaw hero, he both idealizes his squadron and exposes the weaknesses of post–Vietnam American culture striving to preserve his own integrity, while reluctantly helping the group (military) security initiatives, resorting to violent means to do so. His story both scrutinizes and upholds the American involvement in the Vietnam War, and can thus be read as either subversive or conservative propaganda, as Mattes had argued of *Cobra*, cited earlier. Unlike the figurations of the liminal outlaw hero in the urban westerns, Dirty Harry and Paul Kersey, who remain essentially the same from one film to the next, Rambo's is an ongoing story of a conflicted character who strives to resolve his own inner turmoil by coming to terms with the contradictions in himself that are mirrored also in America after Vietnam, and in the difficulties of living in an increasingly complex and shrinking global environment.

Initially recruited to trust in authority and obey it at the risk of his own life while serving as a Green Beret in Vietnam, Rambo's training also requires him to be self-reliant, resourceful, and independent. Rambo provides audiences the opportunity to enjoy vicariously his autonomy from the responsibilities of community and culture, to preserve his cherished independence, while still functioning as the hero who alone can rescue prisoners of war, his former commander, or foolish but sincere missionaries. As he does so, he also wars on the side of freedom for Afghan rebels and persecuted Burmese Christian farmers—all martyrs in the service of a higher spiritual ideal. Rambo acts in accord with his own conscience, looking to his own beliefs to procure justice in a world of deception, covert wars, and false values. In the end, we *want* to see Rambo kill, but he must do so with a *conscience*, that which exacts a heavy personal price. This is the internal struggle with which he must always contend—torn between his own capacity for violence and his respect for life, his own natural goodness. He must dwell in a liminal space, ready to unleash his warrior fury, while keeping it in check most of the time. In order to rescue the missionaries, this warrior fury must be invoked, but as Braudy points out in his discussion of the berserker, after battle his rage must be extinguished, lest it put the community at risk, as it did in the first film. Often, this means isolation and solitude. Rambo's is a sacrificial role, reconciling opposite impulses. On the one hand, we ask him to be a decisive yet discriminating killer, to satisfy our demand for justice. To do so, he must remain in a space apart from the community. Rambo's immediate precursor is, of course, the gunslinger, whose "regeneration through violence," as Slotkin points out, is vital for the preservation of community, and his distant ancestor is the errant knight, whose solitude cultivates a conscience to keep his rage in check.

CHAPTER 8

Dark Days and the Dark Knight in Gotham City (2005–2012)

The Many Faces of Batman

The action hero has enjoyed long-standing success in the world of comics. It is not surprising, then, that the remediation to modern live action films of comic book heroes such as Batman and Superman has also proved to be enormously popular. While it is not unusual for the origin stories of comic book heroes to be embellished or reinvented in order to appeal to new audiences, Batman's has remained stable, even though he has become a mythopoeic hero. His story features a larger-than-life character who lives in a world created for him especially, yet it is also recognizably our own. However, while there is a fixed core of Batman lore and history, it is, like that of the Arthurian legend, always open to renewal. The rich tradition exists as a heterogeneous set of materials from which individual artists can draw to reinvent and reinterpret the story for new generations, while still remaining true to the essential defining features of the character and story. Despite its considerable weight of tradition, one established by multiple artists (another indication of its mythic status)— Batman has been a part of American culture for over seventy years—it is balanced by the flexibility of the story, its cognitive and imaginative power enabling it to be open to new readings. Therefore, attempting to trace the evolution of the character and story across multi-media and seven decades is beyond the purpose and scope of this study. Instead, Batman's incarnation as the Dark Knight, and the modern film trilogy in which he emerges as such— *Batman Begins* (2005), *The Dark Knight* (2008), and *The Dark Knight Rises* (2012)—will be the focus of this discussion. *The Dark Knight* trilogy rejuvenated Batman's character and story; in it, as we shall see, he functions as an especially apt example of a liminal outlaw hero.

Several critics have observed that the Batman/Dark Knight mythos contains features that make its hero an apt example of the liminal outlaw figure. First is the idea of election. Bruce Wayne is called to knighthood, something he shares with the other liminal outlaw heroes we have studied. Randall M. Jensen, in "Batman's Promise," contrasts Batman with other superheroes, such as Spiderman: "Bruce Wayne doesn't acquire superpowers and then later discover how to use them ... he first acquires a mission—a vocation, or a calling, really—and with it, a desperate need for extraordinary abilities" (*Batman and Philosophy: The Dark Knight of the Soul* 86). He has no superhuman powers, per se, however, but perfects his reasoning and agility skills to help him fulfill his particular mission. Another liminal outlaw hero characteristic is Batman's dedication to a higher justice in the face of a corrupt or inept legal system. In his article "Alfred, the Dark Knight of Faith: Batman and Kierkegaard," Christopher H. Drohan remarks, "When the law fails justice, as it sometimes does, Batman is forced to supercede it so as to restore the balance between justice and the law, crime and punishment" (*Batman and Philosophy* 186), noting also that he represents a "metaphysical justice" (194). Despite the fact that he sometimes has a protégé, Batman, like other liminal outlaw heroes, is a solitary figure. In "Notes from the Batcave: An Interview with Dennis O'Neil," the Batman comics writer characterizes Batman as "an obsessed loner" (Roberta E. Pearson and William Uricchio, *The Many Lives of Batman: Critical Approaches to a Superhero and His Media* 19). Moreover, Batman most often remains single, void of a permanent romantic relationship. In "Batman and the Twilight of the Idols: An Interview with Frank Miller," of *The Dark Knight Returns* and *Batman: Year One* fame, Miller points out the importance of the character remaining free of love entanglements: "Notice how insipid are the stories where Batman has a girlfriend or some sort of romance ... he's obsessive," and this intensity prevents him from committing to a long-term relationship that would threaten or curtail his fight for justice (Christopher Sharrett, in *The Many Lives of Batman* 38).

In his insightful study, *Soul of the Dark Knight: Batman as Mythic Figure in Comics and Film*, Alex M. Wainer explores why Batman's is a mythopoeic story: "his essential attraction is based on the appeal of the mythopoeic ... this quality involves the perception of his not being solely human but, rather, a man who transforms himself into a liminal creature" (8). Wainer views the nature of Batman as "liminal," in that, having taken on characteristics of an animal, he is both more and less than man, the bat helping him achieve his end: "This 'mythical effect' ... arises out of Batman's incarnation as an avenging spirit of justice, which has a tremendous appeal to an audience disturbed by the fear of crime and chaos" (9). A bat is a particularly apt animal for this purpose; Wainer points out that it is by its nature a liminal creature, "a mammal that flies" (58).

Batman's persona is thus a literal rendering of his liminal outlaw hero status as it will be examined in detail in this chapter, a view shared by Wainer: "Between law and criminality, Batman stands as a liminal figure necessary in maintaining civilized society through ordered aggression" (73). His liminal nature ("bat man") which nonetheless derives from his own conviction to serve a higher calling, is what makes the Dark Knight exceptional as a liminal outlaw hero, and differentiates him from other comic book superheroes.

With the success of Superman, who had been introduced to the comic book world in June 1938, there was a growing demand for additional action "superheroes." Created by illustrator Bob Kane and writer Bill Finger, Batman, or "The Bat-man," as he was initially named, made his debut in *Detective Comics* Volume 1, #27, its May 1939 issue, in a story called "The Case of the Chemical Syndicate." In it, Bruce Wayne is a young socialite and friend of Commissioner Gordon of Gotham City. At the top of the comic's first page, the caption describes this new hero as "a mysterious and adventurous figure, fighting for righteousness and apprehending the wrong-doer in his lone battle against the evil forces of society." The episode begins *in media res*. While visiting the commissioner one afternoon, the latter confides that he is puzzled by the recent escapades of a vigilante figure known as the "Bat-man." As the story progresses, the mysterious figure, whose "identity remains unknown," solves the murder of the head of the Apex Chemical Corporation, apprehending the villain, Alfred Stryker, and thus preventing further murders. In a struggle inside the chemical plant, Bat-man punches him so forcefully that Stryker falls through a railing and into an acid tank. "A fitting end for his kind," Bat-man tells Rogers, whom he has rescued from Stryker. The Gotham police try and fail to catch the vigilante, but he vanishes through the skylight. At the end of the story, the reader learns that Bruce Wayne is Bat-man, even though Gordon remains in the dark about his identity. In the first episode, then, the defining features of this new action hero include his double life (that of wealthy socialite whose alter ego is the Bat-man in disguise), Bat-man's aggressive vigilantism and willingness to commit acts of violence to stop crime, and his hostile reception by the Gotham police, who attempt but fail to catch him.

The "origin story," as it is widely known in the comic book world, is always crucial to the appeal of a given character. It provides the essential information that explains how and why a particular individual becomes the iconic hero—the set of circumstances that give rise to his new identity, his motivation for his actions, and often also how he acquires his name and his powers. Batman's origin story (the hyphen having been dropped from his name) is first told in *Detective Comics*, Volume 1, #33, the November 1939 issue, "The Batman Wars Against the Dirigible of Doom." In a flashback of fifteen years before the current

8. Dark Days and the Dark Knight in Gotham (2005–2012) 225

adventure, a young Bruce Wayne and his parents are accosted by a mugger as they walk home one night from a movie. The mugger tries to steal his mother's necklace, and Bruce's father, Thomas, is shot trying to protect her. The mother is also shot and killed, and the wealthy young Wayne, having witnessed the murder of his parents, vows to avenge their deaths by fighting crime. As he matures, he trains to stay physically fit, and becomes an excellent scientist. Bruce Wayne decides to adopt the terrifying persona of the Batman when, while sitting in his father's mansion, a bat flies in through an open window, a providential answer to his self-inquiry about an appropriate disguise for his vigilante war against crime.

The origin story presented here provides a powerful motive, essential for the success of any heroic figure, for the transformation of Bruce Wayne into the vigilante hero. The childhood trauma of seeing his parents murdered before his own eyes enlists the reader's sympathy and serves as a justification for his vigilantism. This flashback also provides the rationale for his alter ego; knowing that perpetrators of crime are a "superstitious and cowardly lot," he finds the bat, a "creature of the night, black, terrible" to be capable of "striking terror into their hearts" (dc.wikia.com/wiki/Detective_Comics_Vol_1_33). Later, when *Detective Comics* launched a separate series called *Batman*, this story is embellished by providing the name of Bruce Wayne's mother (Martha), and identifying the mugger as Joe Chill, a criminal who meets his end in the same episode of *Batman*, Volume 1, #47 (June/July 1948). As Paul Levitz, president and publisher of *DC Comics* maintains in a documentary extra for the first film in *The Dark Knight* trilogy, *Batman Begins* (2005): "The magic of the origin story is it provides the most fundamental connection to the character" ("Genesis of the Bat").

From this inception in the comic book world, Batman enjoyed continued success, each new generation of writers and illustrators contributing to the growing mythology of Batman and his Gotham City environment. However, with the advent of the Comics Code Authority in 1954 (defunct in 2011), one devised voluntarily by the Comics Magazine Association of America, the character of Batman was softened somewhat, the violence toned down. This code was instituted to avoid government regulation, a purpose similar to the earlier Motion Picture Production Code (discussed in chapter 4) that lasted from 1930 to 1968. Batman also branched out into other media: television, feature films, graphic novels, animated series, and video games. The television series, comprised of 120 episodes that aired on ABC for three seasons, from 1966 to 1968, rife with puns and juvenile jokes, also contributed to the softening of Batman's character.[1]

As David S. Goyer (co-writer of the first feature film in the trilogy) observes, Batman has "permeated the public consciousness" ("Genesis of the Bat"). Although there were earlier cinematic representations of Batman, his career as a *modern* action hero in film arguably commenced with the Warner Bros. release of *Batman* (1989) directed by Tim Burton and starring Michael Keaton as the titular character, with Jack Nicholson as the Joker, his nemesis. The film enjoyed phenomenal success, breaking several box office records (*Burton on Burton* 70–83), and was followed by *Batman Returns* (1992), also directed by Burton and starring Keaton, but with Danny DeVito as the famed villain, the Penguin. Two additional *Batman* releases were directed by Joel Schumacher, *Batman Forever* (1995) and *Batman and Robin* (1997), with Val Kilmer and then George Clooney replacing Keaton as Batman. The final film was a box office disappointment, and Warner Bros. put the franchise on hold until the rejuvenation of Batman's character by co-writer/director Chris Nolan with the *Dark Knight* trilogy (the name taken from Frank Miller's 1986 *The Dark Knight Returns*) which gleaned its rich archives, drew strength from the mythopoeic nature of the story, and restored something of the original character's vengeful anger. These three films in the trilogy form collectively a coherent representation of a rich and varied tradition, balanced with innovation, to create an intelligible, perhaps even a definitive, version of Batman's epic story. The trilogy incorporates essential plot elements and presents a compelling, complex character rather than a one-dimensional champion of authority. As we shall see, this re-visioning also augmented Batman's status as a liminal outlaw hero.

Batman Begins (2005): Fear and Loathing in Gotham City

"To conquer fear you must *become* fear. You must bask in the fear of other men."

—Henri Ducard to Bruce Wayne

In the documentary, "Genesis of the Bat," the co-writers of *Batman Begins*, Chris Nolan (who also directed the trilogy) and David S. Goyer, maintain that they aimed to be "extremely reverent to the history of the character, the mythology of Batman" (Nolan). From the rich tradition they relied on a few works for inspiration, but also on their own inventiveness to fill some lacunae that opened up the story for a new generation. Some of the Batman comic books of the 1970s inspired them; for instance, the "dark knight" epithet appears in *Batman*, Volume 1, #305, with the story titled "Death Gamble of a Darknight Detective!" (November 1, 1978), although the epithet, the "Dark Knight" appears in *Batman*, Volume 1, #1. Earlier, in issue #232 (June 1971), the character of Ra's al Ghul, the villain in *Batman Begins*, made his first comic book appearance in "Daughter of the Demon," written by Dennis O'Neil and illustrated by Neal Adams, eventually developing his own interesting history and lore. Citing *The Long Halloween*, (1996–1997) a maxi-series by Jeph Loeb and Tim Sale, Goyer said they found it "a very sober, serious approach to Batman, and we really liked that."

The first of two most important sources of inspiration, however, were Frank Miller's comic book mini-series, *The Dark Knight Returns* (1986) and *Batman: Year One* (1987). Goyer commented that what they liked about Miller's approach was that it was "very no-nonsense and very tough." Miller focused on Batman's more sinister side, hence the epithet of the "Dark Knight" in his title, as did the writers of *The Long Halloween*, to which Nolan and Goyer remained faithful in their script. Goyer also notes, "I think Frank was the first one to suggest that the police force in Gotham City was corrupt," which created the need for Batman—and his role as liminal outlaw hero. Dan DiDio, an executive at *Detective Comics*, said of Frank Miller, "He was able to embrace everything that makes the character so strong, so iconic, and so identifiable ... but contemporary at the same time" ("Genesis of the Bat"). Miller's reworking of the material embraced tradition but incorporated innovations that revitalized the character, so essential for the success of the film trilogy that drew inspiration from it.

The outline for the film's plot, however, was derived from a story first published in a *Detective Comics* issue known as *Secret Origins* in 1989. Written by Dennis O'Neil and illustrated by Dick Giordano, "The Man Who Falls" features the episode of the young Bruce Wayne falling down a hole that is inhabited by bats, the first of two traumatic childhood episodes. It also retells the origin story of the murder of Bruce Wayne's parents, but extends the early childhood years to show, as Nolan asserts, "the development along the way of Bruce Wayne into Batman ... that he travels the world and is mentored and tutored." This includes his adventures in Korea, his martial arts training, time spent in a monastery, his encounter with a figure named Henri Ducard in France, his rescue from extreme cold by an Indian Shaman wearing a bat mask sacred to his tribe, and finally his return to Gotham City to fight crime. This adumbration of the plot for the Warner Bros. trilogy would present Batman's as "a story on an absolutely epic scale" (Nolan, "Genesis of the Bat").

This film and the ensuing sequels in the trilogy present an over-crowded scenario of evil forces and at times a convoluted series of events, atypical of a modern action film; they sometimes also over-utilize dialogue, which is frequently avoided in the modern action drama to prevent an over-reliance on too many subtitles for global audiences. However, the expanded setting in Asian countries and cities such as Hong Kong, the incorporation of fast-paced action scenes and special affects, and the use of the *montage*, are typical of the modern action film.

Batman Begins opened in 3,858 theaters on June 15, 2005. Its total box office gross, worldwide, was an astonishing $374,218, 673, ranking number one on its opening weekend and running twenty weeks (www.boxofficemojo.com). Critical reviews were generally favorable, with nods to both Christian Bale's portrayal of Batman and the film's return to the mythic roots of the original comic book character. Roger Ebert awarded the film four out of four stars: "this is the Batman movie I've been waiting for; more correctly, this is the movie I didn't know I was waiting for, because I didn't realize that more emphasis on story and character ... was what was needed." It "penetrates to the dark and troubled depths of the Batman legend, creating a superhero who ... is at least persuasive as a man driven to dress like a bat and become a vigilante" (www.rogerebert.com). In a 2008 interview, Tim Burton likewise praised the film, noting that it "captured the real spirit that these kind of movies are supposed to have nowadays. When I did *Batman* twenty years ago, in 1988 or something, it was a different time in comic book movies. You couldn't go into that dark side of comics yet. The last couple of years that has become acceptable and Nolan certainly got more to the root of what the *Batman* comics are about" "Batman-on-Film: Tim Burton Talks Batman" (www.batman-on-film.com/burton-talks-batman-in-amsterdam).

Batman Begins starts with a brief flashback of Bruce Wayne's first childhood trauma when, having snatched a coveted arrowhead from his playmate, the young Rachel Dawes (Emma Lockhart), he races away, only to tumble down a hole inhabited by bats. The film then cuts to the present, with the adult Wayne being held in a Korean prison, from which he is soon rescued by the enigmatic Henri Ducard (Liam Neeson) who seems to know a great deal about Wayne's identity, his troubled past and present *angst*. Ducard is actually the film's villain in disguise, Ra's al Ghul, who heads a group of vigilante warriors, the League of Shadows. He invites Bruce Wayne to join their organization, instructing him to pick "a rare blue flower that grows in the eastern slopes" and to carry it to the top of the mountain, if he is interested in serving "true justice" by fighting criminals and "devoting himself to an ideal."[2] Upon his promised release the next day, Bruce Wayne locates the blue flower and traverses the rugged terrain to the top of the mountain where lies the monastic fortress occupied by the imposter of Ra's al Ghul (Ken Watanabe), Ducard himself (the true leader), and his followers, ninjas who comprise the feared and legendary League of Shadows.

8. Dark Days and the Dark Knight in Gotham (2005–2012)

Another flashback then resumes with the conclusion of the previous one, and shows the young Bruce Wayne (played by Gus Lewis) being rescued from the hole by his father, a wealthy philanthropic physician. Thomas Wayne (Linus Roache) explains to the boy that the bats attacked him only because they feared him, "All creatures feel fears," and teaches him that the reason humans fall is "So we can learn to pick ourselves back up." A short time later, Bruce Wayne attends an opera with his father and mother, Martha (Sara Stewart), but panics when he sees a scene that portrays bats; he begs to leave immediately and, seeing his distress, his father agrees, shuffling them through the emergency exit into Crime Alley. The flashback concludes with the ensuing trauma of the comic book origin story in which the young Bruce Wayne witnesses his parents' murder by the mugger, Joe Chill (Richard Brake), who is apprehended by a kindly policeman, the future Commissioner Gordon (Gary Oldman). These were dark times in Gotham, brought on by an economic depression that caused an increase in crime, but Bruce carries the guilt of having caused his parents' death because of his irrational fear of bats that he cannot seem to conquer at his young age despite his father's efforts to help him.

Cutting back to the League of Shadows stronghold, Bruce Wayne replies in answer to the question asked upon his arrival, "What are you seeking?" "I seek the means to fight injustice. To turn fear against those who prey on the fearful." He then begins his rigorous *askesis* to perfect his martial arts skills; he will also learn from his mentor, Ducard, the techniques of "theatricality and deception," the virtues of patience and agility, keen powers of observation, and how to "become more than just a man in the mind of your opponent," each of these, powerful weapons. These are skills he employs later when he must fulfill his liminal outlaw hero role, one against many.

Ducard/Ra's al Ghul also begins to indoctrinate his pupil, teaching him the value of being feared, of using his hatred for criminals and his anger at the death of his parents to achieve his goal of eradicating crime and injustice. He proselytizes that "crime cannot be tolerated. Criminals thrive on the indulgence of society's understanding." Ducard encourages Bruce Wayne to cultivate and harness his anger and hatred, to seek vengeance for his parents' death, but we learn in an ensuing flashback that Joe Chill, having spent time in prison, was murdered by Gotham City's reigning crime boss, Carmine Falcone (Tom Wilkinson), upon his early release that was granted in exchange for incriminating testimony against Falcone. For this reason, when Ducard suggests vengeance is the answer to his spiritual malaise, Bruce Wayne reflects, "That's no help to me," since Chill is dead.

Seven years before his meeting with Ducard (and fourteen years after his parents' murder) the next flashback shows us an embittered Bruce Wayne returning from his Princeton studies to the Wayne mansion, very upset because of Chill's impending hearing. Bruce takes a gun to the hearing, intending to murder Chill upon his release. The corrupt presiding official, Jude Faden (Gerard Murphy), grants Chill's petition, ostensibly in exchange for his testimony; however, when he departs the courtroom, before Bruce Wayne can act, Chill is gunned down by a henchman of Falcone (in a scene modeled on Jack Ruby's assassination of Lee Harvey Oswald) who has bribed the judge to release him for this purpose. Rachel Dawes (Katie Holmes) is now an attorney; she argues with Wayne about the difference between justice and revenge, defending the "impartial system." "Well, your system is broken," the disillusioned Wayne replies. Rachel equates justice with due process of the law, but the angry, guilt-ridden Bruce Wayne knows that the legal system does not always render justice, which he wants for his parents' murder. Joe Chill is dead, but not by Bruce Wayne's own hand, or even that of the legal system who set him free. Clearly, at this point he equates justice with revenge, but he will soon see beyond his own personal tragedy and motive, a major step toward his transformation into Batman.

When Rachel points out the rampant crime in Gotham City, the corruption of its officials and their allegiance to the crime boss, Falcone, Bruce Wayne confronts the latter in a restaurant where Falcone holds court. Falcone boasts that in the room are "two councilmen, a union official, a couple of off-duty cops, and a judge" (Faden), and that he could blow Bruce's "head off in front of them" without fear of repercussion. "Now that's a power you can't buy. That's the power of fear." "I'm not afraid of you!" Wayne retorts, but Falcone then threatens Rachel and the loyal family butler, Alfred Pennyworth (Michael Caine), taunts Bruce Wayne by asserting falsely that his father had "begged for his life, like a dog," and has his thugs throw Wayne out of the restaurant into Crime Alley. His humiliation and sense of frustrated helplessness prompts him to depart on his seven-year quest, seeking answers for his anger and despair, and acquiring knowledge that will transform him into Batman, the enemy of crime. He begins to see beyond his desire to avenge only his parents' murder, turning his thirst for vengeance to the world of crime in general, and making distinctions between vengeance and justice. From his travels, Bruce Wayne maintains that he "lost many assumptions about the simple nature of right and wrong," sometimes having to steal like criminals in order to live, but averring that he "never became one of them," a distinction that underscores the liminal space he occupies, even before he transforms into Batman.

Having learned what he can from Ducard, Bruce Wayne undergoes an initiation ritual in which the blue flower he brought with him is brewed into a hallucinogenic, followed by a test of the warrior skills he has mastered. The last test, however, before his induction into the League of Shadows is of his loyalty, what Ducard calls his "commitment to justice." He orders Wayne to behead a local farmer accused of murder, but his inductee declines flatly, "No. I am not an executioner," and insists the accused should have a trial. "By whom? Corrupt bureaucrats? Criminals mock society's laws," Ducard retorts. He then confides in Wayne that he had recruited him to help the League achieve its current objective—the destruction of Gotham City: "Gotham's time has come. Like Constantinople or Rome before it, the city has become a breeding ground for suffering and injustice. It is beyond saving and must be allowed to die." Wayne refuses, a fight ensues, and Ra's al Ghul's fortress goes up in flames, purportedly with him in it, while Wayne carries an unconscious Ducard (the real Ra's al Ghul) to safety before returning to Gotham after his seven-year absence.

Ducard has served as a surrogate father to Bruce Wayne, albeit one who espouses values opposite those of his gentle, philanthropic father, Thomas Wayne, who taught tolerance, understanding, charity, and forgiveness. It was the kindness of Thomas Wayne and other privileged families that averted Gotham's collapse years before. Ducard, we learn, wishes the total destruction of Gotham, seeing it as a cesspool of vice beyond saving, and he attempts to mentor Bruce Wayne so that he can harness his anger to serve that end. Later Ducard tells Wayne, "You were my best student." Clearly Wayne feels some loyalty toward Ducard, and this is why he saves him from the fire before he departs. He will learn to use the superior warrior skills he acquired from Ducard, but he will employ them to serve those who are preyed upon by evil. His individual vigilantism is eclipsed by the terrorist philosophy of the collective group, the League of Shadows, but Wayne has the audacity to use any means necessary to combat the enemies of ordinary, right-thinking citizens of Gotham, including those of his mentor.

Now Bruce Wayne is poised to transform into Batman, the liminal outlaw hero of Gotham City. Upon his return after this long absence, he is reunited with the trustworthy Alfred Pennyworth, who inherited Wayne Manor when the CEO of Wayne Enterprises, the unscrupulous Mr. Earle (Rutger Hauer), had Bruce declared legally dead. He confides in Alfred that he must find a way to shake the citizens of Gotham out of their apathy toward crime (an objective also of Paul Kersey in the first *Death Wish*). He wishes to set an example: "I can't do that as Bruce Wayne. As a man, I'm flesh and blood and can be ignored, destroyed. But as a symbol, I can be incorruptible. I can be everlasting." Alfred asks him what symbol he has in mind, and Bruce Wayne ponders "something elemental, something terrifying." This symbol soon presents itself when, at the Wayne mansion, he sees a large bat fly into the room; he faces his fear by returning to the hole he had fallen into years before and finds it is still occupied by the mammals that had attacked and terrified him. This will soon be transformed into his bat cave, the locale of his alter ego.

He then seeks the expertise of a Wayne Enterprise genius, the inventor Lucius Fox (Morgan Freeman). Fox has developed high-tech military and space exploration equipment that has been put on hold by Earle, and exists as the exiled guardian of the future in an underground laboratory. Fox's function is like that of the "Q" character in the James Bond films, who supplies Bond with all of the high-tech equipment he needs to succeed in his missions. Batman acquires his emblems of election, the special gear he will need to combat crime. His utility harness, survival suit, and retractable claws feature a cutting-edge bio-weave and reinforced joints, constructed from materials called "Kevlar" and "Nomax" (actual registered trademarks of DuPont in the 1960s) designed for "advanced infantry." The gas-powered magnetic grapple-gun will help Batman with quick escapes, and at last Fox shows him the "Tumbler," a yellow vehicle with the extraordinary abilities that will become the Batmobile. Impressed with its performance, Batman asks Fox, "Does it come in black?" With Alfred's help, Batman constructs his theatrical mask, and he himself designs his trademark "batarang," the throwing ranged weapon that becomes his calling card: "Bats frighten me. It's time my enemies share my dread." Later in the film, the Bat-Signal, a distress signal light, will become part of Batman's special accouterments, his way of communicating with Commissioner Gordon. A palpable presence that shines over Gotham, the light serves as a reminder of the watchful eye of Batman, warrior and protective patron saint of the city.

The web of corruption in Gotham City presents a formidable task for Batman. Widespread random crime is only the tip of the iceberg. More menacing is the control exerted by organized crime, in this case represented by Carmine Falcone, who evades prison by bribing officials. The judicial system and the law enforcement are a travesty of justice. Judge Faden is corrupt. City council members and many policemen are in Falcone's pocket. For instance, Detective Flass (Mark Boone Junior) is a member of the police force who moonlights for Falcone, especially in over-seeing the warehouse used for the importation and distribution of drugs. Openly corrupt, Flass steals from food vendors and laughs at their distress. So few are the honest cops that one of his first acts in his Batman persona is to enlist the help of Lieutenant Gordon, whom he no doubt remembers for his kindness when the Waynes were murdered years before. Approaching Gordon by stealth in his office, Batman says, "Don't turn around. You're a good cop, one of the few," and asks how to destroy Falcone's drug operation; Gordon tells him to find leverage against Judge Faden and a district attorney brave enough to prosecute Falcone. When Gordon asks,

"Who are you?" Batman replies, "Watch for my sign." "You're just one man," Gordon remarks, but Batman answers, "Now we're two." It is important to establish Batman's trust and pact with Gordon, as it testifies to his liminal status—the *honest* policeman, and future commissioner trusts him, even though the current regime wrongly treats Batman as a wanted criminal.

As Gordon indicated, Rachel Dawes and her boss, district attorney Carl Finch (Larry Holden) encounter repeated obstacles in their efforts to serve justice, namely that of the false expert testimony of the demented psychiatrist, Dr. Jonathan Crane (Cillian Murphy), who has criminals committed to Arkham Asylum instead of going to prison. There, he conducts experiments on them, using the same hallucinogen from the blue flower that Ra's al Ghul prepared for Bruce Wayne's induction ritual. Crane, who dons a frightening mask and transforms into his alter ego, Scarecrow, is conspiring with Ra's al Ghul to bring down Gotham City by contaminating the water supply with the fear-inducing drug. Ra's al Ghul intends for Gotham to tear itself apart when the insane at the asylum are released and the drug itself, vaporized with a stolen weapon from Wayne Enterprises ("a prototype weapon designed for desert warfare"), will create widespread fear and panic in the city, causing its demise.

An apathetic public has grown to accept this dystopian world of vice and corruption. To combat this helplessness and despair of Gotham, Batman heeds Ducard's advice that to fight crime one must become a legend, "more than just a man," a symbol that will make criminals fear him and inspire citizens to act on their own behalf by setting an example for them to emulate. To restore their faith in the law and justice, its representatives must also be sorted out, the corrupt discarded and the honest recognized. Finally, Batman finds himself at enmity with police officials, when he collars Falcone and breaks up his drug ring. Having defeated several of his henchmen in the warehouse, Batman captures and straps Falcone to a searchlight on the docks; when Gordon finds and arrests him this way, he notices that the projected image of Falcone tied to the searchlight resembles that of a bat. This is the message Batman wishes to send to the public: a fear-inducing symbol of power against crime, and a deliberate image-building to stand in opposition to corruption. At the end of the film, the Bat-Signal is installed on top of police headquarters as a mode of communication between Gordon and Batman, but also as a palpable reminder to the public of the vigilante hero's continued presence in Gotham.

After Batman brings Falcone to justice, newspaper headlines read "Masked Vigilante Exposes Drug Ring." The current police commissioner, Loeb (Colin McFarlane), is outraged and calls a meeting with his officers. He wants the publicity stopped, "off the front page and off the streets," out of the public eye. "No one takes the law into their own hands in my city!" he exclaims. "I don't care if its rival gangs, Guardian Angels, or the god damned Salvation Army." Batman thus becomes the hunted as well as the predator—at odds with the official hero, the Gotham City police force, Gordon excepted. Citizens of Gotham start to take notice of this strange savior, and the beginning of hero worship is evident when Batman encounters a little boy (played by Jack Gleeson) on a tenement house balcony. Mouth agape with wonder, the boy says, "You're him, aren't you?" When the boy says his friends won't believe he saw Batman, the latter tosses him a batarang, his calling card, to use as proof.

Tension between Batman and city hall increases despite and perhaps even because of Batman's growing visibility in the community as an agent that fights crime and corruption. When he rescues Rachel, who has been exposed to the lethal hallucinogenic, from the clutches of Crane/Scarecrow at the asylum, a S.W.A.T. team surrounds the building, intending to capture Batman. With Gordon's help he escapes with Rachel in the Batmobile, and a long police chase ensues, augmenting Batman's liminal hero status. Yet only he can now save Rachel and Gotham City; Batman, having been poisoned by the same drug earlier, was given an antidote created by Lucius Fox, who made it from Batman's own infected blood, an apt metaphor for his sacrificial, redemptive role. Therefore, Batman alone is immune to the affliction that will soon be unleashed on Gotham City, and to which Rachel has been subjected. He takes her to the bat cave and administers the antidote, giving her two vials: one for Lieutenant Gordon, and another to be reproduced for mass distribution to inoculate the city.

The climax of the film, then, features Batman's battle not with one but with several adversaries. He has broken up the Falcone drug operation and found evidence to use as leverage against the corrupt judge, but he is pursued by the police, knows that the insane Dr. Crane/Scarecrow is on the loose, and that Gotham is in imminent danger of being exposed to the deadly hallucinogenic. It is Bruce Wayne's thirtieth birthday, and Gotham's social elite have gathered at his house to celebrate, but the crisis at hand causes Batman to dismiss them all with insults in order to protect them. He calls them "phonies," "sycophants," and "suck-ups" and brusquely orders them to "get out." Ducard and the surviving members of the League of Shadows appear; here, it is revealed to Bruce that the Ra's al Ghul who had perished in the fire earlier was a decoy imposter, and that Ducard himself is the real leader. Boasting that they have been "a check against human corruption for centuries," Ducard takes credit for them having sacked Rome, burned London, and for an earlier attempt to bring down Gotham, using the economic warfare of the depression. Ducard has come to burn Batman's house to repay the earlier favor, and to finish the job of destroying the corrupt Gotham: "We have infiltrated every level of its infrastructure,"

8. Dark Days and the Dark Knight in Gotham (2005–2012)   235

Ducard points out incredulously, when Bruce still maintains it is worth saving. In a struggle, Ducard incapacitates Batman and torches Wayne Manor, but Alfred helps Batman escape through the southeast wing that connects with the underground bat cave. Chaos ensues as the insane are turned loose on the street and Ducard strives to vaporize the contaminated water supply, but Batman defeats him on the train that his own father had built in the earlier depression, bringing Gotham's nightmare to a temporary end. "I won't kill you," he growls at Ducard, "but I don't have to save you," as he exits the doomed runaway train.

As Bruce Wayne he sets matters right, firing Earle, the corrupt CEO of Wayne Enterprises, replacing him with Lucius Fox. He stands among the ruins of Wayne Manor and conspires with Alfred about rebuilding the family home. Having divulged his Batman identity to Rachel earlier, the two meet for a bittersweet parting. He tells her, "Justice is about more than revenge, so thank you." She has helped him channel his own personal vendetta into a more noble pursuit. Rachel has discovered that his example as Batman can work positively. Batman assures her that his mask is "just a symbol," but Rachel understands that the boy she loved as a child has not returned to her, that she cannot be romantically involved with Batman, whose mask criminals now fear. She says to Wayne, "Maybe someday, when Gotham no longer needs Batman, I'll see him again." Batman is a liminal outlaw hero and must remain detached from domestic ties, as Rachel herself recognizes. Although he loves her, he also knows that any permanent relationship with Rachel would both endanger her and make him vulnerable to criminals, an impediment to his crusade for justice. His is a solitary pursuit, aided only by a few: Lucius, Alfred, and most important, the alliance he forms with the future Commissioner Gordon.

In the final oneiric scene of *Batman Begins* (Batman being a figure of night and shadows), Batman meets Gordon (who has been promoted to sergeant) on top of the police headquarters. With the new Bat-Signal installed, Gordon has summoned him: "You started something." There is "hope on the streets" of Gotham. But Gordon is worried about the dual-nature of Batman's inspirational image. It has galvanized the citizens of Gotham and given them hope for the future, but Gordon fears that the power of this symbol, and Batman's methods of fighting crime, might cause an "escalation" in the urban warfare: he fears that violence will beget more violence. Moreover, a caped man in a mask jumping off rooftops can also be a dangerous model for others to emulate. Perhaps the future commissioner even intuits a darker side of this new protector of Gotham. He hints at another menace that threatens Gotham, showing Batman the "calling card" of the Joker. Gordon tells Batman that the Joker "has a taste for the theatrical, like you," anticipating the sequel. "I'll look into it," Batman replies, as he prepares to leap from the roof. "I never said thank you," Gordon

Dark Saint of Gotham City: Lieutenant (and future Commissioner) James Gordon (Gary Oldman) forges an alliance with Batman (Christian Bale) atop police headquarters, where the Bat-Signal beckons the patron warrior of Gotham City. It serves as a reminder to both citizens and criminals of Batman's ever-vigilant eye (*Batman Begins*, Warner Bros., 2005) (Jerry Ohlinger's Movie Materials Store).

calls out, in his new role as official hero. "And you'll never have to," Batman answers, in his signature gruff voice.

Batman, though not yet called the "Dark Knight," clearly has found his role as liminal outlaw hero. His hatred of crime and first motive to fight it is prompted by the same circumstances as those of earlier vigilante incarnations. Like the Lone Ranger, he has witnessed the murder of family members and knows who is responsible for it. He adopts a mask to achieve his revenge, but vows also to despise *all* crime and to strive toward battling it in the name of a higher cause. The personal revenge motive is also true for Paul Kersey, who repeatedly loses loved ones from violent crime and commences vigilante activities in an urban setting. Like Paul Kersey, Batman lives a double life. His is and must be a life on the border of community and family. He can rely on the paternal Alfred, his loyal domestic servant, but cannot enjoy the luxury of a romantic tie.

Moreover, Wayne Manor is a place of seclusion, set apart from the urban hub of Gotham City, underscoring Batman's liminal status. He is the savior and guardian of Gotham, its warrior patron saint, but he resides in a reclusive mansion. In the Batman lore, Wayne Manor is located in a northern area known as the Palisades, apparently just on the border of the city limits. A nocturnal shot of the statuesque Batman atop one of the turrets of Wayne Tower, surveying the city, provides a visual image of this role as Gotham's lonely warrior patron saint. This approximates the errant life of the warrior knight, one that in fact he had led for seven years while coming of age as Batman, the "caped crusader" and future "dark knight," both epithets underscoring his indebtedness to the medieval spiritual knight. Finally, he must confront not only external crime but the demons within, keeping in close check his own darker side. A trained killer, filled with a zealot's thirst for righteous vengeance, Batman knows he must govern his warrior fury carefully, following his own dictate to avoid killing whenever he can. Born into privilege, like the medieval Lancelot, Bruce Wayne comes to understand the most basic tenet of this highest form of spiritual knighthood—that it is a vocation demanding a life of sacrifice and service, rather than being served. In the next chapter of his life, Batman will become even more alienated from the city he has vowed to protect, thus transforming himself into the Dark Knight of Gotham City until he can find a final vindication when the trilogy concludes. As the Dark Knight, he becomes an outlaw, but this is always known to be a false accusation, his true status remaining that of liminal outlaw hero.

"Print the legend": *The Dark Knight* (2008)

> "Because sometimes the truth isn't enough. Sometimes people deserve more. Sometimes they deserve to have their faith rewarded."
> —Batman to Jim Gordon

> "Because he's not a hero. He's a silent guardian, a watchful protector. A dark knight."
> —Jim Gordon to his son, James

The westerns of famed director John Ford frequently explore the importance of heroism and legend in shaping the American consciousness, especially when facts contradict a revered image of a larger-than-life figure or a mythic turn of events. *Fort Apache* (1948) features the redemptive quest of Lieutenant Colonel Owen Thursday (Henry Fonda) who, though a West Point graduate and Civil War veteran, has no experience fighting Indians. He assumes command of Fort Apache, does everything by the book, and seeks a glory that has eluded him, resulting in the slaughter of himself and most of his command in a battle against the Apache. Captain Kirby York (John Wayne) who commands after Thursday's death, has more experience with the Apache, and knows Thursday's decisions to have been foolhardy, costing many lives. Yet, at the end of the film, when a reporter asks him whether "Thursday's Charge," a painting that depicts Thursday as heroic, is accurate, York, knowing it is a distortion, lies and says that it is exactly right, and that the slaughtered men will be remembered as long as the regiment continues. Later, in *The Man Who Shot Liberty Valance* (1962), it is not the future senator, Ranse Stoddard (James Stewart), who kills Liberty Valance (Lee Marvin) even though he gains fame for having done so; instead, it is Tom Doniphon (John Wayne) who rids the town of this unsavory character. A newspaper reporter who learns the truth decides finally "when the legend becomes fact, print the legend." Ford's point is that we need heroes and heroic deeds, models for guidance and inspiration, which outweighs fidelity to truth or facts. It is exactly this belief in the vital importance of a legendary hero that transforms Batman into the "Dark Knight" in the second film of the trilogy.

The Dark Knight resumes the year after *Batman Begins*, as the Joker makes clear when he tells Gotham's mob leaders to "turn the clock back one year" when their troubles began with Batman's arrival in the city. Lieutenant Gordon (Gary Oldman) has been working with the newly elected ambitious district attorney, Harvey Dent (Aaron Eckhart), and Rachel Dawes (Maggie Gyllenhaal) to eradicate the organized crime syndicate in the city. Gordon procures warrants for the Gotham City banks suspected of mob control, but his effort is foiled when the cash is removed from the country by Lau (Chin Han), head of a corrupt Hong Kong investment company. The Joker (Heath Ledger), a sinister master criminal, approaches the already intimidated mob leaders and tells them that Batman, who works outside the legal system, will be able to retrieve Lau in Hong Kong, along with the incriminating cash, and he is proven right when Batman plans and executes a daring kidnapping of Lau, with the help of Lucius Fox (Morgan Freeman). Lau cooperates with authorities to reveal details of the money laundering operation, and the mob members are incarcerated.

The Joker now begins his terrorist threats and attacks against the city and its prominent members: Commissioner Loeb (Colin McFarlane), Judge Surrillo (Nydia Rodriguez Terracina), and District Attorney Dent, Gotham's "White Knight," along with Rachel Dawes, Dent's assistant and love interest. He also plans to create terror and panic in Gotham by pitting individuals and groups against one another. By the Joker's machinations, the kidnapped Rachel Dawes dies in the explosion in which Gordon saves Dent, who is in the same predicament; this leads Dent to become his own dark double, "Two-Face," who wrongly blames Gordon for Rachel's death. He pursues Gordon to exact revenge, while the Joker then focuses on Batman. Eventually, after subduing the Joker and rescuing Gordon and his family from the revenge-crazed Two-Face, Batman convinces the now Commissioner Gordon that, in order to reward the faith of the citizens of Gotham and retain hope for the future, Batman himself should be assigned the blame for the deaths caused by Dent. Hence, he becomes the reviled Dark Knight at the end of the film, preserving the false image of Dent as the "White Knight."

The Dark Knight was released in 4,366 theaters on July 18, 2008. With a production budget of $185 million it ran for 33 weeks, closing on March 5, 2009, and grossed an astonishing $1,004,558,444 worldwide (www.boxoffice mojo.com/movies/?id=darkknight.htm). The film was nominated for eight Oscars, winning for Best Sound Editing and Best Supporting Actor, awarded to Heath Ledger as the Joker, the award accepted posthumously by his father, Ledger having died January 22, 2008, several months before the film's debut. His death was ruled an accidental overdose from a lethal mixture of prescription drugs; doubtless, Ledger's untimely death also added to the dark mystique of the film, and in part, to its phenomenal box office success. Roger Ebert, who was impressed with *Batman Begins*, was even more profuse in his praise of its sequel, calling it "an engrossing tragedy," that transcends its comic book origins, not only because of its complex characters, but also "because of the performances, because of the direction, because of the writing, and because of the superlative technical quality of the entire production" (www.rogerebert.com/reviews/the-dark-knight-2008). Manohla Dargis wrote in "Showdown in Gotham Town," that while the film's "big-bang finish ... is sloppy, at times visually incoherent," *The Dark Knight* is "pitched at the divide between art and industry, poetry and entertainment, it goes darker than any Hollywood movie of its comic book kind—including *Batman Begins*" (www.nytimes.com).

Not only did the film continue to portray the darker side of the original Batman character, the appeal of which was made clear by the reception of the first film, but it featured a villain that drew upon the long cinematic tradition of the "master criminal" with its roots in German Expressionism, in which a charismatic but dangerous master mind (a "Mr. Big") directs a crime from the shadows, often also using various disguises. Certainly the villain in *Batman Begins*, Ra's al Ghul fits in this tradition, his connection with Gotham's impending doom being revealed only at the end of the film, while Dr. Crane/Scarecrow and mob boss Carmine Falcone are his indirect links to the criminal activity in the city. But Ledger's Joker in *The Dark Knight*, the screenplay written by Chris Nolan and his brother Jonathan Nolan (with additional story credit by David S. Goyer), also exploits the master criminal tradition. In an interview,

"The Making of the Joker," first published in December 2009 in *Empire* magazine, Chris Nolan stated that he insisted his brother "watch Fritz Lang's *Dr. Mabuse* prior to writing the Joker." (Lang's 1922 *Dr. Mabuse the Gambler* features a doctor of psychology who uses mind control and various disguises to run counterfeiting and illegal gambling operations in the dark Berlin underworld.) In an interview, the director, Nolan, also remarked that Heath Ledger drew from the character of the sociopathic Alex DeLarge (Malcolm McDowell), leader of the "droogs," a violent juvenile gang in Stanley Kubrick's disturbing film *A Clockwork Orange* (1971), set in a dystopian future in Great Britain (www.empireonline.com/features/heath-ledger-joker).

In the *Empire* magazine interview Chris Nolan avers they returned to the "earliest of comics, really the first few where the Joker appeared" in order to focus on the psychopathic nature of his character and his anarchic thinking to instill terror in the audience. The writers wanted a frightening, and not a comic Joker. In the same interview, Charles Roven, one of the producers of *The Dark Knight*, provided the rationale for the film's main villain, one hinted at in the conclusion of *Batman Begins*. When "Batman began and started to clean the streets of Gotham City, the good news was he was taking on organized crime. But the bad news is that the guy who does it by running round in a bat suit and a cape will attract some pretty fringe people. And the most fringe and most dangerous—but yet the most entertaining—is The Joker. That's why The Joker had to be in *The Dark Knight*."

This draws upon the common western scenario in which a renowned gunfighter is a *persona non grata* in any town he visits because he will attract unsavory characters wishing to challenge him in order to gain fame of their own. The fact that Batman is presented as part of the problem regarding Gotham's crime, as well as its solution, and the continued tension between him and the authorities (with the exception of Gordon) intensifies his liminal outlaw hero status, dramatized by his transformation into the alienated Dark Knight at the film's conclusion. The rationale for his decision to take the blame for Gotham's recent troubles is not, however, brought on directly by the presence of the Joker, but by that criminal's engineering of Harvey Dent's fall from his "White Knight" status.

In truth, *The Dark Knight* thus features an over-crowded scenario in which Batman must continue the fight against organized crime, battle with the Joker, redeem the reputation of the popular new district attorney, Harvey Dent (Aaron Eckhart), who is himself transformed into the villain, "Two-Face," contend with internal corruption in Gotham's police force, and cope with growing pressure from a public divided over his role as vigilante hero. As Gordon tells Dent, when at the beginning of the film the latter insists on meeting Batman:

"Official policy is to arrest the vigilante known as Batman on sight." The Joker dominates the screen time as the main nemesis, but in fact Batman encounters several obstacles in his fight against crime in *The Dark Knight*.

The character of the Joker has enjoyed a venerable tradition in the Batman comics, first appearing in *Detective Comics Batman*, Volume 1, #1 (Spring 1940), a creation of Bill Finger and Bob Kane. The "sources" for his character and appearance are equally rich and varied.[3] The first attempt at an "origin story," also written by Bill Finger, did not appear until issue #168 (February 1951). In this version, a thief known as the Red Hood for the mask he wears, is cornered during a heist at a chemical plant and leaps into a vat to avoid capture by Batman; when he emerges, his hair is green, his lips red, and his face white. He then adopts his name from the playing card that he now resembles, the Ace Playing Card Company being situated next to the chemical plant itself.

The more common origin story, however, derives from the 1988 *Detective Comics* publication *Batman: The Killing Joke* written decades later by Alan Moore and illustrated by Brian Bolland. In it, Batman visits Arkham Asylum, where the Joker has been incarcerated, but learns he has escaped, leaving an imposter in his place. Batman knows he is locked into a deadly struggle with the Joker and pleads with him to seek the help he needs, but the Joker's own psychopathic hatred of order and normalcy prevents this. More important, it adds a strong emotional motivation for the Joker's "origin story": he began as an unsuccessful comedian in need of money to support his pregnant wife, so he agrees to help two mobsters with a chemical plant heist. They provide him with a Red Hood to wear during the robbery. Just before the caper, two policemen inform him that his wife has died from electric shock while trying to operate a baby bottle heater. The mobsters force him to carry through with the robbery, which is foiled by the arrival of Batman, and the future Joker is disfigured in the chemical plant where the action occurs. This story is told in a flashback; in the current time Batman confronts the Joker after rescuing the commissioner whom the Joker has kidnapped and taken to an abandoned amusement park where the Joker once worked as a failed comedian and where he has attempted to drive the commissioner mad. This 1988 version became popular because it provided a motive for the Joker's entrance into the criminal world, a history of his disfigurement, his love of anarchy and hatred for authority. Portrayed here as Batman's dark double, the two are locked in a struggle until one kills the other sometime in the future. However, in "Batman and the Twilight of the Idols: An Interview with Christopher Sharrett," Frank Miller, in assessing Batman's adversaries, rightly points out "the Joker is not so much a Doppelgänger as an antithesis.... He represents the chaos that Batman despises," while Batman is "an absolute control freak." Instead, the true double is Two-Face, who is "identical to Batman in that he's controlled his savage urges" (*The Many Lives of Batman: Critical Approaches to a Superhero and His Media* 36). The Joker nonetheless becomes the archenemy of Batman; the strongest villain in the Rogues Gallery that comprises the many foes Batman faces in his long career.

The opening minutes of *The Dark Knight* confirm the concern Gordon expressed at the end of *Batman Begins*, that Batman's presence in Gotham, while welcome in fighting crime, can also be an adversity. This is shown to be true in two ways. First, Batman's example has spawned a number of amateur "copycat" vigilantes who dress like him and attempt to bring down gangsters in a drug deal, forcing Batman to come to their rescue. One avers, "We're only trying to help," but Batman exclaims he doesn't need that kind of help. "What gives you the right?" the copycat then asks, to which Batman replies wryly, "I'm not wearing hockey pads." Here, they interfere with Batman's efforts to disrupt the drug deal, but later one of the copycats, Brian Douglas (Andy Luther), is shown on a television video; he is incarcerated by the Joker, who tortures and kills him, then demanding that unless Batman reveals himself a dozen people will die each day. As we shall see, Harvey Dent also assumes the identity of Batman as well.

The second negative influence that Gordon has anticipated is the arrival of the Joker himself. In *The Dark Knight*, the Joker and Batman have never met when the former enters the Gotham City crime scene, robbing a mob-owned bank with the intention of taking over the entire crime scene in the city. Knowing of Batman's vigilant watch over the city, a symbol of hope and moral rectitude, the Joker tells Batman late in the film that he came to Gotham because "I wanted to see what you would do. And you didn't disappoint. You let five people die. Then you let Dent take your place. Even to me, that's cold." As Gordon feared, Batman's reputation can actually attract rather than repel psychopaths. The Joker insists that he and Batman are doubles, averring falsely, "I don't want to kill you. What would I do? You complete me," and insisting that while Batman thinks he is like normal citizens, "You're not. To them, you're just a freak—like me. They need you right now. When they don't, they'll cast you out, like a leper. Their moral, their 'code' is a bad joke."[4] Batman knows the Joker to be not his double but his opposite: he scoffs at this that they are alike, and the Joker's underlying philosophical assumption that people act out of selfishness, "They'll eat each other," when faced with a moral dilemma. When the Joker sets up a series of perverse tests to prove that human nature is depraved—that people act only out of animal self-interest—he is the one who is disappointed, his experiments showing instead that people can be decent, even altruistic when their own lives are in danger. Batman believes in goodness and, when the citizens of Gotham uphold his belief, opts to become the Dark Knight in order to help them sustain this optimism.

This is why the Joker is a villain, but Batman is a true liminal outlaw hero. Hunted as an outlaw, he is in fact not one but accepts that part to prevent Gotham from lapsing back into apathy and despair. His personal happiness with Rachel Dawes (Maggie Gyllenhaal replacing Katie Holmes in the role) is foiled. At the end of *Batman Begins* Rachel knows he must remain single in order to fulfill his role as Gotham's protector; in this sequel he sees her die by the machinations of the Joker, unable to protect her from this mad psychopath. In a dilemma set up by the Joker, both Dent and Rachel are in need of rescue, but only one can be saved. Batman also relinquishes his own heroic status and the trust of Gotham's citizens, assuming the sins of Harvey Dent and being outcast from the community at the end of the film, a sacrifice for the greater good of Gotham. Batman preserves the "White Knight" image of the young and popular district attorney Harvey Dent who has become the villain, "Two-Face," becoming himself the hunted and reviled "Dark Knight." Dent is thus cast as the "official hero," but this is just an image, while Batman is vilified, existing in the shadows to protect and encourage the citizens of Gotham. The iconic image of the Bat-Signal, by which Gordon summons Batman, is smashed and replaced by the public image of Dent, "Gotham's White Knight." Batman understands the essential precept of true knighthood—that is a life of service to others, not a pursuit of personal glory or fame.

While the Joker represents an external threat, Dent becomes the enemy within as "Two-Face," acquired long before the explosion engineered by the Joker that hideously disfigures half of his handsome visage. Dent is Batman's true double, the other imitators paling in comparison, with his own over-zealous desire to become Gotham's hero against crime. At the press conference in which citizens call for Batman's arrest, Dent (conspiring with Batman to set a trap for the Joker) even confesses that he is Batman, and allows himself to be arrested. Much earlier, however, he makes clear that he is willing to "take up the mantle" when Batman retires. "You either die a hero or you live long enough to see yourself become a villain," says the politically savvy Dent, words that are presageful of Batman's fall from public grace at the film's conclusion.

The figure of Harvey Dent made his debut in *Detective Comics* #66 (August 1942) in a story called "The Crimes of Two-Face!" First called Harvey "Apollo" Kent, his last name was soon changed to Dent to avoid confusion with Superman's alter ego, Clark Kent. He earned the nickname "Apollo" because of his clean-cut, good looks and reputation as a powerful young district attorney in Gotham. At first he aggressively fought organized crime and formed a strong alliance with Gordon and Batman. During a trial, crime boss Sal Maroni throws acid on his face, disfiguring Dent, who then becomes the disturbed and embittered sociopath, "Two-Face." While the character of Two-Face made only three appearances in the comics of the 1940s and two in the 1950s, it was eventually revived and developed further by Dennis O'Neil in the story titled "Half an Evil," published in *Batman*, Volume 1, #234 (August 1971), making Two-Face an enemy of Batman. Andrew Helfer, in *Batman Annual*, Volume 1, #14 (1990), provided Dent/Two-Face with an abusive alcoholic father and a psychological profile that made him bipolar, updating the character to conform with the 1986 Frank Miller *Batman: Year One* rewrite.

We learn nothing of Dent's early life as an abused child in *The Dark Knight*, nor is he portrayed as a character with a history of bipolar or other mental disease. However, he does display an aggressive pursuit of fame and is shown to be an eccentric risk-taker. Early in *The Dark Knight*, while prosecuting Sal Maroni, a witness who takes the blame for Maroni's crime also pulls out a gun and attempts to assassinate Dent; Dent seizes the weapon and punches out the witness, a very different story than in the comic book version, where Maroni scars Dent with acid. Instead, in *The Dark Knight* the Joker is finally responsible for the explosion that causes the disfigurement. Several times in the film as both Dent and Two-Face he spins his two-headed coin (one of which has a scarred and then later a charred face) to help him make decisions. When he first shows it to his romantic interest, Rachel Dawes, she wonders that he trusts in a coin, but Dent shows her that it has two faces, boasting to her, "I make my own luck." Later, as a vengeful Two-Face out to punish those who betrayed him and were responsible for Rachel's death, he also uses the coin, for instance, with Sal Maroni, whom he then dispenses, and then in the final showdown when he spins it to determine the fates of Batman, and of Gordon and his son. Batman is forced (apparently) to kill Dent, whose memorial service appears as part of the concluding *montage*) to prevent him from murdering Gordon's son, but this truth will be concealed from the public, painting Batman instead as the killer of Gotham's "White Knight."

Batman is uncertain in the beginning about whether Dent can be trusted, as he expresses to both Alfred and Gordon (Michael Caine and Gary Oldman reprising their roles in this sequel). Even though Dent is a rival for Rachel's affections, he earns Batman's trust when he expresses to Bruce Wayne his admiration for the vigilante of Gotham. At a fundraiser he hosts for Dent, Bruce Wayne insists that the district attorney's is "the face of Gotham's bright future." He tells Rachel that Dent has "locked up half of the city's criminals, and he did it without wearing a mask. Gotham needs a hero with a face." Bruce also hopes that if Dent takes his place, he himself might be relieved of his obligation to the public as Batman, freeing himself to marry Rachel. It is interesting that

Dent has Rachel's affections and yet also longs to be Batman, while Batman expresses a wish to retire from his role as Gotham's guardian against crime in order to lead a civilian life with Rachel. Rachel is torn between her affection for the two, but just before her death, she accepted Dent's marriage proposal and wrote a letter to Bruce telling him of her decision (a letter that Alfred withholds).

The Joker attempts to destroy Dent's image in order to undermine Gotham's faith in heroes. He tells Batman, "I took Gotham's white knight and I brought him down to our level." Even Gordon recognizes that when the city learns of Dent's corruption, people "will lose hope." Gordon (now commissioner), the Joker, and Batman all know that Gotham requires an official hero to believe in; as Gordon observes, the fallen Dent is "not the hero we deserved, but the hero we needed. Nothing less than a knight in shining armor." Batman agrees that "the Joker cannot win," and setting aside his personal happiness he tells Gordon, "I'm whatever Gotham needs me to be." In this case, that is a redemptive scapegoat, someone who can sustain the false but necessary image of Dent as the official representative of justice and hope for the future. Batman persuades Gordon to comply with this plan: "You'll hunt me, set the dogs on me, because sometimes the truth isn't good enough. Sometimes people deserve more. Sometimes they deserve to have their faith rewarded." Here, he echoes the view espoused in John Ford's *Fort Apache* and *Liberty Valance*—that treasured myths are more important than literal facts. The Bat-Signal destroyed, Batman vanishes into the night. Gordon's son asks why, and Gordon replies, "Because we have to chase him." A perplexed Jimmy, whose life Batman has just saved, declares that "He didn't do anything wrong." Gordon then tells him that Batman is "the hero Gotham deserves but not the one it needs right now. So we'll hunt him because he can take it … he's not a hero. He's a silent guardian, a watchful protector…. A dark knight." He turns the phrase exactly around from his pronouncement about Dent, thus making clear twice in the closing minutes of the film that Batman is the hero Gotham *deserves* but the image created by district attorney Dent, which instills faith in official judicial and law enforcement channels, is the one it *needs*. It needs order, not justice.

The Joker comes from nowhere, and has no discernible past in the film. A pathological liar, he recites conflicting versions of his own origin story, therefore casting doubt on the veracity of any of them.[5] He expresses a particular kind of mad anarchic drive to destroy a belief in common decency and social order, to bring idols down to his own level, an agency of evil for its own sake. His *modus operandi* is to pose moral dilemmas with impossible choices for others to make; the Joker forces Gordon and Batman to choose between saving Rachel or Harvey Dent, saying that he incarcerated them in different locations with time bombs, so that only one can be rescued. (He reverses the addresses, however, and Batman finds Dent in the location he had thought to find Rachel, resulting in her death.) Later, he tries to pit the passengers on two ferries against each other, sending a message to each ferry that it will explode at midnight if it refuses to detonate a bomb that will blow up the other. In the end, the inhabitants on both ferries refuse to kill in order to save themselves, disappointing the Joker, but affirming Batman's belief in human nature.

As Alfred insists to Batman, some men don't commit crimes for something logical, like money. "They can't be bought, bullied or negotiated with. They just want to watch the world burn." "Everything burns" is the message the Joker wishes to send. As he tells Two-Face, he wishes to "introduce a little anarchy." "I'm an engine of chaos. Chaos is fair." Batman, who ascertains the real reason for this debased behavior, asks the Joker if he wants "to prove that everyone's as ugly as you?" The film concludes, however, not with the capture of the Joker, but with the showdown between Two-Face and Batman, reiterating that it is the internal strife of Gotham, and not the enemy without, that poses the greater threat. The Gotham of *The Dark Knight* is a modern metropolis of 30 million people (according to Lucius Fox's calculations), a thriving urban hub, which nonetheless retains the memory of its recent depression and internal corruption, but with some hope for a better future, guided by its patron warrior, Batman. Organized crime is still a problem and has gone international, as Batman's daring retrieval of a star witness, Lau, who is based in Hong Kong makes clear, and corruption on the police force remains an issue, but Gordon is clearly making strides to clean up the police force. Commissioner Loeb (Colin McFarlane reprising his role from the previous film), the mayor (Nestor Carbonell), and Judge Surrillo (Nydia Rodriguez Terracina), two of whom the Joker assassinates, are honest officials.

In *Batman Begins* it is Batman's own poisoned blood that provides the antidote prepared by Lucius Fox that can save Gotham from the hallucinogenic that threatens them, possibly a literalized version of the sacrificial blood shed by Christ. In *The Dark Knight*, Batman likewise functions as a Christocentric sacrificial savior figure, willingly bringing on the revilement of the crowd and taking on the sins of Dent to save the city's faith in the law and governance of Gotham. (At the press conference conducted by Dent that Batman attends as Bruce Wayne, the crowd of citizens insists: "No more dead cops! Give us Batman!") In *The Dark Knight* actions and methods do "escalate" as Gordon had predicted at the conclusion of *Batman Begins*. Batman resorts to brutality, especially in his interrogation scene of the Joker, when trying to find out where Rachel and Dent are being held. He suffers increasingly greater physical punishment himself; at the start of the film when he breaks up a drug deal between

Scarecrow (again played by Cillian Murphy) and a mobster named Chechen (Richie Coster) he is attacked by dogs. In a scene reminiscent of those in the *Rambo* films, Alfred finds him in his new penthouse headquarters (occupied while Wayne Manor is being rebuilt) sewing up his own wound, but we see old scars along with the new abrasions on his back. Alfred admonishes Bruce, "Know your limits, Master," but this goes unheeded. Batman also relies on more and increasingly sophisticated technology devised by Lucius Fox, and extreme measures to stop the Joker. When he uses technology to spy on the entire city, hitching sonar power to the cell phones of all Gotham citizens to pinpoint the location of the Joker, Lucius agrees to help him, but disapproves of this violation of privacy: "This is too much power for one person ... spying on 30 million people." Batman tells him to type in his own name when the operation is over; Lucius does so, and the system, having served its purpose, is destroyed, to Lucius' own satisfaction, reaffirming his faith in Batman's own ability to keep his powers in check. Lucius sees that such technological surveillance methods in any hands are questionable, but Batman uses this only as a means to an end, and has the system destroyed after the Joker is subdued.

In the end, the Dark Knight remains single and aloof, his hope for domestic happiness even in a distant future is destroyed with Rachel's death, and his ties to the community all but severed, save for his secret alliance with Gordon, the wise counsel of the faithful Alfred and the genius, Lucius Fox. Dark days and dark nights lie ahead for both Batman and Gotham City, but as Dent reminds the citizens at the press conference, "night is darkest just before the dawn." An alienated but just warrior hero, the Dark Knight will continue his lonely vigil as the protector of the city, cherishing an idea of hope for its future, even at the cost of his own happiness.

"Here in thys world he chaunged his lyf": *The Dark Knight Rises* (2012)

GORDON: And now there's evil rising from where we tried to bury it.
 The Batman has to come back.
BRUCE WAYNE: What if he doesn't exist anymore?
GORDON: He must.

The third and final installment of the *Dark Knight* trilogy offers a mythic closure to the epic story envisioned by Christopher Nolan and David S. Goyer, the screenplay (as was *The Dark Knight*) scripted by Nolan and his brother, Jonathan, Christopher Nolan remarked: "I never wanted it to feel like another episode of Batman's or Bruce Wayne's story. This had to feel like the culmination of all of the things he's been dealing with in the first two films" (quoted in Wainer 154). One of the strengths of the trilogy, which becomes apparent in the third film, is the continuity of the main storyline as it hearkens back to *Batman Begins*, along with the fidelity to the main characters—Batman/Bruce Wayne, James Gordon, Alfred Pennyworth, and Lucius Fox—and the fact that the same actors played these essential figure in all three films. But most remarkable is the manner in which the ending of *The Dark Knight Rises* provides closure for Bruce Wayne, while also preserving and continuing the cherished tradition of Batman, whose mythic status demands his immortality.

From the outset the writers knew that it was essential for viewers to invest emotionally in not only in Batman, but in Bruce Wayne as well—to connect with both the human, vulnerable Wayne, orphaned at age eight, and the superhero who acts out the fantasy of personal vengeance while also serving a higher, altruistic cause that espouses justice and order for the citizens of his patron city, Gotham. In earlier films, as Christopher Nolan observed in an interview with Dan Jolin, that viewers waited until the main character donned his costume and transformed into Batman, the rest of the time being simply extraneous to the action. "So we thought if we can get the audience to care about Bruce Wayne ... then we will have properly rehabilitated the franchise." Therefore, Nolan continues, the *Dark Knight* trilogy shows how, "step-by-step, he went from an orphaned child to a man who had a hole in his heart, to eventually become this mythic figure" (quoted in Wainer 146). In other words, the mythic transformation *is* the story itself, the one the trilogy has to tell. This is, of course, why Batman's "origin story" has remained stable, the fixed core of an otherwise rich, varied, and fluid tradition. It is his vengeance motive for his reinvention of himself into a liminal figure—both more and less than man, terrifying to his enemies and reassuring to his allies—that makes both Bruce Wayne and Batman so compelling.

The Dark Knight Rises opened on July 20, 2012; it ran in theaters for twenty-one weeks, grossing $1,084,439,099 worldwide (www.boxofficemojo.com). This staggering gross exceeded that of its billion-dollar predecessor in the trilogy. Kenneth Turan of the *Los Angeles Times* wrote that "the dazzling conclusion to director Christopher Nolan's Batman trilogy is more than an exceptional superhero movie, it is masterful filmmaking by any standard" (www.latimes.com). Writing in the *Chicago Sun Times*, Roger Ebert was not as generous, noting the film starts with a "murky plot and too many new characters," also claiming, "It isn't very much fun, and it doesn't have very much Batman." While "it lacks the near perfection of *The Dark Knight*," Ebert does aver that it "tests the weight a superhero movie can bear," and it "builds to a sensational climax" (www.rogerebert.com).

Eight years after Batman disappears in the shadows as the hunted Dark Knight of Gotham, the opening of *The Dark Knight Rises* shows us that his sacrifice has not been in vain. With the ratification of the Dent Act, named after the dead "white knight" of Gotham, organized crime has come to a halt in the city because the law blocked any hope of parole—convicted crime bosses have been forced to serve their entire sentence. Gotham has declared "Dent Day" an official holiday. The streets are clean, but the conscience of its commissioner, James Gordon (Gary Oldman), is not. He has prepared a speech exposing the cover-up of Dent's criminal activities as Two-Face, and revealing that Batman has been framed for these transgressions, but then changes his mind. Batman has disappeared, and Bruce Wayne (Christian Bale) has for five years been busy in his role as philanthropic billionaire, serving as a benefactor of St. Swithin's orphanage for boys and attempting at Wayne Enterprises to develop a nuclear device that would solve the world's energy problems. However, when a Russian scientist named Dr. Pavel (Alon Aboutboul) publishes an article that details how this energy device might be transformed into a nuclear bomb, Bruce Wayne puts the entire project on hold, and this has devastating financial effects on his company, which in turn, unknown to him, curtails his support of the orphanage.

For the next three years, Bruce Wayne lives the life of a recluse. With the passage of the Dent Act, Gotham no longer needs Batman, and his hope of solving the world's energy crisis likewise hits a snag. Not everyone has forgotten Batman, but for the most part, the Dark Knight is a figure that lives in ignominy or obscurity, loathed by some and forgotten by others. Moreover, he grieves for Rachel Dawes and shows no interest in a social life. The years as Batman have likewise taken their physical toll; Bruce Wayne walks with a cane, is thin and somewhat frail, very much the romantic recluse.

He is jolted out of his torpor when several criminal activities of a new sort converge upon the city and intrude in his personal life. First, during an event at his home, Bruce Wayne walks in on Selina Kyle (Anne Hathaway) a cat burglar posing as a maid at the Wayne mansion; she has just cracked his safe, stolen his mother's pearl necklace, and then absconds with what she really wants—his fingerprints. She also helps John Daggett (Ben Mendelsohn), an assistant of Bruce Wayne's crooked business rival, Phillip Stryver (Ben Gorman), kidnap a congressman in attendance. Selina hands over the congressman and the prints she lifted in the hopes of acquiring a device known as a "clean slate," which would erase her own lengthy criminal record, but when Stryver tries to double-cross her, she uses the congressman's cell phone to tip police to his whereabouts, and herself escapes the scene.

Commissioner Gordon pursues Stryver's men into the dreaded sewers of

Gotham, where he is captured by a remnant band of the League of Shadows, the secret warrior group led by the villain who trained Bruce Wayne, Ra's al Ghul (Liam Neeson), in the first film. It is now commanded by the film's heavy, Bane (Tom Hardy), a formidable figure with a mask over his nose and mouth to control the severe pain he suffered in prison, and a voice like Darth Vader's. The injured Gordon escapes and is rescued by the young police officer, John Blake (Joseph Gordon-Levitt). Blake then visits Bruce Wayne to tell him of Gordon's injury. Having guessed Batman's true identity, Blake pleads for Batman's return and confides that, as an orphaned boy (his mother died in a car accident and his father was killed for a gambling debt a few years later) raised at St. Swithin's he knew back then when he first saw Bruce Wayne that he was Batman. Like Bruce Wayne, Blake felt the anger of his parents' death, and tried without success to move on after he became an orphan. He learned to hide his rage, he avers, with a practiced smile, "like putting on a mask." Thus, his affinity with Batman is established early on. Bruce Wayne also learns that his support of the orphanage has been cut off because of his company's financial straits, as Alfred (Michael Caine) explains. Lucius Fox (Morgan Freeman) tells him that the hold on the new energy device has created the financial distress at Wayne Enterprises.

Alarmed by these developments, Bruce Wayne prepares to act. He first visits his doctor who tells him he has "no cartilage left in his knee, little in his elbows or shoulders, scar tissue on his kidneys, and residual concussive damage to his brain tissue—along with the general scarred-over quality" of his body. But in the same hospital where he learns this, having covered his face with a ski mask, he visits Gordon who responds to his assertion that Batman is no longer needed: "Based on a lie. And now there's evil rising from where we tried to bury it. The Batman has to come back." "What if he doesn't exist anymore?" the masked Wayne asks. "He must" is Gordon's simple reply. Batman's finger prints have been lifted, a Congressman kidnapped, Gordon injured, the city's sewers infested with a new menace, and Wayne Enterprises is at risk. The time is ripe for the return of the Batman, although Bruce Wayne is still a somewhat reluctant hero.

As in the previous films, in *The Dark Knight Rises* all the criminal activities overlap. The master criminal in this case, whose identity is always uncovered late in the film, is the vengeful daughter of Ra's al Ghul, Talia (Marion Cotillard), who, however, is masquerading as Miranda Tate, a philanthropist invited to take over the board of Wayne Enterprises to protect it from falling into the evil hands of the rival company. Bruce Wayne becomes romantically involved with Miranda, in part because Alfred told him of Rachel Dawes' decision to marry Harvey Dent eight years earlier, something that he had withheld to protect his feelings. Alfred knew this disillusionment and his confession of this deception would incur Bruce Wayne's hatred, causing them to part ways, but he thought it best finally, to tell the truth. Batman soon resumes his role as Gotham's protector, foiling Bane's attempt to wreak havoc by taking over the Gotham Stock Exchange. When Batman enlists the help of Selina Kyle in finding Bane, she betrays Batman. Bane reveals his plan to finish the work of Ra's al Ghul by destroying Gotham; he and Batman face off, and Bane badly injures Batman's back, as he does in the comic book tradition, then sends him off to the same remote, ancient prison in which he himself was raised.[6]

With Batman out of commission, Bane terrorizes the city. He entraps most of Gotham's police force in the sewers, forces the Russian physicist Dr. Pavel to convert the Wayne reactor core into a nuclear bomb, and blows up a football stadium, killing the mayor and many others in attendance. Having acquired Gordon's unread speech that tells the truth about Harvey Dent's criminal activities, Bane reads it in public to demoralize Gotham's now isolated citizens, then he proclaims a revolution—intended to start a class war between the rich and the poor—also releasing the criminals held in Blackgate Penitentiary, similar to Ra's al Ghul's release of the criminally insane from Arkham Asylum in *Batman Begins*. Chaos and panic reign: the trapped police force renders the law inept so that widespread looting occurs, and the prominent are dragged to a "trial" that is a mockery of the justice system. Presided over by none other than the mad psychiatrist of the previous films, Dr. Crane/Scarecrow (Cillian Murphy) the guilt of those on trial has already been decided before it begins, and they must choose between exile and death. Stryver opts for exile but falls into the frozen river, while a defiant Gordon, pointing out that the trial is a travesty of justice, chooses death, to which Crane sentences him absurdly to "death by exile." The scenario consciously invokes the terrors of the French Revolution, although looting and vandalism occur in contemporary times of unrest, too. The politics of *The Dark Knight Rises* is a subject of considerable critical debate.[7]

As the nuclear clock ticks away in Gotham City, Bane has arranged for a badly-injured Batman to watch its demise (via a CNN newscast). While imprisoned, he begins his own rehabilitation and learns from other prisoners that one person had ever escaped. Bane had called this prison "home," where he "learned the truth about despair," which is what he wants Batman to experience. All the prisoners hope they can escape by climbing to the top of the well. "There can be no true despair without hope," Bane tells Batman, and this is designed to be Batman's torture. In prison, Batman learns the story of the one escapee: a mercenary employed by a warlord eloped with the warlord's daughter. When the warlord found out, he intended to throw the mercenary into this terrible prison, but exiled him instead when his daughter took his place in the prison to spare her husband. Here, she had a child; the mother died, and one prisoner came to the aid of this child, but suffered a terrible punishment. The child later escaped the prison. As he grows stronger in body and resolve Batman, having tried unsuccessfully to make the climb, is told by a blind sage and fellow inmate that the child succeeded because it used no rope—the fear of plunging to the depths will likewise motivate him to succeed. Indeed, as the fellow prisoners chant "Rise" in Moroccan—the prison apparently being located in the Middle East, although the scene was shot in India—Batman climbs to freedom because he uses no rope. But he throws a liberating rope down to the other prisoners before he departs to return to Gotham.

The bomb is now set to go off, and Gotham's stranded citizens await their doom. Upon his return, Batman enlists the help of Fox, Gordon, Blake and Selina. The trapped police force is liberated, and Batman's palpable presence serves as a rallying cry. The police and Bane's forces clash; this time, Batman defeats Bane in a hand-to-hand struggle, damaging the mask that alleviates Bane's chronic and otherwise unbearable pain. Miranda Tate, now unmasked as Ra's al Ghul's avenging daughter, Talia, emerges as the master criminal, and rescues Bane.[8] Even though Bane is the more compelling and complex villain, Talia reveals that *she* was the child who had escaped the prison, that Bane had been her protector when she was in it, and has been her loyal minion since. "I honor my father by finishing his work," she tells Batman, as she plans to carry out the destruction of Gotham. Talia departs to detonate the bomb, but Selina shows up to rescue Batman from Bane. Talia dies in a chase scene believing the bomb cannot be prevented from exploding, having blocked Lucius' efforts to disarm it.

With only a few minutes left to act, Batman loads it in the "Bat," planning to fly far out over the water where it will detonate. Gordon, believing this is the end, says, "I never cared who you were," but thinks the public should know the identity of the person who is about to save them. "A hero can be anyone. Even a man doing something as simple and reassuring as putting a coat around a young boy's shoulders to let him know the world hadn't ended" is Batman's reply, followed by a brief flashback to the night of his parents' murder, when a young policeman named Gordon did just that for Bruce Wayne. The Bat aircraft laden with the bomb and piloted by Batman explodes in a mushroom cloud out over the open water, presumably killing Batman but saving the city, the ultimate sacrifice.

The coda shows Gordon, newly promoted detective John Blake, Lucius Fox, and Alfred at a memorial for Bruce Wayne. At this eulogy, Gordon recites the concluding lines of the Dickens novel *A Tale of Two Cities* (1859): "I see a beautiful city and a brilliant people rising from this abyss. I see the lives for which I lay down my life, peaceful, useful, prosperous and happy. I see that I hold a sanctuary in their hearts, and in the hearts of their descendants, generations hence. It is a far, far better thing that I do, than I have ever done; it is a far, far better rest that I go to than I have ever known." Lucius has learned that before his apparent demise Bruce Wayne had in fact repaired the Bat's autopilot suggesting his death is not necessarily a *fait accompli*; Batman had also refurbished the Bat-Signal. Wayne Manor, following the instructions of the will, becomes the "Martha and Thomas Wayne Home for Children," and a statue of Batman is erected in Gotham, a tribute to its hero, an honorable legacy for both Bruce Wayne and Batman. Gordon tries to persuade Blake to stay on the police force, but to no avail; the disillusioned young officer repeats Gordon's own earlier words of justification for his secret pact with the liminal outlaw hero, Batman, and their unorthodox methods of fighting crime: "You know what you said that structures sometimes become shackles? You were right, and I can't take the injustice." Blake, whose full name is "Robin John Blake" receives an athletic bag willed to him by Bruce Wayne; it contains the coordinates of the Batcave, which he enters to assume the role of the next Batman, an important feature for the mythic closure of the film.

Alfred learns that he has been forgiven for having told Bruce about Rachel Dawes' decision to marry Harvey Dent, as he is bequeathed the remaining funds from the estate. Earlier, Alfred told Bruce that when his charge was absent for seven years, traveling the world, he often entertained a fantasy that he would see Bruce Wayne with a wife, and perhaps even a family, in a café on the Arno River. He and Alfred would never acknowledge each other, but Alfred would know that Bruce was happy. After the memorial service, we learn Martha Wayne's pearls, stolen by Selina and later retrieved by Bruce, have gone missing once again. In the final shot, Alfred enters a café on the Arno River in Florence; he sees Bruce Wayne in the company of Selina, who is wearing the missing pearls. Bruce Wayne and Alfred only nod in recognition, thus fulfilling Alfred's earlier heart-felt wish for his troubled charge. Bruce Wayne's scientific expertise allowed him to repair the autopilot on the Bat. Theatricality and deception, two warrior traits learned from Ra's al Ghul that have served Batman well in his fight against crime, have apparently also made this ending possible.

"Batman is dead; long live the bat!"

The Dark Knight Rises features the redemptive rise and fall of the mythic hero, and hearkens back to *Batman Begins* to bring closure and coherence to the trilogy. The symmetry of the first and third films is commendable. Each major component of the opening film is referenced in some significant way. The origin story so central to the shaping of Batman's identity in the first film—that of Bruce Wayne's trauma caused by his witnessing of his parents' murder—is invoked in *The Dark Knight Rises*. First, Selina Kyle thieves the pearls for which Joe Chill murdered Martha Wayne. The pearls are recovered, but in the final shot in the Florence café with Bruce Wayne, Selina is shown wearing them. Thomas Wayne gave them as a token of love to his wife Martha; Bruce Wayne gave them as a similar pledge of love to Selina. Robbed of his family in the tragic origin, Bruce Wayne has finally recovered a domestic life that must always remain foreign to Batman. The origin story is also alluded to when Batman finally reveals to Gordon his identity by referencing the night of the murder, and the younger Gordon's kindness to the newly orphaned Bruce Wayne. This is a cipher, proof of his identity that only Batman/Bruce Wayne and Gordon can know, and it underscores the fact that the two were bound together early on in their fight against crime, united by the murder of Bruce Wayne's parents. Remembering his earlier kindness, when in *Batman Begins* the caped crusader chooses Gordon as an ally, he tells Gordon that he is one of only a few honest cops in the city. Finally, the words of Thomas Wayne, having rescued his young son from the hole that becomes the Batcave, "Why do we fall, Bruce? So we can learn to pick ourselves back up again," are remembered by Bruce in the prison, serving as a morale booster to help him make his escape.

The master criminal in *Batman Begins* is Ra's al Ghul, the figure who teaches Bruce Wayne the elite warrior skills he needs to be Batman. In *The Dark Knight Rises* the master criminal is Ra's al Ghul's daughter, Talia, who commands the loyalty of Bane, a former member of Ra's al Ghul's League of Shadows. The return of Ra's al Ghul through his daughter and protégé, Bane, also ties the trilogy together.[9] (Moreover, although he was killed in the first film, Ra's al Ghul appears to the imprisoned Bruce Wayne in the final film.) Both Bane and Bruce Wayne are estranged from their League of Shadows affiliation. In *Batman Begins*, Bruce Wayne aborts his final induction because he refused to execute a man who had not had a fair trial. In *The Dark Knight Rises*, we learn that Ra's al Ghul "excommunicated" Bane from the League because his hideous affliction, obtained in prison, was an unbearable reminder to Ra's al Ghul of his wife's death there. In all three films of the trilogy, the goal is the destruction of Gotham City; in all three the master criminal (Ra's al Ghul, the Joker, Talia) forms an alliance with local criminals (Falcone, the mob bosses, Stryver) and all three films feature the mad psychiatrist, Dr. Crane/Scarecrow.

Another factor that unites the trilogy is the double-edged sword of Wayne Enterprises, along with the recurring importance of Lucius Fox and Batman's own scientific genius. In *Batman Begins*, the military and space technology developed for Wayne Enterprises by its precocious employee, Lucius Fox, head of its "Applied Sciences" division, plays an essential role in the genesis of Batman, providing the weapons, armor, and vehicles he needs to defeat criminals, but a device stolen from Bruce Enterprises is also adapted by Ra's al Ghul to contaminate the city's water supply and bring about its demise. This shows the danger of technology in the wrong hands, as does the third film. Fox then becomes the trusted CEO of the company, appointed by Bruce Wayne at the end of the first film to guard the company from corruption or an economic take-over. Intrigue occurs at Wayne Enterprises in *The Dark Knight*, when the company rejects a business proposition by an unscrupulous Hong Kong banker, Lau, who is also laundering money for the local crime bosses of Gotham. Moreover, an employee, Coleman Reese, learns Batman's identity and threatens to make it public. In *The Dark Knight Rises* Wayne Enterprises' development of the fusion reactor, intended to help the world's energy crisis, backfires when, falling into the wrong hands, it is converted to a weapon of destruction, in part because of a board take-over headed by the disguised master criminal, Talia. In addition, there is the earlier unsuccessful attempt to take over the Gotham Stock Exchange in order to control Wayne Enterprises. Economics and technology are real potential weapons in all three films. Finally, all three films include the release of criminals or the criminally insane at a moment when the city is under its greatest threat. Coupled with either corrupt or incapacitated law enforcement, this results in panic and chaos.

What are we asked to understand about the fates of Bruce Wayne and Batman at the end of the trilogy? Chris Nolan has said, "*The Dark Knight Rises* is specifically and definitely the end of the Batman story as I wanted to tell it, and the open-ended nature of the film is simply a very important thematic idea that we wanted to get into the movie, which is that Batman is a symbol … it all comes back to the scene between Bruce Wayne and Alfred in the private jet in *Batman Begins*, where the only way that I could find to make a credible characterization of a guy transforming himself into Batman is if it was as a necessary symbol, and he saw himself as a catalyst for change and therefore it was a temporary process, maybe a five-year plan that would be enforced for symbolically encouraging the good of Gotham to take back their city. To me, for that mission to succeed … the open-ended elements are all to do with the thematic idea that Batman was not important as a man, he's more than that. He's a symbol, and the symbol lives on" (filmcomment.com/article/cinematic-faith-christopher-nolan-scott-foundas).

Batman emerged as the savior of Gotham City when he averted its first apocalypse in *Batman Begins*. In *The Dark Knight* he, Gordon, and Harvey Dent eradicate the internal threat of syndicated crime, although corruption from within Gotham's law enforcement proves still to be a problem, one exacerbated by Dent's transformation into Two-Face. In the final film the hidden evil surfaces once again, showing it is impossible to build a city on a foundation of deceit and lies. For eight years, Batman thought he was not needed, but the return of the reluctant hero is essential in rectifying the "necessary lie" of the past. The repressed returns to haunt them: as Gordon tells Batman, the evil they have tried to bury is rising up from the city's underground, its unconscious secrets coming to the surface. Gotham needs Batman as a symbol of hope, a guiding light of true justice, a protector against both internal and external enemies. Nolan's point, one made by Batman himself several times in the trilogy, is that *someone* needs to function in that heroic role.

When John Blake assumes this identity at the conclusion of *The Dark Knight Rises*, Batman's mythic status is rendered absolute. Blake enters the Batcave and triggers the mechanism in the floor that elevates him to the new status of Batman, a role for which he has expressly shown an aptitude and sympathy. The now famous epanalepsis, "The king is dead; long live the king," originating in the Middle Ages to guarantee an immediate transferal of sovereignty from a deceased monarch to his successor—a continuum of power—can be aptly applied here. That Blake intends to continue Batman's function as liminal outlaw hero is apparent when he tells Gordon that legal "structures are shackles" and he can't "take the injustice." He will continue Batman's essential work as nocturnal loner who aggressively persecutes evil and is unrelenting in his efforts to bring about a higher justice than the legal system can deliver. Orphaned and single, he is void of domestic obligations that would deter his vigorous pursuit of evil.

What are we to make of Alfred's sighting of Bruce Wayne? Batman was Bruce Wayne's invention, a response to a loss so great it nearly destroyed a young boy's life. The motive for his vow to fight evil is retributive violence. Bruce Wayne attends the release hearing of Joe Chill, his parents' murderers, resolved to kill him, and is only deterred when the mob hit on Chill preempts this act. He then sees that the murder of his parents is part of a larger injustice when he meets the mob boss, Carmine Falcone, who has taken control of Gotham City. Once he has acquired the requisite warrior skills to stand against evil—one against many—Bruce Wayne needs a totemic mask from which he can draw power and instill fear in his enemies. He finds the form this fear should take when a large bat flies into a room at Wayne Manor, a divine portent and approbation of his mission. It is appropriate that the bat, a liminal figure itself, is also a personal fear he must conquer—having fallen down into the batcave as a child, his ensuing anxiety is the reason why the Wayne family left the performance in Gotham and exited into Crime Alley where the murder of his parents occurred years before, becoming the central defining moment of Bruce Wayne's life. Once his identity as Batman is forged in his mind, Bruce Wayne then acquires his many emblems of election that he will need to make a stand against injustice, his mission now transcending personal vengeance. But despite this incarnation into a figure larger than life, Bruce Wayne is mortal. The scars and injuries incurred by Batman, and the spiritual affliction of being the hunted, reviled Dark Knight, takes its toll.

From the first, Bruce Wayne sees an end to his time as the caped crusader, and anticipates the day when he can relinquish the role of patron saint of Gotham to return to a life with Rachel Dawes. This is made explicit in *The Dark Knight* when Bruce Wayne labors to relinquish Batman's function by transferring it to Harvey Dent, the "white knight," so that he can marry Rachel himself. That Dent expressly wishes to be Batman—the aggressive vigilante—is an irony that comes true in a tragic way. Bruce thinks Gotham needs the face of an "official hero," sensing his own separateness from the community he serves, but Dent clearly wishes to *be* Batman and willingly assumes the role, but with the death of Rachel twisting him into his alter ego, Two-Face. Having been healed of the traumatic death of his parents and having earned his salvation through the pain and suffering incurred in his role as Batman, the liminal outlaw hero awaits a worthy successor and a purpose in his life as Bruce Wayne, Rachel's death having left him bereft of that, too.

These gifts are given to him in the final film. Robin John Blake, so like Bruce Wayne in background and beliefs, can assume the essential role of Batman. Selina Kyle—also a liminal figure as the "cat burglar" whose heart is in the right place—is a worthy partner for Bruce Wayne. Like Bruce Wayne, she is given the "clean slate" and thus a second chance to reinvent herself. He dies to the mythic role of Batman, but reinvents himself to enjoy a new life with Selina. His years as Batman were a corrective to Bruce Wayne's earlier tragedy, and he can now enjoy a life he might have expected to live had his parents not been murdered.

It is imperative to remember, then, that it is Batman and not Bruce Wayne who represents the liminal outlaw hero of the trilogy. The figure of Batman remains unattached; he is a loner who dwells apart from the community and avoids domestic entanglements. He does not feel constrained to operate within the confines of the law, but removes those "shackles" to serve a higher justice, a justice that is often retributive. Bruce Wayne can only have domestic happiness once he relinquishes his role as Batman. One is reminded of the mythic King Arthur. After the Battle of Camlann in Malory's *Morte D'Arthur*, in which Arthur slays his wicked son, Mordred, but is himself mortally wounded, we are told that Sir Bedivere, who alone has survived the battle, has it written that Arthur died and was buried by the monks at Glastonbury Abbey. On his grave is a cross that reads, "Hic iacet Arthurus rex quondam rexque futurus" ("Here lies Arthur, once and future king"), the promise of his return. In defiance of his death is the apotheosis of Arthur, made clear in the discursive passage that immediately follows: "Yet somme men say in many partyes of Englond that Kyng Arthur is not deed, but had by the wylle of our Lord Ihesu into another place. And men say that he shal come ageyn and he shal wynne the Holy Crosse. I wyl not say that it shal be so, but rather I wyl say here in thys world he chaunged his lyf" (Sir Thomas Malory, *Le Morte D'Arhtur* Bk. XXI.7.34–37; Bk. XXI.7. 49–53). Like Arthur, Bruce Wayne has indeed "changed his life," reverting from Batman to his mortal self, having escaped death at the last minute in his final heroic act in the role of Batman. But Batman, like the mythic role of the king who creates a utopian Round Table, cannot die, having become something more than man.

This separation between the mortal man and the mythic warrior king is likewise emphasized in John Boorman's *Excalibur* (1981). Before the final battle with Mordred in Boorman's film, Arthur confides to his estranged queen and wife, Guinevere: "I have often thought that in the hereafter of our lives, when I owe no more to the future and can be just a man ... that we may meet, and you will come to me and claim me as yours, and know that I am your husband. It is a dream I have." After the battle, the moribund king commands a reluctant Percival to return his emblem of election, the sword Excalibur, to the water from which it came. Percival is reluctant to discard the last relic of Arthur's reign, but the dying Arthur knows the difference between his own mortality and that of his eternal mythic role: "Do as I command! One day, a King will come, and the sword will rise again," he urges upon his loyal knight. Likewise, Bruce Wayne is no longer Batman, but *someone* is, and so someone else shall be in the future. The Dark Knight knows that true knighthood is a life of service and sacrifice; like the Arthur of *Excalibur* and the liminal outlaw heroes who have preceded him, Batman must remain the solitary figure who looks to the future of the community, perched on top of Wayne Tower, the light of his Bat-Signal a palpable reminder of his presence, but always marginalized, remaining just outside of the community and home. When he sees evil, his actions will be swift and purposeful, as he is certain of his role and his own moral rectitude. Batman imposes order, even when it places him in defiance of the law. He is both more and less than human, a reminder of a cherished ideal.

Like the other action hero, Rambo, discussed in the previous chapter, Batman in *The Dark Knight* trilogy features a liminal outlaw hero who changes and grows, rather than remaining more or less static in the sequel films. Dirty

Harry encounters different enemies and obstacles to justice, but each film shows us the same hero in these various scenarios. Likewise, Paul Kersey in the *Death Wish* franchise undergoes his initial transformation in the opening film; after that, his character does not radically change with each new scenario in the franchise. But the saga of John Rambo shows us a tortured figure trying to work through the initial trauma of his post-war experience and represents his ongoing quest for a resolution of his inner turmoil, one apparently not yet reached, evinced by the upcoming sequel, *Rambo: Last Blood*, although at the end of the fourth film he was shown returning to his Arizona home. The same is true of Bruce Wayne; through his reinvention of himself, first in his incarnation as Batman, and then in relinquishing that role, there is growth and change, yet he is at the end an expatriate, no longer living in his native Gotham, though the "hole in his heart" has now been filled. Batman, however, stands as an icon of what it means to live in a lonely space, ever vigilant, attendant on a transcendent ideal of justice and right, guided by his own conviction and singular purpose.

Chapter Notes

Chapter 1

1. The famous order of the Knights Templar was founded in 1118, for example, the secular orders coming later. King Edward III founded the earliest chivalric order in England, the "Order of the Garter," in 1348. See Kennedy 34–35 for a discussion of the "Order of the Garter" as a possible model for Arthur's Round Table in Malory's text.

2. Two competing manuscript traditions of Malory's Arthurian work are those of its first publisher, William Caxton, who printed the text initially in 1485. Until the discovery of another, the Winchester manuscript in 1934, Caxton's was the only one that readers knew. Which is the most "authentic" is still much debated. I have therefore followed earlier scholars, such as Beverly Kennedy, and provided citations from both manuscripts. The first citation listed after each reference is from the Caxton Malory and the second from Eugene Vinaver's edition of the Winchester manuscript. For a recent, comprehensive appraisal of this issue, see Arthurian Studies XLVII, *The Malory Debate: Essays on the Texts of 'Le Morte Darthur,'* ed. Bonnie Wheeler, Robert L. Kindrick and Michael N. Salda (Cambridge: D.S. Brewer, 2000).

3. For a very helpful discussion of Malory's originality in creating this knight as he compares with the figure in the French Vulgate, see Terence McCarthy's "Malory and His Sources," especially 91–95, and Barbara Nolan's "The Tale of Sir Gareth and the Tale of Sir Lancelot," particularly 174–180, both found in *A Companion to Malory*. More recently, Leah Haught explores the "competing impulses" of Malory's Lancelot, and reasons for them, in "Fleeing the Future, Forgetting the Past: Becoming Malory's Lancelot" (*Parergon* 30, no. 1, 2013).

4. Kennedy also discusses the figure of Gareth as a kind of true knight, but one who emphasizes the courtly more than the religious side; Gareth's story ends in matrimony, suggesting that Lancelot's model of restraint from domestic entanglements is not an absolute requirement of true knighthood, although both maintain a moral virtue above that of the worshipful and heroic knights. Gareth looks to Lancelot, and not his own older brother, Gawain, for his knightly inspiration and instruction. It is Lancelot who knights Gareth and who supports him in his efforts to prove himself a worthy knight. Later, in the episode of "The Great Tournament," Gareth, having recognized his mentor, comes to Lancelot's aid when he is sadly outnumbered by rival knights (XVIII.21–40; XVIII.3). This is what makes Lancelot's accidental slaying of Gareth all the more tragic. For a more complete discussion of Gareth as a true knight, see Kennedy's chapter "Lancelot and Gareth: The Courtly Option," especially 128 and 139.

5. It is significant to take note of the fact that the vocation of knighthood, at its height, was viewed as a sacred trust from God, not unlike the office of the priesthood itself. In his last romance, *Perceval, The Story of the Grail*, composed in the final decade of the 12th century, Chrétien de Troyes has one of his characters assert that chivalry is "the highest honor God had created and ordained," and that it "must be free of all baseness" (*The Complete Romances of Chrétien de Troyes* 360). Kaeuper points out that Goeffroi de Charny expressed a "religious independence" and viewed knighthood as a "divinely ordained" charge to uphold (*A Knight's*

Own Book of Chivalry 32). In her opening chapter, Kennedy shows how the true knight, Lancelot, is modeled on 15th-century notions of the ideal monarch, derived from the 13th-century French king Louis IX (St. Louis) in his piety and his adherence to true justice (22–24). Finally, we will remember that Malory's main source for the character and story of Lancelot, although he made several significant changes to it, was the 13th-century French Vulgate prose romance cycle, which was almost certainly composed by Cistercian monks.

6. In her article "Adultery in Malory's *Le Morte d'Arthur,*" Beverly Kennedy discusses the manner in which each type of knight: the heroic, worshipful, and true knight, regard adultery and its consequences in accordance with their own view of the knightly code. For Gawain, the heroic knight, adultery is only negative when it affects his family (65); for the worshipful knight, the issue of adultery is dependent upon its impact on social institutions such as marriage and vassalage (67), and is a matter between individuals; and for the true knight, whose code is essentially religious, "any sexual act which is sinful is also dishonorable because it is a betrayal of God" (71). *Arthuriana* 7, no. 4 (Winter 1997): 63–91.

7. Two well-researched discussions of Malory's life and times are Felicity Riddy's *Sir Thomas Malory* (Leiden: E.J. Brill 1987), and P.J. C. Field's *The Life and Times of Sir Thomas Malory*, Arthurian Studies XXIX (Cambridge: D.S. Brewer, 1993).

Chapter 2

1. Malory comments on his own time as it contrasts with the Arthurian past: his treatise on love, for instance, through which he praises the enduring, "vertuous love" between Lancelot and Guinevere as it contrasts with the fickle attitude of his own day: "But nowadays men can not loue seuen nyghte, but they must haue alle their desyres.... Ryghte so fareth loue nowadayes, sone hote, soone cold. This is noo stabylyte. But the old loue was not so: men and wymmen coude loue togyders seuen yeres and no lycours lustes were bitwene them; and thenne was loue trouthe and feythfulnes. And loo in lyke wyse was vsed loue in Kynge Arthurs dayes" (XVIII. 25. 28–33; XVIII. IV. 22–29). Another criticism of his own tumultuous day occurs when Malory criticizes those who turn against Arthur and follow the treacherous Mordred, indicating that now, as then, men are too prone to shift loyalties: "Lo, ye al Englisshmen, see ye not what a myschyef here was? For he that was the moost kyng and knyght of the world, and moost loued the felyshyp of noble knyghtes" is betrayed by his followers, and "thys is the grete defaulte of vs Englysshmen, for there may nothynge plese vs noo term" (XXI.1.27–33; XXI.IV. 34–41).

2. In his preface to the 1485 edition, Caxton claims a patriotic motive for choosing Malory's text, indicating that several gentlemen urged him to publish a work about King Arthur, an English hero, perhaps in light of the Hundred Years War between England and France. In her article "Contextualizing *Le Morte Darthur*: Empire and Civil War" Felicity Riddy cautions that Caxton's assertion should "be treated with the skepticism reserved for all publishers' blurbs," suggesting that he had targeted a narrow readership of English knights (*A Companion to Malory* 70–71). Others, however, have shown that Caxton was an editor with integrity, one who took pains to note changes he had made to the manuscript. See, for instance, William Matthews' "The Besieged Printer," in *The Malory Debate: Essays on the Texts of 'Le Morte Darthur'*" (34–64) for the most detailed and complete account of Caxton as a publisher in general, and of Malory's text in particular. The immediate reception of Malory's text was very favorable, and its availability to the public, as well as posterity, was thus boosted by the fact that its composition coincided with the advent of the printing press in England and Caxton's decision to publish Malory's text. As William Matthews so astutely asserts, "Had Caxton's enterprise not been married to Malory's genius, it is by no means impossible that English literature, from Edmund Spenser to T.H. White, might have been most barren of Arthurian inspiration" (*The Malory Debate* 41).

3. For a discussion of the importance of Malory in the post-medieval world, see Chapter 1, "The Mythopoeic Nature of the Arthurian Legend and Its Methods of Transmission" in Rebecca A. Umland and Samuel J. Umland, *The Use of Arthurian Legend in Hollywood Film: From Connecticut Yankees to Fisher Kings* (Westport: Greenwood Press, 1996).

4. Very good studies of the Gothic Revival and the interest in the medieval past include Kenneth Clark, *The Gothic Revival: An Essay on the History of Taste* (New York: Scribner's, 1929), Alice Chandler, *A Dream of Order: The Medieval Ideal in Nineteenth Century English Literature* (Lincoln: University of Nebraska Press, 1978), and Mark Girouard *The Return to Camelot: Chivalry and the English Gentleman*

(New Haven: Yale University Press, 1981). For an excellent study of the roots of the Arthurian Revival, see James Douglas Merriman, *The Flower of Kings: The Growth of the Arthurian Legend in England Between 1485 and 1835* (Lawrence: University of Kansas Press, 1973).

5. For a detailed discussion of the importance Tennyson places on female sexual conduct in his *Idylls*, see my articles, "Tennyson's Hierarchy of Women in *Idylls of the King*" in *History and Community: Essays in Victorian Medievalism*, ed. Florence S. Boos (New York: Garland, 1992 [81–107]) and "The Snake in the Woodpile: Tennyson's Vivien as Victorian Prostitute," in *Culture and the King: The Social Implications of the Arthurian Legend*, ed. Martin B. Shichtman and James P. Carley (Albany: SUNY Press, 1994 [274–287]).

6. In his 1981 epic film *Excalibur*, writer and director John Boorman follows Tennyson's version in portraying, quite poignantly, a final meeting between Arthur and his queen at Almesbury, even though the opening credits indicate it is an adaptation of Malory's text. It is worth noting also that this interpretation of the Arthurian legend makes explicit Lancelot's attraction to the monastic ideal. Guilt-ridden after he succumbs to his passion for the queen, a desire he tries very hard to suppress, Lancelot becomes a religious fanatic and is shown as a nomadic wild man, preaching repentance when the land is laid waste from Arthur's wound. He only returns to his former warrior self when the last battle ensues.

7. See Muriel Whitaker, *The Legends of King Arthur in Art*, Arthurian Studies XXII (Cambridge: Boydell & Brewer, 1990), and Debra Mancoff, *The Arthurian Revival in Victorian Art* (New York: Garland, 1990).

8. The novel has enjoyed such popularity in the cinema that it is the subject of seemingly endless film and television versions. It seems to open itself up to a variety of settings and issues, and the protagonist, Hank Morgan, is also subject to many incarnations, changing gender, age, and ethnicity many times over. See Rebecca A. Umland and Samuel J. Umland, "The Arthurian Legend as Intertexual Collage," in *The Use of Arthurian Legend in Hollywood Film* (21–72) for a full discussion of this enduring subgenre in the Arthurian film tradition.

Chapter 3

1. I follow the poetic tradition, best reconstructed by Joseph Bedier in *The Romance of Tristan and Iseult* (1900). The history of the Tristan material is complicated and even predates the Arthurian legend, but generally the earlier, poetic tradition treats all three characters in the love triangle with greater sympathy than the later prose tradition. For a thorough discussion of the evolution of the Tristan story, see Sigmund Eisner, *The Tristan Story, A Study in Sources* (Evanston: Northwestern University Press, 1969).

2. *Casablanca* has become so iconic as to take on a life of its own. Efforts to continue the story, remake it, or revise its ending are bountiful. Examples are the two television series (1955–1956 and then again in 1983), several feature film remakes, such as *Suspects* (1985) and *Barb Wire* (1996), and a 1998 novel, *As Time Goes By*, written by Michael Walsh, the latter of which attempted to provide a means for Rick and Ilsa to be together. These are only a few instances of the way in which the film enjoys continued attention. www.theweek.com/articles/470740/10-crazy-attempts-continue-thecasablanca-story.

3. *Chisum* (1970), for instance, in which John Wayne plays a New Mexico cattle baron who is locked in conflict with an unscrupulous land developer, Lawrence Murphy, presents the rancher as sympathetic.

4. The film was not shot in that ratio but the negatives were cut to give this effect, which some critics, such as Pauline Kael, found to be substandard. See her review of *Shane* reproduced in her collection *Kiss Kiss Bang Bang* (348).

5. Robert Warshow observes that casting Alan Ladd as Shane added to the mythic dimension of the film because he "is hardly a man at all, but something like the Spirit of the West, beautiful in fringed buckskins" (446).

6. Virginia Woolf's now famous invective against this Victorian model of femininity, seeing her own mother as an example, lays open its destructive potential, when held up as a model to emulate. Woolf focuses on the devastating influence of this "angel in the house on other women," but the threat to the masculine is also very real: "She [the perfect wife] was intensely sympathetic. She was immensely charming. She was utterly unselfish. She excelled in the difficult arts of family life. She sacrificed daily. If there was a chicken, she took the leg; if there was a draught she sat in it.... Above all, she was pure" (Woolf, *Collected Essays* [London: Hogarth Press, 1966] 2, 285). She added that she "bothered me and wasted my time and so tormented me that at last I killed her" (Woolf 2, 285).

7. Film critic Pauline Kael also recognized Shane as a type of knight: "Here's Galahad on the range, in one of those elaborately simple epics American directors love to make" (*Kiss Kiss Bang Bang* 347).

Chapter 4

1. White's novel was first written and published in installments. The first book, *The Sword in the Stone* (1938), recounts, for the first time in literary history, the childhood of Arthur. It is followed by *The Queen of Air and Darkness*, published separately in 1939 under the title "The Witch in the Wood." In this section White focuses on the collective childhood of the Orkney clan (Gawain and his brothers) and concludes with Arthur's unwitting incestuous relationship with his aunt, Morgause. The third book, *The Ill-Made Knight* (1940), portrays the complex love affair between Lancelot and Guenevere, and the final book, *The Candle in the Wind*, was published with the previous three in 1958, as *The Once and Future King*. *The Book of Merlyn*, which White initially intended to be part of *The Once and Future King*, was published posthumously in 1977 and features the final lessons Merlyn imparts to Arthur before the latter's death.

2. In December 1952 Paramount announced that it would produce programs designed for television, and in 1953 Disney made the same claim. A few years later, in December of 1955, RKO (owned by Howard Hughes) was the first studio to sell its library of 740 films to television (*American Cinema of the 1950s: Themes and Variations* xii–xiii).

3. The issue of programming was related to the early debate about the purpose of television, and whether it should be primarily educational or commercial entertainment. Connected with this debate was the role of sponsors, and capital gains. Early broadcasting moguls engaged in theorizing about television's role in the country's economic, ethical, and moral development. For these reasons, the kinds of programs, and the role of censorship, became important. MacDonald discusses this in his section "Shaping of a National Culture" (87–109) and various efforts to codify guidelines for regulating content. For instance, in 1951 the National Association of Radio and Television Broadcasters developed a Television Code for this purpose, largely to address the concerns of television's critics. See especially pp. 101–102 and 107–108.

4. *Gunsmoke* aired for an incredible twenty seasons (1955–1975). As the righteous marshal of Dodge City, Arness as Matt Dillon became an iconic "official hero" in American culture. The series was so popular that it also resulted in five television feature films, which aired from 1987–1994. *Wagon Train* aired from 1957 to 1965 (switching after 1962 from NBC to ABC). Another popular western, *Rawhide* (1959–1966) was similar to *Wagon Train* in its reliance on guest stars for each episode and its use of the trail, the former focusing on the westward expansion and the latter on the cattle drive. *Rawhide's* official hero is the seasoned cattle-drive boss, Gil Favor (Eric Fleming), and also features the young Clint Eastwood as Rowdy Yates, a trail hand. Other official heroes from westerns of the late 1950s on include Lorne Greene as Ben, the patriarchal leader of the Cartwright clan on *Bonanza* (1959–1973) Cheyenne (Clint Walker) whose name is the title of a series that ran from 1955 to 1963, and *Maverick* (1957–1962), starring James Garner as Bret Maverick, a gambler, soon joined in the series by his brother Bart (Jack Kelly). Garner left after season three, so other characters were introduced to fill the void; Roger Moore was introduced as a cousin, Beau Maverick, and Roger Colbert joined the cast as the third brother, Brent. An obsessive, itinerant gambler with a good nature and astute detective skills occupies something of a liminal space, but the show lacks the high moral seriousness of *Have Gun—Will Travel*. *The Rifleman* (1958–1963) starred Chuck Connors as Lucas McCain, a widowed rancher with a young son. Like Paladin, McCain is a crackshot, using a rifle rather than a pistol. But McCain's life is much more domesticated and settled, in large part because of the responsibility of raising his son, Mark (Johnny Crawford). This prevents him from sharing the same liminal space that Paladin occupies, despite their similarities. Closest to *Have Gun—Will Travel* in terms of the type of outlaw hero it featured was *Wanted: Dead or Alive*, which aired also on CBS from 1958 to 1961. As its title indicates, its main character was a bounty hunter, Josh Randall (Steve McQueen), whose profession also placed him in that liminal space of being outside of mainstream culture but not a criminal. Generally, his values and actions coincided with those of the law, and he made efforts to refrain from violence, but bounty hunters, like gunfighters, are not frequently depicted sympathetically in the western genre.

5. See, for instance, Kathleen Spencer's 2014 study, *Art and Politics in Have Gun—Will*

Travel: The 1950s Television Western as Ethical Drama, which devotes lengthy discussions to the social and political issues presented in the western genre of this decade.

6. www.npr.org/templates/story/story.php?storyId=18073741 retrieved January 30, 2015. Part of a special newsmagazine program aired on National Public Radio.

7. www.npr.org/templates/story/story.php?storyId=18073741 retrieved January 30, 2015.

8. The opening sequence was later altered to a full silhouette, apparently to de-emphasize its implicit violence. See Spencer, *Art and Politics* 228, n. 80.

9. Boone agreed to extend his original contract of five years for a sixth season, even though he was ready to move on to other projects, namely *The Richard Boone Show* (1963–964), which attempted to bring live theatre to television. It ran only one season, despite the fact that it won a Golden Globe Award for Best TV Show that year, and was also nominated for several others (www.imdb.com/title/tt0056783). *Have Gun—Will Travel* was wildly popular, and would no doubt have continued longer, but without Boone, there was no Paladin. Several co-workers and acquaintances testify to Boone's control of the series, from production to writing, to casting, and directing, and also to the similarity between the actor and his character. For instance, Johnny Western, an actor who also wrote and recorded the closing song for the series, "The Ballad of Paladin," avers that Boone "had a lot of power regarding the show," and that he was a demanding actor with high expectations for himself and others: "When you are the single character who carries the show—there was no sidekick on *Have Gun*—if the show sucked, you took the blame." Western also observes, "Ninety-five percent of what you saw in Paladin was Richard Boone" (quoted in Rothel 106). Kathleen Spencer asserts that "Boone directed nearly every aspect of the series, choosing scripts, writers, directors, actors, and even costumes" and that "he drew on every aspect of his personality and a lifetime of experiences" for his character in the show (*Art and Politics* 10). Paladin soon entered the culture as a powerful iconic image, appearing on trading cards in boxes of Rinso detergent, Halloween costumes for children and adults, Paladin "kits" with calling cards and moustache, and even an official fan club (Grams and Rayburn 67–73).

10. A succinct summary of MacKenzie's life and career is provided by the Texas State Historical Association at www.tshaonline.org/handbook/online/articles/fma07. Grams and Rayburn note that other episodes that testify to Paladin's military experience and expertise, especially with Native Americans, include "The Yuma Treasure" (season 1, episode 14) "Comanche" (season 2, episode 34) and "The Hunt" (season 2, episode 21) (103).

11. In "The Prophet," his opponent is a beautiful woman, Madam L. (Florence Marly), with whom he has a wager of $100. When the game nears its end, Paladin is summoned by the military intelligence officer who will seek his aid, and the lady, believing she has Paladin's "back against the wall," accuses him of staging the interruption in order to avoid losing. However, after a short pause, Paladin is able to conclude with a "checkmate" by a move known as a "sham sacrifice," in which he sacrifices the most powerful piece, the queen, so that his knight can take the game. Magnanimously, he gives the woman the $100, even though he has won the wager. Although the game is of ancient origin, Chess became popular in the Middle Ages, and is frequently featured in medieval romance: Sir Tristan, Sir Lancelot, and Sir Gawain are all notable chess players; Tristan teaches his lover, Iseult, how to play chess, and in some romances, Sir Gawain goes in search of a magical chess board (a substitute for the grail) on King Arthur's behalf.

12. This is not unlike the famous cut in *Casablanca:* viewers are asked to complete the scene in which Ilsa and Rick rekindle their love, after Ilsa fails to persuade Rick, even at gunpoint, to hand over the letters of transit that will save Victor's life. Rick's elliptical reference to it in the final scene at the airport, "We'll always have Paris. We lost it, but we got it back last night," indicates what happened after the cut, which was required to conform to the Hollywood production code. For the television code which regulated violence and sex, but also politics, see n. 3 above.

13. Frank Pierson, who produced this episode, recalls the inception of its idea: "I remember where that story started. It was *Roman Holiday*" (quoted in Grams and Rayburn 366). In that 1953 feature film, a runaway princess (Audrey Hepburn) falls in love with an American (Gregory Peck). Kathleen Spencer traces the story back to *The Prisoner of Zenda* (*Art and Politics,* n. 17, 239).

14. As James Arness, speaking about his role as the unmarried hero of *Gunsmoke* asserted, "People like westerns because they represent a time of freedom. A cowboy wasn't tied down

to one place or one woman.... They don't want to see a U. S. marshal come home and help his wife wash the dishes" (quoted in MacDonald, *Who Shot the Sheriff?* 75).

15. The series presents other episodes with extenuating circumstances, particularly the juvenile status of the accused and/or his mental or psychological state. In "The Killing of Jessie May" (season 4, episode 8), the titular figure is a young boy (Robert Blake) who, having witnessed his father's punishment for espionage against the Union, begins a string of vengeful slayings of the men who tried and sentenced his father. This young boy, obviously deeply disturbed, wreaks havoc with a Gatlin gun, unremorseful to the end. In "The Prisoner" (season 4, episode 14), Paladin tries to help a boy who, at the age of 13, had been caught with his outlaw brothers, the Groton gang. Two of his brothers were hanged, and the young boy, Justin (Buzz Martin), was sentenced to hang when he turned 21. Justin vowed to avenge the deaths of his brothers, but for eight years he lives peacefully in the community. When the time comes, Paladin gets the sentence revoked, but the community remains hostile to Justin. Paladin convinces him to accept this fact and work towards earning the town's trust.

16. Richard Boone acknowledged the talent of the pool of writers who regularly contributed scripts to the show. Grams and Rayburn quote Boone: "'I'll take Gene Roddenberry, Sam Rolfe, and Harry Julian Fink [three of the most highly regarded and successful writers of series Westerns] and stack them up against Serling, Chayevsky, Vidal, Rose, Foote, and Shaw any day of the week'" (*A Companion* 63–64). In his chapter "The Original Frontier: Gene Roddenberry's Apprenticeship for *Star Trek* in *Have Gun—Will Travel*," Paul Cantor notes that Roddenberry composed 24 out of the 225 episodes for the show. He compares individual episodes of both series to show how Roddenberry's writing for the earlier program was a rehearsal for the later series (*The Invisible Hand* 59–90).

17. In *Who Shot the Sheriff? The Rise and Fall of the Television Western*, J. Fred MacDonald offers a detailed exploration of this issue, tracing the demise of the genre and exploring reasons for it, especially the political and social changes of the 1960s that reshaped the national consciousness on issues of violence, war, politics, and the role of women. See especially pp. 1–13 and 117–127. See also Horace Newcomb, "From Old Frontier to New Frontier," in *The Revolution Wasn't Televised* (287–302) and the final chapters of Kim Newman, *Wild West Movies: Or How the West Was Found, Won, Lost, Lied About, Filmed and Forgotten* (191–205). Cantor maintains that "the simple fact is that television became saturated with westerns, and the American public became bored with them," creating a need to find a new vehicle for the genre itself, as in the example of *Star Trek*, "wagon train to the stars" (*The Invisible Hand* 90).

Chapter 5

1. The serial killer who committed several murders in northern California during the late 1960s and early 1970s—when the first *Dirty Harry* was scripted and filmed—referred to himself as "The Zodiac" in letters he sent to the *San Francisco Chronicle*, the *San Francisco Examiner*, and the *Vallejo Times Herald* as well as to public officials (see Robert Graysmith, *Zodiac Unmasked* 392). Several, but not all communications were encrypted, and of those, most have not been definitely decoded. A Salinas schoolteacher, Don Harden, cracked one coded letter, in which the Zodiac explained in bizarre detail that he was killing people so that they would become his slaves in the afterlife, and that murder was more "thrilling" than sex (Graysmith 40–41), a link with the sadistic pleasure expressed by Scorpio in *Dirty Harry*. In two separate communications, the Zodiac enclosed a bloody swatch from the shirt of Paul Stine, one of his victims, to prove he was the genuine Zodiac killer (Graysmith 46), not unlike Scorpio in *Dirty Harry* sending strands of hair, a molar, and a red bra from one of his victims. The Zodiac may have committed many more murders than those that have been confirmed; the case has never been solved, even though there have been confessions.

2. The film was set in San Francisco even though in the original story treatment it was set in New York. The idea for the abandoned football stadium as a scene for Harry's confrontation with Scorpio was prompted by the fact that both Don Siegel and Clint Eastwood watched the final broadcast of the San Francisco 49ers in Kezar Stadium, and thought it would offer a perfect setting for that scene (Schickel 259).

3. Robert Ray's discussion of films that represent what he calls Left and Right cycles, discussed earlier, and their response to the closing of the frontier, helps to explain how the *Dirty Harry* films could appeal to widely divergent audiences. See *A Certain Tendency of the Hollywood* (306–307).

4. In *Dirty Harry*, when Chico Gonzales (Reni Santoni) is assigned as his partner, Harry mentions the misfortunes of two prior partners: Tom Fanducci (killed) and Fred Dietrich (wounded and in the hospital). Gonzales is wounded and leaves the force. Early Smith (Felton Perry) is blown up by a bomb that has been rigged to his mailbox in *Magnum Force*; Kate Moore (Tyne Daly) is shot and killed in *The Enforcer*, and Horace King (Albert Popwell) has his throat slit in *Sudden Impact*. In *The Dead Pool* Al Quan (Evan C. Kim) is wounded but survives.

5. Gail Morgan Hickman went on to write the screenplay for *Death Wish 4: The Crackdown*. S. W. Schurr is identified as "Scott Shroers" in Schickel's account of the origin of the story for *The Enforcer* (340), although the opening credits of the film list Hickman and Schurr for the story. Perhaps one of the two names, Shroers or Schurr, is a pseudonym.

6. The PRSF (People's Revolutionary Strike Force) in the film may have been modeled loosely on such militant groups as the very famous Symbionese Liberation Army that kidnapped San Francisco newspaper heiress, Patty Hearst, and was responsible also for two murders and a number of bank robberies from 1973 to 1975. The group of black dissenters in the film, whose group is led by Mustapha and is known as UHURU, might be based on an organization like the Black Panther Party, which has been active and undergone various phases from the 1960s on, although Mustapha claims that UHURU is strictly nonviolent, and dresses the part of a guru rather than a militant leader. The group's name, UHURU, sounds very like that of Lt. Uhura (Swahili) of the *Star Trek* television series that aired for three seasons starting in 1966.

7. Marc Eliot cites a contemporary review of *Sudden Impact* by David Denby in *New York Magazine* that claims "Clint Eastwood has attempted to retell the Dirty Harry myth in the style of a forties *film noir*" (*American Rebel* 208).

8. See Schickel 385–387 and Eliot 208 for a discussion of Jennifer's role as a *doppelganger* to Harry.

9. The exact origin of the quotation about 15 minutes of fame is debated, but Andy Warhol did host a radio talk show of that name which aired from 1985 to 1987, the year he died. Since *The Dead Pool* was released in 1988, Warhol and his ideas about popular culture would have been very much in circulation at the time.

10. In July 1974, a Florida newscaster, Christine Chubbuck, shot herself on live TV during a broadcast, evidently in protest against the public's demand for, and the media's catering to, violence. This might well be what prompts Harry to tell Samantha, "All you want is blood," and also the inclusion of the would-be gasoline suicide man episode here. See Christopher Sorrentino, *Death Wish*, 25. An earlier famous case of suicide designed to attract media attention was that of Thích Quảng Đức, the Buddhist monk who set himself on fire in a Saigon street in June 1963. Malcome Browne won a Pulitzer Prize for his photograph of the suicide.

Chapter 6

1. See the entry for "Vigilante" at www.oxforddictionaries.com. for the etymology. For a brief history of vigilante origin in San Francisco and the mining areas in the north, see www.eyewitnesstohistory.com.

2. For a brief history and goals, see www.guardianangels.org.

3. www.biography.com/people/bernhard-goetz.

4. In a 1974 interview with Roger Ebert, Bronson (not at ease with interviews) recalls, "I wore hand-me-downs. And because the kids just older than me in the family were girls, sometimes I had to wear my sisters' hand-me-downs. I remember going to school in a dress. And my socks, when I got home sometimes I'd have to take them off and give them to my brother to wear in the mines" (www.rogerebert.com/interviews). Jill Ireland recounts that Bronson told her when he was a child and believed fervently in Santa, he once "hung up his little black sock ... in a house that was too poor to fill it, or even notice that he did it," so when he awoke on Christmas morning, it was empty. Years later, when they were married, Ireland hung a black stocking crammed with presents that she "thought the child in Charlie would enjoy," with an apology note "from Santa" about having missed doing it years before. She was pleased that he "privately and almost secretly" opened the gifts in it, saying nothing to anyone (*Life Wish* 255–256). Bronson also remembers the horror of his father's slow death and its impact on the family: "I remember my father wheezing and choking away his life in a back bedroom. My mother knew nothing could be done. Death was just a matter of time. At the end, he was choking on every breath, and we

all pretended we didn't hear anything. How do you explain what that does to you? You never forget it" (quoted in Jerry Vermilye, *The Films of Charles Bronson* 12). This must have been particularly difficult for someone with Bronson's sensitivity and artistic aptitude.

5. Only ten years before *Death Wish* was filmed, the famous incident of Kitty Genovese, a woman who was raped and murdered outside of her apartment in New York City on March 13, 1964, despite crying for help. It was initially reported that for various reasons at least 37 witnesses looked on and did not call police, although this has been revised and challenged, especially with its 50th anniversary in 2014. Still, the incident has become known as the "Bystander Effect" or the "Genovese Syndrome," much studied by social psychologists. Paul's reaction in this scene is suggestive of the bystander's reluctance to get involved in crime, and/or the belief that calling authorities would be useless (www.newyorker.com).

6. According to Winner's biographer, Bill Harding, in the original script Paul was to witness a scene similar to this from viewing on television the classic film *High Noon*, but when this was not feasible, Winner, who had visited the Old Tucson set when he had directed *Lawman* (1971) had this re-enactment scene added (Harding, *The Films of Michael Winner* 105). If *High Noon* had been the intended subtext, the cowardice of the town would have been more in accord with the apathy of modern times than the active support for the marshal of the town's bystanders in this scene.

7. In his interview with Roger Ebert during the filming of *Death Wish* (cited above), Bronson's potential for explosive violence, his desire for privacy, and his circumspection become apparent. He discusses the extreme deprivation of his childhood, but also his reclusiveness, wishing only to be close to his wife and children: "I don't have any friends, and I don't want any friends. My children are my friends."

8. This ending, which was Michael Winner's idea, caused considerable divisiveness among the cast and crew. The screenwriter, Wendell Mayes, thought it was inappropriate, and Dino De Laurentiis also thought that "it was over the top and people couldn't possibly accept it." Bronson also objected, refusing to do the scene because it suggested he was enjoying killing people. Winner's response to each was the same: either people are glad he is killing muggers or not. If they are, they will applaud the end, and if not, "we're dead anyway." Winner claims that he won out because Bronson wanted to have a dinner break, and capitulated for that reason (*Winner Takes All* 201).

9. This pattern was established in *The Stone Killer*, the film Winner and Bronson teamed up to do just before they began *Death Wish*. In it, Bronson plays a cop who delivers his own form of justice, released just two years after the first *Dirty Harry* film. In *The Stone Killer*, Bronson and Winner eliminated a female love interest altogether, considering it superfluous to the story. In a 1976 interview, Winner recalls Bronson's anecdote: "Listen: there was no girl in *The French Connection* and no girl in *Dirty Harry*. When I was a miner we used to go to the movies and there was no smoking in the theatre. When the scene came on between the man and the girl we all used to go out of the theatre and stand in the lobby ... when the scene with the girl was over, we'd all put out our cigarettes and go back in." Winner concurred with Bronson: "We had four or five scenes with a girl in *The Stone Killer* and they were all utterly useless. It was complete piffle: nothing to do with the story at all" (quoted in Harding, *The Films of Michael Winner* 98).

10. A motif found in the western genre is that of the motherless family and the efforts to cope with the absence of a maternal presence, borrowed for this second film. Rosario's role in *Death Wish II* resembles that of Guadalupe (Maria Movita Castaneda), the cook and housekeeper of Lieutenant Colonel Owen Thursday (Henry Fonda) in John Ford's *Fort Apache* (1948). Thursday is a widower raising a teenaged daughter, Philadelphia (Shirley Temple). Although neither she nor Philadelphia suffer the terrible fate of Rosario and Carol, Guadalupe functions not only as a servant but as a protective, surrogate mother to the young woman. In the long-running television western, *Bonanza* (1959–1973), the void created by the dead wife and mother of patriarch Ben Cartwright and his three sons was filled by the Chinese cook, Hop Sing (Victor Sen Yung), who was treated more like a family member than a paid servant. Rosario, Guadalupe, and Hop Sing belong to an ethnic minority, but are treated with respect.

11. According to Goldstein, Bronson's physical condition was still impressive, even at this age. He did 100 pushups every day, maintained a 31-inch waist, and had reflexes so quick he could catch a fly with his hands and release it outside. The director also points out that the end credits include an acknowledgment of a company that supplied Bronson with personal gym equipment while shooting the film. Bron-

son wore no make-up, except to darken his eyebrows. (Talbot 109).

12. "A man has to be what he is, Joey, you can't break the mold. I tried, and it just didn't work" is Shane's final appraisal of his failed attempt to join community and his return to his role as itinerant gunfighter. In *The Shootist* (1976), John Wayne's final screen appearance, filmed while he was dying of cancer as was his onscreen persona, legendary gunfighter John Bernard Books, we see him desperately trying to establish some community and family ties, even as he preserves his personal dignity and defends his moral code: "Bond, I don't believe I ever killed a man that didn't deserve it," Books insists, to which Bond Rogers replies, "Surely only the Lord can judge that." Indeed, Books will be judged, but the film shows he has been justified.

Chapter 7

1. In his essay "Rambo and Me: The Story Behind the Story" (e-essay, Morrell Enterprises, April 2012), David Morrell explains the manner in which he named his now iconic hero. When he was in graduate school at Penn State and also writing the novel, his wife brought home some apples she bought from a roadside vendor. Impressed by the taste, he asked her what they were called, and when she replied, "Rambo," he at first thought she said "Rimbaud," whom Morrell describes as the "French poet and mercenary, whose *A Season in Hell* had a big influence on me," but he also liked that the name sounded "like a force of nature." He gave him no first name because he did not wish to "blunt the primal force that his last name signified." Morrell also points out that the Rambo apple was a variety that the mythic Johnny Appleseed planted as he traversed America, even though the name itself is of Scandinavian origin, meaning "mountain dweller," another serendipitous detail that coincides with the fact that the rugged mountainous terrain is where the hero is most at home in the novel. In the essay, Morrell explains that the first name, John, was chosen for the film character as an allusion to the famous Civil War song "When Johnny Comes Marching Home Again," providing an ironic contrast between the celebration of the returning veteran in the song and the hostile reception of Rambo upon his return from Vietnam. By yet another coincidence, there is the name of a John Rambo listed on the Vietnam Memorial Wall, one who did not manage to return ("Rambo and Me").

2. Morrell discusses in detail the true story of war hero turned actor, Audie Murphy (1925–1971), as a partial model for Rambo and his post–Vietnam experiences. Murphy (the son of a poor Texas sharecropper) received the Congressional Medal of Honor and 330 other battlefield decorations, according to Morrell, "as many as the Army could give" ("Rambo and Me"). Like Rambo, he carried both physical and emotional battle scars. Upon his return to civilian life after World War II, for instance, he slept with a pistol under his pillow, once threatened his wife, and assaulted a dog trainer who he thought was overcharging a friend for services. Morrell notes a comment in Murphy's memoir, *To Hell and Back*, first published in 1949 (a best-seller in 1955 and also the basis for a film): "He wished that the Army had spent as much time detraining him as it had preparing him for combat." What we now recognize as Post Traumatic Stress Disorder was only understood as "shell shock" after the first two world wars ("Rambo and Me").

3. Kirk Douglas was cast as the original Trautman, but quit during its production in 1981, purportedly because he disliked the film's altered ending, and was then replaced, happily, by Richard Crenna. See Lambie, "The Rise and Fall of Carolco" (www.denofgeek..com).

4. The first berserkers were probably sent into battle ahead of the cavalry or used as bodyguards for "the royal and the elite," according to Braudy, who describes them as warriors who would go over an "edge" the normal warrior would not traverse in either war or peacetime. Examples of this warrior rage are those of Agamemnon's "inhuman rage" and Achille's "heroic furor" in turn towards Agamemnon in Homer's *Iliad*, and of the ancient Irish hero, Cú Chulainn, whose "warrior fury" is so intense that it threatens his own native city of Ulster upon his return from battle (Braudy 42–45), a parallel to that of the returning veteran, Rambo. Braudy also notes the ancient historian, Tacitus, wrote of the fearsome nature of the berserker in early Germanic tribes, noting they spent most of their time in idleness or hunting (43) yet another parallel to Rambo, one of his weapons being a remarkable hunting knife that he uses in the film to spear a wild pig. Braudy cites historian Georges Dumézil, who notes that in the ancient Indo-European tradition the berserker, drawing so much energy from the "animal and nonhuman world as to become antisocial, so individualist" that his unleashed fury is a menace not only to the enemy but to his own culture (43). Again, one is reminded

of Trautman's admonishment to Rambo that the latter should not be "wasting friendly civilians." Considering this long tradition of which he is a part, one can see why Rambo fears the awakening of this warrior fury in himself.

5. Hawley maintains that Gritz planned several trips into Laos to search for unreturned prisoners, one of which, "Operation Grand Eagle," had "some support from the U.S. government," but never reached fruition. "Operation Lazarus" was supported by donations from Clint Eastwood and William Shatner, but ended in Gritz being swindled out of cash by the Laos boatmen he hired and in the capture of one of Gritz' men (*The Remains of War* 68). A March 28, 1983, article written by John Saar and published in *People Magazine* recounts Gritz' unsuccessful mission in November 1982, citing also the forthcoming Spring 1983 special edition of *Soldier of Fortune* magazine that was preparing a full story on the subject and another story that Gritz falsified his exploits as a Green Beret in 1966 ("A Vietnam Vet Becomes the Hero—or Villain—in a Failed Bid to Find Missing Americans in Laos"). Ted Koppel on ABC's Nightline interviewed Gritz on March 29, 1983, only one day after the *People Magazine* article hit the stands, to determine whether Gritz was a "liar" in his claim about the same 1966 Vietnam experience. Interestingly, Murdock in *Rambo: First Blood Part II* lies to Rambo about his own war activity in 1966. See also Franklin, who points out that Colonel James Braddock, Norris' character in the *Missing In Action* films is a thinly-disguised portrait of Gritz and his missions (Franklin *M.I.A.* 136–140).

6. Franklin's study provides a very convincing discussion of the deliberate obfuscation between MIAs and POWs, and BNR (body not recovered), and how this issue became both an effective political tool and a powerful mythology in the American consciousness. He shows the persistence of the myth as evinced by a poll conducted by the *Wall Street Journal*/NBC News and reported on August 2, 1991, that "69 percent of Americans who were surveyed ... believed that Americans are still prisoners of war in Southeast Asia and that 52 percent of those surveyed are convinced that the government is not doing enough to get them back," prompting the *Journal* to remark, "Bring on Rambo" (*M.I.A.* xi).

7. The Vietnamese foreign minister from 1980 to 1991 was Nguyen Co Thach. "Co" and her son, "Nguyen," collectively borrow two of the minister's names.

8. Franklin avers the United States did accuse the North Vietnamese of "ransoming" American prisoners and using them as "hostages" and "bargaining chips." "The administration's line was parroted by the media. For example, *The Christian Science Monitor* series argued: 'Never before, in any other war (at least as far as State Department officials can ascertain), have prisoners been held as international hostages, ransomed to a political and military settlement of war'" (*M.I.A.* 60). Moreover, the most "committed believers" in POWs maintain "the government is just pretending to be concerned about the POWs, who it knows full well are there but whom it keeps abandoning" (*M.I.A.* 34–35). Nixon wrote a letter to Prime Minister Pham Van Dong of the Democratic Republic of Vietnam on February 1, 1973, that promised a five-year payment for reconstruction of the country, but without any intention of honoring the proposal, the existence of which was denied until it was declassified on May 19, 1977, and published the next day in the *New York Times* (Franklin 122–126). Both of these ideas appear in the film, showing that it reflects the currency and continued persistence of the myth of the MIA.

9. When asked about the disagreement, Stallone recalls that he sent Mulcahy to Israel, where much of the film was shot, to hire actors who would serve as "two dozen vicious looking Russian troops." When Stallone arrived two weeks later, he found instead "two dozen blond, blue-eyed pretty boys that resembled rejects from a surfing contest," scarcely appropriate foes for Rambo. When he expressed his disappointment about the actors who had been hired for such a role in the film, apparently Mulcahy balked at firing them, so Stallone "asked him and his chiffon army to move on" (www.aint itcool.com). MacDonald was a camera operator for both *Superman* and *Superman II* (1978 and 1980, respectively) and photographer for *Excalibur* (1981) as well as for *Gorky Park* (1983) and several other successful films. After *Rambo III*, he continued to direct, his next film being *Mo' Money* (1993).

10. Stallone points out, "*Cobra* was more successful in foreign markets than the last two Rockys." He comments on the rationale for the character: "We seem to be glorifying mass murderers these days," he said. "Manson is on Geraldo Riviera, and I get chastised by the press for not explaining the motives of the killer in my movie. Well, there are no motives. They just kill. And the only way to eradicate them is to find a cop who is a radical eradicator. Power

goes to power. To find a thief, hire a thief" (www.rogerebert.com/interviews). A line at the film's conclusion underscores the conflict between justice and the law, when Cobra answers the villain's over-confident claim that the law will let him go free, "I start where the law stops."

11. David Morrell, who invented Rambo in his novel, *First Blood*, also wrote the novelizations for the second and third films. Having seen "all of the draft versions of the scripts," Morrell remembers that the early versions contained a female French doctor who ministered to the orphaned Afghan children, which "put soul into the action." After Rambo rescues Trautman, the two team up with this character to help guide the children to safety, "In the final draft, all of that was gone" (davidmorrell.net). This would, indeed, have altered the film considerably, as it would have shown audiences explicitly what Trautman meant by getting "soft," invoking again the idea of "Momism" discussed in Chapter 3.

12. One reason for, and evidence of, Rambo's continued iconic status was a result of the many different venues that featured his story and character. "Although *Rambo III* fell short of the domestic grosses enjoyed by the previous movie, its success abroad pretty much guaranteed a profit—and then there were all the videogames, toys and other bits of lucrative merchandising to consider." See Lambie, "The Rise and Fall of Carolco" (www.denofgeek.com). Franklin also points to the pervasiveness of the Rambo figure in American culture, including action toys, bubble gum, clothing, TV cartoons and "Rambo-Grams," delivered by Rambo look-alikes (*M.I.A.* 151–152).

13. One character omitted from the script is Ed Bumgardener, who claims to represent the "Office of Overseas Activities" and is an American Vietnam veteran who now works for the CIA. He "advises" Rambo not to help the missionaries because the corrupt military generals, obviously seen by the CIA as maintaining order in a volatile part of the world, don't need more political turmoil from rebels stirred up by outsiders, or any interference in their export business of "gas, teak, jade and drugs." Many of Bumgardener's negative comments about the "God Squaders" (missionaries) and their meddlesome naiveté, is assumed by the film's mercenary leader, Lewis. Bumgardener continues the motif of the corrupt American government bureaucracy present in the previous films, but not prominent in *Rambo*. Another change is that which relates to the script's title. In a conversation with the missionary, Sarah, while traversing the river, she remarks on an amber stone Rambo wears around his neck. He explains it is a "cobra pearl," sometimes found in the Naga-Mani species, in the "big old ones who've died." Legend has it the stone is a talisman that brings good luck, but it has no power "if you kill them for it." The idea of the majestic, formidable snake producing a magical pearl (the result of irritation and strife) works as a fine metaphor for the troubled warrior Rambo has himself become. He gives this to Sarah at the end. The amber talisman is a nice connection with the jade pendant he had worn (from his dead lover, Co, in the second film) and given to the Afghan boy at the end of the third. Regrettably, this lore is absent in the film. Other than minor changes in dialogue, there are few differences. One is that Sarah is engaged to a lawyer who is not on the mission but has remained in Colorado, so that when the head missionary Michael Burnett is killed (he survives in the film and is Sarah's fiancé) Rambo sends her on a plane back to Colorado, concerned for her safety rather than his own happiness. Vaguely indebted to the buddy movie conclusion of *Casablanca*, after seeing her off, Rambo and Bumgardener leave the airport together, searching for a meal that "doesn't stare back" at them. Still, the script and film both feature an under-stated love triangle (www.screenplaydb.com).

14. David Morrell comments that the cobras recognize in his death-like state and fearlessness "a kindred soul" and therefore refuse to bite Rambo, and also remarks on the fact that as "the Boatman" he is imbued "with all the Greek-myth implications of death on the River Styx" (*Rambo and Me*).

15. I use the theatrical release for my analysis, but the extended cut (7 minutes and 58 seconds longer) offers a more extensive, angry exchange between Sarah and Rambo. In the latter, when she asks him what he means by not being able to change "what is," he replies effusively: "That we're like animals. It's in the blood. It's natural. Peace, that's an accident…. When you're pushed, killing is as easy as breathing." He then launches into a diatribe against a corrupt bureaucratic and political elite: "It ain't your country that's askin' [you to kill in a war]. It's a few men on top who want it. Old men start it, young men fight it. Nobody wins…. And nobody tells the truth. God's gonna make all that go away?" The invective against political corruption and the anti-war sentiment is absent in the theatrical release. "Killing is as easy as breathing" is included in Rambo's voiceover monologue in which he tries to be honest with himself about his own violence.

16. In Chrétien de Troyes' 12th century romance, *Lancelot: The Knight of the Cart*, the besotted Lancelot kisses a single strand of the queen's hair a hundred thousand times, and later kneels before her as though she were a religious shrine, using the language of idolatry to address her.

17. The origin of the prayer, attributed to the medieval founder of the Franciscan Friars, is in fact of much later date. Many politicians have recited the prayer in recent years, including Prime Minister Margaret Thatcher in 1979 and Nancy Pelosi, when she was sworn in as the first female Speaker of the House of Representatives in 2007.

18. In Stallone's script, *Pearl of the Cobra (Rambo 4)*, Burnett is killed, but he is not Sarah's fiancé (see n. 13 above). He relinquishes her more willingly, sending her in a plane back to Colorado, where her future husband has remained. In the extended cut, it is Sarah who turns to Rambo with a sad farewell salute, which he returns.

19. Evelyn Meyer, "Undercutting the Fabric of Courtly Love with 'Tokens of Love' in Wolfram Von Eschenbach's Parzival," *New Research: Yearbook for the Society of Medieval Germanic Studies* 1, no. 1 (2013).

20. "Stallone has completed the script and announced the title for the next Rambo film, *Rambo: Last Blood*, an ominous title. He will direct and star in the role. The title suggests that this will be the final installment" (www.variety.com).

21. The cobra pearl belongs to a revered Hindi tradition. According to David Mead, "Mustika pearls are magical stones which are often thought to originate from inside of living things, and thus include bezoars…. Calling something a mustika pearl emphasizes its spiritual, mystical power. In English the term 'bezoar' is used even by medical professionals" ("Unusual Stones," *Sulang Language Data and Working Papers: Topics in Lexicography* 12 v. 2, Sulawesi Language Alliance 2014) (www.sulang.org).

Chapter 69 of an ancient Sanskrit text, the *Sri Garuda Puranam*, reads, "A man in possession of such a snake pearl will never be troubled by snakes, demonic beings, disease, or disturbances in any form" ("The Other Pearls," www.agt-gems.com). Richard Shaw Brown offers similar testimony to the belief in the gem's power: "Anyone possessing such a naga-mani attains piety, rare good fortune, and eventually becomes illustrious as a leader of men" ("Sacred Vedic Pearls," www.agt-gems.com). The Naga-mani is sacred to the supreme Hindu god, Shiva.

Chapter 8

1. Actor Robert Wuhl, who plays the character of Alexander Knox, a newspaper reporter in the 1989 Warner Bros. release, *Batman*, directed by Tim Burton, explains in an interview with Adam Pirani: "The TV show had *nothing* to do with the comics … it was like a sitcom. It was jokey, like *The Munsters* and *The Addams Family* … it's *not* the Batman comic book, and it's *not* the Batman story." The actor also points out that both the Batman in the film (Michael Keaton), and his adversary, the Joker (Jack Nicholson), are dangerous characters. Wuhl continues in his description of the film: "It's like 'Dirty Harry' meets 'RoboCop'" ("A Dark Knight in Gotham City," *Starlog* #142, May 1989, 37). These comments show artistic efforts to return the character to his darker origins, after its swerve away from this in the television series.

2. The blue flower is a singular image that has enjoyed considerable popularity as a symbol of the ineffable, an aspiration that leads one on a journey of spiritual enlightenment. Its origin is uncertain, but the blue flower as a transcendent symbol of desire was popularized by the German Romantic poet and mystic, Novalis (1772–1801), in his unfinished novel, *Henry von Ofterdingen*. In it, the titular character, a young man who is destined to be a poet, has a dream of the flower: "But what attracted him with great force was a tall, pale blue flower, which stood beside the spring and touched him with its broad glistening leaves. Around this flower were countless others of every hue"; however, "he saw nothing but the blue flower and gazed upon it long with inexpressible tenderness … the flower leaned towards him and its petals displayed an expanded blue corolla wherein a delicate face hovered. His sweet amazement increased with the strange transformation, when suddenly the voice of his mother woke him" (*Henry von Ofterdingen* 17). When Henry relates his dream to his parents, he learns that in his youth his father had experienced a similar dream of the blue flower (22). It instills in Henry a yearning; he undertakes a journey to visit the home of his maternal grandparents and learns his vocation as a poet along the way. He meets and falls in love with Mathilda and concludes, "So do I not feel as I did in that dream when I saw the blue flower? The face that inclined to me out of the flowery calyx, that was Mathilda's heavenly face … she is the visible spirit of song…. She will be my innermost soul, the vestal priestess of my sa-

cred fire" (104). Other writers have employed the blue flower, in like fashion: Walter Benjamin references it and Novalis in his essay on surrealism and the unconscious, *Dream Kitsch* (1925), as does D. H. Lawrence in his story "The Fox" (1922): "The more you reach after the fatal flower of happiness, which trembles so blue and lovely in a crevice just beyond your grasp, the more fearfully you become aware of the precipice below you…. You pluck flower after flower—it is never *the* flower." C.S. Lewis in his autobiographical work, *Surprised By Joy: The Shape of My Early Life* (1955), uses it as a symbol for the desire imposed in the presence of exquisite beauty. In his 1977 novel, *A Scanner Darkly*, Philip K. Dick (who was very interested in German literature and music) includes "Substance D," a drug derived from a plant with a blue flower—a rather close association of its use in *Batman Begins*. Novelist Penelope Fitzgerald's novel about the life of Novalis is titled *The Blue Flower* (1995). A continuing esoteric tradition of the blue flower and its mystical properties is thus employed in the film to show the ardent nature of Bruce Wayne's quest, and the inner knowledge it can provide.

3. The inception and history of the Joker's character is complex and interesting. An obituary of its co-creator, Bob Kane, written by Sarah Boxer and published in the *New York Times*, dated November 7, 1998 contains the following quotation from the then Librarian at *Detective Comics*, Allan Asherman: "Batman's villains also had pedigrees. The Joker is descended not only from the face on playing cards but also, Mr. Asherman said, from "The Man Who Laughs," a 1920's movie based on a Victor Hugo story about a disfigured man in medieval France who moves in royal circles" (www.nytimes.com). Roger Ebert also discusses the Joker's debt in *The Dark Knight:* "His [Ledger's] Joker draws power from the actual inspiration of the character in the silent classic, *The Man Who Laughs* (1928)," directed by Paul Leni and starring Conrad Veidt (who later played the Nazi, Major Strasser, in *Casablanca*) (www.rogerebert.com). Bob Kane cited also Robert Louis Stevenson's archetypal novel, *The Strange Case of Dr. Jekyll and Mr. Hyde* (1886) (www.wikipedia.org). Very fascinating is Chris Nolan's remarks about the creation of the Joker's make-up for *The Dark Knight*, which was inspired by Francis Bacon's 1953 painting titled *Study After Velázquez's Portrait of Pope Innocent X*, referring to the 1650 painting by Diego Velázquez, *Pope Innocent X* (the last Borgia Pope) (www.tate.org.). He commented that the facial make-up was inspired by the way "the paint would run together and the colors would mix" in several of Bacon's paintings. Film shots of the Joker, especially in the chase sequence where he is captured by Gordon and his men, juxtaposed to the Bacon painting, show a striking resemblance between the two.

4. *Unbreakable* (2000) also features two characters locked in a struggle of balanced opposites. Written and directed by M. Night Shyamalan, it stars Bruce Willis as David Dunn, a security guard who discovers he has a super power that makes him unbreakable (being vulnerable only to water) and a sixth sense that allows him to see criminal acts of people he touches. His nemesis, Elijah Price (Samuel L. Jackson), was born with a debilitating disease that makes his bones very fragile. At his comic book exhibition, David Dunn learns that Price orchestrated a number of disasters, including a train wreck in which Dunn was the sole survivor. Price insists that he and Dunn, his antithesis, are mutually linked, like a comic book superhero and the villain. This is what the Joker claims about himself and Batman. A June 2, 2011, *New York Times* article by Gilbert Cruz ranks *Unbreakable* and *The Dark Knight* among the "Top 10 Superhero Films of all Time" (www.entertainmenttime.com).

5. In the film, the Joker recounts two separate origin stories. The first is to the mob gangster, Gambol (Michael Jai White), who puts a price on the Joker's head, only to have it backfire. Based on the story by Andrew Helfer, the Joker tells Gambol that his father, a psychopathic drunkard, knifed the Joker's mother and killed her before the child's own eyes, then turned to him and asked, "Why so serious?" The father then turned the knife on the Joker, carving the trademark permanent smile. Later, however, the Joker relates an alternate story to Rachel Dawes. According to this very different version, the Joker acquired his smile as an adult, and at his own hand. His "beautiful wife" always told him to smile more. She gambled and grew deep in debt to loan sharks, that one day carved her face. Since they had "no money for surgeries," she could not bear her disfigurement. The Joker wanted his wife to smile again, thinking, "I just want her to know that I don't care about the scars. So I stick a razor in my mouth and do this (working his jaws back and forth) to myself." A bitter irony is that she could not stand the sight of the Joker after he disfigured himself, and she left him. This version follows *Batman: The Killing Joke*, in that the Joker has a tragic story of a wife, but the self-disfigurement here is new. Obviously, a trickster

figure, it is impossible to know what to believe.

6. Talia, chosen as the master criminal in the film because she is Ra's al Ghul's daughter, made her comic book debut in Dennis O'Neil's "Into the Den of the Death-Dealers," in *Detective Comics* #411 (May 1971). In ensuing incarnations of her character, Talia has a romance with Batman, one in which they even marry (*DC Special Series* #15, published in 1978) later giving birth to a child she names Ibn al Xu 'ffasch, Arabic for "son of the bat" which she leaves in an orphanage. In other storylines, Talia is romantically involved with Bane. She introduces Bane to her father in "Batman: Bane of the Demon" (1998), and Ra's al Ghul initially wants Talia to wed him but changes his mind. Although his love for Talia is unrequited, Bane's obsession with her continues, as in *Detective Comics* #26, "Birds of Prey" (2001), written by Chuck Dixon.

7. For instance, Scott Foundas' interview with Nolan, "Cinematic Faith," in *Film Comment*, asserts that some read the film as "neoconservative" and "very right-wing," while others have argued it is a "radical leftist film," pointing out that "the political rhetoric of one extreme can be co-opted by the complete opposite extreme." Nolan's response was to point out that the film attempted to "pull off the shackles off everyday life and go to a more frightening place where anything is possible" (www.filmcomment.com). In fact, several anxieties from "everyday life" seem to permeate the film: the banking crisis of 2008 and "Occupy Wall Street," the fear of dictators and terrorists, particularly religious fanaticism, internal political unrest and violence in the streets, particularly clashes between the law and protesters of a perceived misuse of power. For a very insightful discussion of the film's political tenets, see Slavoj Žižek's 2012 article "The Politics of Batman" published in *The New Statesman* (www.newstatesman.com).

8. Bane was introduced two decades after Talia, first appearing in *Batman: Vengeance of Bane*, Volume 1 #1 (January 1993), written by Chuck Dixon. A later addition to Batman's "Rogues Gallery," Bane is a fascinating adversary, sometimes more of a tragic figure than a villain. In his origin story, Bane was born in a fictive Latin American prison, an island called Peña Duro. His father had been a revolutionary in the country of Santa Prisca and died in a failed coup. The mother was imprisoned and gave birth to Bane; according to an old law, a punishment was visited on the children of deceased men who had been sentenced, so Bane was condemned to remain in prison because of his father's actions. His mother died when he was six; surviving the hardships of prison and its brutal inmates, the child grew strong and named himself Bane. Interestingly, the root of bane, "bana," in Old English, meant slayer or killer. Its associations with poison and death (as in "wolf-bane") have now given way to the common meaning of irritant or source of antagonism. Experiments were conducted on Bane later in life, when scientists administered a steroid drug called Venom to prisoners. Only Bane survived these, and the drug gave him extraordinary strength. With his friends, Zombie, Trogg, and a native of Gotham, Bird, Bane escapes the prison. Fascinated by Bird's stories of Batman, Gotham's warrior patron, Bane travels to Gotham in order to learn more about Batman and defeat him. In ensuing episodes (*Batman* #489 and *Batman* #497, for instance), the tension between Bane and Batman increases, Bane eventually breaks Batman's back, and begins his criminal career in Gotham. In the *Knightfall* series, after his rehabilitation, Batman again fights Bane and prevails (www.comicvine.com). Other comic book storylines continue to develop the character of Bane. The film employs several details about his early life in prison and the pain he suffered there. It also hints at his Latin roots. The mask Bane is forced to wear in *The Dark Knight Rises* is for pain control, and not a continued dose of the original drug he was given. Wearing the device gives him his unique voice. Actor Tom Hardy, knowing the character to be "of Latin descent," used as a model a "bare-knuckle fighter," a "sort of Romany Gypsy," named Bartley Gorman. He also acknowledges the influences of Sean Connery and Richard Burton in giving the voice maturity and pain (www.businessinsider.com).

9. After the film's release, Chris Nolan commented: "Moving on to *The Dark Knight Rises*, I knew that the League of Shadows had to come back," he says of the secret society of assassins led by Liam Neeson's Ra's al Ghul. He continues: "I knew that we had to return to *Batman Begins* and those philosophical ideas of Ra's Al Ghul, those challenges—that all had to come back" (www.hollywoodreporter.com).

Works Cited

Acuna, Kirsten. "Here's How Tom Hardy Perfected Bane's Voice in 'The Dark Knight Rises.'" *Business Insider* 28 Nov. 2012. Web.
"The American Film Institute's Top 100 Movie Quotes." 10th Anniversary Edition, 2005. Web.
Aronstein, Susan, and Nancy Coiner. "Twice Knightly: The Democratizing of the Middle Ages in Middle-Class America." *Medievalism in North America*. Spec. issue of *Studies in Medievalism* 6 (1994): 212–231. Web.
Balio, Tino. "A Major Presence in all the World's Important Markets." *The Film Cultures Reader*. Ed. Graeme Turner. New York: Routledge, 2002. 206–18. Print.
"Bane." *Comic Vine*. comicvine.com. Web.
Barber, Richard. "Chivalry and the *Morte Darthur*." *A Companion to Malory*. Ed. Elizabeth Archibald and A.S.G. Edwards. Cambridge: D.S. Brewer, 1997. 19–34. Print.
Batman Begins. Dir. Christopher Nolan. Perf. Christian Bale, Michael Caine, Morgan Freeman, Gary Oldman, Liam Neeson. Warner Bros., 2005. DVD.
"Batman-on-Film: Tim Burton Talks Batman in Amsterdam." 13 Apr. 2008. Web.
Bell, Thomas. "Banned Rambo Film Hot Property in Burma." *The Telegraph* 18 Feb. 2008. Web.
Bernardin, Marc. "Christopher Nolan on 'Extreme Places' in the Making of 'The Dark Knight Rises'" *The Hollywood Reporter* 27 Dec. 2012. Web.
"Bernhard Goetz: Folk Hero." *Bio*. A&E Television Networks. Web.
Boddy, William. *Fifties Television: The Industry and Its Critics*. Urbana: University of Illinois Press, 1993. Print.
Bolter, Jay David, and Richard Grusin. *Remediation: Understanding Media*. Cambridge: MIT Press, 2000. Print.
Boxer, Sarah. Bob Kane Obituary. *New York Times* 7 Nov. 1998. Web.
Braudy, Leo. *From Chivalry to Terrorism: War and the Changing Nature of Masculinity*. New York: Knopf, 2003. Print.
Cameron, James. *First Blood II: The Mission*. Jamescamerononline.com, December 22, 1983. Web.
Cantor, Paul A. *The Invisible Hand in Popular Culture: Liberty vs. Authority in American Film and TV*. Lexington: University Press of Kentucky, 2012. Print.
Chrétien de Troyes. *Perceval, the Story of the Grail. The Complete Romances of Chrétien de Troyes*. Trans. David Staines. Bloomington: Indiana University Press, 1991. Print.
"A Classic Success Story—Charles Bronson." *The Lithuanian Tribune* 23 Jan. 2013. Web.
Cohen, Richard. "The Soviets' Vietnam." *The Washington Post* 22 Aug. 1988. Web.
Gilbert Cruz, "Top 10 Superhero Movies." *Time* 2 June 2011. Web.
Dargis, Manohla. "Showdown in Gotham Town." *New York Times* 18 July 2008. Web.
The Dark Knight. Dir. Christopher Nolan. Perf. Christian Bale, Michael Caine, Aaron Eckhart, Morgan Freeman, Heath Ledger, Gary Oldman. Warner Bros., 2008. DVD.
The Dark Knight Rises. Dir. Christopher Nolan. Perf. Christian Bale, Michael Caine, Tom Hardy, Anne Hathaway, Morgan Freeman. Warner Bros., 2012. DVD.

The Dead Pool. Dir. Buddy Van Horn. Perf. Clint Eastwood, Patricia Clarkson, Liam Neeson. Warner Bros., 1988. DVD.
Death Wish. Dir. Michael Winner. Perf. Charles Bronson, Vincent Gardenia, Jeff Goldblum, Hope Lange. Paramount, 1974. DVD.
Death Wish II. Dir. Michael Winner. Perf. Charles Bronson, Vincent Gardenia, Jill Ireland, Laurence Fishburne. Cannon, 1982. DVD.
Death Wish 3. Dir. Michael Winner. Perf. Charles Bronson, Ed Lauter, Gavin O'Herlihy. Cannon, 1985. DVD.
Death Wish 4: The Crackdown. Dir. J. Lee Thompson. Perf. Charles Bronson, Kay Lenz, John P. Ryan. Cannon, 1987. DVD.
Death Wish 5: The Face of Death. Dir. Allan A. Goldstein. Perf. Charles Bronson, Lesley-Anne Down, Michael Parks. Trimark, 1994. DVD.
Dirty Harry. Dir. Don Siegel. Perf. Clint Eastwood, Andrew Robinson, John Vernon. Warner Bros., 1971. DVD.
Drohan, Christopher M. "Alfred, the Dark Knight of Faith: Batman and Kierkegaard." *Batman and Philosophy: The Dark Knight of the Soul*. Ed. Mark D. White and Robert Arp. Hoboken, NJ: John Wiley & Sons, 2008. 183–197. Print.
Ebert, Roger. "Batman Begins." rogerebert.com, 13 June 2005. Web.
_____. "Charles Bronson: It's Just That I Don't Like to Talk Very Much." Roger Ebert Interviews: 7 Aug. 1974. rogerebert.com. Web.
_____. "The Dark Knight." rogerebert.com, 16 July 2008. Web.
_____. "The Dark Knight Rises." rogerebert.com, 17 July 2012. Web.
_____. "First Blood." rogerebert.com, 1 Jan. 1982. Web.
_____. "Rambo Lets His Guns Do the Talking in Sequel." rogerebert.com, 15 May 1988. Web.
_____. "Roger Ebert Loved Movies: *Shane*." rogerebert.com, 3 Sept. 2000. Web.
Eco, Umberto. "*Casablanca*: Cult Movies and Intertextual Collage." *SubStance* 14, no. 2 (1985). Web.
Edwards, A.S.G. "The Reception of Malory's *Morte Darthur*." *A Companion to Malory*. Ed. Elizabeth Archibald and A.S.G. Edwards. Cambridge: D.S. Brewer, 1997. 241–52. Print.
Eliot, Marc. *American Rebel: The Life of Clint Eastwood*. New York: Harmony Books, 2009. Print.
The Enforcer. Dir. James Fargo. Perf. Clint Eastwood, Tyne Daly, Harry Guardino. Warner Bros., 1976. DVD.
Fagen, Patricia Weiss. "Repression and State Security." *Fear at the Edge: State Terror and Resistance in Latin America*. Ed. Juan E. Coradi, Patricia Weiss Fagen, and Manuel Antonio Garretón. Berkeley: University of California Press, 1992. 39–71. Print.
Field, P.J.C. *The Life and Times of Sir Thomas Malory*. Arthurian Studies XXIX. Cambridge: D.S. Brewer, 1993.
_____. "The Malory Life Records." *A Companion to Malory*. Ed. Elizabeth Archibald and A.S.G. Edwards. Cambridge: D.S. Brewer, 1997. 115–30. Print.
"Film Meets Art: Chris Nolan Inspired by Francis Bacon" The Tate Gallery. 26 Nov. 2013. Web.
First Blood. Dir. Ted Kotcheff. Perf. Sylvester Stallone, Richard Crenna, Brian Dennehy. Carolco, 1982. DVD.
Foundas, Scott. "Cinematic Faith." *Film Comment*. Supplement to November/December 2012. Web.
Franklin, E. Bruce. *M.I.A.: Or Mythmaking in America*. Brooklyn, NY: Lawrence Hill Books, 1992. Print.
"The Guardian Angels." guardianangels.org. Retrieved March 15, 2015. Web.
Geoffroi de Charny. *A Knight's Own Book of Chivalry*. Trans. Elspeth Kennedy. Philadelphia: University of Pennsylvania Press, 2005. Print.
Garfield, Brian. *Death Wish*. New York: The Overlook Press, 1972. Print.
Gies, Frances. *The Knight in History*. New York: HarperCollins, 1985. Print.
Girouard, Mark. *The Return to Camelot: Chivalry and the English Gentleman*. New Haven: Yale University Press, 1981. Print.
Grams, Martin, Jr., and Les Rayburn. *The "Have Gun—Will Travel" Companion*. Arlington, VA: Kirby Lithographic Company, 2000. Print.
Graysmith, Robert. *Zodiac Unmasked*. New York: Berkley, 1987. Print.
Harding, Bill. *The Films of Michael Winner*. London: Frederick Muller, 1978. Print.
Hawley, Thomas M. *The Remains of War: Bodies, Politics, and the Search for American Soldiers Unaccounted For in Southeast Asia*. Durham: Duke University Press, 2005. Print.

Hemmer, Kurt. "Political Outlaws: Beat Cowboys." *American Studies Journal* 50 (2007): 1–21. Web.
Haught, Leah. "Fleeing the Future, Forgetting the Past: Becoming Malory's Lancelot." *Parergon* 30, no. 1 (2013): 159–177. Web.
Holland, Dave. *From Out of the Past: A Pictorial History of The Lone Ranger.* New York: Palladium Media Enterprises, 1988. Print.
Ireland, Jill. *Life Wish.* Boston: Little, Brown, 1987. Print.
Jensen, Randall M. "Batman's Promise." *Batman and Philosophy: The Dark Knight of the Soul.* Ed. Mark D. White and Robert Arp. Hoboken, NJ: John Wiley & Sons, 2008. 85–100. Print.
Jolin, Dan. "The Making of the Joker: An Oral History of the Decade's Greatest Villain: From Playing Card to Oscar History." *Empire Magazine* December 2009. Web.
Kael, Pauline. *5001 Nights at the Movies.* 1982. New York: Holt and Company, 1991. Print.
_____. *For Keeps: 30 Years at the Movies.* New York: Plume, 1996. Print.
_____. *I Lost It at the Movies.* Boston: Atlantic—Little, Brown 1965. Print.
_____. *Kiss Kiss Bang Bang.* Boston: Atlantic—Little, Brown 1968. Print.
Kaminsky, Stuart M. *Clint Eastwood.* New York: New American Library, 1974. Print.
Keen, Maurice. *Chivalry.* New Haven: Yale University Press, 1984. Print.
Kennedy, Beverly. "Adultery in Malory's *Le Morte d'Arthur.*" *Arthuriana* 7, no. 4 (Winter 1997) 63–91. Print.
_____. *Knighthood in the Morte D' Arthur.* Cambridge: D.S. Brewer, 1985. Print.
Klapcsik, Sandor. *Liminality in Fantastic Fiction: A Poststructuralist Approach.* Jefferson, NC: McFarland, 2012. Print.
Lambie, Ryan. "The Rise and Fall of Carolco." 11 Mar. 2014. Web.
Lawrence, John Shelton, and Robert Jewett. *The Myth of the American Superhero.* Grand Rapids, MI: William B. Eerdmans, 2002. Print.
Lemann, Nicholas. "A Call For Help: What the Kitty Genovese Story Really Means." *The New Yorker* 10 Mar. 2014. Web.
Lenz, Timothy O. "Conservatism in American Crime Films." *Journal of Criminal Justice and Popular Culture* 12, no. 2 (Spring 2005). Web.
"The Lone Ranger." *Old Time Radio Westerns.* Web. Retrieved January 28, 2015.
"The Lone Ranger: Justice From Outside the Law." *All Things Considered,* National Public Radio. With Senior Host Robert Siegel. 14 Jan. 2008. Web.
Lynch, Andrew. "Malory's *Morte Darthur* and History." *A Companion to Arthurian Literature.* Ed. Helen Fulton. West Sussex: John Wiley & Sons, 2012. 297–311. Print.
MacDonald, J. Fred. *One Nation Under Television.* New York: Pantheon, 1990. Print.
_____. *Who Shot the Sheriff? The Rise and Fall of the Television Western.* New York: Praeger, 1987. Print.
Magnum Force. Dir. Ted Post. Perf. Clint Eastwood, Hal Holbrook, David Soul, Robert Urich. Warner Bros., 1973. DVD.
Malory, Thomas. *Le Morte Darthur.* Caxton's Malory: A New Edition of *Le Morte Darthur.* Ed. James Spisak and William Matthews. Berkeley: University of California Press, 1983. Print.
_____. *Works.* Ed. Eugene Vinaver. 1954. Oxford: Oxford University Press, 1971. Print.
"Maslin, Janet. "First Blood." *New York Times* 22 Oct. 1982. Web.
_____. "Stallone's 'Rambo III,' Globe-Trotting Cowboy For the 80's Audience." *New York Times* 25 May 1988. Web.
Mattes, Ari. "Turning the Gun on America: *Cobra* and the Action Film as Cultural Critique." *The Australiasian Journal of Popular Culture* 2, no. 3 (2013): 457–470. Web.
Matthews, William. "The Besieged Printer." *The Malory Debate: Essays on the Text of 'Le Morte Darthur.'* Ed. Bonnie Wheeler, Robert L. Kindrick and Michael N. Salda. Cambridge: D.S. Brewer, 2000. 35–64. Print.
McCarthy, Terence. "Malory and His Sources." *A Companion to Malory* Ed. Elizabeth Archibald and A.S.G. Edwards. Cambridge: D.S. Brewer, 1997. 75–95. Print.
Mead, David. "Unusual Stones." *Sulang Language Data and Working Papers: Topics in Lexicography* 12, no. 2 Sulawesi Language Alliance. 2014. Web.
Meyer, Evelyn. "Undercutting the Fabric of Courtly Love with 'Tokens of Love' in Wolfram Von Eschenbach's *Parzival.*" *New Research: Yearbook for the Society of Medieval Germanic Studies* 1, no. 1 (2013). Web.

Millican, Charles Bowie. *Spenser and the Table Round: A Study in the Contemporaneous Background for Spenser's Use of the Arthurian Legend.* Boston: Harvard Studies in Comparative Literature, 1932. Rpt. New York: Octagon Books, 1967. Print.
Moore, Clayton, with Frank Thompson. *I Was That Masked Man.* Dallas: Taylor, 1996. Print.
Morrell, David. "David Morrell on Rambo." davidmorrell.net. Web.
_____. *First Blood.* Greenwich, CT: Fawcett, 1972. Print.
_____. *Rambo and Me: The Story Behind the Story.* E-Essay. Morrell Enterprises, April 2012.
"Myanmar Profile—Overview." bbc.com. Web. Retrieved April 10, 2015.
Nelson, Andrew Patrick. *Contemporary Westerns: Film and Television Since 1990.* Lanham, MD: Scarecrow Press, 2013. Print.
Newcomb, Horace. "From Old Frontier to New Frontier." *The Revolution Wasn't Televised: Sixties Television and Social Conflict.* Ed. Lynn Spigel and Michael Curtin. New York: Routledge, 1997. 287–304. Print.
Newman, Kim. *Wild West Movies: Or How the West Was Found, Won, Lost, Lied About, Filmed and Forgotten.* London: Bloomsbury, 1990. Print.
Nolan, Barbara. "The Tale of Sir Gareth and The Tale of Sir Lancelot." *A Companion to Malory.* Ed. Elizabeth Archibald and A.S.G. Edwards. Cambridge: D.S. Brewer, 1996. 153–82.
Novalis. *Henry von Ofterdingen.* Trans. Palmer Hilty. New York: Frederick Ungar, 1964. Print.
O'Neil, Dennis and Dick Giordano. "The Man Who Falls." *Detective Comics: Secret Origins,* 1989. Rpt. in *Batman Begins: The Movie and Other Tales of the Dark Knight.* New York: DC Comics, 2005. 71–87.
"The Other Pearls." agt-gems.com/Book/OtherPearls.html. Web. Retrieved April 4, 2015.
Patterson, Eric. "Every Which Way But Lucid: The Critique of Authority in Clint Eastwood's Police Movies." *The Journal of Popular Film and Television* (Fall 1982) 92–104. Print.
Pearson, Roberta E., and William Uricchio. "Notes from the Batcave: An Interview with Dennis O'Neil." *The Many Lives of the Batman: Critical Approaches to a Superhero and his Media.* Ed. Roberta E. Pearson. New York: Routledge, 1991. 18–32. Print.
Pirani, Adam. "A Dark Knight in Gotham City." *Starlog* 142 (May 1989): 37–39. Print.
Pitts, Michael R. *Charles Bronson: The 95 Films and the 156 Television Appearances.* Jefferson, NC: McFarland, 1999. Print.
Pomerance, Murray, ed. *American Cinema of the 1950s: Themes and Variations.* New Brunswick: Rutgers University Press, 2005. Print.
Primeau, Ronald. *Romance of the Road: The Literature of the American Highway.* Bowling Green: Bowling Green State University Popular Press, 1996. Print.
Rambo. Dir. Sylvester Stallone. Perf. Sylvester Stallone, Julie Benz, Graham McTavish, Matthew Marsden. NuImage, 2008. DVD.
Rambo: First Blood Part II. Dir. George P. Cosmatos. Perf. Sylvester Stallone, Richard Crenna, Julia Nickson. Carolco, 1985. DVD.
Rambo III. Dir. Peter MacDonald. Perf. Sylvester Stallone, Richard Crenna, Marc de Jonge. TriStar, 1988. DVD.
"Ranald Slidell Mackenzie." *Texas State Historical Association.* Web. Retrieved January 18, 2015.
Ray, Robert B. *A Certain Tendency of the Hollywood Cinema, 1930–1980.* Princeton: Princeton University Press, 1985. Print.
Riddy, Felicity. "Contextualizing *Le Morte Darthur*: Empire and Civil War." *A Companion to Malory.* Ed. Elizabeth Archibald and A.S.G. Edwards. Cambridge: D.S. Brewer, 1997. 55–74. Print.
Rothel, David. *Richard Boone: A Knight Without Armor in a Savage Land.* Madison, NC: Empire Publishing, 2000. Print.
_____. *Who Was That Masked Man?: The Story of the Lone Ranger.* New York: A. S. Barnes and Company, 1976. Print.
Runkle, Patrick. "Cannon Films: The Rise and Fall (A Short History)." cannonfilms.com. Web. Retrieved March 16, 2015.
"Sacred Vedic Pearls." agt-gems.com/Pearls. Web. Retrieved April 10, 2015.
Schaefer, Jack. *Shane: The Critical Edition.* Ed. James C. Work. Lincoln: University of Nebraska Press, 1984. Print.
Schickel, Richard. *Clint Eastwood: A Biography.* New York: Alfred A. Knopf, 1996. Print.
Scott, A. O. "Just When You Thought It Was Safe to Go Back in the Jungle." *New York Times* 26 Jan. 2008. Web.

Sharrett, Christopher. "Batman and the Twilight of the Idols: An Interview with Frank Miller." Ed. Roberta E. Pearson. *The Many Lives of the Batman: Critical Approaches to a Superhero and his Media.* New York: Routledge, 1991. 33–46. Print.
Slotkin, Richard. *Gunfighter Nation: The Myth of the Frontier in Twentieth-Century America.* New York: Atheneum, 1992. Print.
_____. *Regeneration Through Violence: the Mythology of the American Frontier, 1600–1800.* Middleton, CT: Wesleyan University Press, 1973. Print.
Sorrentino, Christopher. *Death Wish.* New York: Soft Skull Press, 2010. Print.
Spencer, Kathleen. *Art and Politics in Have Gun–Will Travel: The 1950s Television Western as Ethical Drama.* Jefferson, NC: McFarland, 2014. Print.
Stallone, Sylvester. *Pearl of the Cobra (Rambo 4).* November 6, 2006. screenplaydb.com. Web.
Steckmesser, Kent Ladd. *The Western Hero in History and Legend.* Norman: University of Oklahoma Press, 1965. Print.
Steinbeck, John. *The Acts of King Arthur and His Noble Knights.* New York: Penguin, 1976. Print.
Sudden Impact. Dir. Clint Eastwood. Perf. Clint Eastwood, Sondra Locke, Albert Popwell. Warner Bros., 1983. DVD.
"Sylvester Stallone." *Bio.* A&E Television Networks, 2015. Web. 13 Apr. 2015.
10th Anniversary Edition of the American Film Institute's 100 Years/100 Movies. 2007. Web.
Talbot, Paul. *Bronson's Loose: The Making of the 'Death Wish' Films.* New York: iUniverse, 2006. Print.
Tennyson, Alfred Lord. *Idylls of the King.* 1885. New York: Penguin. 1983. Print.
Thomas, Kevin. "'Death Wish' Enters Comic-Book Phase." *Lost Angeles Times* 9 Nov. 1987. Web.
Turan, Kenneth. "'The Dark Knight Rises' more than shines, and on many levels." *Los Angeles Times* 18 July 2012. Web.
Umland, Rebecca A., and Samuel J. Umland. *The Use of Arthurian Legend in Hollywood Film: From Connecticut Yankees to Fisher Kings.* Westport, CT: Greenwood Press, 1996. Print.
Vermilye, Jerry. *The Films of Charles Bronson.* Secaucus, NJ: The Citadel Press, 1980. Print.
"Vigilante."oxforddictionaires.com. Web.
"Vigilante Justice, 1851." Eyewitnesstohistory.com. Web. Retrieved March 10, 2015. Web.
Wainer, Alex M. *Soul of the Dark Knight: Batman as Mythic Figure in Comics and Film.* Jefferson, NC: McFarland, 2014. Print.
Warshow, Robert. *The Immediate Experience. Movies, Comics, Theatre, and Other Aspects of Popular Culture.* New York: Atheneum, 1972. Print.
"The Workhouse, The Story of an Institution: Lambeth (Parish of St. Mary), Surrey, London." workhouses.org. Web.
White, T.H. *The Once and Future King.* New York: Berkley, 1958. Print.
Wilmington, Michael. "Why a Rambo Ii? For the Muddiest of Reasons." *Los Angeles Times* 22 May 1985. Web.
Winner, Michael. *Winner Takes All: A Life of Sorts.* London: Robson Books, 2004. Print.
Wright, Will. *Sixguns & Society: A Structural Study of the Western.* Berkeley: University of California Press, 1975. Print.
Woolf, Virginia. *Collected Essays:* London: Hogarth Press 1966. 2: 285. Print.
Wylie, Philip. *Generation of Vipers.* 1942. New York: Pocket Books, 1955. Print.
Žižek, Slavoj. "The Politics of Batman." *The New Statesman* 23 Aug. 2012. Web.

Index

The Acts of King Arthur and His Noble Knights 54
Adams, Neal 227
Alison, Joan 36
Any Which Way You Can 97, 128, 156
Arness, James 60, 264n4, 265n14
Arnold, Matthew 26
Arthur, Jean 48
Arthurian Revival 25

Baden-Powell, Robert 30
Bale, Christian 228, 236, 249
Batman (film): *Batman* 226, 228, 272n1; *Batman and Robin* 226; *Batman Begins* 185, 225–240, 242–243, 246, 248, 251, 253–255, 273n2, 274n9; *Batman Forever* 226; *Batman Returns* 226; *Batman: The Dark Knight* trilogy 5, 6, 92, 225, 247–248, 258; *The Dark Knight* 222, 237–248, 255, 257, 273n3, 273n4; *The Dark Knight Rises* 222–223, 248–256, 274n8, 274n9
Batman (print): *Batman (Detective Comics)* 224; "Batman: Bane of the Demon" 274n6; *Batman: The Killing Joke* 241, 273n5; *Batman: Vengeance of Bane* 274n8; "The Batman Wars Against the Dirigible of Doom" 224; *Batman: Year One* 223, 227, 244; "Birds of Prey" 274n6; "The Case of the Chemical Syndicate" 224; "The Crimes of Two-Face!" 243; *The Dark Knight Returns* 226–227; "Daughter of the Demon" 227; "Death Gamble of a Darknight Detective!" 226; "Half an Evil" 244; "Into the Den of the Death Dealers" 274n6; "The Man Who Falls" 227
The Beguiled 95
Beowulf 11
Bergman, Ingrid 34–35
Bogart, Humphrey 2, 19, 34–35

Bolland, Brian 241
The Book of Merlyn 31, 264n1
Boone, Peter 73
Boone, Richard 58–59, 72–75, 87, 97, 265n9, 266n16
Boorman, John 258, 263ch2n6
The Brave One 180–181
Brinkley, Don 80
Bronson, Charles (Charles Buchinsky) 142–143, 146, 154–156, 162, 164, 166–168, 173–174, 179, 267ch6n4, 268ch6n4, 268n7, 268n8, 268n9, 268n11
Brooks, Richard 189
Buchanan, Edgar 52
Burne-Jones, Edward 25, 30
Burnett, Murray 36
Burton, Tim 226, 228, 272n1

Caine, Michael 230, 244, 250
Camelot (film) 31, 56
Camelot (musical) 31, 56
Cameron, James 197–198, 200–202
Cameron, Julia Margaret 30
The Candle in the Wind 31, 264n1
Cannon Films 154–155, 162, 166–167, 171, 173
Carolco Pictures 189–190, 198, 204, 213; TriStar Pictures 190, 204, 209
Carpenter, John 6
Carver, Steve 173–174
Casablanca 2–4, 19, 33–43, 46, 50, 58, 126, 209–210, 263n2, 265n12, 271n13, 273n3; *Everybody Comes to Rick's* (play) 36
Caxton, William 3, 23–24, 261n2, 262n2
Cimino, Michael 108
Coffin, Tristram 62
Cold War 205, 210
Colleary, Michael 173
Columbia Pictures 189

281

A Connecticut Yankee in King Arthur's Court 30
Conrad, William 73
Coogan's Bluff 90, 94, 97, 146
Cook, Elisha, Jr. 47
Cooper, Gary 102–103
Cosmatos, George P. 197
Cotillard, Marion 250
Courtney, Chuck 68
Crenna, Richard 190–191, 200, 204, 209, 269n3
Crusades 12
Curtiz, Michael 33, 37

Daley, Robert 97
Daly, Tyne 117, 119–120, 127, 267ch5n4
The Dead Pool 125, 128–134, 267ch5n4, 267n9
Death Wish films 5, 92, 104, 154, 161, 163, 165–167, 171–173, 181, 259; *Death Wish* 90, 137–154, 156, 173, 178–181, 198, 231, 268n5, 268n7, 268n9; *Death Wish* (novel) 139–142, 144–145, 147–148; *Death Wish II* 154–162, 164–165, 167, 179, 268n10; *Death Wish 3*, 155, 162- 168, 171–172, 179; *Death Wish 4: The Crackdown* 167–174, 179, 267n5; *Death Wish V: The Face of Death* 173–180, 191
de Charny, Geoffroi 12–13, 15, 261n5
The Deer Hunter 108, 198
The Defence of Guenevere and Other Poems 26–28
De Laurentiis, Dino 143, 268n8
Dennehy, Brian 190, 192
de Troyes, Chrétien 261n5, 2702n16
de Wilde, Brandon 46, 48
Digby, Kenhelm 25
Dillman, Bradford 117, 122, 127
Dirty Harry films 5–6, 87, 92, 94, 98, 105, 116, 118, 121, 126–128, 132–134, 137, 142, 181, 266n3; *Dirty Harry* 90, 95–107, 109–110, 114, 127, 139, 180, 184, 266n1, 267ch5n4; *The Dead Pool* 125, 128–134, 267ch5n4, 267n9; *The Enforcer* 97, 115–122, 125, 127, 134–135, 142, 155, 167, 267ch5n4, 267n5, 267n5; *Magnum Force* 107–115, 117, 122, 125, 134, 137, 267ch5n4; *Moving Target* (screenplay) 115–116; *Sudden Impact* 118, 121–128, 132, 134, 180–181, 267ch5n4, 267n7
Dixon, Chuck 274n6, 274n8
Dore, Gustave 30

Eastwood, Clint 46, 63, 91–97, 100, 102, 104, 108, 115–116, 119, 121, 126–128, 134, 142, 146, 168, 199, 264n4, 266n2, 267n7, 270n5

Eckhart, Aaron 238, 240
Edmonds, Michael 162
The Enforcer 97, 115–122, 125, 127, 134–135, 142, 155, 167, 267ch5n4, 267n5, 267n5
Engelbach, David 155
Epstein, Julius 33, 37
Epstein, Philip 33, 37
Escape from New York 6, 151
Escape from L.A. 6
Everybody Comes to Rick's (play) 36
Excalibur 156, 258, 263ch2n6, 270n9

The Faerie Queene 24
Fargo, James 116
Finger, Bill 224, 241
Fink, Harry Julian 84, 87, 97, 266n16
Fink, R.M. 97
First Blood (film) 189–198, 205
First Blood (novel) 187–192, 194–195, 197, 215–216, 269n1, 271n11
A Fistful of Dollars 91, 125, 168
Fonda, Henry 91, 143, 237, 268n10
Ford, John 89, 134, 237, 245, 268n10
Fort Apache 237, 245, 268n10
Freeman, Morgan 232, 238, 250

Gardenia, Vincent 147, 158
Garfield, Brian 139, 142, 148
Generation of Vipers 50
Giordano, Dick 227
Globus, Yoram 154–155, 162, 167, 173
Goetz, Bernhard 137–138, 162, 181
Golan, Menahem 154–155, 162, 167, 173–174, 179
Goldstein, Allan A. 174, 177
Gordon-Levitt, Joseph 250
Gothic Revival 24
Goyer, David S. 225–226, 239, 247
Great Depression 93
Griffin, Merv 128
Griggs, Loyal 46
Gritz, Lieutenant Colonel James "Bo" 199, 270n5
Guardino, Harry 100
Gunsmoke 58–60, 264n4, 265n14
Guthrie, A.B., Jr. 46
Gyllenhaal, Maggie 238, 243

Hallam, Arthur Henry 27
Hancock, Herbie 143
Hang 'Em High 94, 108
Hardy, Tom 250, 274n8
Harris, Richard 56
Hart, John 62, 69
Hathaway, Anne 249
Have Gun–Will Travel 5, 58–60, 66, 70–87, 97, 264n4, 265n9; "The Bostonian" 73;

"Comanche" 265n10; "Ella West" 76–78; "Fandango" 84–86; "Genesis" 72–75; "The Hanging of Roy Carter" 83–84; "The Hatchet Man" 82; "The Hunt" 265n10; "Justice in Hell" 82; "The Killing of Jessie May" 266n15; "The Last Judgment" 82; "No Visitors" 80; "The Princess and the Gunfighter" 78–80; "The Prisoner" 266n15; "The Prophet" 73, 83, 265n11; "The Return of Dr. Thackeray" 73, 80–81; "Three Bells to Perdido" 72; "The Unforgiven" 72–73, 82; "The Yuma Treasure" 265n10

Heflen, Van 2, 19, 47
Helfer, Andrew 244
Henreid, Paul 2, 19, 34–35
Herrmann, Bernard 71
Hickman, Gail Morgan 115, 167–168, 171–172, 267n5
High Noon 46, 102, 268n6
High Plains Drifter 63
Holmes, Katie 230, 243
Hurd, Gayle Anne 197

Idylls of the King 25–27, 29–30, 43, 49, 263ch2n5
The Ill-Made Knight 31, 55, 264n1
Ireland, Jill 142, 155–156, 167–168, 173, 267ch6n4

Jakoby, Don 162
Jarre, Kevin 197
Johnson, Ben 52
justice 1–8, 16–20, 34, 38, 42, 44, 46, 48, 51–52, 54, 60–61, 63–70, 82, 84–87, 91, 98, 103–107, 112–114, 118, 123–124, 126–127, 132–134, 136–138, 142, 145–146, 149–153, 156, 159, 161, 164, 166, 172, 176, 178–181, 186, 193, 195–197, 203, 210, 221, 223, 228–233, 235, 245, 248, 251, 256–257, 259, 262n5, 268n9, 271n10; and the legal system 1, 3, 5–6, 20, 60, 66, 83–84, 94, 102–107, 109–110, 112–114, 120, 122, 126–127, 134, 137, 141, 146, 160–161, 166, 176–179, 186, 193, 223, 230, 232, 238, 251, 256, 271n10; poetic justice 93–135, 176, 179; retributive justice 85, 104, 120, 127, 134, 136, 256–257

Kane, Bob 224, 241, 273n3
Kassar, Mario 189
Keaton, Michael 226, 272n1
Keats, John 24, 77
Kim, Evan C. 129, 267ch5n4
knighthood 2, 4–5, 11–21, 23, 25, 29, 32–33, 38–39, 49, 52, 70, 74–76, 223, 237, 243, 258, 261n5; definition of 11–13; heroic knight 13, 15, 17, 20, 85, 261n4, 262n6; history of 11–13; knight errant 2, 4, 13, 19, 32, 44, 51, 80, 106, 153, 212, 221; true knight 2–4, 6–8, 13–16, 18–20, 32, 39, 41–42, 45, 48, 52–55, 60, 75, 102, 135, 150, 185, 261n4, 262n5, 262n6; typologies of 2, 4, 7, 11–21, 28, 39, 42, 52; worshipful knight 3, 13–17, 20, 39–40, 42, 46, 52, 261n4, 262n6
Koch, Howard 33–34
Kohner, Pancho 167
Kohner, Paul 167
Korean War 3, 42, 48, 144, 187, 192
Kotcheff, Ted 189, 191, 198
Kozoll, Michael 191

Ladd, Alan 2, 19, 46, 48, 180, 263ch3n5
Landers, Hal 142
Larch, John 84, 100
Ledger, Heath 238–240, 273n3
Leone, Sergio 91, 94, 168
Lettich, Sheldon 204
Lewis, George J. 62
liminality 1; liminal space 1, 4–6, 19–20, 45, 59–60, 66, 83, 96, 103, 134, 167, 186, 194, 197, 202, 212, 214, 220, 230, 264n4; outlaw hero and 1–8, 13, 17–18, 20, 32–33, 41–42, 46–48, 51–52, 58, 60–61, 66, 68–71, 75, 81, 87, 93, 97, 101, 103, 106–107, 113–114, 120–121, 126, 128, 135, 138, 140, 145, 150, 152–154, 161–163, 165–166, 171–172, 174, 179–180, 185–186, 191, 194, 196–197, 201, 203, 210, 216, 218–220, 222–224, 226–227, 229, 231, 234–237, 240, 243, 248, 253, 256–258
Littlefield, Ralph 65
Locke, Sondra 121, 126–127
Logan, Joshua 56
The Lone Ranger 5, 57–72; "Behind the Law" 69–70; "Bullets for Ballots" 69; "Double Jeopardy" 69; "Enter the Lone Ranger" 62–64; "Gold Train" 66; *The Lone Ranger* (film) 62; *The Lone Ranger and the Lost City of Gold* 62; "The Lone Ranger Fights On" 62, 65; "The Lone Ranger's Triumph" 62; "The Masked Deputy" 68; "The Old Cowboy" 69; "The Outcast" 69; "Outlaw of the Plains" 68; radio show 59, 62–63, 65, 67; "Sheep Thieves" 66, 68
Lorre, Peter 34, 37

MacDonald, Peter 204, 270n9
MacKenzie, General Ranald Slidell 73, 265n10
Magnum Force 107–115, 117, 122, 125, 134, 137, 267ch5n4
Malory, Sir Thomas 2–4, 13–18, 20–25, 27–32, 40, 54–56, 185, 257–258, 261n1,

261n2, 261n3, 262n5, 262n7, 262n1, 262n2, 262n3, 263ch2n6
The Man Who Shot Liberty Valance 238, 245
Mariscot, Mariel 108
Mason, Martin 52
Matter of Britain 24, 29, 56
Mayes, Wendell 142, 268n8
McFarlane, Colin 233, 238, 246
McQueen, Steve 189, 264n4
Meadow, Herb 58, 72
medievalism 22–32; and the American west 32–87; contemporary culture 31–32; definition of 23; 19th century revival 4, 24–30
Meyer, Emile 47
Middle Ages 4, 11–13, 21, 23, 30–32, 39, 75, 186, 256, 265n11
Milius, John 107–108, 112
Miller, Frank 223, 226–227, 241, 244
Milton, John 24
Missing in Action 198, 270n5
modern action film 3, 87, 89, 92, 183–259; Pacific Rim and 184, 186; definition of 184–185; rise of 183–186
Monterastelli, Art 213
Monzano, Sonia 143
Moore, Alan 241
Moore, Clayton 61, 62, 64, 68
Moore, Wildey J. 164
Morrell, David 187–192, 194, 198, 215–217, 269n1, 269n2, 271n11, 271n14
Morris, William 25–26, 30
Le Morte D'Arthur 2–4, 13–14, 16, 18, 20–23, 32, 40, 54–56, 106, 257–258; Winchester manuscript 54, 261n2
Moving Target (screenplay) 115–116
Mulcahy, Russell 204, 270n9
Murphy, Cillian 233, 247, 251

Neeson, Liam 129, 228, 250, 274n9
Nero, Franco 56
Nicholson, Jack 226, 272n1
Nixon, Richard 91, 104, 199, 270n8
Nolan, Christopher 226–228, 239–240, 247–248, 255–256, 273n3, 274n7, 274n9
Nolan, Jonathan 239, 247
Norris, Chuck 155, 173, 184, 198, 270n5

Oldman, Gary 229, 236, 238, 244, 249
The Once and Future King 30–31, 55–56, 264n1; *The Book of Merlyn* 31, 264n1; *The Candle in the Wind* 31, 264n1; *The Ill-Made Knight* 31, 55, 264n1; *The Queen of Air and Darkness* 31, 264n1; *The Sword in the Stone* 31, 264n1
Once Upon a Time in the West 91, 143
O'Neil, Dennis 227, 244

Page, Jimmy 155
Palance, Jack 47–48
Paradise Lost 24
Paramount Pictures 48, 57, 146, 264n2
Patmore, Coventry 49
Pearl of the Cobra (Rambo 4) script 213, 220, 271n13, 272n18
Pearson, Durk 128
Perry, Felton 109, 267ch5n4
Pierce, Charles B. 121
Pierson, Frank 265n13
Play Misty for Me 95, 97, 127
Popwell, Albert 111, 118, 124, 127, 267ch5n4
The Poseidon Adventure 116, 142
Post, Ted 108

The Queen of Air and Darkness 31, 264n1

Rains, Claude 37
Rambo films 5, 92, 213, 247; *First Blood* (film) 189–198, 205; *First Blood* (novel) 187–192, 194–195, 197, 215–216, 269n1, 271n11; *Pearl of the Cobra (Rambo 4)* script 213, 220, 271n13, 272n18; *Rambo* 190, 211–220, 271n13; *Rambo: First Blood Part II* 190, 197–203, 208, 219, 270n5; *Rambo: Last* 220, 272n20; *Rambo III* 13, 186, 190, 204–211, 214, 218–219, 270n9, 271n12
Rawhide 93, 97, 108, 264n4
Redgrave, Vanessa 56
remediation 54–87, 222; definition of 56
Renaissance 24
Restoration 24
Riesner, Dean 97, 116, 142
Roberts, Bobby 142, 150
Robinson, Andy 100
Robinson, Casey 36–37
Rocky films 189–190, 205
Roddenberry, Gene 76, 83, 87, 266n16
Rolfe, Sam 58, 72–73, 80, 266n16
Rossetti, Dante Gabriel 30
Roven, Charles 240
Ruskin, John 25
Russell, Kurt 6

Sackheim, William 191
Sande, Walter 65
Santoni, Reni 99, 267ch5n4
Schaefer, Jack 42–44, 46–48, 50
Schroeder, Barbet 155
Schurr, S.W. (Scott Shroers) 115, 267n5
Scott, Walter 25, 27
The Searchers 46, 134
Shane (film) 2–5, 19, 33, 41–53, 58, 60, 140, 144, 180, 263ch3n4
Shane (novel) 42–44, 46–48, 50–51
Sharon, Steve 128

Shatner, William 199, 270n5
Shaw, George Bernard 76
Shaw, Lou 83
Shaw, Peggy 83
Shaw, Sandy 128
The Shootist 180, 269n12
Siegel, Don 94–95, 97, 102, 142, 266n2
Silliphant, Stirling 116, 142, 155
Silverheels, Jay 62, 64
Silverman, Stanley 80
Simms, Jay 72
Smith, Earl E. 121
Society for Creative Anachronism 30–31
Southey, Robert 24
Spaghetti Western 91, 94
Spenser, Edmund 24, 262n2
Stallone, Sylvester 155, 183–184, 189–191, 197–198, 202, 204–206, 209–214, 270n9, 270n10, 272n18, 272n20
Steinbeck, John 54, 56, 59
Stevens, George 41, 46
Stinson, Joseph C. 121
The Stone Killer 142–143, 268n9
Strachey, Edward 25
Strange, Glenn 62
Striker, Fran 61–62, 65, 67
Striker, Fran, Jr. 64–65
Sudden Impact 118, 121–128, 132, 134, 180–181, 267ch5n4, 267n7
Swinburne, Algernon Charles 26
The Sword in the Stone 31, 264n1
The Sword in the Stone (1963 film) 31, 56

The Tale of Balen 26
The Taming of the Shrew 76
Tennyson, Alfred Lord 25–31, 43, 49, 263ch2n5, 263ch2n6
Terracina, Nydia Rodriguez 238, 246
the Tudors 23–24, 30
Thompson, J. Lee 167, 171
Thompson, Robert E. 78
Trendle, George 61, 67, 70
Tristan and Iseult 26
TriStar Pictures 190, 204, 209

Tristram of Lyonesse 26
Twain, Mark 19, 30, 41

Unbreakable 273n4
Universal Studios 97
urban western 3–6, 33, 87, 89–181, 184, 221; definition of 4, 91; rise of 89–181

Vajna, Andrew 189
Van Horn, Buddy 128
Veidt, Conrad 35, 273n3
Vernon, John 100
Vietnam War 5, 185, 187–188, 191, 198–199, 220
vigilantism 113, 136–137, 150, 153, 161, 163, 167–168, 180–181, 224–225, 231; definition of 67, 136; history of 136–137
vigilante 6, 8, 66–67, 82, 107, 112–114, 122, 134, 136–138, 140–141, 143, 146–150, 153, 157–161, 163, 166, 168–169, 171–172, 175–177, 180–181, 185, 188, 224–225, 228, 231, 233, 236, 240–242, 244, 257, 267n1
Vinaver, Eugene 54, 261n2

Wallis, Hal 37
War of the Roses 3, 16, 23–24, 55
Warhol, Andy 129, 131, 267n9
Warner Brothers 33–34, 36, 57, 97, 116, 119, 174, 189, 226, 227, 236, 272n1
Wayne, John 180, 206, 238, 263n3, 269n12
White, T.H. 30–31, 55–56, 262n2, 264n1
Willis, Bruce 6, 184, 273n4
Wilson, Charles Nesbitt 205
Wilson, Dooley 34
Wincelberg, Shimon 82–83
Winner, Michael 142–143, 149–150, 155, 162, 166–167, 171, 181, 268n6, 268n8, 268n9
Woolf, Virginia 263ch3n6
Wordsworth, William 24–25
World War II 3, 42, 55, 57, 144, 208, 269n2
Wright, Thomas 25
Wuhl, Robert 272n1
Wylie, Philip 50

www.ingramcontent.com/pod-product-compliance
Lightning Source LLC
Chambersburg PA
CBHW051211300426
44116CB00006B/523